DECISIVE GAMES IN CHESS HISTORY

DECISIVE GAMES IN CHESS HISTORY

Luděk Pachman

Translated by A. S. Russell

TM

Dover Publications, Inc., New York

Published in Canada by General Publishing Company, Ltd., 30 Lesmill Road, Don Mills, Toronto, Ontario.
Published in the United Kingdom by Constable and Company, Ltd.

This Dover edition, first published in 1987, is an unabridged and unaltered republication of the English language edition first published by Pitman Publishing, London, England in 1975 under the title, *Pachman's Decisive Games*, which was an enlarged and updated edition of *Entscheidungspartien*, published in 1972 by Walter Rau Verlag, Düsseldorf, West Germany. The Dover edition is reprinted by special arrangement with A & C Black (Publishers) Ltd., London, England.

Manufactured in the United States of America
Dover Publications, Inc., 31 East 2nd Street, Mineola, N.Y. 11501

Library of Congress Cataloging-in-Publication Data

Pachman, Luděk.
    Decisive games in chess history.

    Reprint. Originally published: Pachman's decisive games. London : Pitman, 1975.
    "The English language edition . . . was an enlarged and updated edition of Entscheidungspartien"—T.p. verso.
    Includes indexes.
    1. Chess—Collections of games. I. Title.
GV1452.P2913 1987   794.1′52   86-29272
ISBN 0-486-25323-6 (pbk.)

Preface

Luděk Pachman is not only an international grandmaster of many years' standing but also a well-known theoretician and writer.

In this present book he has drawn on his great experience and knowledge to give a vivid account of the highlights of the most important tournaments and matches from Baden-Baden 1870 to the 1972 World Championship match between Spasski and Fischer. The course of each event is described in such a way as to bring out the drama surrounding it, and this is followed in each case by the decisive game or games, deeply annotated.

The whole is a balanced mixture of chess information and instruction which should appeal to players of all levels.

A. S. Russell
Translator

Contents

DECISIVE GAMES IN
CHESS HISTORY

1 Introductory

Moments of Decision

A glance at a tournament table gives the impression that every game is of equal importance; after all, in the final reckoning every win counts as a full point and every draw half a point. In actual fact, however, there is a great difference between a game played at the beginning of a tournament, when everything is open, and one played in the last two rounds, where a special effort often has to be made to obtain a particular result. Towards the end of a tournament or match a player is frequently in a situation in which he has to win at all costs. Then he faces a task that puts not only his chess knowledge and ability to the test but even more so his nerves. Such games are convincing proof of the fact that chess is neither a science nor an art, but rather a battle of minds.

In this book I have analysed sixty-five games played in an exceptionally tense atmosphere; each one had a decisive bearing on the outcome of an important international tournament or match. None of the games is technically or aesthetically outstanding; in fact, many of them contain bad mistakes. That, however, makes them all the more instructive. These games show how players of differing styles tackle the extremely difficult problem of winning a game that has to be won.

A perusal of tournament books shows us an interesting fact. Many games played at a decisive phase contain mistakes that are hardly to be expected of a player of the calibre making them. Obviously nervous tension, often coupled with fatigue following the previous games, influences the quality of play. There are even cases where unbelievable blunders have decided a match for the world championship title.

1. Steinitz-Chigorin

Position after Black's 8th move

This position occurred in the twenty-second game of the world championship match in 1892. With rules stipulating that the first player to win ten games was the victor, the match was now nearing its climax, eight games having been won by both players and six drawn. On his ninth move Chigorin, who had Black, made an elementary mistake.

| 9 PxP | NxP? |

This loses at least a pawn without the slightest compensation. It is interesting to note that in this game Chigorin chose a defence to the Queen's Gambit that was later adopted by Tartakower and which now bears his name.

10 NxN	BxN
11 BxB	QxB
12 RxP	Q-Q3
13 R-B3	BxP?

It is possible that, when making his ninth move, Tartakower assumed that he would recover his pawn by capturing with the bishop on QR7. However, by so doing, he loses a piece, for the bishop cannot escape.

14	P-K4	Q-N5
15	Q-R1	B-N6
16	N-Q2	B-B7

There is no way of avoiding loss of material: e.g. 16 ... Q-R5 17 NxB or 16 ... B-R5 17 R-B4.

17	R-B4	Q-Q3
18	RxB	QxQP
19	0-0 and wins.	

In the next game of the same match Chigorin had White, and it was to be expected that he would make every effort to draw level, as his choice of opening, a

2. Chigorin–Steinitz

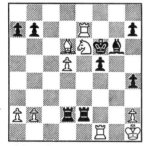

Position after Black's 31st move

King's Gambit, seemed to indicate. Steinitz was not in his best form on that day and got into the hopeless endgame shown in diagram 2. Chigorin, a piece up, should have played 32 RxNP, after which his material superiority would have ensured victory, for 32 ... RxQP? is answered by 33 N-B4. Instead the game took an unexpected turn: **32 B-N4?? RxPch**, and White resigned. Steinitz thus retained his title.

During his world championship match against Tal in 1960 Botvinnik made an incomprehensible mistake which may

well have cost him his title. He did the same against Petrosian three years later.

In the match against Tal, Botvinnik, although two points behind after sixteen games, was by no means without hope, as his strong finish showed. In the seventeenth game, however, where he had won

3. Tal–Botvinnik

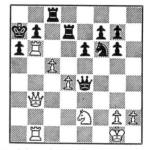

Position after White's 39th move

two pawns in a safe position (see diagram 3), he played **39 ... Q-Q4**, and after **40 RxRPch K-N1** (40 ... PxR 41 Q-N6ch K-R1 42 QxRPch R-R2 43 QxR (B8) mate) **41 Q-R4** resigned. Instead he could have countered White's threat of 40 P-B6 by 39 ... K-R1, e.g. 40 P-B6 RxBP 41 RxNP R-B8ch! 42 RxR (42 NxR Q-K8 mate) 42 ... RxR, etc. As it was, he found himself three points down with seven rounds to go, which virtually assured his opponent of victory.

In his match with Petrosian Botvinnik was one point down after fifteen games,

4. Botvinnik–Petrosian

Position after Black's 38th move

having won two, lost three and drawn ten. In the position in diagram 4 Botvinnik could have won by 39 RxP R-QB1 40 K-R2 R(B1)-B7 41 R-KN1, etc. However, he was in time-trouble and played the faulty 39 P-K6. Now 39 . . . K-B3 40 RxP RxKP 41 RxRch KxR 42 R-QN4 P-QN4, etc., would have sufficed to draw, but instead Petrosian chose to go on with his original plan, which was also adequate: 39 . . . R-QB1 40 K-R2 R(B1)-B7 41 R-KN1 (Botvinnik had obviously just realized that 41 P-K7 RxNPch 42 K-R3 is answered by 42 . . . P-KN4 43 P-K8=Nch K-B1.) 41 . . . R-Q7 42 R(Q1)-K1 K-B1 43 P-K7ch K-K1 44 K-N3 P-Q6 (threatening R-K7) 45 R-K3 R(R7)-N7 46 K-B4 RxKNP 47 R-Q1 R(QN7)-Q7 48 RxR RxR 49 K-N5 (the last chance) 49 . . . R-Q8 50 K-B6 (avoiding 50 KxP? R-KN8ch 51 K-B6 P-Q7 52 R-B3 R-N3ch! with a win for Black) 50 . . . P-B5 (not 50 . . . P-Q7 51 R-Q6 winning) 51 R-K4 R-QB8 52 R-Q4 R-B3ch 53 K-N5 R-B6 54 K-B6 drawn.

In the 1956 Candidates' Tournament in Amsterdam Keres was one point behind the leader, Smyslov. In the penultimate round he sacrificed a pawn in his game against Filip to create complications. From the position shown in diagram 5 he went on the attack.

5. Keres–Filip

Position after Black's 32nd move

| 33 N-K6! | PxN |
| 34 BxB | N-Q3 |

Not, of course, 34 . . . KxB? 35 RxNch R-B2 36 Q-QB3ch! winning.

| 35 B-K5 | R-B1?? |

Filip is the first to go wrong. Much better is 35 . . . N-B2, after which Black has a defensible position.

| 36 Q-B4 | N-B2 |
| 37 R-N7 | Q-B1 |

Or 37 . . . NxB 38 QxN Q-B1 39 QxKPch, etc. After the text-move White could have attained a winning position by 38 Q-B6 NxB 39 QxN. Instead he made an indecisive move, which had a big effect on the outcome of this important game.

| 38 K-R2?? | R-B5! |
| 39 Q-B6 | NxB |

Now if White takes the knight, Black replies 40 . . . Q-B5ch exchanging queens.

| 40 QxKPch | N-B2 |
| 41 P-N3 | RxP |

and Black won on the 91st move.

6. Anderssen–Paulsen

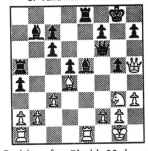

Position after Black's 23rd move

This game had a decisive bearing on the first prize in the London Tournament of 1862, a tournament which went down in history as the first in which chess clocks were used. Black won a pawn, but in doing so he weakened his king's side and allowed his bishop to be subjected to a deadly pin. White should now have continued 24 RxR! RxR 25 P-KB4!, after which both 25 . . . PxP 26 BxR and 25

... QxP 26 R-KB1 would have led to a decisive win of material. Instead Anderssen made an interesting mistake.

24 Q-K2?   ...

Now Black is given an opportunity to save the game by sacrificing his bishop to pin his opponent's: 24 ... Q-N3! 25 BxB P-B3!

24 ...   **Q-R1??**

Black sacrifices in the wrong way, allowing his opponent to exploit the weakness of his king's side.

25 BxB	P-B3
26 Q-R5	RxB
27 RxR	PxR
28 Q-K8ch	K-N2
29 N-B5ch	Resigns

The outcome of many a tournament is influenced by the unsuccessful attempts of players to win at all costs in an important game.

7. Bogolyubov–Vidmar

Position after Black's 16th move

After the logical 17 B-K3, developing a piece, White would have a slight advantage. Instead he weakens his position by initiating a completely unwarranted attack.

17 P-B4?	N-B4!
18 NxN	BxNch
19 B-K3	B-Q5
20 Q-KB2?	

Realizing that he has already squandered his advantage, Bogolyubov makes a bad mistake, which leads to the clear loss of a pawn. However, after 20 BxB QxBch 21 K-R1 KR-Q1 Black would have had the slightly better position.

20 ...	BxNP!
21 QR-Q1	

Or 21 QxB QxB 22 B-B5 QxP! etc.

21 ...	B-B6!
22 B-B5	

After 22 BxP Q-B1 23 BxB QxB Black would win either the QRP or the KP.

22 ...	R-K1
23 B-B2	Q-B2
24 B-N6	Q-B5
25 B-Q3	Q-B3

and Black won in the endgame.

This game was played in the last round of a tournament in Sliac in 1952. By winning it Vidmar succeeded in sharing first prize with Flohr, while Bogolyubov had to be content with eighth place.

In spite of what was said above, attack in decisive games tends to have the upper hand over defence. To defend correctly demands great precision and a cool head, requirements which are difficult to fulfil at a time when everything is at stake.

The Paris Tournament of 1878 ended in a tie between Zukertort and Winawer.

8. Zukertort–Winawer

Position after White's 33rd move

In accordance with the rules at that time a play-off took place to split the tie. The first two games were drawn, but the remaining two, after taking a dramatic course, were won by Zukertort. The result, however, was not a real reflection of the play on the board.

In the third game, for example (see diagram 8), Zukertort had made an incorrect pawn sacrifice. His opponent, however, defended inaccurately.

33 ...   P-R4?

Seriously weakening the king's side. Better was 33 . . . B-B1!

34 B-B1   R-K2

If 34 . . . N-Q5, then 35 RxNP NxB 36 RxPch K-N1 37 R-R8ch K-B2 38 RxRch winning.

35 BxN   R(K2)xB??

Black should have taken with the other rook.

36 B-N2   R-B2

Black would have had better prospects after 36 . . . R-K4. On the other hand, 36 . . . R-B1 37 RxPch PxR 38 BxBch would win for White.

37 RxNP   RxR
38 RxPch   K-N1
39 R-R8ch   BxR
40 QxB mate

In the fourth and final game Zukertort made an incorrect piece sacrifice.

9. Winawer–Zukertort

Position after White's 23rd move

23 ...   RxP?
24 RxN!   B-N2
25 N-K4?

Here White had two winning lines, the quiet 25 R-K2 R-KB1 26 PxP BxP 27 B-K7 and 25 R-K4 R-KB1 26 B-K7 RxKNPch 27 KxR Q-B6ch 28 K-R3 B-B1ch 29 Q-N4, etc.

25 ...   RxKNPch!
26 KxR   QxR

Now White's knight is subjected to an unpleasant pin and the king is badly exposed. There is no way for White to avoid a loss of material.

27 R-K1   R-K1
28 K-B3   P-KR3
29 B-Q2   K-N1!

Threatening 30 . . . P-N4.

30 P-KR3?

White prepares the defensive manoeuvre Q-N4, but in so doing fails to see a second threat, which quickly decides the game.

30 ...   Q-B4ch
31 Q-B4   QxPch
32 K-B2   R-KB1
33 QxRch   KxQ
34 B-B4   Q-B4

and Black won.

In the Vienna Tournament of 1908 Duras needed to win in the last round to

10. Duras–Bardeleben

Position after White's 31st move

catch Schlechter and Maróczy, who were half a point in front of him and who both drew in the final round. That explains why the Czech grandmaster, playing the white pieces, embarked on such a doubtful enterprise in the following game.

31 ...	NxB
32 RxR	RxR
33 QxRP?	NxP!
34 KxN	Q-B5

All at once the situation looks bad for White, for 35 QxR is answered by 35 . . . Q-N5ch 36 K-R1 (36 K-B1 B-N4ch) 36 . . . QxNch 37 K-N1 B-B3 38 K-B1 Q-R6ch 39 K-K2 B-N4ch 40 K-Q1 (40 K-Q2 B-R3ch) 40 . . . Q-B6ch, etc.

35 P-R3	B-B3
36 R-K3	R-QN1
37 Q-B4	B-QR1
38 Q-KB7	R-Q1
39 B-R2	RxP??

Once again fortune favours the bold, for Black now goes wrong. He should first have played 39 . . . B-K5!, after which RxQP really is a threat.

40 Q-N8ch	K-R3
41 QxB(R8)	R-Q8
42 R-K8	Resigns

The next example is from the game between the favourites and leaders in the ninth round of a tournament at Mayren-Ostrau in 1923.

11. Réti–Lasker

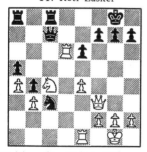

Position after White's 27th move

The former world champion, Lasker, is in a difficult situation, being faced by the threat of 28 P-K5, which would give his opponent a considerable advantage in space. He therefore decides on a counterattack, after which the game takes a dramatic turn. It should be noted that 27 . . . NxRP? 28 R(K1)-Q1 N-B4 29 N-N6 loses the exchange.

27 ...	P-K4!?
28 Q-B5	N-K7ch?!?
29 K-B1	

White rightly avoids losing the exchange by 29 RxN QxR 30 QxBPch K-R1! However, the continuation he chooses isn't good either. He could have refuted Black's combination by moving the king in the other direction, e.g. 29 K-R1 N-Q5 30 QxKP NxP 31 N-N6 Q-B6 32 QxQ PxQ 33 NxQR P-B7 34 P-R3 P-B8=Q 35 RxQ RxRch 36 K-R2 remaining a pawn up.

29 ...	N-Q5
30 QxKP	NxP
31 N-N6	N-Q7ch!
32 K-N1	N-B5

The tempo that Black gained by checking from Q7 decides the game in his favour, for his passed pawn on the QN file is a very strong weapon.

33 NxN	QxN
34 Q-KB5	QR-N1
35 P-K5	P-N6
36 P-K6	PxP
37 R(Q6)xP	R-KB1
38 Q-K5	Q-B7
39 P-B4	P-N7
40 R-K7	Q-N3
41 P-B5	Q-KB3
42 Q-Q5ch	K-R1
43 R-N7	Q-B6
44 Resigns	

The final result of the tournament was Lasker 10½, Réti 9½, Grünfeld 8½, etc.

Even the best players in the world are not immune to mistakes while defending in important games. In the key game of the tournament at Margate 1935, Capablanca defended accurately for a long time against Reshevsky. In the end, however, he made a bad mistake.

12. Reshevsky–Capablanca

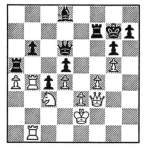

45 ...   BxP?

By playing 45 . . . Q-K3 followed by Q-B4 Capablanca could have obtained the draw which was so vital to him.

46	RxNP	Q-R6
47	K-Q2	B-K2
48	R-N7	

Not, of course, 48 NxP? Q-Q6ch.

48	...	RxRP
49	QxP	R-R4
50	QxP	R-KR4
51	K-Q3	Q-R1
52	Q-K6	Q-R6
53	R-Q7	R(R4)-KB4
54	R-N3	Q-R8
55	RxB	Q-KB8ch
56	K-Q2	Resigns

Reshevsky won the tournament with 7½ points, just half a point in front of Capablanca, who was well ahead of the other participants. The former world champion was thus very near to winning. A single accurate defensive move would have sufficed.

A very important asset for tournament play is the ability to overcome a state of depression caused by a loss. Some players lose their self-confidence after

being defeated and choose to play for a draw in the next round in the hope of getting over their depression. Others act as though the loss had given them new energy and increased their physical strength enormously. Bogolyubov belonged to this second category. A classic example is his performance at the Karlsbad Tournament of 1923. He lost in the tenth, twelfth and fourteenth games but was the winner in those that followed, including that in the fifteenth round in which he had the black pieces against Rubinstein.

13. Rubinstein–Bogolyubov

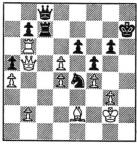

35 ...   Q-KR1!

A remarkable way of getting the queen into play. White cannot now continue with 36 RxNP because of 36 . . . QxP! 37 RxRch K-R3 38 Q-Q3 Q-B7ch 39 K-R3 P-N4 with a mating attack.

36	Q-Q3	PxP
37	R-N5	Q-QB1
38	RxQP	R-B7
39	Q-N5	K-R3
40	K-B3	R-Q7

Threatening Q-B8. White, however, has an adequate defence.

41	Q-B4	QxQ
42	BxQ	RxP

Black has made the most of the position. Even so, after the correct continuation 43 B-Q3 the game should have ended in a draw, e.g. 43 . . . R-N6 44

K-K3 P-N3 45 R-N5 RxR 46 BxR NxP
47 P-Q5, etc.

| 43 P-N4?? | N-Q7ch |
| 44 Resigns | |

The result of this important game depended on a blunder. The remarkable fact is that it should have been committed by such a sound player, especially as he was already out of the running for a high place. Bogolyubov's tenacity, on the other hand, was rewarded, for Alekhin, who with three rounds to go had a clear lead of one point, lost in the penultimate round with the white pieces in a nervously played game to Spielmann, who shared last place in the tournament.

Queen's Gambit

Alekhin	Spielmann
1 P-Q4	N-KB3
2 P-QB4	P-K3
3 N-KB3	P-Q4
4 N-B3	QN-Q2

5 B-B4?	PxP
6 P-K3	N-N3
7 KBxP	NxB
8 Q-R4ch	P-B3
9 QxN	N-Q4
10 B-K5	P-B3
11 B-N3	Q-N3
12 Q-K2	B-N5
13 R-QB1	NxN
14 PxN	B-R6
15 R-Q1	Q-N4
16 P-B4	Q-QR4ch
17 N-Q2	0-0
18 0-0	P-QN3
19 P-B4	B-R3
20 B-K1	Q-R5
21 R-B2	QR-Q1
22 R-N1	P-QB4
23 PxP	B(R6)xP
24 N-N3	B-R6
25 N-Q4	BxP

and Black won after 62 moves.

The final result of the tournament was 1-3 Alekhin, Bernstein and Bogolyubov!

2 Baden-Baden 1870

An Incorrect Sacrifice Leads to a Tournament Victory

The first part of the 1870 international tournament, which was held in July and August at the German spa of Baden-Baden, later the venue for many a chess contest, proved to be most interesting. A system of matches consisting of two games each having been adopted, Anderssen defeated his main rival, Steinitz, before causing the greatest surprise of the whole tournament by losing 2:0 to Neumann.

One of the participants, the German master Stern, had to leave after playing four games. The war between France and Prussia had just broken out and Stern was given the opportunity of seeking fame in the uniform of a Prussian officer but had to forgo the attempt to achieve less glorious, but also less dangerous, success in the tournament.

The outbreak of war caused a lively discussion among the participants about whether or not the tournament should be continued. Baden-Baden was not far from the French border, and, as the French army was still of high repute, the possibility of the town being occupied could not be ignored. However, professional solidarity, or the desire to win the prizes, prevailed, and the tournament continued, though, according to press reports, in a fairly nervous atmosphere.

After ten rounds the position was as follows: Neumann 7½, Anderssen and Blackburne 7, Steinitz 6. Then, however, Neumann dropped back. First he lost two games to Steinitz and then one each to Rosenthal and de Vère. Steinitz, on the other hand, played with great energy and at the beginning of the last round was only half a point behind the leader,

Anderssen. In the seven games from rounds eleven to seventeen he scored 5½ points and in the last round had to face an opponent who was in the lower half of the table—de Vère. Anderssen also had to play someone who was not in the best of form, though his opponent was one of the leading players of that time. This game between two old rivals was to determine the winner of the tournament.

Ruy Lopez

Anderssen	Paulsen
1 P-K4	P-K4
2 N-KB3	N-QB3
3 B-N5	P-QR3
4 B-R4	N-B3
5 P-Q3	P-Q3
6 BxN	

Anderssen again adopts the system he had successfully employed in London eight years previously against the same opponent in an equally vital game. On that occasion the exchange BxN occurred one move earlier, for Paulsen had played 3 . . . N-KB3, omitting 3 . . . P-QR3.

| 6 . . . | PxB |
| 7 P-KR3 | P-N3 |

In London Paulsen had developed the bishop to K2, but now he improves on his defence by adopting a fianchetto, which is still considered strong today in such positions.

| 8 N-B3 | |

More than three decades later, Duras was very keen on such attacks against the castled king as played here by Anderssen.

The only difference was that he first made the advance P-QB4 and then developed by N-QB3, B-K3, Q-Q2, etc.

8 . . .	B-KN2
9 B-K3	0-0
10 Q-Q2	K-R1!

A good manoeuvre. It is clear that Paulsen, who was one of the greatest theoreticians of his time, had done his homework.

| 11 B-R6 | N-N1 |
| 12 BxBch | KxB |

Black is now ready to play P-KB4, which White must prevent. If he tries to counter in the centre with 13 P-Q4 Black gets a very good game after 13 . . . PxP 14 QxPch Q-B3 15 Q-Q2 (15 Q-R4 N-K2) 15 . . . R-K1 or 14 NxP Q-K1 15 Q-B4 N-B3.

| 13 P-KN4 | Q-B3 |

A debatable move. Black invites the pawn advance P-KN5 so that, after withdrawing his queen, he can break up White's pawns by P-KB3. However, the queen is not well placed on KB3, because the logical freeing move P-KB4 is prevented. In view of the fact that neither side has completed his development 13 . . . P-KB4!? would have been possible without undue risks. A good alternative is 13 . . . P-QB4 followed by N-K2-B3-Q5

| 14 Q-K3 | B-K3 |
| 15 N-K2 | |

If 15 P-N5 Q-K2 16 P-Q4, then PxP 17 QxPch P-B3 and Black frees himself by P-QB4 and PxP.

15 . . .	P-B4
16 0-0-0	P-QR4
17 P-B4	R(B1)-N1
18 R(Q1)-N1	Q-Q1
19 P-N5	

If White plays 19 P-KR4, Black can reply P-KR3 and prevent a file on the king's side being forced open. However,

after the text-move, White's attack is not particularly effective.

19 . . .	Q-QB1
20 N-B3	P-R5
21 N-Q2	N-K2
22 P-B3?	

A move not in keeping with Anderssen's style. Perhaps it was intended as a trap, though a chess player of master class is hardly likely to take the pawn on Black's KR6 thereby opening a line of attack for his opponent (e.g. 22 . . . BxRP 23 P-B4 or 23 R-R2). Better would have been 22 P-B4, although after 22 . . . PxP 23 QxKBP N-B3 Black would have had a sound position (e.g. 24 Q-B6ch K-N1 25 P-R4 Q-Q1 or 24 P-R4 N-K4 25 Q-B6ch K-N1 26 P-R5 Q-Q1! 27 PxP QxQ 28 PxRPch K-R1 29 PxQ NxQPch).

22 . . .	Q-N2
23 N-Q1	N-B3
24 P-R4	N-Q5

With the pretty threat of 25 . . . P-R6 26 P-N3 NxNP 27 NxN QxN! 28 PxQ P-R7.

| 25 P-R3 | Q-R2? |

Now the queen will be out of play for a considerable time. It would have been better to transfer the king to K2 at once.

26 P-R5	Q-R4
27 R-R2	K-B1
28 PxP	RPxP
29 P-B4	PxP
30 QxP	K-K2

The point of Black's defence. His king can take refuge on the queen's side.

31 N-KB3	K-Q2
32 K-N1	R-N6
33 NxN	PxN
34 K-B2	Q-K4
35 Q-B2	

Black's pieces are actively placed, and an objective evaluation would indicate an exchange of queens for White to ensure a draw. However, Anderssen had to win this game to be sure of first place. On the other hand, defeat could have meant dropping back to fourth place.

35 ...	R(R1)-QN1
36 R-R7	K-B3
37 Q-Q2	K-Q2
38 R-B1	K-B3
39 R-B6	R(N6)-N2
40 Q-B2	

White is obviously trying at all costs to upset the equilibrium. Black cannot now play 40 . . . QxNP? 41 QxP Q-K4 42 QxQ PxQ 43 R(R7)xP, etc.

40 ...	R-N6

Instead of this, Black could transfer his king to KR2 and thus prevent White's exchange sacrifice, for after 40 . . . K-N3 the continuation 41 N-B3 K-R4! 42 N-N5? fails to 42 . . . P-B3. The exchange sacrifice, however, should be no real danger for Black.

14. Anderssen–Paulsen

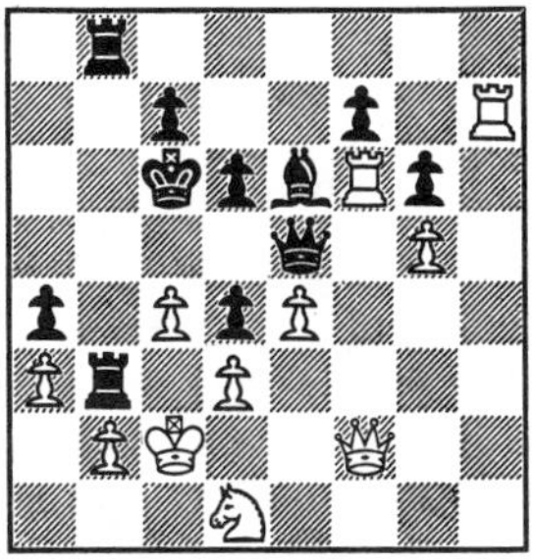

41 R(B6)xBP!?

Objectively this move deserves a question-mark. For the daring way in which Anderssen proceeds, an exclamation mark is called for. In this game, whose loss would have cost him a lot, both from the point of view of chess and financially, he risked a great deal. But here again fortune favoured the bold.

41 ...	BxR
42 QxB	R(N6)-N2
43 Q-Q7ch	K-N3
44 QxRP	QxNP
45 P-N4	Q-K4??

Paulsen overlooks the only real, and not very complicated, threat. After 45 . . . R-R2 Black would have had a won game, for the passive retreat 46 Q-N3 is obviously hopeless, and if instead White tries 45 Q-Q7, there follows 46 . . . R-Q1 47 Q-N7 (47 Q-B7 Q-N7ch 48 K-N3 Q-Q7) 47 . . . Q-K4 48 Q-B7 (48 QxNP RxP) 48 . . . R-KR1! etc.

46 N-N2!

Now there is no defence to the terrible threat of 47 P-B5ch PxP 48 N-B4 mate. Black's next few moves only succeed in prolonging the game a little.

46 ...	R-R2
47 P-B5ch	K-N2
48 Q-N5ch	K-R1
49 Q-B6ch	R(R2)-N2
50 RxP	Resigns

Baden-Baden 1870

	1	2	3	4	5	6	7	8	9	10	Pts	Prize
1 Anderssen	–	1 1	1 ½	0 0	1 1	½ 1	1 0	1 1	0 1	1 1	13	I
2 Steinitz	0 0	–	0 ½	1 1	1 1	1 1	1 1	0 ½	1 ½	1 1	12½	II
3 Blackburne	0 ½	1 ½	–	½ 0	0 1	1 1	1 ½	1 1	½ ½	1 1	12	III, IV
4 Neumann	1 1	0 0	½ 1	–	0 1	0 1	1 1	1 1	½ 0	1 1	12	III, IV
5 L Paulsen	0 0	0 0	1 0	1 0	–	1 0	½ 1	1 ½	1 ½	1 1	9½	V
6 de Vère	½ 0	0 0	0 0	1 0	0 1	–	1 0	0 1	1 1	1 1	8½	
7 Winawer	0 1	0 0	0 ½	0 0	½ 0	0 1	–	1 1	1 ½	1 1	8½	
8 Minckwitz	0 0	1 ½	0 0	0 0	0 ½	1 0	0 0	–	1 1	1 1	7	
9 Rosenthal	1 0	0 ½	½ ½	½ 1	0 ½	0 0	0 ½	0 0	–	1 1	7	
10 Stern	0 0	(½ 0)	0 0	0 0	0 0	0 0	0 0	(1 0)	0 0	–	–	

The German player Stern played only the four games shown in brackets. Then he had to leave because of the outbreak of war. All his games were deemed to have been won by his opponents.

3 Vienna 1873

Failure at the Post

Cases in which a mistake unexpectedly upsets the result of a tournament at the last moment are by no means unusual, and no one seems to worry about them except those immediately concerned. However, it does sometimes happen that an unexpected set-back, a falling off in form or a loss to a much weaker opponent can influence the outcome of the tournament to such an extent that historians cannot simply gloss over it.

One such case occurred in the first international tournament in the Austrian capital, which was later, at the turn of the century, to become a focal point of world chess.

The English master Blackburne was on the point of becoming the hero of the tournament. He was within inches of achieving the major success of his life. His failure was all the more tragic.

The tournament was played on a system of matches consisting of three games, only the matches being counted, so that, if a player won the first two games, the third was not played. This system tended to confuse the true performance of the players, for a victory by 2:0 or 2½:½ was valued no higher than the less deserving 2:1.

Soon after the start the English master Blackburne faced Steinitz, and caused the first great sensation of the tournament by beating him in the first and third games, where he had White, and drawing in the second, where he had Black. Then he continued his run of victories. He defeated players as renowned as Paulsen and Bird, and finally won the match against his second most difficult opponent, Anderssen.

There remained only one more match—against Rosenthal—and a victory or a draw in that would have ensured him first prize and the greatest success of his chess career.

A present-day grandmaster or master would approach such a decisive match with caution and possibly be content with three draws against the weaker player. Such tactics, however, were unknown to the chess generation of the 1870s. At that time it was not only victory that counted; the beauty of its conception, a convincing win and the applause of the whole chess world played their part.

Blackburne sacrificed two pawns in the first game and after move thirty had a lost position (see diagram 15).

15. Blackburne–Rosenthal

Black has several ways of winning. For the reasons mentioned Rosenthal chooses the most showy.

32 ...	NxBP
33 BxBPch	K-R1?

This leads to unnecessary complications, which Black could avoid by playing his king to KB1.

34 NxR

A move of despair, which fails by a hair's breadth to bring victory. Blackburne had obviously worked out that the following continuation loses: 34 KxN B-B4ch 35 RxB RxQ 36 RxR (36 NxR Q-K6ch and mate in two moves) 36 ... RxR 37 R-Q8ch K-R2 38 B-N8ch K-N3 39 R-Q6ch K-R4 40 B-B7ch P-KN3 41 RxNP R-B7ch 42 K-K1 R-B8ch! 43 K-Q2 (43 K-K2 Q-B8ch) 43 ... Q-Q2ch 44 KxR QxB.

| 34 ... | NxQ |
| 35 RxN | P-B6?? |

An unbelievable mistake. Now after the obvious 36 RxP and the forced continuation 36 ... B-B4ch 37 K-R1 Q-B1 38 P-N4 Q-B2 39 N-N6ch K-R2 40 PxB White has a rook and two minor pieces for the queen.

Although there was only a draw to be had from 35 ... B-B4ch 36 RxB RxR 37 N-N6ch with perpetual check, Black could have won without difficulty by 35 ...Q-B4 36 N-N6ch K-R2 37 RxR RxR 38 N-B8ch K-R1.

The surprises, however, are not yet over.

36 NxP??	BxPch
37 NxB	QxR
38 R-B1	Q-K6ch
39 K-R1	R-Q7
40 B-N6	RxNch
41 KxR	Q-K7ch
42 Resigns	

How can such a case be explained? It is obvious that Blackburne had already written off the game and so failed to take the unexpected chance that he was later given.

The English master failed to recover from this defeat. The second game was drawn, and the third, which he had to win, had all the appearances of having been played in a coffee-house.

King's Gambit

Blackburne	Rosenthal
1 P-K4	P-K4
2 P-KB4	PxP
3 N-KB3	P-KN4
4 P-KR4	P-N5
5 N-K5	Q-K2
6 NxNP?	

The correct continuation is 6 P-Q4 P-Q3 7 NxNP P-KB4 8 N-B2, which incidentally was well known at the time the game was played.

6 ...	P-KB4
7 N-B2	PxP
8 N-B3	

Or 8 Q-R5ch K-Q1 9 Q-KB5 P-K6!

| 8 ... | N-KB3 |
| 9 N-N4? | |

Or 9 N-Q5 NxN 10 Q-R5ch Q-B2 11 Q-K5ch Q-K3 12 QxR N-KB3 with advantage to Black.

9 ...	N-R4
10 N-K3	N-N6
11 Q-N4	NxR
12 QxBP	P-B3
13 N-B5	Q-K3
14 B-K2	P-Q4
15 B-N4	Q-B3
16 P-Q4	BxN
17 BxB	B-Q3
18 Q-N4	R-B1
19 Q-R5ch	Q-B2
20 B-N4	QxQ
21 BxQch	K-Q2
22 B-R6	N-R3
23 B-N4ch	K-B2
24 BxR	RxB
25 N-K2	N-N6
26 Resigns	

The top two players had thus lost one match each, so in accordance with the rules a play-off took place. In their previous match Steinitz had drawn one game and lost two. Now, however, his opponent was in bad psychological shape, and the match proved to be an un-expected walk-over.

Ruy Lopez

	Blackburne	Steinitz
1	P-K4	P-K4
2	N-KB3	N-QB3
3	B-N5	P-QR3
4	B-R4	N-B3
5	Q-K2	P-QN4
6	B-N3	B-N2

It is interesting to note that this method of development has occurred frequently in tournaments recently.

7 P-Q3

Quiet development like this is not likely to cause Black any great trouble. White has greater chances with 7 P-B3 followed by 0-0, R-Q1 and P-Q4.

7	...	B-B4
8	P-B3	0-0
9	B-N5	P-R3
10	B-KR4	B-K2

Black has, it is true, lost a tempo; on the other hand, White's bishop on KR4 is by no means brilliantly placed. Another possibility is 10 ... P-Q3 followed by B-N3, N-N1 and QN-Q2.

11 QN-Q2   K-R1

A move that is difficult to understand. Black perhaps intends to reply to 12 0-0 by N-KN1 and, after White's retreat 13 B-N3, regroup his minor pieces (B-B3, KN-K2). The move 11 ... P-Q3 looks better.

12 N-B1

Contemporary annotators considered this move to be bad and possibly even the cause of White's defeat—to my mind wrongly, however. Black has also devel-

oped slowly (B-K2, K-R1), so White can quite safely postpone castling.

12	...	P-QR4!?
13	P-R4	PxP
14	BxRP	P-Q4!?

Steinitz obviously makes a correct assessment of the psychological condition of his opponent and decides to embark on a cut and thrust affair. If White now accepts the pawn sacrifice (15 KBxN BxB 16 NxP) Black has, after B-N2, an active game as well as the two bishops.

15	Q-B2	PxP
16	PxP	N-Q2
17	B-KN3?	

A bad mistake. The tempo lost through retreating with the bishop will have serious consequences. The correct continuation is 17 BxB QxB 18 N-N3 (better than 18 N-K3 N-B4 19 0-0 N-Q1! with unpleasant pressure on the KP) 18 ... N-B4 19 0-0 with approximate equality.

17	...	N-B4!
18	R-Q1	Q-K1!

16. Blackburne–Steinitz

With this move Black gives additional protection to his knight on QB3 and thus paves the way for B-R3. Naturally he has nothing to fear from White taking his king's pawn: 19 NxP NxB 20 QxN NxN 21 QxQ R(B1)xQ 22 BxN BxP, etc.

| 19 | N-K3 | B-R3! |

If now 20 BxN QxB 21 NxP, Black can choose between an exchange of queens (21 ... QxP 22 QxQ NxQ 23 R-Q7 B-B3 24 N(K3)-N4 QR-N1) and the promising pawn sacrifice 21 ... Q-K3 22 P-KB3 QR-N1

20 N-Q5?	B-Q3
21 N-R4	

The continuation 21 BxN QxB 22 NxKP can be answered by 22 ... Q-K1 or 22 ... BxN 23 BxB R-K1, in both cases with advantage to Black. White's only chance lies in artificial castling—P-KB3 and K-B2—though there is not really enough time for it.

21 ...	R-QN1
22 N-B6!?	

Answering the threat of 22 ... NxB 23 QxN RxP. Black cannot accept the sacrifice: e.g. 22 ... PxN 23 Q-B1 N-K3 24 QxPch K-N1 25 N-B5 RxP 26 RxB! PxR 27 BxN Q-Q1 28 B-KR4, etc., or 25 ... B-N4 26 B-N3! Q-Q2 27 B-KR4, etc.

White's impressive-looking move, however, merely leads to an exchange of pieces, which in no way improves his situation.

22 ...	Q-K3!
23 BxN	QxN
24 P-B3	R-N3
25 B-Q5	R(B1)-QN1
26 P-N3	NxNP
27 N-B5	N-B4
28 P-QB4	R-N7
29 NxB	PxN

Or 29 ... RxQ 30 NxPch K-R2 31 BxP Q-K2.

30 Q-B3	KR-N6
31 QxRP	R-K6ch
32 K-B1	RxBPch
33 K-N1	RxB
34 Resigns	

In the second game Blackburne again failed to put up any resistance. Steinitz even played an irregular opening, which was something very unusual for him.

Irregular

Steinitz	Blackburne
1 P-QR3	P-KN3
2 P-Q4	B-N2
3 P-K4	P-QB4
4 PxP	Q-B2
5 B-Q3	QxBP
6 N-K2	N-QB3
7 B-K3	Q-QR4ch
8 QN-B3	P-Q3
9 0-0	B-Q2
10 P-QN4	Q-Q1
11 R-N1	P-N3?

Black should play 11 ... N-B3 at once.

| 12 N-Q5 | N-B3 |

Better is 12 ... P-K3!

13 NxNch	BxN
14 B-KR6!	N-K4
15 P-R3	R-KN1
16 P-KB4	N-B3
17 Q-Q2	Q-B2
18 P-B4	N-Q1
19 R(B1)-QB1	N-K3
20 N-B3	Q-N2
21 N-Q5	B-R1
22 K-R1	R-QB1
23 Q-KB2	B(Q2)-B3
24 Q-R4	N-Q5
25 B-N5	BxN
26 BPxB	K-Q2
27 BxP	RxR
28 RxR	R-QB1
29 R-Q1	R-B6
30 B-B6	Q-B1
31 Q-N4ch	N-B4
32 B-QN5ch	K-B2
33 BxR	P-KR4
34 Q-B3	N-R5
35 BxB	QxB
36 R-QB1ch	K-N2
37 Q-B3	Q-Q1
38 Q-QB6ch	K-N1
39 B-R6	Resigns

Vienna 1873

	1	2	3	4	5	6	7	8	9	10	11	12	Pts	Prize
1 Steinitz	—	0 ½ 0	1 1	1 1	1 1	1 1	½ 1 ½	1 1	½ 1 ½	1 1	1 1	1 1	10	I
2 Blackburne	1 ½ 1	—	0 1 1	0 ½ 0	1 1	1 0 1	1 0 1	1 1	1 1	½ 1 1	1 0 1	1 0 1	10	II
3 Anderssen	0 0	1 0 0	—	0 1 1	0 1 1	1 1	0 1 ½	0 1 1	½ ½ 1	1 1	0 1 1	½ 1 1	8½	III
4 Rosenthal	0 0	1 ½ 1	1 0 0	—	0 0	1 0 ½	1 1	1 0 1	1 1	1 0 1	1 1	1 1	7½	IV
5 Bird	0 0	0 0	1 0 0	1 1	—	0 0	1 1	0 ½ 1	1 1	1 1	1 1	1 1	6½	V, VI
6 L Paulsen	0 0	0 1 0	0 0	0 1 ½	1 1	—	1 1	0 1 ½	½ 1 1	1 1	1 0 ½	1 1	6½	V, VI
7 Fleissig	½ 0 ½	0 1 0	1 0 ½	0 0	0 0	0 0	—	0 ½ 1	0 1 1	1 0 0	0 ½ 1	1 1	3½	
8 Heral	0 0	0 0	1 0 0	0 1 0	0 ½ 1	1 0 ½	1 ½ 0	—	0 ½ 1	½ 0 1	½ 1 0	0 1 0	3	
9 Meitner	½ 0 ½	0 0	½ ½ 0	0 0	0 0	½ 0 0	1 0 0	1 ½ 0	—	½ 1 ½	½ 1 1	1 1	3½	
10 Gelbfuss	0 0	½ 0 0	0 0	0 1 0	0 0	0 0	0 1 1	½ 1 0	½ 0 ½	—	½ ½ ½	½ 1 1	3	
11 Schwarz	0 0	0 1 0	1 0 0	0 0	0 0	0 1 ½	1 ½ 0	½ 0 1	½ 0 0	½ ½ ½	—	½ 1 ½	3	
12 Pitschel	0 0	0 1 0	½ 0 0	0 0	0 0	0 0	0 0	1 0 1	0 0	½ 0 0	½ 0 ½	—	1	

In this tournament, matches of three games were played. If the first two games were won by the same player the third was not played. In the final result only the matches, and not the games, counted. There was a play-off between Steinitz and Blackburne, which ended 2:0 in favour of Steinitz.

4 The First World Championship Match

Cool Calculation versus Attacking Élan

The 1870s and 1880s were dominated by two players of entirely different character. The cosmopolitan Steinitz, who was born in Prague, was too far ahead of his time to enjoy any particular popularity in the chess world. He played a ponderous type of chess, thinking over his moves slowly and calculating accurately. He preferred dour defence and positional manoeuvres to brilliant attacks, indulging in combinations only when the result could be clearly foreseen.

Zukertort, who was six years younger, played an elegant type of chess that was understood by his contemporaries. He never had difficulties with his clock, he worked out impressive combinations at lightning speed, and he played for the spectators, with whom he was very popular. In 1878 and 1883 Zukertort won two great international tournaments, in Paris and in London, the latter by a margin of three clear points from Steinitz. In London and the previous year in Vienna these two players faced each other a total of four times, Zukertort winning twice, Steinitz once, with one game drawn.

After extensive negotiations they met in 1886 in the first match recognized by the chess world as a world championship title match. It was played in the three American towns of New York, St Louis and New Orleans. Steinitz made a tragic start, being 4:1 down after losing four and winning one of the five games played in New York. Not a single game was drawn. That was the position on 20 January. The scene then moved to St Louis, where play in the sixth game began on 3 February. Here Steinitz managed to level matters by 10 February, winning three and halving one. After a fortnight's break the match was continued in New Orleans, where the tenth game was drawn. This was virtually the start of a new match of ten games, with chances equal. In the eleventh game Zukertort had White, and it was assumed that he would make a renewed effort to go into the lead.

Four Knights Game

Zukertort	Steinitz
1 P-K4	P-K4
2 N-KB3	N-QB3
3 N-B3	N-B3
4 B-N5	B-N5
5 0-0	0-0
6 N-Q5	

Such sallies were very popular in the last century. Current theory gives this move a question-mark, though it should be remembered that the experience of several generations was necessary for this conclusion to be reached. Correct is 6 P-Q3, but 6 BxN QPxB 7 P-Q3 is also good.

| 6 ... | NxN |
| 7 PxN | P-K5! |

A discovery of Steinitz's, which is the reason why 6 N-Q5 has completely disappeared.

8 PxN

The best way of attaining equality is 8 N-K1 N-K2 9 P-Q3. Now, however, the initiative goes over to Black.

| 8 ... | PxN |
| 9 QxP | |

18

Not, of course, 9 PxNP BxP or 9 PxQP
PxNP! etc.

9 . . .	QPxP
10 B-Q3	B-Q3
11 P-QN3	

White is too much occupied with
completing his development. The correct
move is 11 P-B3 followed by B-B2 and
P-Q4.

| 11 . . . | Q-N4! |

With the unpleasant threat of Q-K4.
White could now prevent a loss of
material by 12 R-N1, but then his opponent would have a considerable lead in
development after 11 . . . B-KN5. True to
form Zukertort therefore sacrifices a
pawn and hopes for attacking chances.

| 12 B-N2 | QxQP |
| 13 B-B1 | |

Played with the intention of preventing the Black queen from retreating
to KR3. The continuation 13 Q-R5
P-KN3 14 Q-R4 Q-B5 is not particularly
good either, although it is possible that a
modern master might choose such a line
in the hope of achieving a draw following
an exchange of queens. In the last century, however, such tactics were considered degrading.

13 . . .	Q-R4
14 B-KB4	B-K3
15 QR-K1	KR-K1!

It would be a mistake to take the
second pawn, for after 15 . . . QxP? 16
B-Q2! White threatens to win the queen
(17 R-R1 Q-N7 18 B-B3!), and if 16 . . .
Q-R6, White replies with 17 P-QN4!,
shutting Black's queen dangerously out of
play.

| 16 R-K3 | B-Q4? |

When making his last move Steinitz
was probably convinced that his opponent would now sacrifice his bishop, a

Pachman's Decisive Games

17. Zukertort–Steinitz

Position after Black's 16th move

sacrifice which Steinitz regarded as un-
sound. Objectively best, however, is 16
. . . QxP!, for the rook on K3 prevents
White from trapping Black's queen. A
possible continuation is then 17 BxB PxB
18 Q-K4 P-KN3 19 Q-Q4 Q-R6 20 P-QN4
P-QR4!

17 BxPch?

A move typical of the times and of
Zukertort's style. A better continuation
was 17 Q-R3 P-KN3 18 RxRch RxR 19
BxB PxB 20 Q-Q7 with good drawing
chances.

17 . . .	KxB
18 Q-R5ch	K-N1
19 R-R3	P-B3
20 Q-R7ch	K-B2
21 Q-R5ch	K-B1
22 Q-R8ch	K-B2

This series of checks requires an explanation. In the last century the rules of
play were laid down before each match or
tournament, and in world championship
matches a draw could be claimed only
after the same moves had been repeated
six times. Moreover, the first time-control
was after thirty moves, so that Steinitz
could repeat moves until then to allow
himself to work out the best continuation
at home.

23 Q-R5ch	K-B1
24 Q-R8ch	K-B2
25 Q-R5ch	K-B1

26	Q-R8ch	K-B2
27	Q-R5ch	K-B1
28	Q-R8ch	K-B2
29	Q-R5ch	K-B1
30	Q-R8ch	K-B2
31	Q-R5ch	K-K2!

The game is not drawn although the position has been repeated six times, the rules at that time requiring that the moves of both sides be repeated six times. Steinitz avoids this and embarks on a difficult winning manoeuvre.

18. Zukertort–Steinitz

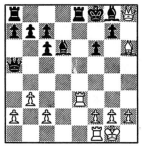

Position after White's 34th move

32	R-K3ch	K-B1
33	Q-R8ch	B-N1
34	B-R6!	

Suddenly the position looks dangerous for Black. After 34 . . . PxB?? 35 QxBPch B-B2 White would not even have to be content with perpetual check, but could win by 36 QxPch K-N1 37 R-R3 B-K4 38 Q-N5ch K-B1 39 R-R8ch! BxR 40 QxQ. But clearly Steinitz had worked that out.

34	. . .	R-K2!
35	RxR	KxR
36	BxP	Q-KB4
37	R-K1ch	K-B2
38	B-R6	Q-R2
39	QxQ	BxQ
40	P-QB4	P-R4
41	B-K3	P-QB4
42	R-Q1	P-R5
43	Resigns	

The psychological effect of this game was considerable. Zukertort, with White, lost the next game and only succeeded in winning once in the rest of the match. The final result was 10:5 with five draws.

5 World Championship 1894

Tactics Victorious over Strategy

When Steinitz defended his title in a match against Dr Emanuel Lasker, he was fifty-eight years old. His twenty-six year old opponent was his first pupil. Among their contemporaries, Lasker was the first to recognize the depth of Steinitz's strategical conceptions, but he was also aware of the difficulties of their practical application. Steinitz belonged to the nineteenth century and now found himself faced by a thinker of the twentieth, who was a fighter too, for Lasker always considered chess to be a fight more than anything else.

The year 1894 was really the start of Lasker's chess career, and the result of this contest between years of experience and youthful élan was quite open.

The first person to win ten games was to be the winner. In the first four games both players managed to use the advantage of the white pieces to force wins. The next two games were drawn. There followed a break of three days (31 March–2 April), after which the match was resumed at the New York Union Square Hotel, where the seventh game was played. Here the match really got going. Few people realized that that day was virtually to decide the outcome of the match and the world championship title.

Ruy Lopez

	Lasker	Steinitz
1	P-K4	P-K4
2	N-KB3	N-QB3
3	B-N5	P-Q3

The defence named after Steinitz. It is interesting to note that his pupil and

opponent, Lasker, also used it consistently.

4	P-Q4	B-Q2
5	N-B3	KN-K2

Later this development of the knight became popular in the line 3 . . . P-QR3 4 B-R4 P-Q3 5 P-B3 B-Q2 6 P-Q4 KN-K2, for the pawn on QB3 hampers White's development, allowing Black the privilege of adopting a slow mobilization of his forces.

6	B-K3

In the fourth game Lasker had played 6 B-QB4 PxP (answering the threat of N-KN5) 7 NxP NxN 8 QxN N-B3 9 Q-K3 B-K3 10 N-Q5 B-K2 11 B-Q2 0-0 12 0-0 N-K4 13 B-N3 BxN 14 BxB P-QB3 15 B-N3, and gained a slight though lasting advantage. Nevertheless the game ended in a draw. This time Lasker hopes to achieve more.

6	. . .	N-N3
7	Q-Q2	

Again a move of a decidedly aggressive character. White prepares to castle long, so that he can launch a king-side attack. The quiet continuation 7 0-0 would have given him a slight advantage in space.

7	. . .	B-K2
8	0-0-0	P-QR3
9	B-K2	PxP
10	NxP	NxN
11	QxN	B-KB3
12	Q-Q2	B-B3
13	N-Q5	0-0

In spite of White's slight advantage in space, due to the so-called little centre (pawn on K4 against one on Q3), the game is more or less equal, for Black's minor pieces are actively placed. From now on Lasker plays in a way quite contrary to his usual style. The unprepared attack, signalled by his next two moves, is an isolated occurrence in his games.

| 14 | P-KN4!? | R-K1! |
| 15 | P-N5? | |

The previous move did not in itself compromise White's position unduly. But now Lasker fails to strengthen the centre by 15 P-KB3, which was really necessary.

| 15 | ... | BxN |
| 16 | QxB | |

The line 16 NPxB BxKP 17 P-KB3 B-B3 18 PxP Q-K2 loses at once, and after 16 KPxB Black has the interesting positional exchange sacrifice 16 ... RxB!, which White could hardly accept, for 17 PxR (17 QxR?? BxKNP) 17... BxKNP followed by N-K4 and B-B3 leaves Black's pieces actively placed, whereas White's bishop is powerless. On the other hand, 17 PxB R-K4 18 PxP Q-B3 followed by R(R1)-K1 and N-B5 gives Black an obvious advantage.

| 16 | ... | R-K4 |
| 17 | Q-Q2 | |

Lasker had obviously overlooked the temporary piece sacrifice that now allows Black to win material. Otherwise, he would have played 17 QxNP, which leads to complications. In this case, however, Black could have sacrificed a pawn to gain a strong attack: 17 ... R-N1 18 QxRP BxP 19 Q-Q3 N-B5 20 BxN BxBch 21 K-N1 R-N5 22 P-KB3 Q-N1, etc.

17	...	BxP!
18	P-KB4	RxP!
19	PxB	Q-K2
20	R(Q1)-B1!	

Strategically the game is already lost, and Lasker can only hope to make the conversion of Black's advantage as difficult as possible. A player of lesser stature would probably have tried to reduce the material disadvantage by 20 B-B3 RxB 21 BxP, but then, after 21 ... R-K7! 22 QxR QxQ 23 BxR Q-K6ch 24 K-N1 QxP or 22 QR-K1 RxQ 23 RxQ NxR 24 KxR R-R2, the position would be fairly straightforward.

| 20 | ... | RxB |
| 21 | B-B4 | N-R1 |

A well-known principle postulated by Steinitz is that defence should be as economical as possible, that is it should tie up the minimum of one's own forces. For that reason, he protects the pawn with a knight and not a rook (R-KB1), so that the rook can control the open king's file.

| 22 | P-KR4 | P-QB3 |
| 23 | P-N6!? | P-Q4 |

The simplest reply. Also possible is 23 ... RPxP 24 P-R5 P-KN4 (not, however, 24 ... P-Q4 25 PxP! NxP 26 B-Q3, which gives White good attacking chances for his three pawns).

24	PxRPch	KxP
25	B-Q3ch	K-N1
26	P-R5	R-K1
27	P-R6	P-KN3
28	P-R7ch	K-N2
29	K-N1	Q-K4
30	P-R3	P-QB4
31	Q-B2	P-B5
32	Q-R4	

19. Lasker–Steinitz

| 32 | ... | P-B3 |

Contemporary annotators regarded this move as incorrect, but quite wrongly, for it was the quickest way to win. Naturally 32 ... K-B1 is also good enough, for 33 BxNP NxB 34 P-R8=Qch NxQ(R1) 35 QxNch QxQ 36 RxQch K-K2 leaves Black with a won endgame and the stronger 33 B-B5! can be answered by P-B3 or P-Q5, not, however, by 33 ... PxB? 34 R(R1)-N1.

33 B-B5!   K-B2?

In attempting to drive off the troublesome bishop, Steinitz has chosen the wrong plan. The correct, and winning, line is 33 ... Q-N6! 34 Q-R6ch K-B2 followed by R-K8ch.

34 R(R1)-N1!   PxB?

His previous move had made the task of winning more difficult, for after the correct 34 ... P-KN4 35 Q-R5ch K-K2 36 Q-R6 it is no easy matter to convert the advantage of the two pawns. Taking the bishop, however, leads to a quick and unexpected change of fortune.

35	Q-R5ch	K-K2
36	R-N8	K-Q3
37	RxP	Q-K3
38	RxR	QxR(K1)
39	RxBPch	K-B4
40	Q-R6!	

20. Lasker–Steinitz

A curious situation. Black is a full piece up but cannot win. The reason is not so much the strong pawn on R7 or the unfortunate position of Black's knight on R1 but rather the exposed position of the Black king. White's king, on the other hand, is quite safe, as a result of the remarkable cool-headedness displayed by Lasker in making his twenty-ninth and thirtieth moves.

40 ...   R-K2?

When a player has had a winning position for most of the game it is difficult for him to readjust his thinking and be satisfied with a draw. Black could have attained this by 40 ... Q-K2, for 41 R-B8 K-K3 42 R-B8ch R-QB3 leads nowhere and 41 Q-B8 QxQ 42 RxQ N-N3 43 R-KN8 R-R6 44 RxN RxRP 45 P-B3 is a typically drawn rook endgame. Steinitz, however, was still dreaming about winning and wanted to prepare the manoeuvre Q-Q2 and RxP. He saw that 41 R-B8 RxP! was not possible for White, but he failed to see the main danger—his exposed king.

41 Q-R2!   Q-Q2

There is no way of saving the game, e.g. 41 ... R-K3 42 Q-B2ch K-B3 43 R-B8 or 41 ... Q-Q1 42 Q-N1ch K-N4 43 P-R4ch KxP 44 Q-B5! R-K8ch 45 K-R2 QxR 46 P-N3ch, etc.

42	Q-N1ch	P-Q5
43	Q-N5ch	Q-Q4
44	R-B5	QxR
45	QxQch	K-Q3
46	Q-B6ch	Resigns

The result of this dramatic game was tragic for Steinitz. He failed to recover quickly enough from the depression it caused, and he lost four more times, playing well below his usual standard. That virtually decided the outcome. The match was continued in Philadelphia and Montreal, and seven weeks later Lasker had won the world championship title by 10:5 with four draws.

6 Hastings 1895

Failure of the New World Champion

The name of the English seaside resort of Hastings is now automatically linked with the traditional annual chess congress, which first took place in 1895. A year previously Lasker had gained the world championship title by his victory over the ageing Steinitz. But the chess world was not yet convinced of his supremacy. He needed to win a great tournament in which the élite of the chess world had participated.

The Hastings organizers succeeded in the by no means easy task of creating such a tournament. There were thirty-eight entries from the best chess masters of the time, sixteen of whom had to be turned down. Only in one case was this for reasons other than playing ability or previous performance. The Polish master Winawer was not accepted because the organizers refused to accept his demand to play under a pseudonym. Clearly masters of that era also had strange wishes at times!

Chigorin was the hero of the first part of the tournament. In the first round he defeated Pillsbury and in the second Lasker, who, as it later turned out, were his main rivals for first place. In the fourth round, however, he suffered a defeat at the hands of his fellow-countryman Schiffers, the game lasting only twenty moves. Then there followed a series of victories, which was ended by a loss in the thirteenth round, an Evans Gambit, to his opponent in a previous world championship match, Steinitz.

After his set-back in the first round, Pillsbury began to catch up by winning against Tarrasch, Pollock, Albin, Mieses, Steinitz, Schiffers, Janowski, Mason and Teichmann. His run of victories was quite a sensation in the chess world.

The world champion, Lasker, began very badly, losing to Chigorin in the second round and Bardeleben in the fourth. He then improved his position by victories over Bird, Janowski, Pollock, Walbrodt, Steinitz and Gunsberg. He also won the important twelfth round game against Pillsbury.

In the seventeenth round Pillsbury had a walkover, his opponent, Bardeleben, failing to turn up for the game—a rare occurrence in such a tournament. However, this was characteristic of Bardeleben: in his game against Steinitz he simply walked out of the tournament hall, leaving his opponent the task of showing the spectators the final phase of the mating sequence.

At the start of the twentieth and penultimate round of this historic tournament the position was as follows: Chigorin 15, Lasker and Pillsbury 14½. The next two, Tarrasch and Steinitz, were two and a half points behind. In the last two rounds Chigorin had White against Janowski and Black against Schlechter, while Lasker had White against Blackburne and Black against Burn. In the twentieth round Pillsbury faced by far the weakest participant in the tournament, Vengani, and had White in the last round against Gunsberg. It was thus clear that Chigorin and, even more so, Lasker would have to play for a win in the twentieth round, for their games in that round were of great importance in determining the final victor.

Vienna Game

Chigorin	Janowski
1 P-K4	P-K4
2 N-QB3	N-KB3
3 P-Q3	

The choice of such an opening by so aggressive a player as Chigorin is hard to understand, especially as he was in the lead. It is one of those mysteries that occur at exciting and exhausting moments of a tournament.

3 ...	P-Q4
4 PxP	

The move 4 P-KB4 leads to a well-known theoretical position, in which Black obtains a good game by either 4 ... PxBP 5 P-K5 P-Q5 or 4 ... N-QB3.

4 ...	NxP
5 Q-K2	

A move that will be justly punished.

5 ...	N-QB3
6 B-Q2	B-K2
7 0-0-0	0-0
8 Q-B3(?)	

White is having difficulty in completing his development, but this only makes matters worse. Chigorin was evidently not enamoured of the continuation 8 N-KB3 B-KN5 9 P-KR3 N-Q5 10 QxP BxN 11 PxB N-N5, and, of course, 8 P-KN3 NxN 9 BxN Q-Q4! is bad.

8 ...	B-K3
9 KN-K2	P-B4
10 Q-R3	

More logical is 10 P-KN3. It is, however, difficult to comment on Chigorin's individual moves in this game. He seems to have played as if in a dream.

10 ...	Q-Q3
11 NxN	QxN
12 N-B3	Q-R4
13 P-R3	

This makes Black's elegant finish possible. However, 13 K-N1 is not much better on account of 13 ... P-QN4! 14 P-QN3 B-N5 15 K-N2 N-Q5 with the threat of 16 ... Q-R6ch and (after 17 K-N1) a double piece-sacrifice on QN6.

21. Chigorin–Janowski

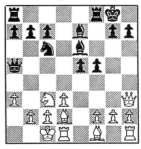

13 ...	BxP!

A normal piece-sacrifice. After 14 PxB QxPch 15 K-N1 N-N5 16 R-B1 (meeting the threat of 16 ... B-R7ch 17 K-R1 B-N6dis ch 18 K-N1 BxP mate) 16 ... B-R7ch 17 K-R1 R-B3! Black wins.

14 N-N1	BxPch!
15 KxB	Q-R7ch
16 K-B1	

A real problem mate would be 16 K-B3 Q-R8 mate.

16 ...	N-Q5
17 Resigns	

Lasker's task in his game was by no means easy either, especially from the psychological point of view. In the previous round, he had had much the best of the play for most of the game, his opponent having to struggle for a draw in the ending; then he blundered and actually lost. So the present game was his last opportunity. He had to win to remain in the running.

Ruy Lopez

Lasker	Blackburne
1 P-K4	P-K4
2 N-KB3	N-QB3
3 B-N5	P-Q3

Lasker himself was very fond of the Steinitz Defence. Now he had to fight against his own weapon.

4 P-Q4	B-Q2
5 N-B3	PxP
6 NxP	NxN
7 QxN	BxB
8 NxB	N-K2
9 0-0	

The first inaccuracy. It would have been better to develop the queen's bishop so that the queen can move to Q2. Theory recommends 9 B-K3 or, even better, 9 B-N5.

9 ...	N-B3
10 Q-B3	P-QR3
11 N-R3	

After 11 N-Q4 Q-B3! 12 B-K3 Black has no difficulty in completing his development.

11 ...	Q-B3!?
12 Q-QN3(?)	

If the game had been played in an earlier round Lasker would have certainly exchanged queens, which incidentally would have accorded well with his style. After 12 QxQ PxQ 13 N-B4 White has the better of it, and an endgame expert like Lasker would still have had winning chances despite the simplification.

12 ...	0-0-0
13 P-QB4(?)	

Another nervous move, after which Black has the advantage. After 13 N-B4 Q-K3 the game would have been equal.

13 ...	R-K1
14 R-K1	Q-N3
15 B-Q2!?	

After 15 P-B3 P-KB4 White would have had an isolated king's pawn. However, the sacrifice is not correct. Black could now have played 15 ... RxP 16 RxR QxR 17 R-K1 (17 Q-R3ch Q-K3) 17 ... Q-B4 18 R-K8ch K-Q2. If then White

tries 19 Q-K3 the reply is 19 ... P-KN3! and if 20 B-B3 then B-R3! Blackburne, however, chooses a quieter continuation, evidently out of respect for his great opponent.

15 ...	B-K2
16 Q-B2	B-B3
17 QR-N1	B-Q5
18 P-QN4	N-K4

Black's pieces are ideally centralized, and there is, moreover, the threat of N-B6ch. Lasker now had a last chance to avert the threatening defeat by adopting an active defence, e.g. 19 R-N3 (and if 19 ... N-N5 then 20 R-KB3).

22. Lasker–Blackburne

19 R-K2?	N-B6ch
20 K-R1	NxP

Black is content with winning a pawn, but there was more to be had. He could have won at least the exchange by 20 ... Q-R4!, e.g. 21 B-B4 B-K4 22 BxB RxB 23 P-R3 N-Q5 or 21 P-R3 N-N8! 22 R(K2)-K1 NxP! 23 PxN QxPch 24 K-N1 R-K3 or 22 R-K3 BxR 23 BxB NxP 24 PxN QxPch 25 K-N1 R-K3 26 B-B4 R-N3ch 27 B-N3 R-R3.

21 B-B4	N-N5
22 B-N3?	

Here 22 R-N3 was necessary. After the move played Black could have won quickly by 22 ... Q-R4ch 23 K-N1 R-K3! 24 KR-K1 BxPch! 25 BxB Q-R7ch 26 K-B1 R-B3 or 24 R-Q2 BxPch! 25

BxB (25 RxB R-R3 26 K-B1 N-K6ch) 25
... Q-R7ch 26 K-B1 R-B3, and White is
helpless against the threats of N-K6ch and
Q-R8ch.

| 22 ... | B-K4? |
| 23 Q-Q3 | BxB |

Again Black could have gone on the
offensive: 23 ... Q-R4ch 24 K-N1 R-K3.
At several stages Blackburne misses the
strongest continuation, though, unfortunately for Lasker, without throwing away
his great advantage.

| 24 QxB | N-B3! |

Naturally not 24 ... RxP?? 25 RxR
QxR 26 P-B3, etc.

| 25 Q-R3ch | K-N1 |
| 26 P-B3 | N-R4 |

A very strong continuation is 26 ...
R-K4 27 P-N4 P-KR4, after which White
has nothing better than to give up a
second pawn: 28 R-N1 R-R2 29 P-KN5.

27 R-Q2	R-K4
28 K-N1	N-B5
29 Q-R4	N-K3
30 R-Q5	N-N4
31 Q-N3	RxR
32 BPxR	P-KR4!
33 P-N5	P-R5
34 Q-N4	PxP
35 NxP	P-R6
36 R-N2	PxP
37 RxP	N-R6ch
38 K-B1	Q-B3?

This enables White to prolong the
game even further. There was a quicker
win to be had by 38 ... Q-R3! (threatening 39 ... Q-B8ch) 39 R-QB2 Q-K6 with
the threats of R-R3 and N-B5.

| 39 P-K5! | PxP |

If Black were to take with the queen,
White would reply 40 QxP.

40 R-R2	P-K5!
41 RxN	Q-R8ch
42 K-N2	PxPch
43 K-N3??	

Pachman's Decisive Games

After Blackburne had obtained a decisive advantage he played the whole time
as if he did not intend to win and
repeatedly gave the world champion
chances to defend. The latter, however,
had evidently lost the desire to continue
the fight and now makes a mistake that
loses out of hand. The correct, and
obvious, continuation, 43 QxP Q-N7ch
44 K-N3 RxRch 45 KxR QxN 46 QxP
Q-Q6ch, leads to a queen endgame which
Black, with accurate play, should win.
But it would have been the best position
that White had had since his twelfth
move.

43 ...	Q-K4ch
44 KxP	QxPch
45 Resigns	

Saturday, 31 August 1895, was certainly one of the American master Pillsbury's lucky days. Both his main rivals
lost and opened the way for the greatest
success of his life. To attain this, however, he required a little luck in the last
round.

The following position occurred after
his 25th move in his game with Gunsberg.

23. Pillsbury–Gunsberg

Black does not face any particular
threat. A possible continuation is 25 ...
N-N1 26 BxBch KxB 27 N-B5 P-K4,
though 25 ... NxB 26 NPxN B-B2 27
P-KR3 P-QR4 is even better. The line

Hastings 1895

		1	2	3	4	5	6	7	8	9	10	11	12	13	14	15	16	17	18	19	20	21	22	Pts	Prize
1	Pillsbury	—	0	0	1	1	1	1	1	0	½	½	1	1	1	1	1	1	½	1	1	1	1	16½	I
2	Chigorin	1	—	1	1	0	0	1	1	1	1	½	1	0	1	½	1	½	1	1	½	1	1	16	II
3	Lasker	1	0	—	0	1	1	0	1	1	0	1	1	1	½	1	1	½	1	1	½	1	1	15½	III
4	Tarrasch	0	0	1	—	1	1	½	0	½	1	1	1	1	0	1	½	1	1	0	½	1	1	14	IV
5	Steinitz	0	1	0	0	—	1	1	½	½	1	1	½	0	1	0	1	1	1	0	½	1	1	13	V
6	Schiffers	0	1	0	0	0	—	½	½	0	1	1	½	1	½	1	1	0	½	1	½	1	1	12	VI
7	Bardeleben	0	0	1	½	0	½	—	½	½	0	0	1	½	1	½	1	½	1	1	1	0	1	11½	VII, VIII
8	Teichmann	0	0	0	1	½	½	½	—	½	0	0	1	½	1	1	0	½	1	½	1	1	1	11½	VII, VIII
9	Schlechter	1	0	0	½	½	1	½	½	—	½	½	1	0	1	½	½	½	½	½	½	1	0	11	IX
10	Blackburne	½	0	1	0	0	0	1	1	½	—	0	1	1	0	½	0	1	0	1	0	1	1	10½	X
11	Walbrodt	½	½	0	0	0	0	1	1	½	1	—	0	0	½	½	½	0	½	½	1	1	1	10	XI
12	Burn	0	0	0	0	½	½	0	0	0	0	1	—	1	0	½	0	1	1	1	1	1	1	9½	
13	Janowski	0	1	0	0	1	0	½	½	1	0	1	0	—	½	½	0	0	1	½	1	0	1	9½	
14	Mason	0	0	½	1	0	½	0	0	0	1	½	1	½	—	1	0	½	0	1	1	0	1	9½	
15	Bird	0	½	0	0	1	0	½	0	½	½	½	½	½	0	—	1	1	½	0	½	½	1	9	
16	Gunsberg	0	0	0	½	0	0	0	1	½	1	½	1	1	1	0	—	1	½	0	1	0	0	9	
17	Albin	0	½	½	0	0	1	½	½	½	0	1	0	1	½	0	0	—	0	0	1	1	½	8½	
18	Marco	½	0	0	0	0	½	0	0	½	1	½	0	0	1	½	½	1	—	1	1	0	½	8½	
19	Pollock	0	0	0	1	1	0	0	½	½	0	½	0	½	0	1	1	1	0	—	0	0	1	8	
20	Mieses	0	½	½	½	½	½	0	0	½	1	0	0	0	0	½	0	0	0	1	—	1	1	7½	
21	Tinsley	0	0	0	0	0	0	1	0	0	0	0	0	1	1	½	1	0	1	1	0	—	1	7½	
22	Vergani	0	0	0	0	0	0	0	0	1	0	0	0	0	0	0	1	½	½	0	0	0	—	3	

28

chosen by Gunsberg is by no means bad either.

| 25 ... | BxB |
| 26 NPxB | N-N1? |

This, however, loses surprisingly quickly. The correct continuation would have led to a draw: 26 ... P-QR4! 27 P-B5 P-N4! 28 P-B6 N-N3 29 N-B5 PxP 30 PxP K-Q3 31 N-N7ch KxP 32 NxPch K-B2 followed by N-B5.

| 27 P-B5! | P-N4 |

Otherwise Black loses the QP: 27 ... P-QR4 28 N-B4! (28 PxKP P-N4!) or 27 ... KPxP 28 PxP PxP (28 ... P-N4 29 N-N4) 29 N-B4.

28 N-N4	P-QR4
29 P-B6	K-Q3
30 PxP	NxP

Naturally not 30 ... PxN 31 P-K7 KxKP 32 P-B7.

31 NxN	KxN
32 P-K4	PxP
33 P-Q5ch	K-Q3
34 K-K3	P-N5
35 KxP	P-R5
36 K-Q4	P-R4

Breaking through with his pawns does not save Black, e.g.

(i) 36 ... P-B4 37 PxP K-K2 (37 ... P-R4 38 P-B6 P-N5 39 P-B7 K-K2 40 P-Q6ch) 38 K-B5 P-N6 39 P-Q6ch K-Q1 40 P-Q7 K-B2 (40 ... K-K2 41 P-B6ch) 41 PxP PxP 42 P-B6 P-N7 43 P-B7 P-N8=Q 44 P-N8=Q, etc.

(ii) 36 ... P-N6 37 PxP P-R6 38 K-B3 P-B4 39 PxP K-K2 40 P-N4 P-R4 41 P-N5 P-R7 42 K-N2 P-N5 43 P-N6, etc.

37 PxP	P-R6
38 K-B4	P-B4
39 P-R6	P-B5
40 P-R7	Resigns

7 International Tournament in Vienna 1898

The Great Chess Marathon

The history of chess tournaments in the nineteenth and the early twentieth centuries was marked by a series of real marathons. The most important of these, both from the point of view of its length and the strength of the competitors, was the Emperor's Anniversary Tournament in Vienna, which took place at the Vienna Chess Club from 31 May to 25 July. With twenty competitors playing each other twice there were thirty-eight rounds plus the four games of the play-off for first place. Apart from Lasker, all the leading masters of the world were present, making it virtually a review of the possible candidates for a world-championship match.

It is interesting to note that after the first half of the tournament the position of the first four players was the same as at the end. After the 19th round the leading scores were: Pillsbury and Tarrasch 15, Janowski 13½, Steinitz 12½, Chigorin 12, Alapin 11½, Lipke 11, Burn, Maróczy and Schlechter 10½.

For the rest of the tournament the two rivals for first place ran neck and neck. They either had the same score, or one of them—usually Pillsbury—had a lead of half a point. In the 33rd round they met for the second time, when Tarrasch, avenging his defeat in the 14th round, took the lead, which he lost in the next round by failing to score against Janowski. At the end of the 35th round Pillsbury, with 26½ points, was half a point ahead of Tarrasch and seemed to have a very good chance of securing first place. Apart from his lead, he had much easier opponents in the next three rounds—Burn, Trenchard and Baird,

whereas Tarrasch was drawn against Chigorin, Alapin and Walbrodt. Moreover, Pillsbury had White in two of his games and Tarrasch Black in two of his. The very next round, however, changed the situation somewhat, for although Tarrasch only drew his game with Chigorin he nevertheless caught up with his rival, who had one of his worst days in the tournament.

24. Pillsbury–Burn

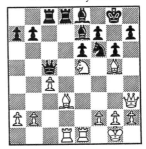

White has no real prospects of a king-side attack, so his next move is not very accurate.

19 R-K3(?)	N-Q2!
20 BxB	QxB
21 N-N4?	

One of those automatic moves often made without much thought and which sometimes cause irreparable damage. After the correct 21 NxN or 21 R(Q1)-K1 the game is even and Pillsbury would have stood to win an extra 2,000 Austrian crowns, for the first prize (apart from the gold cup) was 6,000 crowns, the second "only" 4,000.

21 ...	P-KR4!
22 N-K5	

30

It is probable that Pillsbury only now realized that the attack 22 N-R6ch K-N2 23 N-B5ch NPxN 24 QxRP is simply answered by 24 ... Q-B3, when the Black king escapes via KB1. After the text-move, however, White loses a pawn.

22 ...	NxN
23 RxN	RxP
24 R(Q1)-K1	R(B5)-Q5

White has not got the slightest compensation for his pawn. After a long struggle (ninety moves), Burn managed to convert his advantage into a win.

Both Tarrasch and Pillsbury won their remaining games, so that the chess marathon had to be continued. According to the rules, the first prize could not be shared, so a play-off consisting of four games had to take place. It began after a break of one day on 27 July and ended on 30 July. Tarrasch won the first game, Pillsbury the second. Thus, after nearly three months' play, no decision had been reached. The third game was played on 29 July.

Four Knights Game

Tarrasch	Pillsbury
1 P-K4	P-K4
2 N-KB3	N-QB3
3 B-N5	N-B3
4 N-B3	

Transposing into the Four Knights Game. In the first game Tarrasch had played 4 P-Q3 B-B4 5 B-K3 and in the 33rd round the classical 4 0-0 NxP 5 R-K1. Both players had mutual respect for each other's theoretical ability and each tried to upset his opponent right from the opening.

4 ...	B-N5
5 0-0	0-0
6 P-Q3	P-Q3

| 7 B-N5 | BxN |
| 8 PxB | N-K2 |

This manoeuvre was introduced by Pillsbury. Today it is considered satisfactory, though without the exchange on the previous move.

9 B-QB4

This quiet continuation, stemming from Janowski, should not cause Black any real trouble. A much stronger line is 9 N-R4 N-N3 10 NxN BPxN 11 B(QN5)-B4ch K-R1 12 P-B4 or 10 ... RPxN 11 P-KB4 P-B3 12 B-B4 Q-N3ch 13 K-R1 N-N5 14 Q-K1 and if 14 ... N-K6 then 15 P-B5! NxR 16 P-B6! winning.

9 ...   B-K3?

This is a severe weakening of Black's king-side pawns. In 1909 Lasker, in his match with Janowski, played 9 ... N-N3! 10 N-R4 N-B5! 11 BxN(B4) PxB 12 N-B3 B-N5 with a very good game.

10 BxN!	PxB
11 BxB	PxB
12 N-R4	N-N3
13 NxN	PxN

It was Tarrasch who discovered that this position is not even. Here we have a good example of how exposed the castled king is when the pawns in front of it have left their original squares. In a strategic-

25. Tarrasch–Pillsbury

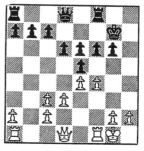

Position after Black's 14th move

Vienna 1898

	1	2	3	4	5	6	7	8	9	10	11	12	13	14	15	16	17	18	19	Pts	Prize
1 Tarrasch	–	0 1	1 0	1 ½	1 ½	1 ½	½ 1	½ ½	½ 1	½ 1	½ ½	1 1	1 1	1 1	½ 1	1 ½	1 1	1 1	1 ½	27½	I, II
2 Pillsbury	1 0	–	1 0	½ 1	1 ½	0 1	½ 0	1 ½	0 1	½ 1	1 1	1 1	1 ½	½ 1	1 1	1 1	1 1	1 1	1 1	27½	I, II
3 Janowski	0 1	0 1	–	1 1	1 ½	1 1	1 ½	0 0	½ ½	1 1	½ 0	1 1	1 ½	1 1	1 1	0 0	½ 1	1 1	1 1	25½	III
4 Steinitz	0 ½	½ 0	0 0	–	½ 1	1 0	½ ½	1 1	1 ½	½ 1	½ ½	0 1	1 1	1 1	0 1	1 ½	1 ½	1 1	1 1	23½	IV
5 Schlechter	0 ½	0 ½	0 ½	½ 0	–	½ ½	1 1	½ ½	½ ½	½ 1	0 ½	1 ½	½ 1	1 ½	1 1	0 ½	½ 1	1 1	1 1	21½	V
6 Chigorin	0 ½	1 0	0 0	0 1	½ ½	–	1 0	0 1	1 ½	1 ½	½ 0	1 0	0 1	1 1	1 0	1 1	1 0	0 1	1 1	20	VI, VII
7 Burn	½ 0	½ 1	0 ½	½ ½	0 0	0 1	–	1 ½	0 ½	½ ½	½ ½	½ 0	½ 0	1 1	0 1	1 1	1 ½	1 1	1 1	20	VI, VII
8 Lipke	½ ½	0 ½	1 1	0 0	½ ½	1 0	0 ½	–	½ ½	½ ½	½ 0	1 ½	1 1	1 ½	0 ½	½ 1	½ ½	1 1	½ ½	19½	VIII, IX
9 Maróczy	½ 0	1 0	½ ½	0 ½	½ ½	0 ½	1 ½	½ ½	–	½ ½	1 ½	1 1	½ ½	0 1	0 ½	0 1	1 ½	½ ½	1 1	19½	VIII, IX
10 Alapin	½ 0	½ 0	0 0	½ 0	½ 0	0 ½	½ ½	½ ½	½ ½	–	½ 1	1 ½	1 1	0 0	1 0	1 1	½ 1	1 0	1 1	18	
11 Blackburne	½ ½	0 0	½ 1	½ ½	1 ½	½ 1	½ ½	½ 1	0 ½	½ 0	–	½ ½	½ 0	0 ½	½ 0	½ ½	0 0	1 1	½ 1	17	
12 Schiffers	0 0	0 0	0 0	1 0	0 ½	0 1	½ 1	0 ½	0 0	0 ½	½ ½	–	0 1	1 ½	1 1	½ 1	½ 1	1 1	½ 1	17	
13 Marco	0 0	0 ½	0 ½	0 0	½ 0	1 0	½ 1	0 0	½ ½	0 0	½ 1	1 0	–	1 1	½ 1	1 ½	½ 1	½ 1	1 0	16½	
14 Showalter	0 0	½ 0	0 0	0 0	0 ½	0 0	0 0	0 ½	1 0	1 1	1 ½	0 ½	0 0	–	½ 1	1 1	1 1	0 1	1 1	15	
15 Walbrodt	½ 0	0 0	0 0	1 0	0 0	0 1	1 0	1 ½	1 ½	0 1	½ 1	0 0	½ 0	½ 0	–	0 0	1 1	½ 0	1 1	14½	
16 Halprin	0 ½	0 0	1 1	0 ½	1 ½	0 0	0 0	½ 0	1 0	0 0	½ ½	½ 0	0 ½	0 0	1 1	–	½ ½	1 ½	½ 1	14	
17 Caro	0 0	0 0	½ 0	0 ½	½ 0	0 1	0 ½	½ ½	0 ½	½ 0	1 1	½ 0	½ 0	0 0	0 0	½ ½	–	1 1	½ 1	12½	
18 Baird	0 0	0 0	0 0	0 0	0 0	1 0	0 0	0 0	½ ½	0 1	0 0	0 0	½ 0	1 0	½ 1	0 ½	0 0	–	½ 1	8	
19 Trenchard	0 ½	0 0	0 0	0 0	0 0	0 0	0 0	½ ½	0 0	0 0	½ 0	½ 0	0 1	0 0	0 0	½ 0	½ 0	½ 0	–	5	

Play-off for the first prize: Tarrasch 1 0 1 ½ – Pillsbury 0 1 0 ½ ally similar position Tarrasch also defeated Janowski at Ostend in 1907.

14 P-KB4   K-N2?

This only helps White's attack. A better move is 14 . . . P-KB4, though after 15 Q-K2 Q-Q2 16 K-R1 White has a positional advantage.

15 P-B5!   KPxP
16 PxP   R-R1

The advance 16 . . . P-KN4 is not good on account of 17 P-KR4!, for 17 . . . PxP can be answered by 18 Q-N4ch. The line 16 . . . PxP 17 RxP Q-K1 18 Q-B3 P-B3 19 R-KB1 gives White a strong attack.

17 PxP   R-R3
18 R-N1   P-N3
19 R-N4!

Black intends to capture the pawn on KN3 with his rook, which can then be used to defend the king. Tarrasch therefore prepares to exchange off the rook, e.g. 19 . . . RxNP 20 Q-B3! R-N1 (preparing Q-Q2 or Q-K2. The alternative 20 . . . Q-K1 can be answered by 21 R-KR4) 21 R-KN4, etc.

Black's best defence is 19 . . . Q-K2!, and if 20 R-KN4 then 20 . . . QR-KR1, after which he has drawing chances. His mistake on the next move leads to a definite loss of the game and of the three months' struggle for first place.

19 . . .   Q-Q2?

Black apparently only considers the continuation 20 Q-B3? RxNP. The attack on his KBP, however, can be carried out by energetic means.

20 R(B1)xP!   KxR
21 Q-B3ch   K-N2

Pachman's Decisive Games

Capturing the pawn would lead to mate: 21 . . . KxP?? 22 R-KN4ch K-R2 23 Q-K4ch, etc.

22 QxR   P-B4
23 R-N1   PxNP
24 R-KB1   Q-K2
25 P-B4   P-K5!?

This attempt to gain counter-play does not save Black. But, in the situation he is in, there is no great difference between being one pawn down or two.

26 QxKP	QxQ
27 PxQ	R-N5
28 R-K1	K-B3
29 P-N3	K-K4
30 P-B3	R-N2
31 K-N2	R-QN2
32 P-QR4	P-R3
33 P-R4	P-N4
34 RPxP	PxP
35 PxP	RxP
36 K-R3	P-B5
37 K-N4	R-N7
38 P-R5	R-QB7
39 R-KR1	R-QR7
40 P-R6	R-R1
41 P-R7	R-KR1
42 K-N5	KxP
43 K-N6	K-Q6
44 K-N7	RxPch
45 KxR	KxP
46 R-Q1	Resigns

The last game did nothing to alter the final result. Pillsbury played the Queen's Gambit, against which Tarrasch, again out of respect for his opponent's theoretical preparations, chose a defence that for him was quite unusual: 1 P-Q4 P-Q4 2 P-QB4 P-K3 3 N-QB3 P-QN3. In trying to force the pace, Pillsbury lost two pawns, but in the double rook endgame Tarrasch remained content with a draw in view of the state of the match.

8 Barmen 1905

Six Endings Decide

The international Barmen Congress, 1905, brought together a greater number of masters and strong amateurs than any other event of that time. In addition to the tournament to which the leading international masters had been invited, there was a masters' B Tournament. There were also eight other main and subsidiary tournaments, in one of which, Main Tournament A, two players who were soon to become top rankers, Rubinstein and Duras, were fighting to gain the master's title. These two tied for first place, and the play-off also ended in a tie.

In the international tournament there were two notable absentees, Lasker and Tarrasch, who three years later were to play a match for the world championship title. But, apart from these two, the tournament was exceptionally strong. Among the participants there were four masters who had either played, or were later to play, a world championship title match: Chigorin, Janowski, Marshall and Schlechter.

At the end of the thirteenth round, with two rounds to go, the leading scores were Janowski 9½, Marshall 9, Maróczy

26. Leonhardt–Schlechter

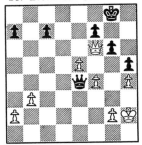

Position after Black's 45th move

and Schlechter 8½. It is a remarkable fact that the final placings of the first four all depended on intricate endings. Here Maróczy was the most successful, and as a result managed to share first place, the final scores being Janowski and Maróczy 10½, Marshall 10, Schlechter 9.

White is a pawn up and Black's queenside pawns are isolated. The win, however, is not easy, for the active position of the Black queen means that White may have problems in safeguarding his king. The continuation 46 Q-Q8ch K-N2 47 Q-Q2 P-QB4 followed by P-B5 allows Black to get rid of one of his weaknesses. Leonhardt finds the most promising line.

46 P-K6!   PxP

The pawn ending after 46 ... QxKP 47 QxQ PxQ is lost for Black in view of his three pawn weaknesses. An important factor here is that White has the tempo move P-KN3 in reserve, e.g. 48 K-N3 K-B2 49 K-B3 K-B3 50 K-K4 P-R4 51 P-R3 P-B3 (51 ... P-B4 52 P-R4 K-B2 53 K-K5 K-K2 54 P-N3) 52 P-QN4! P-R5 (52 ... PxP 53 PxP K-B2 54 K-K5 K-K2 55 P-N3) 53 K-Q4 K-B4 54 K-B5 KxP 55 KxP P-K4 56 P-N5, and White queens with check. Or 50 ... P-B4 51 P-R3 P-R3 (51 ... P-R4 52 P-R4) 52 P-QN4 PxP (52 ... P-B5 53 P-R4 P-B6 54 K-Q3 K-B4 55 P-N5) 53 PxP K-K2 54 K-K5 K-Q2 55 K-B6 K-B3 56 KxKP K-N4 57 P-B5 PxP 58 KxP KxP 59 P-N4 winning.

47	Q-Q8ch	K-B2
48	QxPch	K-B3
49	Q-Q8ch	K-B2
50	Q-Q2	K-K2!

34

Black needs to get rid of the weak KP. After 50 ... K-B3 51 K-N3 there is no suitable continuation, e.g. 51 ... P-K4? 52 Q-Q6ch or 51 ... Q-B4 52 Q-Q4ch or 51 ... K-B4 52 Q-R5ch (or 52 P-R4).

51 P-QN4	P-K4
52 P-N3?	

With this move White weakens his pawns and throws away all his winning chances. He should have played 52 K-N3!, e.g. 52 ... PxPch 53 QxP or 52 ... Q-B4 53 PxP Q-N5ch (53 ... QxPch 54 Q-B4) 54 K-R2 QxPch 55 K-N1 Q-N6 56 Q-Q6ch, etc.

52 ...	PxP
53 PxP	P-R3
54 P-R4	Q-B5
55 Q-K3ch	K-Q2
56 Q-R7ch	K-Q1
57 Q-N8ch	K-Q2
58 Q-N7ch	K-Q1
59 Q-N6 ch	K-Q2
Drawn	

27. Janowski–Berger

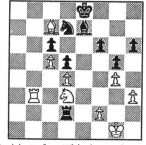

Position after White's 42nd move

For a long time Janowski had tried to force a win, but after the endgame stage was reached, Black managed to activate his rook and exploit the weakness of the enemy QP.

42 ...	N-B1!

Threatening 43 ... N-K3, after which White has no way of saving his QP. It is therefore essential to look for counter-play. The continuation 43 B-Q6 BxB 44 PxB K-Q2 45 R-N8 N-K3 46 N-B5ch KxP is inadequate, because Black retains his extra pawn.

43 N-N4!	RxQP
44 NxBP	R-Q8ch
45 K-N2	BxP
46 R-N7!	

With his last few moves White has achieved counter-play. If now 46 ... R-Q7, then 47 B-N6!, when 47 ... RxPch fails to 48 K-N3, winning (e.g. 48 ... BxB? 49 R-K7 mate or 48 ... N-Q2 49 BxB NxB 50 R-K7ch). And if 46 ... K-Q2, the reply 47 N-Q8! is very unpleasant.

46 ...	N-Q2
47 B-N3	P-Q5
48 K-B3	R-K8
49 R-B7!	P-Q6?

This over-hasty pawn advance should have cost Black half a point. There was a win to be had by 49 ... B-N3!, e.g. 50 R-B8ch K-B2 51 N-N4 N-K4ch 52 BxN PxB 53 R-B6 P-K5ch 54 K-N2 P-Q6! etc.

50 R-B8ch	K-B2
51 R-Q8?	

But now it is Janowski who makes a mistake, and one, moreover, which means that he will only share first place instead of being its sole occupier. There was a draw to be had by 51 R-B7 K-K3 52 N-Q8ch K-K2 53 N-B6ch K-K1 54 R-B8ch with repetition of moves.

51 ...	N-K4ch
52 BxN	PxB

Janowski has originally overlooked the fact that the QP cannot be taken because of an elementary pawn fork—a further example of chess hallucination.

53 K-N3	P-K5
54 N-N5ch	K-B3
55 NxP	PxN
56 RxP	K-K3

57	R-KB3	R-K5
58	R-QB3	K-Q4
59	R-B2	B-Q3ch
60	K-N2	R-QB5
61	R-R2	R-KB5
62	R-R6	R-B3
63	R-R2	B-B4
64	K-N3	B-Q5
65	K-N2	K-K5
66	K-N3	R-B6ch
67	K-N2	R-QN6
68	R-K2ch	K-Q6
69	R-K8	R-N3
70	R-Q8	R-KB3
71	K-N3	R-B5
72	R-Q6	K-K7
73	R-K6ch	K-B8
74	P-B3	B-B7ch
75	K-R2	RxBP
76	RxP	B-N8ch
77	K-R1	R-B7
78	Resigns	

28. Marshall–Chigorin

Position after White's 24th move

Black is undoubtedly in the better position. He has a superiority on the queen's wing, and White's bishop on QN2 is a passive piece in view of the potential blockade of the QP. The accurate way in which Black makes use of his advantage reminds one of Capablanca's later performances.

24	...	P-QN4
25	N-K5	P-B3
26	N-B3	R-QB1!

In addition to his other advantages Black now takes control of the open QB file. Although Marshall defends accurately he cannot avert defeat.

27	N-K1	N-Q7
28	P-B3	N-B5
29	P-N3	

The only way of staving off immediate defeat. The alternatives 29 R-N1 NxB 30 RxN R-B8 31 K-B2 RxN! and 29 B-B1 N-K7ch 30 K-B2 NxQP lose quickly.

29	...	N-K3
30	B-B3	N-N3
31	B-N2	R-B5
32	R-Q1	N-B2!
33	K-B2	N(B2)-Q4
34	P-B4	K-B2
35	R-Q2	N-R5
36	N-N2	P-QR3
37	N-K3	NxN

This wins just as safely as 37 ... NxB 38 RxN RxP 39 NxN RxN 40 R-B2 R-Q6.

38	KxN	NxB
39	RxN	K-K3
40	R-N3	K-Q4
41	R-Q3	P-B4
42	P-R3	P-KR4

White is now in *zugzwang*.

43	K-K2	RxP
44	R-QB3	R-K5ch
45	K-Q2	P-R5
46	R-B7	PxP
47	RxP	RxP
48	RxP	K-K4
49	K-K2	R-QB5
50	R-N6	R-QR5
51	R-N3	P-B5
52	R-QN3	R-B5
53	K-Q1	K-K5
54	P-KR4	P-B6
55	K-K1	K-B5
56	P-R5	R-B8ch
57	K-B2	R-B7ch
58	K-K1	K-N6
59	P-R6	R-K7ch

60 K-Q1	R-KR7
61 P-R4	P-N5
62 P-R7	RxP
63 RxNP	R-R8ch
64 K-Q2	P-B7
65 R-N8	P-B8=Q
66 Resigns	

29. Mieses–Maróczy

Position after Black's 25th move

Although Black is not at the moment threatening to win the QRP—26 . . . RxP? 27 BxN loses a piece and 26 . . . NxP? is answered by 27 N-Q3, after which Black must return the pawn to prevent the loss of his pinned knight, e.g. 27 . . . P-N5! 28 NxP R-R2 29 N-B2 N-N4—the simplest way for White to draw is 26 P-QR4!

26 N-Q3? **RxP!**

But after White's mistake the pawn can be taken, for 27 BxN can now be answered by 27 . . . RxP. The game, however, is not necessarily lost.

27 RxR	NxR
28 B-R2	B-Q2
29 K-B2	P-B3
30 K-K3	K-K2
31 K-Q2	K-Q3
32 K-B1	B-B4
33 N-N4	B-B1
34 N-Q3	B-B4
35 N-N4	P-N4
36 K-N2	N-B5ch
37 BxN	QPxB

The long trek by the White king was for the purpose of exchanging off Black's

knight, an unnecessary course, for Black could not in any case have utilized his pawn majority. Nevertheless there is still a draw to be had if White places his KBP and KNP on black squares to prevent them being blocked, e.g. 38 K-B1 B-B1 39 P-N3! P-KB4 40 P-B4 draw.

38 N-R6? **P-R4?**

Black does not make full use of his chances either. He should have played 38 . . . B-B1! 39 N-N4 P-KB4 followed by P-B5.

39 K-B1	B-K3?
40 K-Q2?	P-KB4
41 K-K3	

It is now too late for P-N3, e.g. 41 P-N3 P-B5!

41 . . .	B-B1
42 N-N4	P-B5ch
43 K-K4?	

After this "active" move White gets unexpectedly caught in a mating net and has to sacrifice a second pawn to extricate himself. However, even after the stronger 43 K-K2 or K-B2 Black also wins. First he plays 43 . . . P-B4 44 PxPch KxP, then he places his bishop on QN2 and advances with his king (K-N3-R4-R5). If White counters by transferring his king to Q2, Black breaks through on the king-side with P-KN5. It is obvious that such a plan would not be possible if White's pawns were on black squares.

43 . . . **P-R5!**

Not 43 . . . B-Q2 at once because of 44 P-N3. After the text-move the game is virtually over.

44 P-R3	B-K3
45 N-R6	B-Q2
46 N-N4	B-B1
47 N-R2	K-K3
48 P-Q5ch	

Or 48 N-N4 B-N2 49 P-Q5ch PxPch 50 K-Q4 K-Q3 51 N-B2 B-B1.

48 ...	PxP
49 K-Q4	K-Q3
50 N-N4	B-K3
51 N-B2	B-B4
52 N-N4	B-Q6
53 NxP	B-B8
54 N-B6	BxP
55 N-K4ch	K-K3
56 K-B5	K-B4
57 N-Q6ch	K-N3
58 NxNP	BxRP
59 K-Q4	B-N7
60 Resigns	

30. Schlechter–Janowski

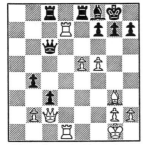

Position after Black's 28th move

At first sight it looks as if Black has quite an advantage in view of his potential passed pawn on the queen's wing and his opponent's apparently immobile central pawns. But matters are not so simple.

29 P-K6!   **P-B3**

Black cannot reply 29 ... PxKP because of 30 P-B6! K-R1 31 B-K5!

30 P-N3?

With his previous move White obtained a strong protected passed pawn. There is no reason to allow his opponent to do the same. He should therefore have continued with 30 PxP and if 30 ... QxBP then 31 Q-K4 with the better game.

30 ...	R-R1
31 P-R3	R-R4
32 K-R2	Q-R1!
33 Q-Q3	R-R7

34 Q-Q5	QxQ
35 R(Q1)xQ	QR-R1!

Both 35 ... P-B7 36 R-QB7 and 35 ... R-B1? 36 R-Q8 R(R7)-R1 37 P-K7 are weak.

36 R-Q1?

Schlechter's first move in this endgame is a mistake that leads to a loss. After the correct 36 B-Q6! Black would have had to be content with a draw (36 ... BxB 37 R(Q5)xB R(R1)-B1 38 R-N6! P-B7 39 R(N6)-N7), for the attempt to force a win loses, e.g. 36 ... R(R1)-B1? 37 BxB P-B7 38 RxPch K-R1 39 R(Q5)-Q7 P-B8=Q 40 RxPch K-N1 41 B-R6! or 37 ... KxB 38 R-KB8ch K-N1 39 R(Q1)-Q7 P-B7 40 RxPch, etc.

36 ...   **P-N3!**

This undermines the foundation of White's position—the KBP. If now 37 PxP, then both 37 ... PxP and 37 ... RxP 38 PxPch K-R1 give Black the advantage.

37 B-B4	PxP
38 R-K1	R-K2
39 R-Q3	R(R1)-K1
40 R-N3ch	R-KN2!
41 R-Q3	P-R4
42 B-Q6	BxBch
43 RxB	R-QN2
44 R-Q5?	R-N3!
45 P-K7	K-B2
46 RxP	RxP
47 R(K1)-KB1	K-N3
48 R(B5)-B4	R-K7
49 Resigns	

In spite of all his efforts in the previous 81 moves, Maróczy had not been able to achieve more than the position in the diagram. He had tried everything— apart from a piece sacrifice on K6, which is his only chance. If Black had now reacted correctly and played 81 ... N-B7, then neither the bishop nor the knight sacrifice would have led to anything, e.g.

31. Maróczy–Gottschall

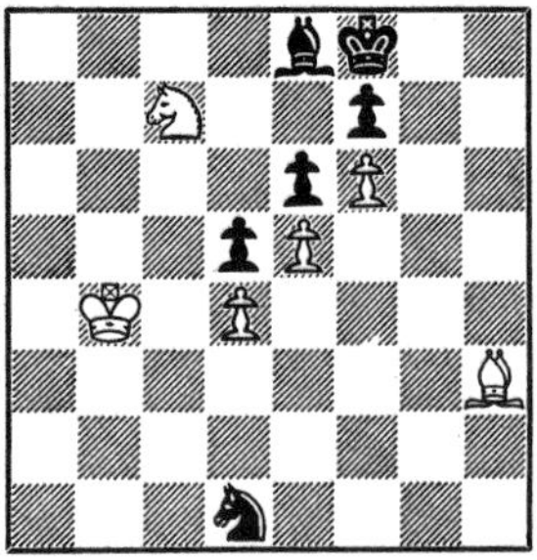

Position after White's 81st move

82 BxP PxB 83 NxKPch K-B2 84 N-B7 B-B3 85 K-B5 B-N2 86 K-N6! (86 NxP N-K5ch!) 86 . . . B-B1 87 NxP N-K5, draw, or 82 NxKPch PxN 83 BxP B-B2, draw.

81 . . . **N-K6?**

This gives White an opportunity to prepare the sacrifice, after which there is no way of saving the game.

82 K-B5!	**B-R5**
83 BxP!	**PxB**
84 NxKPch	**K-N1**

or 84 . . . K-B2 85 N-N5ch K-N3 86 P-B7 K-N2 87 P-K6 winning.

85 N-B4 **K-B2**

The QP cannot be saved, e.g. 85 . . . B-N6 86 P-K6 winning.

86 NxP **N-B4**

After 86 . . . NxN 87 KxN there is a theoretically won position of three pawns against a bishop similar to that occurring later.

87 N-B3	**B-N6**
88 N-K4!	**B-R7**
89 N-Q6ch	**NxN**
90 KxN	**B-N6**
91 P-Q5	**B-B5**
92 K-B6	**B-N6**
93 P-Q6	**K-K3**
94 P-Q7!	**B-R5ch**
95 K-B7	**BxP**
96 P-B7	**Resigns**

Maróczy thus managed to gain two full points from two drawn endings, which helped him to his great success. The final result was: Janowski and Maróczy 10½, Marshall 10, Bernstein and Schlechter 9, etc.

Barmen 1905

	1	2	3	4	5	6	7	8	9	10	11	12	13	14	15	16	Pts	Prize
1 Janowski	–	½	1	0	1	0	1	1	½	1	1	1	1	1	0	½	10½	I, II
2 Maróczy	½	–	½	½	1	½	0	1	½	1	1	1	½	½	1	1	10½	I, II
3 Marshall	0	½	–	1	1	0	1	1	0	½	1	½	½	1	1	1	10	III
4 Bernstein	1	½	0	–	0	½	1	0	1	½	1	0	1	1	½	1	9	IV, V
5 Schlechter	0	0	0	1	–	0	1	½	1	½	1	1	1	½	½	1	9	IV, V
6 Berger	1	½	1	½	1	–	½	0	1	½	½	½	0	0	½	½	8	VI
7 John	0	1	0	0	0	½	–	0	½	1	1	0	1	0	1	1	7	VII
8 Leonhardt	0	0	0	1	½	1	1	–	0	½	0	½	1	0	1	½	7	VII
9 Chigorin	½	½	1	0	0	0	½	1	–	0	0	½	½	½	1	1	7	VII
10 Wolf	0	0	½	½	½	½	0	½	1	–	½	½	½	1	½	½	7	VII
11 Bardeleben	0	0	0	0	0	½	0	1	1	½	–	1	½	1	1	0	6½	
12 Süchting	0	0	½	1	0	½	1	½	½	½	0	–	½	1	½	0	6½	
13 Alapin	0	½	½	0	0	1	0	0	½	½	½	½	–	½	½	1	6	
14 Burn	0	½	0	0	½	1	1	1	½	0	0	0	½	–	1	0	6	
15 Gottschall	1	0	0	½	½	½	0	0	0	½	0	½	½	0	–	1	5	
16 Mieses	½	0	0	0	0	½	0	½	0	½	1	1	0	1	0	–	5	

9 Match Tournament Ostend 1907

First against Last

Normal tournaments are not always an accurate measure of the strength of the participants. As a rule there is quite a difference between the players at the top and the bottom, so that a chance result in a game between a strong player and a considerably weaker one can affect the order at the top of the table. Those who can consistently win against outsiders are at an advantage compared with those who play best against strong opponents. In addition, the draw is of considerable importance. It is by no means immaterial whether one has White or Black against one's main rivals.

For these reasons there have occasionally been tournaments with a small number of evenly matched players where each played the others several times. Some of these tournaments of the élite have been a virtual prelude to a world championship title match, for, in the opinion of the public, the winner had a greater moral right to such a match than the winner of a normal international tournament.

One of these forerunners of the candidates' tournaments took place from May to June 1907 at the Belgian seaside resort of Ostend. The world's six strongest players were invited: Lasker, Tarrasch, Janowski, Marshall, Schlechter and Maróczy. Two of these, Lasker and Maróczy, declined the invitation and were replaced by masters of the older generation, Chigorin and Burn. The competition was too strong for these two, however, and they finished in the last two places. Nevertheless, one of them, Chigorin, who was at the bottom, was involved in a

dramatic game which had a vital bearing on the final result.

For nearly the whole of this four-round match tournament, the lead had been held by Dr Tarrasch, who, incidentally, was to play a world championship match with Dr Lasker one year later. Two rounds before the end the position was as follows: Tarrasch 11½, Janowski 11, Schlechter 10½, Marshall 9½, Burn 7, Chigorin 4½. A dramatic finish was on the cards. As Tarrasch had Black against Schlechter in the last round—a very difficult task—he needed to win his game in the previous round to be sure of first place. Here he was to play Chigorin, while Janowski and Schlechter were drawn against each other. In his previous games with Chigorin in the tournament, Tarrasch had lost one, drawn one (after reaching a theoretically won game) and won one. So his task here was by no means easy.

Queen's Pawn Opening

Tarrasch	Chigorin
1 P-Q4	P-Q4
2 N-KB3	P-QB3

This move has the slight disadvantage that White can, if he chooses, continue with 3 B-B4, after which Black will sooner or later have to play P-QB4, involving a loss of a tempo.

White can, of course, opt for 3 P-B4, going into the normal position of the Slav Defence. Tarrasch chooses another course, a completely innocuous line which permits the active development of Black's queen's bishop.

3 P-K3(?)	B-N5
4 P-B4	P-K3
5 N-B3	N-Q2
6 B-Q3	KN-B3
7 0-0	B-Q3
8 PxP	

This exchange leads to an isolated QP. On the other hand, the immediate 8 P-K4 gives Black an excellent game after 8 . . . PxBP 9 BxBP P-K4.

8 . . .	KPxP
9 P-K4	PxP
10 NxP	NxN
11 BxN	0-0
12 Q-B2(?)	

After the game Tarrasch called this a pawn sacrifice. But it is more likely that it was an oversight. White gets no adequate compensation for the pawn.

| 12 . . . | P-KB4? |

In the tournament book Tarrasch wrote: "The immediate BxN followed by Q-R5 would not be good because White can play P-KR3 and, if QxQP, then R-Q1 followed by Q-Q3, winning a piece, even if Black should play Q-K4 and check on KR7." Such an imprecise note on the part of a well-known theoretician is quite a surprise. Let us look at it a little closer. First 12 . . . BxN 13 BxB Q-R5 14 P-KR3 QxQP! 15 R-Q1 Q-K4 16 Q-Q3 Q-R7ch 17 K-B1 KR-K1! Now Black is threatening mate and after the forced 18 B-K3 can cover his piece with 18 . . . R-K3 (19 B-N4 N-K4). The overall verdict must therefore be that the immediate exchange (i.e. 12 . . . BxN) would have won Black a pawn without weakening his pawns.

13 Q-N3ch	K-R1
14 B-B2	BxN
15 QxB	Q-R5
16 P-KN3	QxQP
17 R-Q1	Q-B4

17 . . . N-K4? would have been a bad mistake on account of 18 Q-K2 Q-B4 19 B-K3 Q-N5 20 P-QR3, when Black loses a piece. After the text-move, on the other hand, Black has nothing to fear. If, for example, 18 Q-Q3, then 18 . . . N-K4 19 QxB QxB.

18 Q-K2	N-B3!
19 B-K3	Q-K4
20 Q-Q3	

White could have won back the pawn but only at the cost of a positional disadvantage: 20 BxBP B-B4 21 B-Q3 BxB 22 PxB QR-K1.

| 20 . . . | N-Q4 |
| 21 B-Q4 | Q-K2 |

32. Tarrasch–Chigorin

The first phase has ended with a clear success for Black. His opponent's two bishops are inadequate compensation for the pawn. It is true that White's bishop on the long diagonal is very active; on the other hand, Black's knight is also powerfully placed.

22 R-K1	Q-N4
23 P-QR3	QR-Q1
24 K-R1	Q-R3

Threatening 25 . . . P-B5 26 P-KN4? P-B6. White cannot forestall this by 25 P-B4? because of 25 . . . NxP 26 PxN BxBP 27 R-K2 P-B4.

| 25 Q-KB3 | Q-Q7 |

Now 25 . . . P-B5 would no longer have been good because both White's bishops would become very active after 26 P-KN4.

26 Q-Q1	Q-N4?

Chigorin obviously overrates his position. After an exchange of queens White would have had to fight for a draw, which he should have attained in view of his two bishops. But he could not have hoped for more.

27 P-B4!	NxP?

Although Black gets three pawns for the piece, the sacrifice is nevertheless wrong, for White's pieces soon become very active. Black should have played 27 ... Q-N3, though it must be admitted that his previous queen manoeuvre has, in view of the loss of tempo, already deprived him of the advantage he had.

28 B-K3

Not 28 PxN QxP 29 B-KN1 B-N5 30 Q-K2 BxR 31 RxB QR-K1! 32 Q-B2 QxQ, and Black wins.

28 ...	Q-B3
29 PxN	BxBP
30 Q-B3	BxB
31 QxB	QxP
32 QR-B1	P-QR3?

This pawn is not important; Black has more to fear from the threat Q-K7. The correct defence is 32 ... P-KN3! 33 Q-K7 Q-N2, after which Black has almost equalized.

33 Q-K7!

Now White has two strong threats: 34 QR-Q1 and 34 BxP.

33 ...	Q-B6
34 R-K3	

Preventing 34 ... Q-KB6ch.

34 ...	Q-B5
35 R-KN1	Q-Q4ch
36 R-N2	Q-B2

36 ... R-B2 would not save the game, for after 37 Q-R4 White has two strong threats, 38 R-Q3 and 38 B-N3. If Black

then tries 37 ... Q-R4 there follows 38 B-N3 R(B2)-Q2 39 QxPch KxQ 40 R-R3 mate.

33. Tarrasch-Chigorin

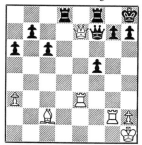

37 B-N3!	QxQ
38 RxQ	P-KN3
39 RxQNP	R-QN1
40 RxR	RxR
41 R-N3!	

41 B-B4 would be wrong because then Black could force an exchange of rooks and secure a draw. With the rooks on the board, on the other hand, White undoubtedly has the upper hand, mainly because of Black's broken pawns (QR3 and QB3).

41 ...	P-B4
42 R-Q3	P-QR4
43 K-N2	K-N2
44 K-B3	K-B3
45 P-KR4	R-N3
46 B-B2	K-K4
47 B-N3	K-B3
48 B-B4	P-R3
49 K-K3	P-N4
50 P-R5!	R-B3
51 R-Q7	R-N3
52 R-KR7	

There is a quicker win by 52 R-QB7, which leaves Black without counter-play.

52 ...	K-K4
53 R-K7ch	K-Q3
54 R-K6ch	K-B2
55 R-K5	P-B5ch
56 K-K4	R-QB3

57	R-K7ch	K-Q1?	60	B-Q5	P-B6
58	R-KN7	R-Q3	61	K-Q6	K-B1
59	K-K5	R-Q5	62	R-N8 mate	

Ostend 1907

		1	2	3	4	5	6	Pts	Prize
1	Tarrasch	– –	½ ½	½ 1	½ 1	1 ½	1 ½	12½	I
		– –	1 0	½ ½	½ 1	1 0	0 1		
2	Schlechter	½ ½	– –	½ 0	1 1	½ 1	½ ½	12	II
		0 1	– –	1 0	½ ½	½ ½	1 1		
3	Marshall	½ 0	½ 1	– –	0 1	0 ½	½ ½	11½	III
		½ ½	0 1	– –	0 1	1 1	1 1		
4	Janowski	½ 0	0 0	1 0	– –	1 1	1 1	11½	III
		½ 0	½ ½	1 0	– –	1 1	½ 1		
5	Burn	0 ½	½ 0	1 ½	0 0	– –	½ 1	8	
		0 1	½ ½	0 0	0 0	– –	1 1		
6	Chigorin	0 ½	½ ½	½ ½	0 0	½ 0	– –	4½	
		1 0	0 0	0 0	½ 0	0 0	– –		

10 St Petersburg 1909

A Reputation Saved in the Last Round

The years in which Dr E. Lasker held the world championship title proved to be rather barren as regards world title matches. Steinitz had in his time sought out those opponents he considered to be most dangerous. Lasker, on the other hand, avoided matches with players of his own strength. He only agreed to a match with Tarrasch when the German grandmaster was already past his peak, and Marshall and Janowski were not really in the same class.

In the first decade of the present century, a dangerous rival appeared on the scene, the Polish player Akiba Rubinstein. The latter was noted for his wonderful knowledge of the mysteries of the positional game; he was, moreover, an endgame virtuoso who had the ability to utilize minute advantages to secure a win. In that respect he was unrivalled until the appearance of J. R. Capablanca.

For years Lasker had managed to avoid a title match with Rubinstein, although the latter had been victorious in several important international tournaments and had won matches against both Marshall (twice) and Schlechter—two players against whom Lasker defended his title! Rubinstein also defeated Bogolyubov, Teichmann, Mieses and Salwe in matches.

Once, however, it looked as though Lasker's delaying tactics might fail to work. In the great St Petersburg tournament, played in February and March 1909, there was a keen duel between the world champion and his would-be challenger. Soon after the start—in the third round—they faced each other, and Rubinstein emerged victorious, the game

going down in many books of instruction as a brilliant example of active defence.

Prior to the last round the leading scores were Rubinstein 14, Lasker 13½, Spielmann 11, Duras and Teichmann 10. The superiority of the top two was clear; so too was the importance of the final result, for if Rubinstein, after his victory over Lasker in their individual game, were also to come out ahead of him in the tournament, then a world title match would be inevitable.

Lasker had White in the last round against Teichmann, one of the leaders and a player, moreover, who was well known for his ability to put up stubborn defence in inferior positions. Rubinstein had Black, though against a much weaker opponent, the twenty-two year old Tartakower. The latter only reached the ranks of the chess élite after the war and in the St Petersburg tournament ended up in the bottom half of the table.

It looked very much as though Rubinstein had everything in his favour. However, in past tournaments a serious weakness had shown up in his armour—his nerves. In vital games he tended to make elementary mistakes that were unworthy of a player of his ability. Lasker, on the other hand, had the knack of applying all his energies at decisive moments and concentrating fully on the task in question. The difference in purely sporting qualities made itself felt in this case. Rubinstein only just managed to share first place, thus failing to demonstrate his superiority over the world champion. It was perhaps the decisive moment of his chess career, for he was never given an opportunity to measure swords with

Lasker in a world championship title match.

Ruy Lopez

Lasker	Teichmann
1 P-K4	P-K4
2 N-KB3	N-QB3
3 B-N5	P-QR3
4 B-R4	N-B3
5 0-0	B-K2
6 Q-K2	

At the time the game was played a completely unknown system. Lasker evidently wanted to confuse his opponent in the opening, which he managed to do.

6 ...	P-QN4
7 B-N3	P-Q3
8 P-B3	0-0
9 P-Q4	PxP
10 PxP	B-N5
11 R-Q1	P-Q4
12 P-K5	

There is nothing to be feared from this move, which is one reason why 12 PxP has been tried several times. If then 12 ... KNxP, White secures a slight advantage by 13 Q-K4 B-B3 14 N-B3. However, Black has a stronger counter in 12 ... N-QR4! 13 B-B2 R-K1.

12 ...	N-K5
13 N-B3	NxN
14 PxN.	P-B3?

34. Lasker–Teichmann

For present-day annotators there is nothing simpler than to call this move a serious mistake. However, it must not be forgotten that all the question and exclamation marks of chess theory have first to be discovered, which often takes generations. The correct continuation is 14 ... N-R4 15 B-B2 Q-Q2 (or P-KB3).

15 P-KR3	B-R4

Here Black cannot play 15 ... BxN because his QP is under attack after 16 QxB. The retreat 15 ... B-K3 is not good either on account of 16 PxP RxP 17 B-N5 R-N3 18 B-B2! And the passive 15 ... B-B1 16 P-QR4 is advantageous to White.

16 P-N4	B-B2

Black entices the KP to advance in the hope that it will prove to be a weakness and give Black's pieces access to the square Q3. The only problem is that Black's king is open to attack. However, after the alternative, 16 ... B-N3, White has two good continuations, 17 N-R4 and 17 PxP RxP 18 N-K5.

17 P-K6	B-N3
18 N-R4	N-R4
19 NxB	PxN
20 B-B2	P-KB4
21 K-R1!	

White's plan of attack is now clear: after exchanging pawns on KB4 he will play R-KN1 and Q-R5, e.g. 21 ... N-B5 22 PxP PxP 23 R-KN1 N-Q3 24 Q-R5 B-B3 25 B-R6 Q-K1 26 R-N6! followed by 27 QR-KN1 (26 ... QxP 27 BxNP!).

21 ...	B-Q3
22 PxP	Q-R5
23 Q-B3	PxP
24 R-KN1	

Threatening both 25 BxP and 25 B-N5. If Black replies with 24 ... Q-B3 White has several possibilities, among them the elegant 25 B-N5 QxKP 26 QR-K1 Q-Q2 27 B-R6 R-B2 28 BxNP! RxB 29 BxP R-KB1 30 RxRch winning.

24 ...	P-B5
25 R-N4	Q-R3
26 P-K7!	BxP
27 BxP	Q-K3

Or 27 . . . Q-KB3 28 QR-KN1 R-B2 29 Q-N3. Immediately after making his move Black resigned in anticipation of the pretty finish 28 RxPch! KxR 29 R-KN1ch.

French Defence

Tartakower	Rubinstein
1 P-K4	P-K3
2 P-QB4	

Even at that time Tartakower had leanings towards experiment. Black, however, gets a very comfortable game.

2 ...	P-Q4
3 KPxP	PxP
4 P-Q4	N-KB3
5 N-KB3	B-K2
6 B-K2	0-0
7 0-0	PxP

Black has the choice of several very good plans. One possibility is 7 . . . P-B3, but the most active line seems to be 7 . . . N-B3 followed by B-KN5.

8 BxP	QN-Q2
9 N-B3	N-N3
10 B-N3	B-KN5

At this stage of the game this otherwise quite natural move is not good. Black should have blocked his opponent's isolated pawn by either 10 . . . P-B3 or 10 . . . N(N3)-Q4.

11 P-KR3	B-R4

A better continuation is 11 . . . BxN 12 QxB P-B3. The two bishops are not nearly as important as the blocking of the QP.

12 P-N4!	B-N3
13 N-K5	

35. Tartakower–Rubinstein

Now it is too late to think about stopping the QP, for White is already threatening 14 P-KB4. In such positions the bishop on KN3 is badly placed. Rubinstein therefore decides to open the game, though this does not lead to equality, for his opponent secures the advantage of the two bishops.

13 ...	P-B4
14 NxB	RPxN
15 PxP	BxP

Black cannot exchange queens at once, for after 15 . . . QxQ 16 BxQ! BxP 17 B-B3 the QNP is unprotected (17 . . . R-N1 18 B-B4). Nevertheless an exchange of queens actually does take place a few moves later, though in more favourable circumstances.

16 Q-B3	Q-B2
17 B-KB4	Q-B3
18 QxQ	PxQ
19 QR-B1	B-Q5
20 N-K2!	

Apparently illogical, for White rids his opponent of his weak pawn. On the other hand, the move forces Black's strong centrally posted bishop to depart and also enables White to eliminate Black's QBP, which could have made the latter's Q4 into a strong square for a knight.

20 ...	BxNP
21 RxP	QR-B1
22 RxR	RxR
23 R-Q1	N-B5(?)

A more active plan is 23 . . . P-R4! threatening P-R5. It is possible that Rubinstein wanted to avoid the continuation 24 R-N1 B-R6 25 BxPch KxB 26 RxN, though after 26 . . . R-B7 he would have recovered the pawn and had an easy draw.

24	K-N2	N(B5)-R4
25	R-QN1	B-R6?

Black misses an opportunity to exchange off White's dangerous bishop and Tartakower does not give him a second chance. The correct line is 25 . . . NxB! 26 PxN (26 RxB N-B4) 26 . . . B-R6 27 R-QR1 B-B4 28 B-K3! BxB 29 PxB R-B2 30 N-Q4 N-Q4, when White's advantage is very slight.

26	B-K3	R-B2
27	P-N5	N-K1
28	B-Q5	B-B4
29	R-N8	K-B1
30	B-KB4	R-Q2
31	B-B3	B-Q3

Black has succeeded in neutralizing one of his opponent's advantages—the two bishops. This, however, is not sufficient to equalize, for the pin on the knight is very troublesome. Moreover, the other knight is out of play, which White

36. Tartakower–Rubinstein

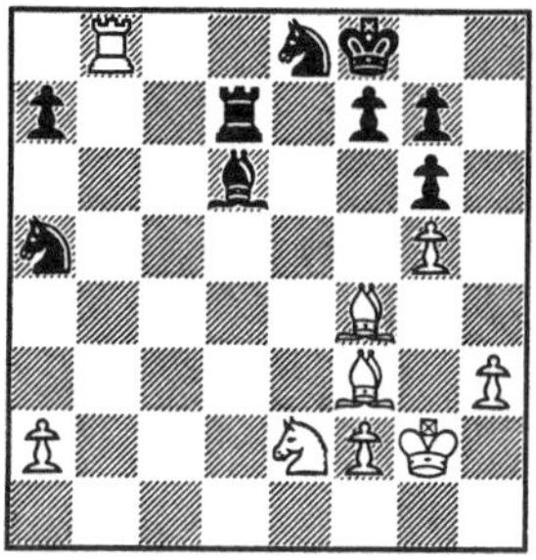

Position after Black's 31st move

should be able to capitalize upon. If White were now to continue 32 R-B8!, preventing the knight from getting into play, Black would have a difficult game; e.g. 32 . . . K-K2? 33 B-Q2 N-N2 34 B-B6, winning, or 32 . . . BxB 33 NxB R-B2 34 R-R8 N-B5 35 N-Q5 R-Q2 36 K-N3 N-K4 37 B-K4 N-B5 38 K-B4 N-Q7 39 P-KR4 (E. Lasker's analysis). In this second variation Black cannot very well exchange on K5, for after 39 . . . NxB 40 KxN he would be forced to alternate his rook between Q2 and QN2, when White could strengthen his position by advancing his QRP to QR6 and then playing R-QN8-N7.

St Petersburg 1909

		1	2	3	4	5	6	7	8	9	10	11	12	13	14	15	16	17	18	19	Pts	Prize
1	Lasker	–	0	1	½	½	1	1	1	1	½	1	1	0	1	1	1	1	1	1	14½	I, II
2	Rubinstein	1	–	1	1	½	½	½	1	1	1	1	½	0	1	½	1	1	1	1	14½	I, II
3	Duras	0	0	–	0	0	1	½	0	1	½	1	0	1	1	1	1	1	1	1	11	III, IV
4	Spielmann	½	0	1	–	0	1	1	½	½	1	½	½	1	0	½	1	½	½	1	11	III, IV
5	Bernstein	½	½	1	1	–	0	1	0	1	1	1	1	½	0	0	0	½	½	1	10½	V
6	Teichmann	0	½	0	0	1	–	0	½	½	½	1	½	1	½	1	½	1	1	½	10	VI
7	Perlis	0	½	½	0	0	1	–	½	1	½	1	½	1	½	1	½	0	0	1	9½	VII
8	Cohn	0	0	1	½	1	½	½	–	0	0	½	1	½	0	½	½	½	1	1	9	VIII
9	Salwe	0	0	0	½	0	½	0	1	–	0	1	½	1	1	½	0	1	1	1	9	VIII
10	Schlechter	½	0	½	0	0	½	½	1	1	–	0	0	1	1	½	0	1	½	1	9	VIII
11	Mieses	0	0	0	½	0	0	0	½	0	1	–	1	½	1	1	1	0	1	1	8½	
12	Tartakower	0	½	1	½	0	½	½	0	½	1	0	–	0	0	½	1	1	1	½	8½	
13	Dus Chotimirski	1	1	0	0	½	0	0	½	0	0	½	1	–	½	½	½	1	0	1	8	
14	Forgacs	0	0	0	1	1	½	½	1	0	0	0	1	½	–	½	½	½	0	½	7½	
15	Burn	0	½	0	½	1	0	0	½	½	½	0	½	½	½	–	1	½	½	0	7	
16	Vidmar	0	0	0	0	1	½	½	½	1	1	0	0	½	½	0	–	½	1	0	7	
17	Speyer	0	0	0	½	½	0	1	½	0	0	1	0	0	½	½	½	–	½	½	6	
18	Freymann	0	0	0	½	½	0	1	0	0	½	0	0	1	1	½	0	½	–	0	5½	
19	Snosko-Borowski	0	0	0	0	0	½	0	0	0	0	0	½	0	½	1	1	½	1	–	5	

32 R-R8?	N-B5!

After White's mistake, everything is now in order for Black. He has no difficulty in achieving a draw.

33 BxBch	N(B5)xB
34 N-Q4	R-B2
35 N-B6	N-B1

36 P-QR4	N-N3
37 R-N8	NxP
38 NxP	RxN
39 B-B6	K-K2
40 RxNch	K-Q3
41 BxN	RxB

Drawn

A Strange Conclusion to a Strange Match

The world championship match between
Dr Emanuel Lasker and C. Schlechter,
which took place in Vienna in January
1910, was unusual in one respect. It was
played over ten games, the shortest title
match in the history of chess.

C. Schlechter was a player with an
unusually solid style; he rarely lost a
game, but, on the other hand, had a large
percentage of draws, which reduced the
number of his successes in tournament
play. To be faced by such a player in a
short match was extremely risky for the
world champion, and it is a great mystery
why Lasker agreed to such conditions. A
chance loss could easily have been decisive. And that is what very nearly
happened!

The first three games were on the
whole quite even and without any great
complications, all of them ending in
draws. The fourth was also drawn, though
not without some very dramatic
moments. Lasker, who had White, won a
pawn, and after simplifying reached a
won endgame. But then he made a single
mistake, which allowed his opponent to
achieve a draw. In the fifth game Lasker
again made the running, reaching a position in which his heavy pieces gave him
the upper hand. Then Schlechter sacrificed a pawn for some nebulous attacking
chances. In time-trouble Lasker
blundered twice, which changed the situation completely, and Schlechter was able
to press home a mating attack.

The rest of the match was characterized by Lasker's onslaught and some
hard-fought games. In the sixth
Schlechter managed to save a game in
which he was a pawn down, and in the

ninth he drew a lost ending when his
opponent blundered. Prior to the last
game, Schlechter was thus still in the lead
(5:4) and very close to becoming world
champion. He only needed to hold the
last game, in which his opponent had
White. Everyone expected him to remain
true to style and play cautiously. What
actually happened is therefore an almost
inexplicable psychological mystery.

Queen's Gambit

Lasker	Schlechter
1 P-Q4	P-Q4
2 P-QB4	P-QB3
3 N-KB3	N-B3
4 P-K3	P-KN3

Later the system was named after
Schlechter, and it still enjoys a good
reputation. But the simplest way to
equalize is 4 . . . B-B4.

5 N-B3	B-N2
6 B-Q3	0-0
7 Q-B2	

If 7 0-0, Black can reply 7 . . . B-N5,
which is why 6 B-K2 is nowadays preferred to 6 B-Q3.

7 . . .   N-R3(?)

Black could have attained equality
quite easily by 7 . . . PxP 8 BxBP P-B4 9
PxP QN-Q2 or 8 . . . B-B4 and if 9 P-K4
then 9 . . . B-N5 with a good game.
Instead of choosing a quiet continuation,
Schlechter starts off on his first adventure
on the queen's wing. How can such a
decision be explained? Schlechter's contemporaries, among them the well-known

chess annotator G. Marco, attributed it to a desire to avoid having the outcome of the match depend entirely on the chance win in the fifth game. But is it possible that a chess player would be influenced by such exaggerated scruples? I consider it to be unlikely. A more logical explanation is that both players were labouring under such nervous stress that their power of judgment was not working as well as it normally did.

| 8 P-QR3 | PxP |
| 9 BxBP | P-N4 |

The logical continuation in view of his previous decision. Nevertheless the passive 9 . . . N-B2 is objectively better.

10 B-Q3	P-N5
11 N-QR4	PxP
12 PxP	B-N2
13 R-QN1	Q-B2
14 N-K5!?	

Lasker can hardly be criticized for going in for this sharp attack instead of striving to maintain his small positional advantage by 14 0-0 followed by B-Q2. The game soon takes on an exciting character.

| 14 . . . | N-R4 |

Not, of course, 14 . . . N-Q2? 15 RxB! QxR 16 BxN.

37. Lasker–Schlechter

15 P-N4!?

Again the sharpest continuation. After 15 P-B4 Black could have started a

counter action on the queen's wing, e.g. 15 . . . KR-N1 16 P-N4 BxN 17 BPxB N-N2, threatening P-QB4 and B-B1.

15 . . .	BxN
16 PxN!	B-N2
17 PxP	RPxP
18 Q-B4	B-B1

White was threatening both 19 RxB and 19 BxP. Apart from being a direct answer to the first of these threats, the text-move deals with the second indirectly, e.g. 19 BxP B-K3! 20 QxN PxB, giving Black the strong pair of bishops for the pawn. White dare not try to win a second pawn, e.g. 20 BxPch? RxB 21 QxN B-Q4.

| 19 R-N1 | Q-R4ch |

Not 19 . . . QxP? 20 RxP. Black needs the queen for the defence of the king-side and, as we shall see later, for a counter-attack there.

| 20 B-Q2 | Q-Q4 |
| 21 R-QB1 | |

White has no objection to an exchange of queens, provided, of course, it does not improve his opponent's pawn position.

| 21 . . . | B-N2 |
| 22 Q-B2 | Q-KR4 |

38. Lasker–Schlechter

The first crisis in the game. After 23 R-N1! QxP 24 K-K2 White would have the better of it, e.g. 24 . . . Q-B2 25 BxP PxB 26 Q-N3ch R-B2 27 QxB QxQ 28

RxQ P-K4! or 24 ... QR-N1? 25 RxB QxR 26 BxN Q-N5ch 27 K-B1 Q-R6ch 28 K-K1 Q-R8ch 29 K-K2 Q-R4ch 30 P-B3, though in the first variation his advantage would hardly be sufficient to win. Another possibility is 23 Q-N3 QxP 24 RxNP QR-N1, which leaves Black with a playable game. Lasker tries a third line, a dangerous-looking sacrifice, which, however, can be adequately countered.

It is almost unbelievable that Black's unusual piece configuration cannot be exploited in any way. But that nevertheless seems to be the case. However, Lasker can hardly be blamed for failing to foresee this when choosing the line of play that led to the position.

23	BxP!?	QxP
24	R-B1	PxB
25	Q-N3ch	R-B2
26	QxB	QR-KB1!

After the game Lasker admitted that he had simply overlooked this move. The knight cannot be taken because Black can reply RxP with a mating attack.

Black now has the advantage, though not necessarily a decisive one if White continues correctly with 27 P-B4 forcing his opponent to make the passive retreat 27 ... N-N1. Lasker, however, chooses an inaccurate continuation, which gets him into a critical situation. As things turned out the mistake actually enabled him to win the game and save his title, for it evidently encouraged his opponent to play for a win at any price, which in turn led to an error at the decisive point of the struggle.

27	Q-N3?	K-R1
28	P-B4	P-N4!
29	Q-Q3	PxP!
30	PxP	Q-R5ch
31	K-K2	Q-R7ch
32	R-KB2	Q-R4ch
33	R-KB3	N-B2!

The weakness of White's 27th move becomes apparent, for the Black knight is ready to go to Q4 or QN4. Moreover, White's pieces lack co-ordination, and the White king is exposed. Can White still hope to offer resistance?

34 RxP

"You might as well be hanged for a sheep as a lamb." In any case, after 34 N-B3 Black's knight would also be very effective in operating from K3.

| 34 ... | N-N4! |

Objectively the best move, though 34 ... N-Q4 would virtually have ended the match, for White would then have had nothing better than to go into an unfavourable endgame by 35 Q-N6 QxQ 36 RxQ NxPch 37 BxN RxB 38 R-R3ch K-N1 39 R(R3)-KN3. It should be noted that 35 R-B5 could have been answered by 35 ... RxP! 36 BxR NxBch 37 K-Q1 P-K4! with a decisive attack.

35 R-B4

39. Lasker–Schlechter

| 35 ... | RxP? |

Schlechter's desire to attain an elegant, rather than a straightforward win leads to disaster. The search for beauty has often been severely punished. After the fairly obvious 35 ... R-Q1, White has no real defence, e.g. 36 B-K3 (36 R-B5 NxQPch 37 QxN QxR(B6)ch) 36 ... P-K4 37 P-Q5 N-Q3, and Black wins the exchange.

36	BxR	RxB
37	R-B8ch	B-B1
38	K-B2	

The only adequate defence; it gives White a draw, though nothing more. In his notes on the game Schlechter stated that he had originally planned 38 ... Q-R5ch but now noticed the interesting refutation 39 K-N2! Q-N5ch 40 R-N3 QxR(B1) 41 Q-N6!

38	...	Q-R7ch!
39	K-K1	Q-R8ch?

One mistake leads to another. Black had already missed the win, but there was still a draw to be had, and with it the world title: 39 ... Q-R5ch! 40 K-Q2 Q-R7ch 41 K-K3 RxRch 42 KxR Q-R6ch 43 K-K2 QxR 44 QxN or 40 K-B1 Q-R6ch 41 K-B2 (41 K-K2?? Q-N7ch) 41 ... RxRch 42 QxR QxR 43 Q-R5ch. (On the other hand, an attempt to win by 40 R-N3? fails: 40 ... Q-R8ch 41 K-K2 Q-KB8ch 42 K-Q2 R-B7ch.) How can we explain Schlechter's tragic mistake? Certainly fatigue played its part; but so too did the disappointment caused by the fact that the "winning" sacrifice had actually thrown away the win.

40	R-KB1	Q-R5ch
41	K-Q2!	RxR

Of course, not 41 ... RxP 42 R(B8)xBch K-N2 43 R(B1)-B7ch K-R3 44 R-KR8ch.

42	QxR	QxPch
43	Q-Q3	Q-B7ch
44	K-Q1	N-Q3
45	R-B5	B-R3

White's material advantage is very slight. But with correct play it is sufficient to win, as Lasker proves in what turns out to be the longest game of the match.

46	R-Q5	K-N1
47	N-B5	

For a long time White had had difficulties with his king. Now, however, it is Black who is faced by this problem. The threat is 48 Q-N6ch.

47	...	Q-N8ch
48	K-B2	Q-QB8ch
49	K-N3	B-N2
50	N-K6	Q-N7ch
51	K-R4	K-B2
52	NxB	QxN
53	Q-QN3!	

Virtually the end of the game, for Black has to choose between exchanging queens (after K-N3 or K-B3) and losing the QRP.

53	...	K-K1
54	Q-N8ch	K-B2
55	QxP	Q-N5ch
56	Q-Q4	Q-Q2ch
57	K-N3	Q-N2ch
58	K-R2	Q-B3
59	Q-Q3	K-K1
60	R-KN5	K-Q2
61	R-K5	Q-N7ch
62	R-K2	Q-N5
63	R-Q2	Q-QR5
64	Q-B5ch	K-B2
65	Q-QB2ch	QxQ
66	RxQch	K-N3
67	R-K2	N-B1
68	K-N3	K-B3
69	R-QB2ch	K-N2
70	K-N4	N-R2
71	K-B5	Resigns

12 San Sebastián 1911

J. R. Capablanca's Début

Prior to the start of the first international tournament in the Spanish town of San Sebastián, there was some disagreement about one of the participants. The Cuban champion, J. R. Capablanca, at that time unknown, had been brought in at the last moment and was in the opinion of some of the other competitors, especially Dr Bernstein, not up to world standard. As luck would have it the renowned grandmaster was drawn against the youngest competitor in the very first round.

40. Capablanca–Bernstein

Position after White's 22nd move

White undoubtedly has the better of it; his second knight is now threatening to join in the attack against the king. Black's best policy is to simplify by 22 . . . Q-N3, which would allow him to equalize, the game probably resulting in a draw. But the grandmaster did not want to drop half a point against his young opponent and so he embarked upon an over-risky adventure.

22 . . .	QxP?
23 N(K2)-N3	QxBP
24 R-QB1	

White is two pawns down and must prevent an exchange of queens (24 . . . Q-B4). Bernstein obviously assumed that his queen would become active on the long diagonal, but it is already too late for such a procedure.

| 24 . . . | Q-N7 |
| 25 N-R5! | R-KR1 |

Not 25 . . . P-N3 26 QxKRPch K-N1 27 P-K5 PxN(R4) 28 NPxP, when Black has no defence against the manoeuvre 29 K-R1 followed by R-KN1ch.

| 26 R-K2 | Q-K4 |
| 27 P-B4 | Q-N4 |

The Black queen must now leave the long diagonal, giving White the opportunity to make one of his well-known "minor combinations", a favourite tactical feature of Capablanca's play throughout his career.

| 28 N(B5)xNP! | N-B4? |

With this move Black more or less resigns himself to his fate. However, the alternative, 28 . . . NxN 29 N-B6ch K-N3 30 NxB P-B3 31 P-K5!, would leave his king in a somewhat exposed position, so that his chances of organizing a successful defence would not be very great, e.g. 31 . . . BPxP 32 Q-K4ch K-B2 33 RxP.

29 NxR	BxN
30 Q-QB3!	P-B3
31 NxPch	K-N3
32 N-R5	R-N1
33 P-B5ch	K-N4
34 Q-K3ch	Resigns

This first victory was, from the psychological point of view, extremely important. In the further course of the tournament Capablanca played calmly and thoughtfully, losing only one game, and getting into danger in only one other (against Janowski). After his victory over Bernstein he drew with Marshall; then he defeated Burn and drew with Tarrasch. He continued with two victories against Janowski and Leonhardt respectively, and after drawing with Duras he defeated Nimzowitsch. There followed two draws, against Maróczy and Schlechter, and then with a bit of luck he netted another full point, this time against Spielmann. In the thirteenth round he made his task more difficult by losing to Rubinstein, who thereby caught up with him, both having 8½ points. However, the latter had a bye in the final round, so that Capablanca had one more game to play. At this stage of the tournament Capablanca adopted the correct psychological plan and played cautiously against Teichmann, the game ending in a colourless draw. In the same round Rubinstein had a considerable advantage over Spielmann, but at the decisive moment he played weakly and dropped half a point.

French Defence

Spielmann	Rubinstein
1 P-K4	P-K3
2 P-Q4	P-Q4
3 N-QB3	N-KB3
4 B-KN5	PxP
5 NxP	QN-Q2
6 N-KB3	

More accurate is the immediate NxNch, for one move later Black can, if he wishes, retake with the bishop.

6 ...	B-K2
7 NxNch	NxN
8 B-Q3	P-QN3(!)

Rubinstein's innovation—obviously prepared for an encounter with a dangerous opponent. In view of the replies 9 B-N5ch and 9 N-K5, the text-move looks rather dangerous, but actually Black gets a good game in both cases. White should therefore have gone on with his development, e.g. 9 0-0 0-0 10 Q-K2 B-N2 11 QR-Q1, etc.

9 N-K5

If 9 B-N5ch, Black can simply play 9 ... B-Q2. Even now Black can ignore the threat 10 B-N5ch.

9 ...	B-N2
10 B-N5ch	P-B3!

The point of the whole set-up. Black can recover the pawn with an excellent game: e.g. 11 BxPch (11 NxQBP Q-Q4) 11 ... BxB 12 NxB Q-Q4 13 N-K5 QxNP 14 Q-B3 QxQ 15 NxQ, etc.

11 Q-B3	Q-Q4!
12 BxN	

Or 12 QxQ NxQ 13 BxB NxB.

12 ...	BPxB
13 BxP	

This allows Black to transpose into a favourable endgame, where he has the two bishops. The correct continuation is 13 QxQ BxQ 14 BxB KxB.

13 ...	QxQ
14 PxQ	R-KN1
15 B-R6	P-B3
16 N-Q3	BxP
17 R-KB1	R-N5!

This rook manoeuvre will eventually win the KRP. The game is strategically decided, and in view of his excellent technique Rubinstein should have had no great difficulty in turning his material advantage into a win. However, at this decisive phase he began to feel the effects of the strain of being in the struggle for first prize.

18 B-B4	R-Q1
19 P-B3	P-K4
20 B-K3	P-K5
21 N-N4	B-Q3

Although this wins a pawn, there is an even stronger move in 21 . . . P-B4!, which prevents his opponent from castling artificially (K-Q2) and consolidating his position.

22 **P-KR3**	**R-R4**
23 **R-KN1**	**K-B2**
24 **K-Q2**	**RxP**
25 **P-R4**	**P-B4**
26 **N-B6**	**R-Q2**
27 **P-Q5**	**P-B5**
28 **B-Q4**	

41. Spielmann–Rubinstein

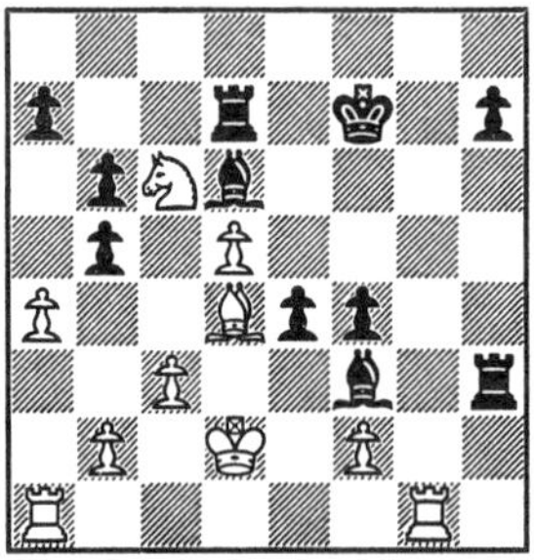

28 . . .	**P-K6ch!**

A strong move, which Rubinstein fails to follow up correctly.

29 **PxKP**	**PxKPch?**

This allows White to save half a point. There was a clear win by 29 . . . R-R7ch! 30 K-B1 BxP 31 RPxP (31N-K5ch BxN 32 BxB B-K5, etc.) 31 . . . P-B6 or 30 K-Q3 B-K7ch followed by P-B6, and the passed KBP soon decides the issue.

30 **BxKP**	**R-R7ch**
31 **K-B1**	**R-K7**
32 **B-R6!**	

Preventing Black from advancing his KRP. The game is now virtually even, for there is no way in which Black can use his very slight advantage.

32 . . .	**BxP**
33 **PxP**	**P-R4**
34 **R-R4!**	**R-K5**
35 **RxR**	**BxR**
36 **R-N7ch**	**K-K1**
37 **R-N8ch**	**K-B2**
38 **R-N7ch**	

Drawn

42. Vidmar–Capablanca

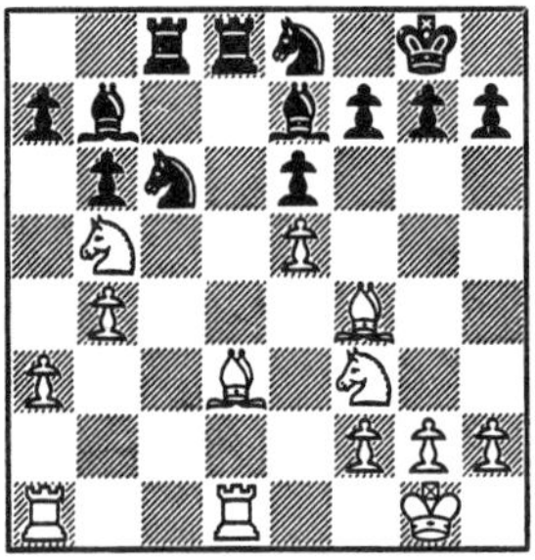

Position after White's 17th move

San Sebastian 1911

		1	2	3	4	5	6	7	8	9	10	11	12	13	14	15	Pts	Prize
1	Capablanca	—	0	½	½	1	½	½	1	1	½	1	½	1	½	1	9½	I
2	Rubinstein	1	—	½	½	½	½	½	½	½	½	1	½	½	1	1	9	II, III
3	Vidmar	½	½	—	0	½	½	½	1	½	½	1	½	1	1	1	9	II, III
4	Marshall	½	½	1	—	½	½	½	½	½	1	1	½	½	0	1	8½	IV
5	Nimzowitsch	0	½	½	½	—	½	0	½	1	1	½	½	½	½	1	7½	V-VII
6	Schlechter	½	½	½	½	½	—	½	0	½	½	1	½	½	1	½	7½	V-VII
7	Tarrasch	½	½	½	½	1	½	—	1	½	0	½	½	1	0	½	7½	V-VII
8	Bernstein	0	½	0	½	½	1	0	—	1	1	½	1	0	1	0	7	
9	Spielmann	0	½	½	½	0	½	½	0	—	½	½	1	½	1	1	7	
10	Teichmann	½	½	½	0	0	½	1	0	½	—	0	½	½	1	1	6½	
11	Janowski	0	0	0	0	½	0	½	½	½	1	—	0	1	1	1	6	
12	Maróczy	½	½	½	½	½	½	½	0	0	½	1	—	½	½	0	6	
13	Burn	0	½	0	½	½	½	0	1	½	½	0	½	—	0	½	5	
14	Duras	½	0	0	1	½	0	1	0	0	0	0	½	1	—	½	5	
15	Leonhardt	0	0	0	0	0	½	½	1	0	0	0	1	½	½	—	4	

In the last round Capablanca had an easier task. He only needed a draw to win the tournament, and he achieved this with the help of one of his typical minor combinations.

Black's position looks uncomfortable, for his opponent's knight is threatening to go to Q6. Fortunately for him there is an effective defence.

17 ...	R-Q4!
18 N-Q6	NxN

19 PxN   BxP

Has Black perhaps failed to see the imminent loss of the exchange?

20 BxB   R-Q1!

Not of course 20 . . . RxB?? 21 BxPch winning. At this stage the game was agreed drawn, for White has nothing better than 21 BxPch KxB 22 RxR PxR, when the bishops of opposite colours ensure a draw.

13 Karlsbad 1911

Two Miniatures Decide

Karlsbad was beginning to make a name for itself. For the second time it was the venue of a great international tournament with a distinguished field (21 August–24 September 1911). It was generally expected that Schlechter, Rubinstein, Duras and Marshall would fight it out for first place. Surprisingly, however, other names appeared among the leaders, and at the end of the 17th round the position was: Rotlevi, Schlechter and Teichmann 12½, Rubinstein, Marshall 10½, etc.

The issue was virtually decided in the 18th round, where two of the leaders were drawn against each other; the third suffered an unexpected defeat at the hands of a player who had been in the bottom half of the table for the whole of the tournament.

Decisive games between players of the same strength are generally long and tough struggles. The encounter between Teichmann and Schlechter was the exception to the rule. The game that was to determine the leader, and eventual winner, turned out to be a miniature. So, too, did the other key game of the round.

Ruy Lopez

	Teichmann	Schlechter
1	P-K4	P-K4
2	N-KB3	N-QB3
3	B-N5	P-QR3
4	B-R4	N-B3
5	0-0	B-K2
6	R-K1	P-QN4
7	B-N3	P-Q3
8	P-B3	0-0
9	P-Q3	N-QR4

10	B-B2	P-B4
11	QN-Q2	Q-B2(?)

The first of a series of inaccuracies leading to Schlechter's unexpectedly speedy defeat. The queen is better placed on Q1 than QB2, and for that reason the line recommended today is 11 ... N-B3 12 N-B1 R-K1! 13 N-K3 B-B1, etc.

12	N-B1	N-B3
13	N-K3	B-N2(?)

In the present variation, where White plays 9 P-Q3, Black's bishop is usually badly placed on QN2, the main reason being that White's knight has easy access to KB5. The correct continuation is 13 ... B-K3 and if 14 N-N5 then 14 ... P-Q4! 15 PxP BxP! 16 P-Q4 BPxP 17 BxPch K-R1.

14	N-B5	KR-K1
15	B-N5	N-Q2

Black intends to exchange off his passive bishop, but thereby allow his opponent to get a dangerous attack with his pieces. A safer continuation is 15 ... B-Q1.

16	B-N3!	N-B1

Black would have more chances of putting up a successful defence by 16 ... B-KB1.

17	B-Q5!	N-N3?

White was threatening 18 BxN followed by NxBch, winning the exchange. There was, however, a better counter in 17 ... B-Q1! A defence that is less good, on the other hand, is 17 ... BxB 18 NxB N-Q1 19 Q-N4! N-N3 20 BxB NxB 21

P-KR4 (or 21 R-K3), with a violent attack.

18 BxB	N(N3)xB

Not, of course, 18 ... N(B3)xB 19 BxB QxB 20 NxQP, when White wins the exchange and a pawn.

43. Teichmann–Schlechter

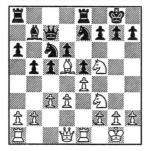

19 BxPch	KxB
20 N-N5ch	K-N1

Other king moves do not help either, e.g. 20 ... K-N3 21 Q-N4 P-KR4 22 N-R4ch or 20 ... K-B3 21 NxRPch K-B2 22 N-N5ch K-B3 23 NxNP!, winning easily.

21 Q-R5	NxN
22 QxPch	K-B1
23 QxNch	K-N1

The Black king cannot escape from the mating net. If 23 ... K-K2, then 24 Q-K6ch K-Q1 (24 ... K-B1 25 N-R7 mate) 25 N-B7ch, winning the queen.

24 Q-N6!

The most accurate move. There were, however, also wins to be had from 24 R-K3 P-N3 25 QxNPch Q-N2 26 Q-R5 and 24 Q-R7ch K-B1 25 R-K3, etc.

24 ...	Q-Q2
25 R-K3	Resigns

In view of 25 ... N-Q1 26 R-R3 N-B2 27 NxN QxN 28 R-R8ch! etc.

French Defence

Dus Chotimirski	Rotlevi
1 P-K4	P-K3
2 P-Q4	P-Q4
3 N-QB3	PxP

It was thanks to Rubinstein that this defence became popular at the time this tournament was played. Réti later "improved" the order of moves: 3 ... N-KB3 4 B-KN5 PxP.

4 NxP	N-Q2
5 B-Q3	KN-B3
6 NxNch	NxN
7 N-B3	B-K2

Rubinstein used to play 7 ... P-QN3 instead. In the 1912 San Sebastián tournament Schlechter tried to refute this by 8 N-K5, which was answered by B-N2! 9 B-QN5ch P-B3 10 BxPch. At this stage 10 NxQBP Q-Q4 11 NxPdis ch K-Q1 is bad for White. A playable alternative, however, is 10 Q-B3 Q-Q4 11 QxQ NxQ 12 BxPch BxB 13 NxB R-B1 14 NxP RxP, when Black has counter-play for the pawn. Another possibility for Black on the seventh move is P-QB4.

8 0-0	0-0
9 B-KN5	P-QN3

The continuation 9 ... P-B4 10 PxP BxP merely wastes a tempo.

10 Q-K2	B-N2
11 QR-Q1	Q-Q4?

White's eleventh move prevented 11 ... P-B4. Black could, however, play 11 ... P-B3 followed by Q-B2, QR-Q1 and P-B4, after which he has a passive but sound position. Another possibility is 11 ... BxN 12 QxB Q-Q4!, forcing an exchange of queens. Then after 13 QxQ NxQ (or 13 ... PxQ) 14 B-Q2 his position is only slightly inferior.

12 P-B4	Q-Q3
13 N-K5	QR-Q1
14 KR-K1	N-Q2

Karlsbad 1911

	1	2	3	4	5	6	7	8	9	10	11	12	13	14	15	16	17	18	19	20	21	22	23	24	25	26	Pts	Prize
1 Teichmann	—	1	1	1	½	1	½	1	1	½	0	1	½	½	½	1	0	½	½	1	½	1	½	1	1	1	18	I
2 Schlechter	0	—	½	0	½	½	½	1	½	1	0	½	1	1	1	1	1	0	½	1	1	1	½	1	1	1	17	II, III
3 Rubinstein	0	½	—	½	0	½	½	1	½	1	1	0	½	1	1	½	1	1	1	½	½	½	1	1	1	1	17	II, III
4 Rotlevi	0	1	½	—	1	1	0	0	1	0	½	1	1	0	1	1	0	1	1	1	1	0	0	1	1	1	16	IV
5 Marshall	½	½	1	0	—	½	0	½	½	½	1	½	½	½	1	1	½	1	0	½	1	1	0	1	1	1	15½	V, VI
6 Nimzowitsch	0	½	½	0	½	—	½	½	0	0	0	½	1	1	1	½	½	1	1	½	1	1	1	1	1	1	15½	V, VI
7 Vidmar	½	½	½	1	1	½	—	0	½	0	1	1	½	0	1	½	1	0	0	½	½	1	1	½	1	1	15	VII
8 Alekhin	0	0	0	1	½	½	1	—	1	0	1	0	0	1	½	1	0	½	0	1	0	1	1	1	½	1	13½	VIII–XI
9 Tartakower	0	½	½	0	½	1	½	0	—	½	1	½	½	½	½	1	0	1	1	1	1	0	1	0	0	1	13½	VIII–XI
10 Leonhardt	½	0	0	1	½	1	1	1	½	—	0	½	½	0	0	½	1	½	1	1	0	0	1	1	1	0	13½	VIII–XI
11 Duras	1	1	0	½	0	1	0	0	0	1	—	0	½	1	0	0	½	1	1	½	½	1	½	1	½	1	13½	VIII–XI
12 Spielmann	0	½	1	0	½	½	0	1	½	½	1	—	0	1	1	½	½	½	1	½	½	1	0	0	1	0	13	XII
13 Perlis	½	0	½	0	½	0	½	1	½	½	½	1	—	½	1	½	1	1	0	½	1	0	0	0	0	1	12	XIII
14 Cohn	½	0	0	1	½	0	1	0	½	1	0	0	½	—	½	½	1	0	1	0	1	0	½	1	1	0	11½	
15 Löwenfisch	½	0	0	0	0	0	0	½	½	1	1	0	0	½	—	1	1	½	½	1	½	1	1	0	1	0	11½	
16 Süchting	0	0	½	0	0	½	½	0	0	½	1	½	½	½	0	—	1	1	0	0	½	1	½	1	1	1	11½	
17 Burn	1	0	0	1	½	½	0	1	1	0	½	½	0	0	0	0	—	0	½	½	1	1	1	1	0	0	11	
18 Salwe	½	1	0	0	0	0	1	½	0	½	0	½	0	1	½	0	1	—	1	½	½	0	½	½	1	½	11	
19 Johner	½	½	0	0	1	0	1	1	0	0	0	0	1	0	½	1	½	0	—	1	½	0	1	1	0	0	10½	
20 Kostić	0	0	½	0	½	½	½	0	0	0	½	½	½	1	0	1	½	½	0	—	½	½	1	1	0	1	10½	
21 Rabinowitsch	½	0	½	0	0	0	½	1	0	1	½	½	0	0	½	½	0	½	½	½	—	1	½	0	1	1	10½	
22 Dus Chotimirski	0	0	½	1	0	0	0	0	1	1	0	0	1	1	0	0	0	1	1	½	0	—	1	0	0	1	10	
23 Alapin	½	½	0	1	1	0	0	0	0	0	½	1	1	½	0	½	0	½	0	0	½	0	—	½	½	0	8½	
24 Chajes	0	0	0	0	0	0	½	0	1	0	0	1	1	0	1	0	0	½	0	0	1	1	½	—	0	1	8½	
25 Fahmi	0	0	0	0	0	0	0	½	1	0	½	0	1	0	0	0	1	0	1	1	0	1	½	1	—	0	8½	
26 Jaffe	0	0	0	0	0	0	0	0	0	1	0	1	0	1	1	0	1	½	1	0	0	0	1	0	1	—	8½	

If 14 ... P-B4, White's next move would be even stronger. There can be no doubt that Black's queen is rather badly placed.

| 15 B-B4 | NxN |
| 16 BxN | Q-B3 |

If Black's queen withdraws to Q2, the well-known combination 17 BxRPch! KxB 18 Q-R5ch K-N1 19 BxNP! KxB 20 R-Q3, etc., is decisive.

| 17 Q-N4 | P-B3 |

After 17 ... P-N3 18 B-K4 Black would lose a piece. Now, however, 18 B-K4 can be answered by 18 ... QxBP.

44. Dus Chotimirsky–Rotlevi

18 P-Q5!

An excellent break-through, which wins a pawn. If now 18 ... PxP, then 19 PxP Q-B4 (19 ... RxP 20 B-QB4 or 19 ... Q-Q2 20 B-B5) 20 R-QB1! followed by 21 BxQBP.

| 18 ... | Q-Q2 |
| 19 PxP | Q-B3 |

Again the only move to prevent immediate disaster. The tournament book gives the following alternative: 19 ... Q-R5 20 BxQBP R-B1 21 Q-R5! P-B4 (21 ... P-N3 22 BxKNP) 22 BxBP KRxB 23 QxR RxB 24 Q-B7ch K-R1 25 R-Q8ch! BxR 26 Q-B8 mate.

| 20 B-B3 | Q-B4 |
| 21 P-KR4 | |

Now that the Black queen cannot go to KN4, White is threatening to win it by 22 P-QN4.

| 21 ... | P-QR4 |
| 22 P-R3 | K-R1 |

If the king were left on KN1, White would have a discovered attack on the queen after 23 P-N4 Q-B3 24 B-K4 QxBP 25 BxRPch.

| 23 R-K3 | R-KN1 |

There is no adequate defence to White's king-side attack, e.g. 23 ... P-N3 24 P-N4 Q-B3 25 B-K4 QxBP 26 RxR BxR (26 ... RxR 27 Q-B3) 27 P-K7 BxP 28 Q-Q7 BxB 29 QxB winning.

| 24 BxKRP! | RxRch |
| 25 QxR | R-Q1 |

After 25 ... KxB 26 R-K5! Black would either lose his queen or be mated.

26 B-Q3	K-N1
27 Q-N4	Q-B3
28 R-N3	Resigns

14　San Sebastián 1912

More Haste Less Speed

Neither the hero of the first tournament, J. R. Capablanca, nor the world champion, Dr E. Lasker, took part in the second international tournament in the casino of the Spanish seaside resort of San Sebastián. Their absence was due in part to negotiations that were taking place on a world championship title match. If, however, Capablanca had hopes that these negotiations would quickly prove successful, he was soon to find that his rival was not only an excellent chess player but that he also excelled in the field of chess diplomacy. The match did not take place until 1921.

Apart from these two grandmasters—the strongest at that time—the rest of the world's chess élite assembled at San Sebastián. The tournament was a double-round affair, and at the half-way stage it looked as if there were not going to be any real struggle for first place, the leading scores being Spielmann 8, Marshall and Nimzowitsch 5½, Rubinstein and Tarrasch 5. In the second half the scene changed radically, for Spielmann did not even manage to score 50 per cent from his remaining games. He was still in the lead with three rounds to go, but then he lost with White to Tarrasch and scored only half a point from the last two games, losing with White to Rubinstein and drawing with Leonhardt.

The position prior to the last round was Nimzowitsch 12, Spielmann 12, but with one more game, for the Hungarian player Forgács had withdrawn after the first half, Rubinstein 11½. As Rubinstein and Nimzowitsch were to play each other, Spielmann was already out of the running for first prize.

Nimzowitsch only needed a draw to win the tournament, but his opponent, who was at the peak of his career, had White. Moreover, the latter had just had an excellent run of victories, which had netted him 6½ points from his last eight games, so he must have been full of confidence at the start of the game.

Old Indian

Rubinstein	Nimzowitsch
1 P-Q4	N-KB3

It is amusing to see what the world champion, Dr Lasker, wrote in the tournament book: "This is also possible, if you have patience and then play very well. But 1 ... P-Q4 is less of a commitment."

A few years later, Lasker was to witness the upsurge of the Indian systems arising from 1 ... N-KB3, propagated by those grandmasters, of whom Nimzowitsch was one, who called themselves neo-romanticists and who revolutionized chess theory. Their period of fame, however, did not arrive until after the first world war. In fact the name "Indian system" did not exist in 1912, when this game was played, and Nimzowitsch used a set-up (2 ... P-Q3) that had been played by Chigorin and Burn among others in the previous century.

2 P-QB4	P-Q3
3 N-KB3	QN-Q2
4 N-B3	P-K4

5	P-K4	B-K2
6	B-K2	0-0
7	0-0	R-K1
8	Q-B2	B-B1
9	P-QN3	P-B3
10	B-N2	N-R4?

Up to this move the game could easily have been played by present-day grandmasters. But the attempt to attack on the king-side is not sufficiently well prepared, and Black soon gets into an inferior position. It is apparent that, in the struggle for first place, Nimzowitsch did not succeed in keeping a cool head. He had already proved in earlier games that he understood how to handle such positions—first concentrating on patient defence and only at a later stage striving for active play. Nowadays, instead of 10 ... N-R4, Black either plays 10 ... P-QR3, preparing P-QN4, or the waiting move 10 ... P-KN3.

11	P-N3	N-N1

Black wants to exploit the slight weakness in his opponent's king-side position, but neglects his own development on the queen's wing. A better continuation is 11 ... P-KN3.

12	QR-Q1	Q-B3
13	N-N1!	

When two players do the same thing, the result is not necessarily the same. Unlike Black's knight move, this one does not shut the rook out of play. Besides, it is part of a concrete tactical plan.

13	...	B-R6
14	KR-K1	N-B5

Although this move leads to a lost position it is difficult to attach a question mark to it, for it is the logical continuation of the manoeuvre started on move 10. If Black did not continue like this, the set-up with his knight on KR4 and his queen on KB3 would be pointless.

15	PxP	PxP
16	NxP!	

A pretty combination which completely thwarts Black's plans. As a result of neglecting his development Black will now be unable to consolidate the position of his minor pieces.

16	...	RxN
17	B-KB1	

Another strong continuation is 17 BxR NxBch (17 ... QxB? 18 PxN QxBP 19 Q-B3) 18 QxN QxB 19 R-Q8, which prevents Black from completing his development, e.g. 19 ... P-KN3 20 Q-K3 Q-K2 (20 ... K-N2 21 RxB KxR 22 Q-R6ch) 21 KR-Q1, and 21 ... B-Q2 is answered by 22 R(Q1)xB!

17	...	N-Q2
18	Q-Q2?	

This is rather too subtle. After the simple continuation 18 BxB NxBch 19 K-N2, there are two Black pieces under attack. Black's only reasonable chance of attack is then 19 ... Q-K3 20 RxN! N-B5ch!, but White has no difficulty in beating it off: 21 PxN Q-N5ch 22 K-B1 R-KR4 23 R-Q3 RxP 24 R-N3 QxP 25 B-Q4. If Black deviates with 20 ... QxR (instead of N-B5) he is admittedly only a pawn down after White's reply 21 BxR, but all his attacking chances have gone.

18	...	BxB
19	RxB	

As a result of White's mistake on the previous move, Black has strong counterplay. If 19 KxB, Black can reply 19 ... N-R6 20 K-N2 B-B4!, e.g. 21 KxN Q-K3ch 22 K-N2 RxP 23 RxR QxRch 24 P-B3 Q-K2 25 QxN Q-K7ch or 21 BxR NxB 22 KxN N-B6.

19	...	N-R6ch
20	K-N2	N-N4

Threatening mate in two and enabling Black to exploit the tactical weakness of White's KP after the forced reply.

62

21 P-B4	Q-N3!
22 PxN	RxKP!

An excellent move. A speedy loss would result, on the other hand, from 22 . . . QxKPch 23 K-R3! R-K2 24 KR-K1, when Black loses a knight.

23 QxN	R-K7ch
24 R-B2	Q-K5ch
25 K-N1	

45. Rubinstein–Nimzowitsch

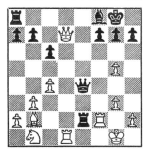

It is quite clear that Black will have to attack the weakened king's position, after which a perpetual check is on the cards. Of course, 25 . . . R-K8ch 26 RxR QxRch 27 K-N2 Q-K5ch (27 . . . QxN? 28 QxKBPch) 28 K-R3 is not good for Black, but after the correct 25 . . . RxR! 26 KxR Q-B7ch! (not 26 . . . B-B4ch? 27 B-Q4) 27 Q-Q2 B-B4ch 28 K-N2 Q-K5ch 29 K-R3 Q-B4ch, White is faced with

perpetual check. If he tries to avoid it, he has to resort to the risky 30 K-R4, when Black has good chances with 30 . . . B-K2! threatening P-KR3, e.g. 31 Q-B4 Q-B7 32 Q-Q4 QxRPch 33 K-N4 Q-K7ch 34 K-B4 P-B3! or 31 P-KN4 Q-B6! (31 . . . BxPch? 32 K-N3!), and Black has the strong threat of BxPch!

25 . . .	B-B4??
26 B-Q4??	

One of the most unbelievable examples of chess blindness in a grandmaster game. First Black opens himself to a simple mate in two that even a rabbit would see (26 QxBPch K-R8 27 QxKNP mate), and then White fails to take advantage of it. Luckily for Rubinstein his continuation also wins.

26 . . .	BxB
27 QxB	R-K8ch
28 R-KB1	RxR(B8)ch
29 KxR	Q-R8ch
30 K-B2	QxPch
31 K-B3	P-B3

Parrying the threatened mate (32 Q-Q8ch) and at the same time trying to initiate an attack on the KB file. White must now refrain from 32 PxP on account of 32 . . . R-KB1!

32 Q-Q2!	Q-R6
33 Q-Q7!	P-KB4

34 N-B3	Q-R4ch
35 K-N2	QxP
36 Q-K6ch	K-R1
37 N-K2	

Preventing 37 ... P-B5, which would

deprive the White king of the last pawn protecting it.

37 ...	Q-R4
38 R-Q7	R-K1
39 N-B4!	RxQ
40 NxQ	Resigns

15 St Petersburg 1914

Drawing Variation—The Way to Victory

Since 1911, Lasker's dominance in world chess had not remained uncontested. A great rival had entered the scene in the person of the young Cuban grandmaster, J. R. Capablanca, and it seemed only a matter of time before a world championship match between them would take place. That the chess world had to wait ten years for this meeting was mainly due to external circumstances. For four years there was a struggle on a much bigger chessboard, and altogether more than half a decade passed without a major chess event.

Virtually on the eve of the less noble world confrontation, Lasker and Capablanca met in the strong St Petersburg Grandmaster Tournament, for which invitations had only gone out to those chess masters who had already had at least one victory in an international tournament to their credit. The system of play was unusual. First, all eleven contestants played each other in a one-round tournament; then the top five went on to play a two-round final, the points obtained in the preliminary tournament also being counted.

At the end of the preliminary tournament, the situation was fairly clear: first, Capablanca with 8 points, equal second, Lasker and Tarrasch with 6½ points, equal fourth, Alekhin and Marshall with 6 points. Bernstein, Rubinstein, Nimzowitsch, Blackburne, Janowski and Gunsberg were eliminated.

In the first half of the restricted tournament the position changed only slightly. Lasker played with great élan. (His historic game against Alekhin is found in many books of instruction.) But Capablanca did not falter either. He had White against his main rivals and subjected them to considerable pressure. In fact he was within an ace of inflicting defeat on Lasker, which would have virtually decided the tournament.

Towards the end of the first four rounds Lasker managed to reduce the lead by half a point, the scores being Capablanca 11, Lasker 10, Alekhin 8½, Marshall 7, Tarrasch 6½.

There were only four rounds to go when Lasker and Capablanca sat down to play each other for the last time in the tournament. It was clear that Lasker's only chance lay in winning that game. This time he had White, but Capablanca was already well known for his excellent technique and his powers of defence.

How does one win a game that really has to be won? That is a problem of the most difficult kind. In fact, between high-class players of the same level it is an almost insoluble problem if one of the two is content with a draw. In such situations most chess players choose the obvious and logical way: they go in for sharp play. However, not everyone is a natural attacking player, and anyone who tries too much in a sphere in which he does not feel at home has little chance of success.

Lasker's strength lay in positional play, especially defence. This fact alone reduced his prospects against such a perfect master of technique as Capablanca. The world-champion, however, had one advantage. There was one sphere where he was undoubtedly superior to his opponent—the field of psychology and its application to chess. In a note to one of his games he once wrote: "This move is very good against Tarrasch; in the game against Janowski it would have been a grave error." Lasker did not consider a game of chess to be something objective, bound by scientific laws. It was, rather, a fight waged by means of a strategy which varied with the opponent and his momentary mental state.

Ruy Lopez

Lasker	Capablanca
1 P-K4	P-K4
2 N-KB3	N-QB3
3 B-N5	P-QR3
4 BxN	QPxB
5 P-Q4	PxP
6 QxP	QxQ
7 NxQ	

There can be no‑doubt that the opening moves, which had been awaited with enormous interest, proved to be a disappointment to the spectators. Even at that time the exchange variation of the Ruy Lopez was considered to be a colourless drawing system. It looked very much as if Lasker had given up the struggle to win the tournament and, by avoiding risks, was intent on making sure of second prize. Yet nothing could be further from the truth. The choice of the colourless opening system was in reality an ingenious idea: it was a psychological attack on his opponent.

46. Lasker–Capablanca

Position after White's 7th move

In order to get a better understanding of Lasker's strategy, let us have a close look at the position in diagram 46.

White has a favourable pawn structure. His king-side pawn majority will enable him, after further simplification, to advance his pawns and eventually attain an important strategic goal—the creation of a passed pawn. Black's queen-side majority, on the other hand, suffers from the fact that it includes doubled pawns on the QB file, so that a passed pawn cannot be created without tactical measures (support from pieces). I recommend the reader to make the following interesting experiment: Remove all the pieces except the king and the pawns. It is then quite easy to show that the pawn ending is won for White.

White's strategy in the diagrammed position is clear‑cut: he must exchange off as many pieces as possible and after the simplification make use of his mobile pawn majority. What should Black do? His highest card is his bishop pair, for in open positions two bishops are stronger than a bishop and a knight. In order to make use of this advantage he must be active and go on to the attack.

Capablanca, however, had not had any thoughts of attack in mind when he started the game. He had sat down at the chessboard intent on avoiding complications; he wanted to simplify and was content to draw, seeing this as a means of making sure of first place. But that is exactly what Lasker had been counting on. The intentions of his opponent were in complete contrast to the requirements of the position on the board.

7 ...   B-Q3

This quiet development move is not, of course, a mistake, but Black could have continued much more energetically. According to present-day theory both 7 ... B-Q2 8 B-K3 0-0-0 and 7 ... P-QB4 8 N-K2 B-Q2 followed by 0-0-0 are better.

8	N-QB3	N-K2
9	0-0	0-0
10	N-N3	R-K1

Here Black could also have proceeded more actively. After 10 ... P-KB4 he would have gained more space for his pieces, which is important if he wants to make the most of his two bishops.

11	P-B4	P-B3

Black could again have played 11 ... P-KB4, which, after 12 P-K5 B-QN5 13 B-Q2 BxN 14 BxB P-QN3 followed by P-B4, would have given him a satisfactory position.

12	P-B5!?

This move is at first sight a paradox, for White immobilizes his own KP. On the other hand, Black's pieces (with the bishop on QB1 and the knight on K2) are very cramped.

12	...	P-QN3

Strangely enough Capablanca fails to produce a single good idea in the whole game. The bishop fianchetto is intended to put pressure on the KP, but it merely allows White's knight to penetrate to K6. After 12 ... B-Q2 the game would still have been level. Another possibility is 12 ... P-KN4!, as recommended by Réti. Then after 13 PxP NxP 14 RxP B-K4 followed by BxN and RxP Black recovers his pawn.

13	B-B4	B-N2?

Continuing his passive and faulty strategy. With 13 ... BxB 14 RxB B-Q2 followed by QR-Q1 Black would still have had chances of equalizing.

14	BxB!	PxB
15	N-Q4	QR-Q1

By exchanging on Q6 White has undoubled his opponent's pawns. However, Black's QP is now a serious weakness, and in addition there is no way

for Black to defend the point K3. If now 15 ... B-B1, White wins the QP by 16 QR-Q1 followed by R-Q2 and KR-Q1.

16	N-K6	R-Q2
17	QR-Q1	N-B1
18	R-B2	P-QN4
19	R(B2)-Q2	R(Q2)-K2

The intermediary move 19 ... P-N5 would have offered Black better prospects of holding out, for after 20 N-K2 QR-K2 he could advance his QBP, thus activating his bishop.

20	P-QN4!	K-B2
21	P-QR3	B-R1
22	K-B2	R-R2
23	P-N4	P-R3
24	R-Q3	P-QR4?

Black's first really active move in this game is not particularly fortunate, for the opening of the QR file will be to White's advantage. However, White could also have played to open the QR file himself by means of P-QR4 and PxNP.

25	P-KR4	PxP
26	PxP	R(R2)-K2
27	K-B3	

The straightforward way is 27 R-KN1 followed by P-N5. Lasker, however, obviously wants to get his king into the most active position possible before opening the game.

27	...	R-N1
28	K-B4	P-N3
29	R-N3	P-N4ch

If White were now forced to exchange, Black's troubles would be at an end; e.g. 30 PxP RPxPch 31 K-B3 R-R1. By delaying the exchange for one move, however, White gains control of the rook file himself.

The alternative 29 ... PxP would not save Black, for White then plays KPxP followed by N-K2-Q4 and R(Q1)-KN1, preparing the break-through P-KN5, which would give him a vicious attack.

30 K-B3! N-N3!

Of course, not 30 ... PxP 31 R-R3 followed by RxRP, after which the KRP is soon lost. The text-move is an attempt to gain counter-play in return for a pawn. If now 31 RxP, then 31 ... N-B5 followed by N-K4ch.

31 PxP RPxP
32 R-R3 R-Q2

If Black had not opened the QR file he could now have played 32 ... N-B5, which is, however, faulty in the present situation because of the interesting

47. Lasker–Capablanca

Position after Black's 34th move

tactical manoeuvre 33 R-R7ch K-K1 34 R-QR1! B-N2 35 N-B7ch K-Q2 36 RxRch KxR 37 R-R7 R-QN1 38 N-R6, winning.

33 K-N3! K-K1
34 R(Q1)-KR1 B-N2
35 P-K5

The only inactive White piece is the knight on QB3, which is now brought into action by means of this typical break-through. The idea behind White's 33rd move now becomes clear.

35 ... QPxP
36 N-K4 N-Q4
37 N(K6)-B5!

For fully twenty moves this knight remained on its advanced post. Now it nets White the exchange, for the rook cannot be withdrawn because of 38 NxB RxN 39 N-Q6ch.

37 ... B-B1
38 NxR BxN
39 R-R7 R-B1
40 R-QR1 K-Q1
41 R-QR8ch B-B1
42 N-B5 Resigns

St Petersburg 1914

	1	2	3	4	5	6	7	8	9	10	11	Pts
1 Capablanca	—	½	½	1	½	1	½	1	1	1	1	8
2 Lasker	½	—	½	½	½	0	1	½	1	1	1	6½
3 Tarrasch	½	½	—	½	½	1	½	1	1	0	1	6½
4 Alekhin	0	½	½	—	1	½	1	½	½	½	1	6
5 Marshall	½	½	½	0	—	1	½	½	1	1	½	6
6 Bernstein	0	1	0	½	0	—	½	½	½	1	1	5
7 Rubinstein	½	0	½	0	½	½	—	½	½	1	1	5
8 Nimzowitsch	0	½	0	½	½	½	½	—	0	½	1	4
9 Blackburne	0	0	0	½	0	½	½	1	—	0	1	3½
10 Janowski	0	0	1	½	0	0	0	½	1	—	½	3½
11 Gunsberg	0	0	0	0	½	0	0	0	0	½	—	1

After the first part of the tournament the top five played a double round all-play-all for the prizes, the results from the preliminary being added to their scores.

	Prelim	1	2	3	4	5	Pts	Prize
1 Lasker	6½	— —	½ 1	1 1	1 ½	1 1	13½	I
2 Capablanca	8	½ 0	— —	½ 1	1 0	1 1	13	II
3 Alekhin	6	0 0	½ 0	— —	1 1	1 ½	10	III
4 Tarrasch	6½	0 ½	0 1	0 0	— —	0 ½	8½	IV
5 Marshall	6	0 0	0 0	0 ½	1 ½	— —	8	V

With this victory Lasker caught up with his rival, who was so depressed that, on the following day, he lost with the white pieces to Tarrasch. The final result was: Lasker 13½, Capablanca 13, Alekhin 10, Tarrasch 8½, Marshall 8. The decisive game is still regarded as one of the finest examples of a game conducted on psychological principles.

16 Teplitz-Schönau 1922

Dramatic Last Round

In the Teplitz Tournament played in October 1922 some notable grandmasters were missing: Capablanca, Lasker, Alekhin, Bogoljubov, Nimzowitsch and Vidmar. Nevertheless it was in its way an important tournament, for it was one of the first confrontations between the representatives of the neo-romantic school, led by Réti and Tartakower, and the grandmasters of the pre-war generation, for example Tarrasch and Teichmann, both of whom had passed their peak. Rubinstein does not fit snugly into either of these categories. To judge from his style he belonged to the new generation; on the other hand, he had already notched up a number of important victories before the war and was considered by many to have been the world's number two of the pre-war period (behind Lasker).

For almost the whole of the tournament the running was made by two players of completely different styles, the classical romantic with a fondness for aggressive chess, Spielmann, and the neo-romantic Tartakower. With one round to go they were caught by Réti, all three players having scored 8½ from twelve games. Half a point behind were Rubinstein and Grünfeld, both of whom had only theoretical chances of ending up in first place, for it was unlikely that none of the leading three would win his game.

Rubinstein once again demonstrated that such situations did not appeal to him or his nerves. He had Black against Kostić and, after a series of complications, he blundered away a piece on the 47th move in an unclear position, resigning a few moves later.

Réti had White against Grünfeld. This

48. Réti–Grünfeld

Position after Black's 41st move

key game ended in a draw following a complicated positional struggle. The critical point was reached after Black's 41st move (diagram 48). Here White can sacrifice a piece for three pawns: 42 BxP!? PxB 43 QxBPch K-N1 44 QxP. Subsequent analysis showed that Black would then have had to defend very accurately, the only way being 44 ... N-B2!, e.g. 45 BxNch KxB 46 Q-N3 (46 P-Q6 Q-B3!) 46 ... Q-R3! 47 P-K5 Q-R7ch 48 K-B3 Q-Q7, after which White is forced to take perpetual check. Or 45 Q-N3 N-N4! 46 P-B6 B-Q3! 47 QxB (47 P-K5 Q-R1!) 47 ... QxPch, again with perpetual check. In such an important game Réti could not bring himself to risk playing for the win in this way—which actually was no risk at all—and the draw was agreed after the following moves: 42 K-B3 K-N1 43 Q-B2 Q-R3 44 B-B5 Q-R8 45 BxN QxPch 46 Q-K3! QxQch 47 KxQ BxB 48 B-K8 draw.

Spielmann in his game was lucky to save half a point. He had Black in the position in diagram 49, which in spite of the unlike bishops is favourable to White in view of the weaknesses on Black's

49. Wolf–Spielmann

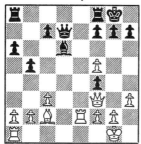

Position after White's 22nd move
Black to play

queen-side. As White has the unpleasant threat of 23 P-QR4 (after moves like 22 ... Q-Q1), the logical continuation for Black is 22 ... QR-K1, after which White can, however, play 23 B-K4 Q-K2 24 QR-K1 Q-B3 25 B-N7. Instead of choosing this line Spielmann made a blunder that, far from harming him, actually proved beneficial. He played 22 ... KR-K1, whereupon his opponent missed the correct reply, the game ending in a draw after 23 QR-K1? K-B1 24 K-B1 (24 B-K4 QR-Q1 25 B-B6 RxR) 24 ... QR-B1 25 RxRch RxR 26 RxRch QxR 27 Q-K4 QxQ 28 BxQ. What White failed to see is that after 23 B-K4! Black has to give up the exchange by 23 ... RxB in view of the decisive threat 24 B-B6, which cannot be countered by 23 ... Q-K2 because of 24 P-B6! PxP 25 BxPch, winning the queen.

Of the three leaders, Tartakower had the best chance of winning. He was opposed by Teichmann, a master of the older generation whose chess career was drawing to a close and who in this tournament had at the most prospects of gaining the last (seventh) prize. Moreover, Tartakower had White.

Bird's Opening

Tartakower	Teichmann
1 P-KB4	

This opening, which had previously been neglected, was adopted by both Tartakower and Nimzowitsch. It fitted in with the ideas of the "neo-romantics", according to whom a more effective strategy than the traditional fight for control of the centre should be aimed at. This consisted in allowing the opponent to set up a pawn centre and then seeking to control the centre squares from the wings.

1 ...	P-Q4
2 N-KB3	P-KN3

One of the most effective defences against this opening. Black makes it difficult for his opponent to fianchetto his queen's bishop, a course which in some variations is very strong, e.g. 2 ... P-QB4 3 P-K3 N-QB3 4 B-N5 B-Q2 5 P-QN3 P-K3 6 B-N2. A defence which has been popular of late is 2 ... N-KB3.

3 P-K3

Probably more promising than 3 P-KN3 followed by B-N2.

3 ...	B-N2
4 P-Q4	

Tartakower decides to adopt the Stonewall System, a line commonly chosen by Black in the Dutch Defence after 1 P-Q4 P-KB4. Another possibility is to copy Black's moves in the closed system of the Dutch, e.g. 4 B-K2 N-KB3 5 0-0 0-0 6 P-Q3. In neither of these cases, however, does the additional tempo that White has, compared with Black in the Dutch, suffice to achieve the initiative.

4 ...	N-KB3
5 B-Q3	

This looks more active than 5 B-K2, though it has its disadvantages, one of them being that Black can oppose the bishop with his own (5 ... B-B4). The pawn weakness that Black gets after the exchange of bishops (6 BxB PxB) is less important than the fact that he has got rid of his opponent's active piece and has increased his control over K5.

5 ...	0-0
6 QN-Q2	P-N3
7 Q-K2	P-B4
8 P-B3	B-N2
9 0-0	N-K5

50. Tartakower–Teichmann

A further disadvantage of White's fifth move (B-Q3) becomes apparent. Black does not need to worry about NxN, which means that his knight is secure on its advanced post.

10 BxN?

It is not clear whether this move is a blunder or a dubious combination. Whatever it is, White loses either a pawn or the exchange without any adequate positional compensation.

10 ...	PxB
11 N-N5	B-QR3
12 Q-B2	

It would be hopeless to give up the pawn by 12 P-B4 PxP 13 QNxP P-Q6 followed by 14 ... BxBP. After the text-move White at least gets a pawn for the exchange and can maintain his pawn structure in the centre.

12 ...	BxR
13 QxB	N-Q2
14 QNxP	P-KR3

A superfluous move. After 14 ... N-B3 15 NxNch BxN (or PxN) the knight would have to retreat in any case.

| 15 N-B3 | N-B3 |
| 16 NxNch | PxN!? |

This move is not actually bad: Black gives his opponent a passed pawn, but in return gets pressure along the K-file on his opponent's weak KP. However, it would have been simpler to take with the bishop and then play P-K3 and Q-B2. White would then have had no real chances on the king's wing in spite of the needless weakness caused by Black's 14 ... P-KR3.

17 B-Q2	R-K1
18 R-Q1	QR-B1
19 B-B1	Q-K2
20 P-Q5	

If White tries 20 P-B4, with the intention of getting a protected passed pawn by P-Q5, Black continues 20 ... PxP 21 PxP Q-K7! But after the text-move, Black can stop White from protecting his passed pawn, which can then be subjected to attack.

20 ...	P-B5!
21 N-Q4	Q-Q2
22 N-B6	P-QN4

The simplest way to win is to return the exchange and exploit the passive position of White's queen's bishop. True, this should not be done at once (22 ... RxN? 23 PxR QxP 24 R-Q4 P-QN4 25 Q-B3!), but should be preceded by 22 ... R-K5!, after which White soon gets into a

51. Tartakower–Teichmann

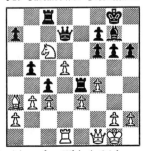

Position after White's 24th move

72

Pachman's Decisive Games

hopeless position, e.g. 23 P-QN3 RxN! 24
PxR QxP 25 PxP RxQBP 26 B-Q2 P-B4
or 25 P-QN4 P-B4 26 Q-K1 (26 B-Q2
Q-R5) 26 ... Q-R5 27 R-Q2 (27 Q-Q2
BxP! or 27 P-QR3 Q-N6) 27 ... K-R2!

23 P-QN3   R-K5
24 B-R3!

One of Tartakower's strongest
weapons throughout his career was the
ingenious tactical trap. Here he tries to
induce his opponent to go in for the
following combination: 24 ... RxKP 25
PxP RxP 26 N-K7ch K-R2 27 NxR RxB,
and the White knight is lost. It is by no
means easy to resist such a temptation
and calculate a little further, after which
the result looks very different: 28 P-Q6
QxN 29 P-Q7 Q-Q1 30 Q-K2 followed by
31 Q-K8, winning.

24 ...   P-B4
25 PxP   PxP
26 B-N4   K-R2
27 Q-K1   P-R3?

The point of White's last move was to
relieve the bishop of the duty of
defending the QBP so that it could be
moved to QB5, attacking Black's QRP.
Black therefore decides to take preventive
action. However, it is pointless to waste
time defending the unimportant QRP;
there was a much quicker way to victory
by 27 ... QR-K1 28 B-B5 RxBP 29 BxP
R(B5)-K5, threatening P-B5.

28 Q-Q2   B-B3
29 P-N3   P-KR4?

This should have robbed Black of all
winning chances. Attack on the king-side
is, it is true, the only effective plan. But
the order of moves is wrong. Correct is
first 29 ... P-KN4 followed by P-N5, and
only then P-KR4 and P-R5.

30 K-B2?

A mistake that can only be attributed
to time-trouble and nervousness. By 30
P-KR4! White could have secured the

king's wing and practically freed himself
of all his troubles.

30 ...   P-R5!
31 B-B5   K-N1?

Black still does not see the right
continuation and unnecessarily loses two
tempi, a fact which Tartakower correctly
uses to secure his position on the other
wing.

32 P-R4!   K-R2
33 P-QR5   P-N4!

This should, of course, have been
played two moves earlier.

34 B-N6   P-N5
35 N-N4   K-N3
36 NxP   PxPch

52. Tartakower–Teichmann

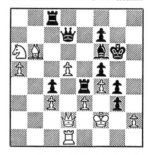

As a result of Black's indecision, the
scene has changed considerably: White
has two passed pawns, and Black's only
chance lies in a king-side attack. The
apparently logical 37 PxP is a mistake, as
the game shows. After the correct 37
KxP! Black would have been hard put to
it to save the game, getting into difficulty, for example, by 37 ... R-KR1 38
K-N2! (38 N-B5? Q-K1 39 NxR QxN,
etc.) 38 ... Q-K1 39 N-B7 Q-KB1 40
P-R6 Q-R3 41 K-N1 P-N6 42 P-R7. His
best continuation is 37 ... B-K2! 38
P-Q6 Q-N2! 39 PxB RxP(K2) 40 P-K4!
QxN (40 ... QxP 41 Q-KN2) 41 PxPch
K-R2, when he should get a draw even
though White has the better position.

37 PxP? R-KR1
38 K-N2?

After this second mistake there is no saving the game. Correct was 38 R-KN1 R-R7ch 39 R-N2 R-R8! 40 R-N1! R-R7ch, with a draw by repetition.

38 . . . R-R6
39 R-KR1

It is too late to try and exchange off the Black rook, but there is no other adequate defence, for Black is threatening Q-K1 followed by Q-KR1, and if 39 N-B5, 39 . . . Q-K1 is also decisive.

39 . . . BxP

A pretty move; after 40 QxB QxP 41 N-N4 Q-R1 White has no defence to the withdrawal of Black's rook. There was, however, a quicker, and no less elegant win by 39 . . . R-Q5!

40 N-B5! BxQ
41 NxQ RxR
42 KxR P-B6
43 N-B5 P-B7
44 N-N3 R-N5
45 P-Q6 RxN
46 P-Q7 P-B8=Qch
47 Resigns

Teplitz-Schönau 1922

	1	2	3	4	5	6	7	8	9	10	11	12	13	14	Pts	Prize
1 Réti	–	1	½	1	1	1	1	½	1	0	0	1	1	0	9	I, II
2 Spielmann	0	–	1	½	½	1	½	1	1	½	1	½	½	1	9	I, II
3 Grünfeld	½	0	–	½	½	1	½	1	½	½	1	1	½	1	8½	III, IV
4 Tartakower	0	½	½	–	1	1	0	1	0	1	1	1	1	½	8½	III, IV
5 Rubinstein	0	½	½	0	–	0	1	1	½	1	1	½	1	1	8	V
6 Kostić	0	0	0	0	1	–	1	½	1	1	½	½	½	½	6½	VI
7 Teichmann	0	½	½	1	0	0	–	½	½	½	½	1	½	½	6	VII
8 Maróczy	½	0	0	0	0	½	½	–	1	½	1	0	½	1	5½	
9 Treybal	0	0	½	1	½	0	½	0	–	1	1	0	1	0	5½	
10 Wolf	1	½	½	0	0	0	½	½	0	–	½	½	½	1	5½	
11 Mieses	1	0	0	0	0	½	½	0	0	½	–	1	½	1	5	
12 Sämisch	0	½	0	0	½	½	0	1	1	½	0	–	0	1	5	
13 Tarrasch	0	½	½	0	0	½	½	½	0	½	½	1	–	½	5	
14 Johner	1	0	0	½	0	½	½	0	1	0	0	0	½	–	4	

17 New York 1924

Victory in Danger

Capablanca had been world champion for three years, but in the chess world his dominance was not beyond all doubt. His match with Lasker in 1921 had not had the appearance of a real fight. On that occasion it had seemed as if Lasker had handed over his title rather than losing it in a match between equals. Nor had the 1914 St Petersburg Grandmaster Tournament been forgotten, in which the ex-world champion with a unique show of will-power had defeated and overtaken his great opponent. The question Capablanca or Lasker had not been unequivocally decided.

On 15 March 1924 in New York, eleven of the very top grandmasters and masters met in a tournament that turned out to be a further round in the duel between the two giants of the early twentieth century. Only Nimzowitsch and Rubinstein were missing, and this, in view of the other participants, was not sufficient to detract from the enormous importance of the tournament.

The final table gives no indication of the dramatic struggle for first place, and yet the tournament was marked by a duel which was much closer than the result suggests. In the penultimate round Lasker's victory was in great danger.

In the first half of the tournament the ex-world champion produced a magnificent performance. He scored 7½ points from ten games and was the only competitor to go through undefeated. Capablanca suffered a defeat at the hands of Réti in the fourth round, the game later appearing in many books of tuition as an example of the strategical concept of the neo-romantics. He remained one point behind Lasker and only half a point ahead of Réti.

It soon became apparent, however, that the world champion intended to fight hard. He proceeded to win three games in a row, the last in a dramatic encounter with Lasker. Typically, the latter refused to be intimidated and by the beginning of the nineteenth round had again achieved a lead of one point. In that round, however, he was in danger, for both his game and Capablanca's could have easily ended differently.

53. Yates–Capablanca

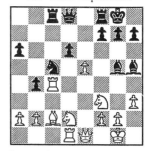

In the opening Capablanca had secured the two bishops, which gave him a distinct advantage. Now he exploits the exposed position of Black's rook by means of a pawn sacrifice.

| 21 ... | P-Q4! |
| 22 RxP | Q-K2? |

An inaccuracy. The correct way to exploit the exposed rook is 22 ... B-K2!, threatening N-Q6 or N-K3. Black then attains a decisive advantage, as the following variations, given by Alekhin, show:
(i) 23 P-N4 N-K3 24 R-N7 RxB 25 PxB B-B4 26 N-K4 PxN! 27 RxQ RxR 28

QxP RxBP or 26 R-B1 RxR 27 QxR
Q-B1! threatening QxR and BxPch.

(ii) 23 N-B4 BxN 24 PxB N-Q6! 25
BxN BxR 26 QxB Q-N4ch 27 K-R1 PxN
and wins.

23 NxB!

This shows up the difference between
22 . . . Q-K2 and B-K2. By means of a
simple tactical thrust, White forces a
draw. In the tournament book Alekhin
maintained that Black could have
retained winning chances by playing 23
. . . QxN. He then analysed the possibilities arising from 24 P-KN4 B-N3 25
BxB BPxB! He overlooked, however,
that White does not need to weaken his
king-side but can cope with all tactical
threats by 24 R-B1. If then 24 . . . B-N3,
White first plays 25 R-N4 and then BxB.

23 . . .	BxR
24 BxPch	K-R1
25 R-KR4!	

But not 25 P-B4 P-N3 26 Q-R4 B-R4
27 P-KN4 N-K3! 28 PxB NxN 29 PxN
QxKP 30 PxP Q-K6ch, and Black wins.

25 . . .	QxN
26 P-B4	Q-K2
27 B-B2dis ch	K-N1
28 B-R7ch	K-R1
29 B-B2dis ch	
	Drawn

Capablanca thus unnecessarily
dropped half a point. Lasker, on the
other hand, was blessed by good fortune
in his game and gained the full point.

French Defence

Lasker	Maróczy
1 P-K4	P-K3
2 P-Q4	P-Q4
3 N-QB3	B-N5

At the time the game was played this
system, which was adopted consistently

by Nimzowitsch, was still in its infancy.
Lasker never bothered much about the
latest discoveries of chess fashion, a fact
which led to several unpleasant defeats.

| 4 P-K5 | P-QB4 |
| 5 P-QR3 | |

Partly as a result of this game, 5 B-Q2
was, for some time, considered stronger
and more solid.

5 . . .	PxP
6 PxB	PxN
7 PxP?	

It was later discovered that Black
should reply to 5 P-QR3 by 5 . . . BxN
and not, as in this game, by 5 . . . PxP.
The reason is that White could now either
go in for the very promising pawn sacrifice 7 N-B3 Q-B2 8 Q-Q4! N-K2 9 B-Q3
N-Q2 10 0-0 PxP 11 BxP, which gives him
excellent attacking chances, or continue 7
Q-N4 K-B1 8 N-B3, which may even be
better. The move played by Lasker, 7
PxP, is a serious waste of time, for White
has no good way of holding the pawn on
QB3.

| 7 . . . | Q-B2 |
| 8 N-B3 | N-K2! |

White's weak pawn on QB3 cannot run
away; Black therefore first goes after the
more important KP.

| 9 B-Q3 | N-N3 |
| 10 0-0! | N-Q2 |

Black wisely refrains from capturing
the KP, for the continuation 10 . . . NxP
11 B-KB4 NxNch (11 . . . P-B3 12 NxN
PxN 13 Q-R5ch) 12 QxN P-K4 (12 . . .
Q-K2 13 Q-N3 N-B3 14 QxP) 13 KR-K1
P-B3 14 QxP would be favourable to
White.

11 R-K1

White can only avoid the loss of a
pawn by giving up his active bishop, but
then, after 11 BxN RPxB 12 Q-Q4 N-N3
followed by B-Q2, Black has the advan-

tage thanks to his control of the weak points QN4 and QB5. After the text-move, taking the KP is not good (11 . . . QNxKP 12 NxN NxN 13 B-KB4), so Black must content himself with lesser things.

11 . . .	QxBP
12 B-Q2	Q-B2
13 Q-K2	0-0
14 Q-K3	N-N3
15 Q-N5	N-QB5
16 B-B3	

On 16 B-QB1 Lasker was obviously afraid of 16 . . . P-B3! 17 PxP PxP (better than 17 . . . RxP 18 Q-R5) 18 Q-R5 Q-B2 or 18 Q-R6 Q-N2, though it is quite possible that this line would have given him more attacking chances than the one he chose in the game.

16 . . .	P-KR3!

Black can only play this move because the White bishop has left the diagonal QB1-KR6. The reply 17 Q-R5 is not possible because of 17 . . . N-B5.

17 Q-N4	N-K2
18 Q-R5	B-Q2
19 P-N4	

54. Lasker–Maróczy

Black's position now looks precarious in view of the threat 20 P-KN5. But here an old maxim proves true: the best defence to some threats is simply to ignore them.

19 . . .	B-N4!

Maróczy quietly improves the position of his pieces and prepares to return the pawn, after which he succeeds in gaining the initiative. That is a well-known counter to opening gambits, and Maróczy was one of the first masters to perfect the idea.

The tactical considerations behind the move can be seen from the following variation: 20 N-Q4 B-K1 21 P-N5 NxP! (21 . . . P-B3 22 Q-R3) 22 PxP P-B4 23 Q-N5 N(K2)-N3, and Black escapes by a hair's breadth.

20 P-N5	P-KN3!
21 QxRP	N-N3!

An excellent defensive manoeuvre. After the exchange of bishops White's attack is virtually at an end, whereupon he is left with incurable pawn weaknesses.

22 R-R3	BxB
23 PxB	N-B4
24 Q-R3	Q-K2?

Here Black begins to play irresolutely and gradually throws away his advantage. The open QB file is an important operation base, and its control would soon lead to a decisive advantage. Alekhin gives the following continuation: 24 . . . N-QR5 25 R-QB1 P-N4 26 B-Q2 Q-N3 27 R-R2 KR-B1 28 R(R2)-B2 Q-N2, etc.

Just as good is the continuation 24 . . . KR-B1, e.g. 25 R-QB1 Q-Q2 followed by N-QR5. In both cases Black can soon bring about an exchange of rooks and reach an endgame which, in view of his superiority on the queen's wing, is clearly advantageous to him.

25 Q-N4	K-N2

There was still time for 25 . . . KR-B1.

26 KR-R1	KR-B1
27 P-R4	N-R5!
28 B-Q2	P-N4
29 R(R3)-R2	R-R1
30 K-N2	

White, who is not quite out of the

wood yet, could not solve all his problems by exchanging knights: 30 N-Q4 NxN 31 QxN QR-QB1. On the other hand, after the text-move, the king is ill-placed on KN2, a fact which Black should exploit by means of the manoeuvre Q-Q2, P-Q5, Q-Q4.

| 30 ... | QR-QB1 |
| 31 R-R1 | Q-B2? |

An unnecessary loss of tempo. The immediate 31 ... Q-Q2 was called for. Now White succeeds in levelling the game.

| 32 N-Q4! | Q-Q2 |

When making his previous move Maróczy had obviously overlooked the fact that White's KP cannot be taken, for after 32 ... QxKP 33 N-B3 Q-Q3 34 B-B4 followed by 35 B-K5ch White wins the exchange.

| 33 NxNch | KPxN |
| 34 Q-Q4 | Q-K3 |

55. Lasker–Maróczy

35 QxRP?

Lasker considers the situation ripe for an attempt to seize the initiative and in doing so makes one of those mistakes that have so often led to victory. Disturbing the equilibrium of the position often upsets the opponent to an extent that is more significant than the positional or material disadvantage incurred.

| 35 ... | P-Q5! |

Of course, not 35 ... QxP?? 36 B-K3, etc.

| 36 R(R2)-R1 | QxP? |

The first of a series of mistakes that loses the game and assures his opponent of first place in the tournament. There was still a win to be had by 36 ... R-B7, e.g. 37 B-B4 Q-Q4ch 38 K-N3 N-B6, with the irresistible threat of 39 ... N-K7ch. Or 37 QR-Q1 Q-Q4ch 38 P-B3 QxKP 39 K-B1 N-B6 40 R-K1 Q-Q4, winning.

| 37 QR-K1 | Q-Q4ch |
| 38 K-N3 | |

The disappearance of the KP has proved advantageous to White, for now there is the threat of 39 B-B4 followed by B-K5ch.

38 ...	KR-K1
39 P-R5!	PxP
40 RxR	RxR
41 RxP	N-B6?

White would have had a much tougher task after 41 ... P-KB5ch!, in reply to which both 42 BxP R-K8 and 42 KxP R-K7 would lose. White's best reply is 42 K-R4!, after which Black has no time for a quiet queen move (Q-B6 or Q-N7) on account of the danger to his pawn on Q5. By checking, however, he could get a draw, though nothing more: 42 ... Q-R8ch 43 K-N4 Q-N7ch 44 K-B5 Q-Q4ch 45 K-N4 R-K7 46 Q-N8.

| 42 Q-N6 | N-K7ch |
| 43 K-R2 | Q-K3?? |

This incomprehensible move leads to a loss. Instead 43 ... R-K3! 44 Q-N8 Q-Q3ch 45 QxQ RxQ 46 K-N2 R-QR3 47 R-R4 R-R7 would have resulted in a drawn ending.

| 44 QxNP! | Q-Q3ch |
| 45 K-N2 | N-B5ch |

It is difficult to understand what Black had in mind when making his 43rd move. At any rate he gets no compensation for the pawn, since both kings are equally

exposed. The text-move leads to a queen
ending in which Black loses another
pawn.

46	BxN	QxB

47	QxR	Q-N5ch
48	K-B1	QxR
49	Q-K5ch	K-N1
50	QxBP	Resigns

New York 1924

		1	2	3	4	5	6	7	8	9	10	11	Pts	Prize
1	Lasker	– –	½ 0	1 ½	½ 1	1 1	1 1	1 1	½ 1	½ 1	½ 1	1 1	16	I
2	Capablanca	½ 1	– –	½ ½	½ ½	0 1	½ 1	1 1	1 1	1 ½	½ 1	½ 1	14½	II
3	Alekhin	0 ½	½ ½	– –	½ ½	1 0	1 ½	½ ½	½ ½	1 1	½ ½	1 1	12	III
4	Marshall	½ 0	½ ½	½ ½	– –	½ 1	0 ½	0 1	½ 0	½ 1	1 ½	1 1	11	IV
5	Réti	0 0	1 0	0 1	0 ½	– –	½ ½	0 1	1 1	1 0	1 0	1 1	10½	V
6	Maróczy	0 0	½ 0	0 ½	1 ½	½ ½	– –	0 1	½ ½	1 1	½ 1	1 0	10	
7	Bogoljubov	0 0	0 0	½ ½	1 0	1 0	1 0	– –	0 1	1 1	½ 1	0 1	9½	
8	Tartakower	½ 0	0 0	½ ½	½ 1	0 0	½ ½	1 0	– –	1 0	½ 0	½ 1	8	
9	Yates	½ 0	0 ½	0 0	½ 0	0 1	0 0	0 0	0 1	– –	1 1	½ 1	7	
10	Ed. Lasker	½ 0	½ 0	½ ½	0 ½	0 1	½ 0	½ 0	½ 1	0 0	– –	0 ½	6½	
11	Janowski	0 0	½ 0	0 0	0 0	0 0	0 1	1 0	½ 0	½ 0	1 ½	– –	5	

18 International Tournament, Semmering 1926

Sensational Victory by an Outsider

It was the intention of the organizers of the tournament at the Austrian mountain hotel of Panhans on the Semmering to bring together the élite of the chess world. Only after the withdrawal of Capablanca and Lasker and the refusal of the Soviet chess organization to allow Bogolyubov to participate was a player brought in who had originally been left out because of his poor results prior to the tournament. That player proved to be the eventual winner. Although not an unique case—there had been doubts as to Capablanca's skill prior to the San Sebastián tournament—it was nevertheless unusual.

The tournament was played from 6 to 30 March 1926, and the closing phase was exceptionally dramatic. After the eleventh round Tartakower was in the lead with 9 points, ahead of Nimzowitsch (8½), Spielmann and Alekhin (both 8). The first four had opened up such a gap from the rest of the field (Rubinstein, Tarrasch and Vidmar 6½ each) that it was almost certain that one of them would emerge victorious.

The first victim of the hard and at

56. Vidmar–Nimzowitsch

Position after White's 33rd move

times nervous fight for top place was Tartakower. In the twelfth round he lost to Réti in an endgame with bishops of opposite colours which could have been drawn in several ways. The same round also proved tragic for Nimzowitsch.

As a result of an earlier positional advantage Black is a pawn up. He now breaks open White's king-side position, which induces the latter to go in for a desperate counter-action.

33 ...	P-R5!
34 P-Q5!?	PxNP
35 N-Q4	QxBP
36 R-KB1	Q-Q3??

This converts a won position into a lost one. After the correct 36 ... Q-K4! the game would have been virtually decided (e.g. 37 N(Q2)-B3 Q-Q3! 38 PxP PxP 39 N-KN5 R-K1) and Nimzowitsch would have had good prospects of winning first prize.

| 37 N-K4 | Q-B2 |

Here 37 ... NxN is not possible because of 38 N-B5dbl ch followed by mate. And 37 ... Q-K4 38 NxN NxN 39 NxPch loses Black his queen.

| 38 NxN | NxN |
| 39 N-N5 | |

There was a quicker win to be had by 39 NxPch PxN 40 QxNch K-N1 41 QxNPch Q-KN2 42 QxKPch K-R1 43 R-B6 or 40 ... K-R2 41 R-B4, etc. The text-move, however, wins a piece without complications.

| 39 ... | Q-K2 |
| 40 P-Q6 | Q-B1 |

41	QxNch	K-N1
42	R-B4!	R-Q2
43	R-R4	Q-N2
44	QxQch	KxQ
45	R-Q4	P-R3
46	N-B7	K-B3
47	R-Q1	K-K4
48	N-K8	P-R4
49	KxP	P-R5
50	K-N4	P-R6
51	R-QR1!	K-Q5
52	N-B6!	RxP
53	R-Q1ch	KxP

If 53 . . . K-K4, then 54 N-Q7ch, and if 53 . . . K-B4, then 54 N-K4ch.

54	RxR	P-R7
55	R-B6ch!	K-N4
56	R-B1	K-R5
57	N-Q7	P-QN4
58	N-B5ch	K-R6
59	N-Q3	K-N6
60	N-B5ch	K-R6
61	N-Q3	K-N6
62	K-B3	Resigns

The other two leaders, Alekhin and Spielmann, both won (against Tarrasch and Kmoch respectively) in spite of having Black. But in the next round Alekhin dropped out of the race. He lost to Nimzowitsch's conqueror, not, however, as the result of a blunder but through trying too hard for a win.

57. Alekhin–Vidmar

It looks as if White's risky play in this important game is paying off, for he is threatening both 41 QxN and 41 Q-R8ch. Black, however, has a pretty counter.

40 . . .	B-N2!
41 QxB?	

This is being a little too ambitious. Although a piece down Alekhin continues to play for a win, trusting that Black's badly placed knights will be unable to stop the White passed pawns. The correct continuation is 41 QxN! BxP 42 Q-QB5! (not 42 Q-KB5? B-K5 43 Q-B8ch K-R2 and White loses his bishop on N2) 42 . . . Q-K8ch 43 K-B4 B-K7ch 44 K-Q5 B-B6ch 45 K-B4 Q-K7ch 46 K-B3 draw.

41 . . .	Q-K8ch
42 K-B4	QxR
43 B-B3	Q-KB4
44 Q-N8ch	K-R2
45 P-R5	QxBP
46 Q-B7	NxP
47 K-N4	N-B5!
48 K-R3	N-K3
49 Q-K5	N-K5
50 B-N4	Q-Q6
51 K-R4	N-Q5!

Both knights have performed excellently, which enables Black to win the game.

52 Q-Q5	P-B4
53 Q-B4	Q-Q8
54 B-R3	Q-QR8
55 P-R6	N-QB6ch
56 K-N4	N-B7ch
57 K-B5	QxBch
58 K-N6	N-K6!
59 Resigns	

In the same round Spielmann drew with Réti and Nimzowitsch with Kmoch. By virtue of his victory over Vajda, Tartakower took the lead with 10 points followed by Spielmann with 9½. The next round brought these two together. Whereas many of his grandmaster contemporaries would have been content with a lead of half a point and laid out the key game of the tournament solidly,

Tartakower decided to use the advantage of the White pieces to put matters beyond all doubt.

Queen's Gambit

	Tartakower	Spielmann
1	N-KB3	P-Q4
2	P-Q4	N-KB3
3	P-B4	P-K3
4	B-N5	QN-Q2
5	P-K3	P-B3
6	QN-Q2	

Even at that time many masters considered the orthodox Queen's Gambit to be too hackneyed, which explains the search for new paths. The development of the knight to Q2 instead of QB3, however, allows Black to reach equality at an early stage by means of the advance P-QB4.

6	. . .	P-KR3
7	B-R4	B-K2
8	B-Q3	0-0
9	0-0	P-B4!
10	R-B1	P-QN3
11	PxQP	KPxP
12	N-K5(?)	

This sharp continuation is out of key with White's previous development (QN-Q2). The less ambitious 12 Q-K2 followed by KR-Q1 would have been better.

12	. . .	NxN
13	PxN	N-N5
14	B-N3	P-B3
15	PxP	BxP
16	P-KR3(?)	

An unnecessary loss of time, for the White bishop on Q3 will in any case have to be withdrawn to K2 on the next move. By playing 16 B-K2 White would have saved a whole tempo. It is possible that Tartakower was afraid of 16 B-K2 P-KR4, though he would then have had a good reply in 17 P-KR3 P-R5 18 B-KB4.

16	. . .	N-K4
17	B-K2	B-B4
18	N-B3	NxNch
19	BxN	BxNP!
20	BxPch	K-R1

58. Tartakower–Spielmann

The first critical moment. White could now have played 21 BxR, e.g. 21 . . . QxB 22 Q-N3 (22 R-B4? R-Q1 23 Q-N3 B-Q6!) 22 . . . BxR 23 RxB or 21 . . . BxR 22 QxB QxB 23 Q-B3, when, in view of the unlike bishops, a draw would have been the likeliest outcome. The attempt to seize the initiative ends badly, for White fails to win the exchange and gives his opponent a positional advantage.

21	R-B4?	R-B1
22	P-K4	B-R2
23	Q-K2	

White now has two threats, 24 QxB and 24 B-N7, both of which Black counters by means of an interesting manoeuvre.

23	. . .	Q-B3!
24	P-K5	Q-Q1!

Now 25 B-N7 is answered by 25 . . . B-Q6, when it is Black who wins the exchange. And 25 QxB QxB followed by B-Q6 does not allow White to equalize either.

25	R-Q1	B-Q5
26	B-B3	

At this stage White should have opted for an exchange sacrifice, viz. 26 QRxB

PxR 27 RxP, which would have given him more counter-play than he got in the game.

| 26 ... | Q-K2 |
| 27 B-N4 | QR-K1 |

Of course, not 27 ... B-B4? 28 BxB RxB 29 R(Q1)xB! etc.

| 28 B-R5 | R-Q1 |
| 29 K-R2? | |

A bad mistake, which leads to an immediate loss of material. White intends to play P-B4, which is the correct plan, but he goes wrong in preparing the way. The king should have been played to KR1 and not KR2. The difference will become apparent on the next move.

| 29 ... | BxBP! |

If White's king were on KR1, this move would be wrong because of the reply 30 RxR. As it is, the exchange of rooks is not possible because of 30 ... BxBch.

| 30 BxB | RxR |
| 31 B-R4 | |

The best chance. If instead 31 QxR RxB or 31 BxP PxB 32 QxR QxPch, Black, although only a pawn to the good, has an easy win.

31 ...	Q-K3
32 QxR	QxR
33 Q-Q6!	

59. Tartakower–Spielmann

| 33 ... | R-B8? |

Spielmann had obviously worked out the queen sacrifice that this move involves. Such a course, however, unnecessarily makes the win more complicated. Although neither 33 ... Q-B5ch 34 B-N3 Q-B4 35 P-K6 nor 33 ... R-R1 34 B-B3 R-K1 35 B-QB6 is good for Black, the deceptively passive retreat of the rook to KN1 wins easily, e.g. 33 ... R-KN1! 34 B-N3 B-K5! threatening Q-B7.

34 P-K6!	QxB
35 P-K7	QxB
36 Q-Q8ch	B-N1
37 P-K8=Q	QxQ
38 QxQ	P-B5

Black has the better endgame, though, in view of the mobility of his opponent's queen, his advantage should not lead to a win. White, however, must not play passively, e.g. 39 Q-K3? (the move recommended in the tournament book) 39 ... R-QN8! (threatening R-N7) 40 Q-Q4 P-QN4! 41 P-N4 P-N5 42 P-KR4 P-B6 43 P-N5 PxP 44 PxP P-B7 45 Q-R4ch B-R2 46 P-N6 R-KR8ch! winning.

| 39 P-N4! | P-B6 |
| 40 Q-QB8 | R-B6 |

Better than 40 ... R-QB8 41 P-N5!, when Black cannot prevent perpetual check after either 41 ... P-B7 42 PxP or 41 ... PxP 42 Q-K8.

| 41 P-N5 | |

Even better is 41 P-KR4!, which forces a draw if Black replies 41 ... P-QN4 (42 P-N5). Black's best chance is instead 41 ... R-B5 42 QxBP RxP 43 Q-QR3! RxPch 44 K-N3 or 43 ... P-QR4 44 Q-K7, though even here a draw is likely.

| 41 ... | PxP |
| 42 K-N2? | |

After this mistake the game is lost. A much stronger line is 42 Q-K8! R-B3 43

Q-QB8!, when Black has nothing better
than 42 ... R-B7ch 43 K-N3 RxP 44
QxP. Then, in view of the threats Q-K5
and Q-B3, a draw seems likely.

42 ...	R-Q6
43 Q-K8	R-Q3
44 Q-QB8	R-Q7ch

The difference between the line
chosen and the missed opportunity 42
Q-K8! is now clear. In the latter case the
king could have evaded the check by
moving to KN3, attacking the rook at the
same time and thus preventing the pawn
reaching the seventh rank.

45 K-B3	P-B7
46 K-K3	

If 46 Q-K8, Black wins by means of
the study-like 46 ... R- Q1!!

46 ...	R-R7
47 P-KR4	R-R6ch
48 K-K4	

A little better is 48 K-Q4 RxPch 49
K-K5 R-QB5 50 Q-K8 R-K5ch! 51 KxR
P-B8=Q 52 Q-R5ch B-R2ch, though Black
still wins. After the text-move, however,
there is a quicker win by 48 ... R-R8! 49
QxP B-R2ch.

48 ...	RxPch
49 K-B5?	

Or 49 K-K5 R-QB5 50 Q-K8 R-K5ch!,
etc.

49 ...	R-R8!
50 Resigns	

Tartakower completed his unfortunate
hat-trick in the sixteenth round, losing
to Alekhin. Spielmann, on the other
hand, finished the tournament in top
form. In the last round he defeated his
other rival, Nimzowitsch, though
admittedly not without a bit of luck.

60. Spielmann–Nimzowitsch

Position after White's 17th move

Black has a very promising game. If he
wants he can transpose into an ending in
which he has a slight advantage, e.g. 17
... QxPch 18 KxQ N-N5ch 19 K-N1 NxQ
20 PxB NxB 21 R-K1 B-B4. Or he can try
for even more by 17 ... N-N5 18 Q-N3
QR-B1 19 B-QB4 (19 P-B3 B-K3 20
B-QB4 BxB 21 NxB RxN) 19 ... B-KB4,
etc. Instead he chooses a weak continuation.

17 ...	QR-B1?
18 B-Q3!	B-KB4
19 BxB	RxB
20 Q-B4!	P-N4
21 Q-KN4	Q-B2
22 KR-N1!	

As White cannot in any case hold the
pawn in view of the threats N-N5 and
N-K4, the best plan is to aim for a quick
mobilization of his pieces.

22 ...	N-N5
23 P-B3	NxPch
24 K-N1	P-N5

The piece sacrifice on QB6 is incorrect: 24 ... NxPch 25 PxN RxQBP 26
B-Q4, etc.

25 B-Q4	B-N4?

This move loses. Instead 25 ... B-B1!
26 P-QB4 P-N6! 27 NxP N-N5 leaves the
game quite open.

26 P-QB4	P-N6
27 N-K4!	

Semmering 1926

	1	2	3	4	5	6	7	8	9	10	11	12	13	14	15	16	17	18	Pts	Prize
1 Spielmann	—	½	1	1	1	0	½	½	1	1	1	1	1	½	1	½	½	1	13	I
2 Alekhin	½	—	0	0	1	1	1	1	1	½	1	½	1	0	1	1	1	1	12½	II
3 Vidmar	0	1	—	1	1	½	0	1	½	1	1	½	1	1	½	1	½	½	12	III
4 Nimzowitsch	0	1	0	—	½	1	½	1	0	1	½	1	1	1	½	½	1	1	11½	IV, V
5 Tartakower	0	0	0	½	—	½	1	0	1	1	1	1	½	1	1	1	1	1	11½	IV, V
6 Rubinstein	1	0	½	0	½	—	½	1	1	0	½	0	1	½	1	½	1	1	10	VI, VII
7 Tarrasch	½	0	1	½	0	½	—	1	0	0	0	1	½	1	1	1	1	1	10	VI, VII
8 Réti	½	0	0	0	1	0	0	—	1	1	1	0	½	1	1	½	1	1	9½	VIII
9 Grünfeld	0	0	½	1	0	0	1	0	—	0	½	½	1	1	1	1	½	1	9	IX
10 Janowski	0	½	0	0	0	1	1	0	1	—	½	0	½	0	1	1	1	1	8½	
11 Treybal	0	0	0	½	0	½	1	0	½	½	—	1	1	1	0	1	½	½	8	
12 Vajda	0	½	½	0	0	1	0	1	½	1	0	—	0	½	½	½	½	1	7½	
13 Yates	0	0	0	0	½	0	½	½	0	½	0	1	—	½	½	1	1	1	7	
14 Gilg	½	1	0	0	0	½	0	0	0	1	0	½	½	—	½	0	½	1	6	
15 Kmoch	0	0	½	½	0	0	0	0	0	0	1	½	½	½	—	1	½	1	6	
16 Davidson	½	0	0	½	0	½	0	½	0	0	0	½	0	1	0	—	1	1	5½	
17 Michel	½	0	½	0	0	0	0	0	½	0	½	½	0	½	½	0	—	1	4½	
18 Rosselli	0	0	½	0	0	0	0	0	0	0	½	0	0	0	0	0	0	—	1	

The end. White has the two threats, NxB and N-Q6.

27 ...	Q-N3
28 QxB!	RxQ
29 RxR	Q-B2
30 N-Q6	QxKBP
31 BxNPch	K-N1

32 B-K5dis ch	K-B1
33 R-B5ch	QxR
34 NxQ	RxP
35 R-Q8ch	Resigns

With this victory the outsider, Spielmann, overcame the last obstacle on his path to victory.

World Championship 1927

Why Did Alekhin Win?

The encounter between Capablanca and Alekhin in Buenos Aires in 1927 is still considered by many to have been the greatest of all world championship matches.

The Cuban grandmaster was at the peak of his career. Since 1921, when he had won the title from Lasker without any great resistance on the latter's part, he had raced from success to success. For years he had not made a single serious mistake, and his opponents were faced with the seemingly impossible task of beating a "chess machine", as he was often called.

In February and March 1927 there had been a match tournament contested by the strongest grandmasters of the time, the four-round system guaranteeing an objective assessment of the individual performances. The result had been plain for all to see: Capablanca 14, Alekhin 11½, Nimzowitsch 10½, Dr Vidmar 10, Spielmann 8, Marshall 6. Not only had Capablanca succeeded in gaining first place; he had also defeated each of the other contestants in their individual matches.

Six months later, on 16 September, the match between the top two in that tournament began. The victor was to be the first player to win six games, irrespective of the number of draws. This system seemed to be very much in favour of Capablanca, for no one could imagine that a player who had hardly lost a game for years could lose six in a single match.

Even today there is no agreement on why Capablanca was defeated. Most chess historians are of the opinion that in 1927 Capablanca possessed the greater chess ability. They explain his defeat by saying that he did not prepare himself sufficiently for the match, that his opening repertoire was not sophisticated enough or that he simply underestimated his opponent. My opinion is that the explanation for the unexpected result has to be sought in the realm of psychology. In the years preceding the match Capablanca had become so unaccustomed to losing that he was badly affected not only by the loss of a game but also by any set-back at all, such as the failure to exploit a decisive advantage, for example.

The first game of the match was won by Alekhin. This did not upset Capablanca as much as what later followed, for it was a chance result caused by a blunder on the sixteenth move, and the reigning world champion succeeded in squaring the match in the third game. In the sixth he successfully parried Alekhin's violent attack, and thereafter there followed a series of draws. The first really critical stage was reached in the eleventh game. Capablanca came out of the opening with a clear superiority in space, but as a result of three mistakes he conceded his opponent an unmistakable advantage. Although Alekhin then played a little inaccurately, giving his opponent drawing chances on several occasions, the latter failed to hold the game. This second defeat with White affected Capablanca considerably. In the next game he had a wonderful opportunity to square matters again, but he missed his way and got no more than a draw. After a long series of draws, most of them colourless, Capablanca lost his third game, again with White. Of course, that did not by any means signify the end of the match. In the 31st game, with the score 4:3 in Alekhin's favour, Capablanca was a pawn up in the endgame, and the win was so easy that even a player of much inferior playing strength should have had no difficulty in winning. But two moves before the time-check, he threw the win away and with it the chance of squaring the match. Undoubtedly that was a great disappointment for the Cuban, and he was clearly suffering from depression when, after a break of three days, the match was resumed. The game that follows was without doubt the one that virtually decided matters.

Queen's Gambit

Alekhin	Capablanca
1 P-Q4	P-Q4
2 P-QB4	P-K3
3 N-QB3	N-KB3
4 B-N5	QN-Q2
5 P-K3	P-B3

The first surprise and at the same time an indication of Capablanca's bad mental state. Up to this moment he had stuck to the Orthodox Defence (5 . . . B-K2), and not without success. The Cambridge Springs Variation, which is introduced by 5 . . . P-B3, had been tried a few times by Alekhin, though in the eleventh game he had not come out of the opening too well. Capablanca had made some scathing remarks about this defence, and yet here he was adopting it himself in the decisive phase of the match.

6 PxP

In the eleventh game the main variation had been played: 6 N-B3 Q-R4 7 N-Q2 B-N5 8 Q-B2 PxP 9 BxN NxB 10 NxP Q-B2 11 P-QR3 B-K2. Today the continuation 7 PxP NxP 8 Q-Q2 is considered stronger.

| 6 . . . | KPxP |

| 7 B-Q3 | B-K2 |
| 8 KN-K2 | |

Developing the knight on K2 has become popular here—mainly as a result of Alekhin's success in this game.

| 8 . . . | 0-0 |
| 9 N-N3 | |

Today 9 Q-B2 or 9 0 0 is usually played. The text-move is the prelude to a king-side attack, which does not really correspond to the character of the position. White has the choice between two logical plans: the preparation of the minority attack (P-QN4-N5) and an action in the centre (P-B3 and P-K4).

| 9 . . . | N-K1 |

Black could also play 9 . . . R-K1 10 N-B5 B-B1.

| 10 P-KR4! | QN-B3! |

Black reacts accurately to White's aggressive move. If instead 10 . . . P-KR3, White can successfully sacrifice his bishop: 11 BxP! PxB 12 Q-R5.

11 Q-B2	B-K3
12 N-B5	BxN
13 BxB	N-Q3
14 B-Q3	

If 14 BxN, Black equalizes at once by 14 . . . NxB!

| 14 . . . | P-KR3 |
| 15 B-KB4 | |

61. Alekhin–Capablanca

Position after White's 15th move

The bishop was not yet in danger. However, 15 0-0-0 would have allowed Black to simplify by 15 . . . N(B3)-K5!

In this position White has the two bishops, though that can hardly be considered an advantage in this opening, for Black's queen's bishop is usually the latter's most passive piece and its exchange for the White knight is generally an advantage to him. The only real danger for Black is his opponent's pawn attack on the king-side, which could lead to the opening of the KN or KR file. After the correct 15 . . . R-K1! Black would have a good game, for 16 P-KN4? NxP 17 R-KN1 P-KR4 is bad for White and 16 0-0-0 gives Black a chance to simplify: 16 . . . N(B3)-K5! 17 B(Q3)xN NxB 18 NxN PxN 19 QxKP BxP 20 Q-B3 B-N4 with an even game.

| 15 . . . | R-B1? |

Anticipating his opponent castling long and preparing the logical counter P-QB4. In his normal mental state Capablanca would hardly have overlooked the fact that this unfortunate placing of the rook gives his opponent the opportunity to make an immediate thrust on the king's side.

| 16 P-KN4! | N(B3)-K5 |

Black must do something about White's threat to advance further. 16 . . . N(B3)-K1 17 P-N5 P-KR4 18 P-N6! is not good for Black and 16 . . . NxP 17 BxN BxB 18 B-B5 loses the exchange, though admittedly White would have some difficulty in turning his material advantage to account. The line chosen by Capablanca gives up a pawn for chances in the endgame.

| 17 P-N5! | P-KR4 |

Black cannot allow his opponent to open the rook file: 17 . . . PxP 18 PxP BxP 19 B(Q3)xN NxB 20 NxN PxN 21 QxKP P-KN3 22 0-0-0 with an irresistible attack, e.g. 22 . . . BxB 23 QxB R-K1 24

R-R7! or 22 . . . R-K1 23 B-K5 B-B3 24 R-R3! followed by R(Q1)-KR1.

18 BxN	NxB
19 NxN	PxN
20 QxKP	Q-R4ch
21 K-B1	

Of course not 21 K-K2? Q-N4ch 22 K-B3 KR-K1 23 Q-B2 P-QB4! and if 24 P-Q5 then 24 . . . Q-Q2.

| 21 . . . | Q-Q4 |

Capablanca had already anticipated this manoeuvre when making his sixteenth move. The penetration of the rook to QB7 compensates for the loss of a pawn.

| 22 QxQ | PxQ |
| 23 K-N2! | |

Much weaker is 23 P-B3 R-B7 24 R-R2 on account of 24 . . . RxR 25 BxR P-B3! 26 P-N6 R-B1 27 R-K1 P-B4! 28 B-N3 R-B3 with a quick draw.

| 23 . . . | R-B7 |
| 24 KR-QB1! | |

If Black were given a free hand to double rooks (after QR-QN1, for example), he would have nothing to worry about, for the rooks would thwart any attempt by White to turn the pawn majority to account. The text-move, however, virtually forces an exchange of one set of rooks, for capturing the QNP would allow White control of the QB file with fatal consequences, e.g. 24 . . . RxNP 25 R(B1)-QN1! RxR 26 RxR P-QN3 27 R-QB1 (threatening R-B7) 27 . . . B-Q1 28 R-B8 (threatening 29 B-Q6 R-K1 30 B-B7). In this line, the move given by Alekhin, 28 R-B6, is less accurate on account of 28 . . . P-B3! 29 R-Q6 B-B2 30 RxQP BxB 31 PxB P-N3.

24 . . .	R(B1)-B1
25 RxR	RxR
26 R-QN1	K-R2?

A bad mistake and an unusual one for an endgame virtuoso like Capablanca. The

correct move is 26 ... P-QN4!, preventing White's queen-side pawns from
getting out of range of the Black rook
and making it almost impossible for
White to turn his material advantage to
account.

| 27 K-N3 | K-N3 |
| 28 P-B3 | P-B3 |

It is possible that, when making his
26th move, Black had intended to play
28 ... K-B4 but now realized that this is
answered by 29 P-K4ch!, and if 29 ...
PxKP, then 30 PxKPch KxKP 31 R-K1ch.

29 PxP	BxP
30 P-R4!	K-B4
31 P-R5	R-K7
32 R-QB1?	

An unnecessary pawn sacrifice, which
leaves White with only slight winning
chances. According to Alekhin, he had
originally planned 32 P-N4 R-QB7 33
R-N3 followed by 34 B-N8 and then
after 34 ... P-R3, 35 P-N5, opening lines
for his rook. But at the last moment he
was frightened by the reply 32 ...
P-KN4. His fears, however, were ground-
less, for after this the endgame is easily
won, e.g. 33 PxP BxNP (33 ... BxQP!?
34 R-Q1!) 34 BxB KxB 35 P-B4ch K-B4
36 K-B3 R-KR7 37 R-N1.

32 ...	RxNP
33 R-B5	K-K3
34 P-K4	

62. Alekhin–Capablanca

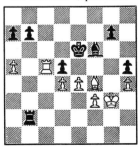

The reason behind the sacrifice now
becomes clear. White has mobilized his
rook and can create a passed pawn.

| 34 ... | BxQP |

This is not really a mistake. On the
other hand, there was a forced draw by
34 ... PxP 35 P-Q5ch K-B4 36 P-Q6dis
ch K-K3 37 PxP R-N6ch 38 K-N2 R-N7ch
39 K-R3 R-N5 40 R-B8! RxP 41 R-K8ch
K-Q4 42 RxR KxR 43 B-N5 B-B6 44
P-R6! (up to here given as a winning line
by Alekhin) 44 ... P-QN4! (not 44 ...
PxP? 45 P-Q7 B-R4 46 K-N2! B-N3 47
K-B1! winning) 45 P-Q7 B-R4 46 B-K7
(an immediate draw results from 46
P-Q8=Q BxQ 47 BxB P-N5 48 B-R5 P-N6
49 B-B3 P-N3) 46 ... K-Q4! (answering
White's threat of B-B5) 47 K-N3 K-B5.

| 35 RxP | B-B6? |

This does not actually lead to a forced
loss, but it makes Black's task very
difficult indeed. It is hard to understand
why Capablanca did not maintain
material equality by 35 ... B-B7ch 36
K-R3 R-N6 37 R-K5ch K-B3! (better
than the line given by Alekhin: 37 ...
K-B2 38 B-N5!, when Black cannot play
38 ... RxP because of 39 K-N2 and
White wins a piece) 38 R-B5ch K-K3 39
B-N5 P-N4!, when it is difficult to see
how White can progress.

| 36 RxP | P-R3 |

Threatening 37 ... R-N4. Advancing
the QNP would no longer have been
sufficient, e.g. 36 ... P-QN4 37 PxP e.p.
PxP 38 R-Q5 P-QN4 39 R-Q6ch K-K2 40
R-QN6 P-N5 41 K-N4 followed by 42
K-B5. Neither would an attack on the
KBP have helped: 36 ... B-K8ch 37
K-R3 R-KB7 38 R-K5ch K-B3 39
R-KB5ch K-K3 40 B-N3 or 38 ... K-Q2
39 R-Q5ch K-K3 40 R-Q3.

| 37 B-B7 | B-K8ch |

Here 37 ... R-N4 would allow the simple reply 38 R-KN5! because the QRP is protected.

38	K-N4	R-N7ch
39	K-R3	R-KB7
40	K-N4	R-KN7ch
41	K-R3	R- KB7
42	P-B4!	R-B6ch

At the moment Black is operating with mate threats. For example, on move 39 or 41, White could not have played K-B4 because of B-Q7 mate. Now there is another such threat: 43 K-N4?? R-KN6 mate.

43	K-N2	R-B7ch
44	K-R3	R-B6ch
45	K-N2	R-B7ch
46	K-N1	R-B7
47	B-N6	

63. Alekhin–Capablanca

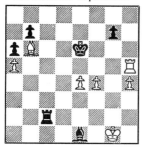

47 ...   R-B5?

Here Capablanca fails to see a simple tactical twist which enables his opponent to get a won position. The last hope of saving the game, and the title, lay in 47 ... B-N6! 48 R-K5ch K-Q3! (not 48 ... K-B2? 49 P-R5!) 49 R-KN5 BxBP 50 RxP R-B5 51 RxP RxP 52 R-QR7 K-B3! 53 RxP K-N4 54 R-R7 (or R8) B-Q7 55 P-R5 R-KR5 draw.

48 K-N2!

Even a world-class player can overlook such a simple reply. The KP is taboo (48 ... RxP 49 K-B3 and after the withdrawal of the rook White wins a piece by

R-K5ch). Now White's king enters the game with decisive effect.

48 ...	P-N3
49 R-K5ch	K-Q2
50 P-R5!	PxP
51 K-B3	P-R5
52 R-R5	R-B6ch
53 K-N4	R-B5
54 K-B5!	BxP!?
55 R-R7ch!	

Care is still required. An attempt to win the piece would lead to a catastrophe: 55 BxB R-B4ch 56 K-N4?? RxR 57 KxR P-R6.

| 55 ... | K-B3 |
| 56 BxB! | |

White avoids falling into the last trap: 56 R-QB7ch? K-N4 57 RxR KxR 58 BxB and White cannot stop the KRP.

56 ...	R-B4ch
57 K-K6!	RxB
58 P-B5	

In such positions it is not the number of pawns that counts but the pace at which they can advance.

58 ...	R-R6
59 P-B6	R-KB6
60 P-B7	P-N4
61 R-R5!	P-R6
62 R-KB5	RxR
63 PxR	Resigns

Because of 63 ... P-R7 64 P-B8=Q P-R8=Q 65 Q-QR8ch.

After this tragic encounter, the match only lasted two more games. There was a colourless draw in eighteen moves in the next game, in which Capablanca had White. The one after, the 34th, ended in a victory for Alekhin following a long and interesting struggle over eighty-two moves. A return match never took place, for the two adversaries could not agree on the conditions. Subsequently Capablanca's career soon took a marked downward turn.

20 Karlsbad 1929

Only Three Rounds in the Lead

Until the sixteenth round of the tournament at Karlsbad, played from 31 July to 26 August, it looked as if the chess machine that had suffered a reverse in the match with Alekhin was still going strong. It is true that, in a field containing all the world's strongest players apart from the new and the former world champions, Alekhin and Dr Lasker, Capablanca began modestly with five draws. In the second game he was even lucky to save half a point against Thomas, and in another one he defended excellently against Rubinstein. In an exciting encounter with Bogolyubov he failed to make the most of his chances.

From the sixth round, however, it was the Capablanca of old. His excellent positional performance enabled him to notch up one point after the other, and he climbed higher and higher up the table, going into the lead in the thirteenth round. This he maintained until the end of the fifteenth round, where he defeated his old rival Marshall. He and Spielmann had 11 points, a full point ahead of Nimzowitsch, who was followed by Rubinstein, Vidmar and Euwe.

What happened in the sixteenth round has gone down in chess history as one of the most unbelievable blunders ever perpetrated by a grandmaster. Capablanca, who had Black against Sämisch, made a mistake on his ninth move that lost a piece. The game went 1 P-Q4 N-KB3 2 P-QB4 P-K3 3 N-QB3 B-N5 4 P-QR3 BxNch 5 PxB P-Q3 6 P-B3 P-K4 7 P-K4 N-B3 8 B-K3 P-QN3 9 B-Q3 B-R3?? 10 Q-R4 B-N2 11 P-Q5. Although he struggled on valiantly until the 62nd move, even getting his opponent into dire

time-trouble on two occasions, he finally had to submit to the inevitable.

Spielmann took the sole lead by drawing his game, though he was caught by Capablanca again in the eighteenth round. Then began the final drama. Capablanca drew with Vidmar in the nineteenth round, where he was joined in the lead by Nimzowitsch, who defeated Spielmann in a double rook ending after winning a pawn. In the last round but one, Nimzowitsch only managed to draw against Maróczy owing to an inaccuracy in a won endgame. Capablanca, however, lost from the following position and so dropped out of the running.

64. Spielmann–Capablanca

Such a position is unusual after twenty-two moves in the Orthodox Queen's Gambit. Black's pieces lack co-ordination, and in spite of the forced transposition into an endgame White has a clear advantage.

23 R-Q6	QxQch
24 KxQ	R-K1
25 BxP	

There was a more stylish win by 25 K-Q3 N-K3 26 B-Q5 R-K2 27 R-K1 R(R1)-K1 28 P-KN4.

25 ...	R-K7ch
26 K-Q3!	RxBP
27 R-K1	R-B3

White was threatening 28 B-Q5ch K-N2 29 R-K7ch. After the exchange of the active rook Black will have absolutely no counter-play.

28 B-Q5ch	K-N3
29 RxRch	KxR
30 R-K8!	P-KR4

The knight cannot move because of 30 ... N-N3 31 RxR NxR 32 K-Q4 followed by K-B5.

31 R-R8	P-R5
32 PxP	PxP

White could now finish the game off quickly by 33 K-K4. Instead he adopts an inaccurate continuation which makes the win more difficult.

33 RxP(?)	K-K4
34 B-B6	P-R6
35 PxP	RxPch
36 K-B2	P-N5!
37 PxP	N-K3
38 B-R4	N-B5
39 R-K7ch	K-Q3
40 R-Q7ch	K-K4
41 B-B6	R-R3
42 P-N5	R-Q3
43 R-K7ch	R-K3
44 R-QB7	K-Q3
45 R-B8	R-K7ch
46 K-B3	R-K6ch
47 K-B4	R-K7
48 R-Q8ch	K-B2
49 R-Q7ch	K-B1
50 K-B5	RxP
51 K-N6	R-K7
52 R-B7ch	K-Q1
53 R-Q7ch	K-B1
54 R-Q4	N-K3
55 B-N7ch	K-N1
56 R-QB4	Resigns

Prior to the last round Spielmann and Nimzowitsch were leading with 14 points, Capablanca being one point behind. Spiel-

mann did not manage to repeat his success at Semmering 1926, though in the last round he got very near to doing so.

65. Mattison–Spielmann

As Spielmann pointed out immediately after the game, there is an easy win by 22 ... RxP 23 RxR PxR 24 N-N2 Q-R3, when Black has no problem in retaining his extra pawn, for 25 NxP fails to 25 ... NxB!

22 ...	NxB(?)

This does not throw away the win, though it was not necessary to mobilize White's QR.

23 N-N2	Q-N5
24 QRxN	PxP(?)

Another mistake. Much stronger is 24 ... RxP 25 RxR PxR 26 R-KB1 R-KB1 threatening 27 ... P-B6 or 25 P-R3 RxRch followed by QxPch. However, Black still has winning chances.

25 P-KR3	Q-B4!

Much better than 25 ... Q-N4? 26 R-B3 followed by QR-KB1.

26 QxQ	RxQ
27 RxP	RxR?

Spielmann admitted later that he had been suffering from hallucinations when he made this move. The correct line is 27 ... QR-KB1! 28 RxR RxR 29 R-Q1 R-B6 30 P-KR4 K-N2, and the king has a free hand. Deviating on the 28th move does not help White: 28 R-N4ch K-R1 (threatening R-B7) 29 R-N2 R-B6.

28	NxR	NxQP
29	R-Q1	N-B6ch
30	K-B2	NxP

When making his 27th move Spielmann had planned 30 ... N-N4? 31 P-KR4 N-K5ch followed by K-B2. Now he realizes that 30 ... N-N4 is answered by 31 R-KN1.

31	NxKP	R-K1
32	N-B4	
	Drawn	

As a result of the faltering of his two main rivals, Nimzowitsch, who had gone into the lead just two rounds earlier, was given a chance to win the tournament outright. His last hurdle was, like himself, an apostle of the neo-romantic school.

King's Indian

	Nimzowitsch	Tartakower
1	P-Q4	N-KB3
2	P-QB4	P-KN3
3	P-B3	

An innovation aimed at avoiding the Grünfeld Defence (3 N-QB3 P-QB4), which at that time was quite new. It was later discovered, however, that 3 ... P-Q4 is even better after 3 P-B3 than 3 N-QB3.

3	...	B-N2
4	P-K4	P-Q3
5	N-B3	0-0
6	B-K3	QN-Q2

This move is still sometimes seen as an alternative to the usual 6 ... P-K4.

7 N-R3

Nimzowitsch was very fond of this original way of developing. It proves good if the game continues 7 ... P-B4 8 P-Q5, when the knight can head for Q3, where it should have a fine future. Today the preferred lines are 7 Q-Q2 P-B4 8 KN-K2 followed by 9 0-0-0 and 7 B-Q3 P-B4 (or K4) 8 KN-K2.

7	...	P-K4
8	P-Q5	P-QR4

The present-day devotee of the King's Indian would, at this stage, have no hesitation in playing 8 ... N-R4! and, after 9 P-KN4, sacrificing a pawn by 9 ... N-B5 for excellent counter-play.

9	N-B2	P-N3(?)

Such positions should not be handled so passively. Either here or on the next move N-R4 was called for.

10	Q-Q2	N-B4?
11	B-N5!	B-Q2

The manoeuvre N-R4 has now become more difficult. Nevertheless Black should at any rate have tried to prepare the way for it by unpinning the knight by 10 ... Q-Q2. If then 11 P-KN4, Black could play 11 ... N-K1.

12	P-KN4	Q-B1
13	P-KR4	K-R1

It is now too late to prepare the freeing advance P-KB4, for 13 ... N-K1 is answered by 14 P-R5 P-B4 15 PxNP, when the Black king is left without the protection of his pawns.

14	P-R5	PxP
15	BxN	

There is time for this later. Much stronger is 15 0-0-0. Then, of course, Black cannot reply 15 ... PxP?? 16 BxN BxB 17 Q-R6, and after 15 ... N-N1 16 RxP P-KB3 17 B-K3 White retains his active bishop in a position otherwise similar to that in game.

15	...	BxB
16	RxP	

Dr Lasker, who subjected the games of his past and future opponents to a thorough examination, suggests a different, and very strong, continuation: 16 Q-R6 B-N2 17 QxP(R5) P-R3 18 P-N5 P-B4 19 PxBP e.p.! (better than 19 PxRP

66. Nimzowitsch–Tartakower

Position after Black's 15th move

B-KB3) 19 ... RxP 20 B-R3 B-K1 21 BxQ BxQ 22 RxB RxB 23 K-K2, and White has a considerable advantage in the endgame thanks to the weak white squares in Black's position.

| 16 ... | B-N2 |
| 17 N-R1! | |

The knight is heading for KB5. It could also choose another route, passing through Q1 and K3, but Nimzowitsch was particularly fond of the move N-KR1. Two years previously he had used it to win an important game against Rubinstein.

17 ...	P-KB3
18 Q-R2	P-R3
19 N-N3	K-R2
20 B-K2	

Another strong continuation is 20 N-Q1 followed by N-K3, threatening N-B5. In this case Black would be hard put to it to defend the square KR3.

| 20 ... | KR-N1 |
| 21 K-B2! | |

Nimzowitsch was the first to formulate the strategic principles of positional play, which he did in his book *My System*. One of the most important things about so-called "positional tacking" is that, in the absence of a disturbance of the equilibrium, a single weakness is usually not sufficient for success.

According to Nimzowitsch it is necessary to operate against two weaknesses at the same time. In the present position White needs to complement his king-side action by one on the other wing (P-QN3, P-QR3, P-QN4), where he can prepare the breakthrough P-QB5. If, therefore, he were to castle long, his king would be in the way. So he leaves it in the middle.

21 ...	R-R1
22 R-R4!	Q-K1
23 R-KN1	B-KB1
24 K-N2	N-N2!

The knight is urgently needed for the defence of the king's wing. However, its removal from the queen-side will later help White's action there.

25 N-R5!

In the circumstances a justified change of plan. Before occupying KB5 White will first increase his pressure by the advance P-KB4.

25 ...	Q-N3
26 P-B4	N-Q1
27 B-B3	N-B2
28 N-K2	B-K2

Exchanging would not really ease Black's position: 28 ... PxP 29 N(R5)xP(B4)! Q-N2 30 N-Q4 N-N4 31 N-B5 BxN 32 KPxB followed by 33 N-K6.

29 K-R1	K-N1
30 N(K2)-N3	K-B1
31 N-B5	R-KN1

Black would lose his queen by 31 ... BxN? 32 NPxB Q-R2 33 R-N7, and the attempt to increase the activity of his knight by removing White's KBP would lose a pawn: 31 ... PxP 32 NxP(B4) Q-N4 33 R-R5 Q-N1 34 NxRP or 32 ... Q-R2 33 N-K6ch BxN 34 PxB N-K4 35 RxP.

32 Q-Q2	R-B1
33 R-R2	K-K1
34 P-N3!	K-Q1

Karlsbad 1929

	1	2	3	4	5	6	7	8	9	10	11	12	13	14	15	16	17	18	19	20	21	22	Pts	Prize
1 Nimzowitsch	–	½	1	½	½	1	1	1	½	½	1	½	½	1	½	1	0	1	½	1	½	1	15	I
2 Capablanca	½	–	0	½	1	½	½	½	½	½	1	1	1	½	1	0	1	1	1	1	½	1	14½	II, III
3 Spielmann	0	1	–	0	½	½	½	½	1	0	½	1	1	½	1	1	½	1	1	1	1	1	14½	II, III
4 Rubinstein	½	½	1	–	½	½	½	½	1	1	1	½	½	½	1	½	½	1	½	0	½	1	13½	IV
5 Becker	½	0	½	½	–	1	1	1	0	0	1	½	½	½	½	½	1	½	1	1	½	0	12	V–VII
6 Euwe	0	½	½	½	0	–	0	½	½	1	½	1	½	½	1	½	½	1	½	½	1	1	12	V–VII
7 Vidmar	0	½	½	½	0	1	–	½	½	½	½	1	½	1	0	½	½	0	1	1	1	1	12	V–VII
8 Bogolyubov	0	½	½	½	0	½	½	–	½	½	½	1	0	0	1	1	1	0	½	1	1	1	11½	VIII
9 Grünfeld	½	½	0	0	1	½	½	½	–	½	½	0	1	½	½	0	1	½	1	½	1	½	11	IX
10 Canal	½	½	1	0	1	0	½	½	½	–	1	0	0	½	½	½	0	1	0	½	1	1	10½	X, XI
11 Mattison	0	0	½	0	0	½	½	½	½	0	–	1	1	1	0	1	1	1	½	0	½	1	10½	X, XI
12 Colle	½	0	0	½	½	0	0	0	1	1	0	–	1	½	1	½	1	0	½	0	1	1	10	
13 Maróczy	½	0	0	½	½	½	½	1	0	1	0	0	–	½	0	0	1	½	1	1	½	1	10	
14 Tartakower	0	½	½	½	½	½	0	1	½	½	0	½	½	–	½	½	½	½	½	½	½	1	10	
15 Treybal	½	0	0	0	½	0	1	0	½	½	1	0	1	½	–	½	½	0	1	1	½	1	10	
16 Sämisch	0	1	0	½	½	½	½	0	1	½	0	½	1	½	½	–	½	0	½	½	1	0	9½	
17 Yates	1	0	½	½	0	½	½	0	0	1	0	0	0	½	½	½	–	1	½	½	1	1	9½	
18 Johner	0	0	0	0	½	0	1	1	½	0	0	1	½	½	1	1	0	–	½	0	½	1	9	
19 Marshall	½	0	0	½	0	½	0	½	0	1	½	½	0	½	0	½	½	½	–	1	1	1	9	
20 Gilg	0	0	0	1	0	½	0	0	½	½	1	1	0	½	0	½	½	1	0	–	½	½	8	
21 Thomas	½	½	0	½	½	0	0	0	0	0	½	0	½	½	½	0	0	½	0	½	–	1	6	
22 Menschik	0	0	0	0	1	0	0	0	½	0	0	0	0	0	0	1	0	0	0	½	0	–	3	

35	P-R3	R-QR1
36	Q-B1	

67. Nimzowitsch–Tartakower

36 ...	B-KB1??

This makes the win much easier and assures Nimzowitsch of first prize in the tournament. Tartakower intends to counter White's positional threat of P-QN4, P-QB5 by preventing the exchange of his king's bishop, but completely overlooks that he thereby loses the exchange and a pawn. After the game he recommended a re-grouping of Black's pieces by 36 ... Q-KR2 followed by

Q-R1 and B-KB1. In this case White could have broken through on the queen's side; e.g. 36 ... Q-R2 37 P-N4 RPxP 38 RPxP Q-R1 39 P-B5! and both 39 ... QPxP 40 NxB KxN 41 NPxP and 39 ... BxN 40 KPxB NPxP 41 NPxP are positionally hopeless for Black. In the latter variation 41 ... QPxP? would be answered by 42 P-Q6.

37	N-R4!	Q-R2
38	NxP	Q-R1
39	NxR	QxN
40	P-N5!	KPxP
41	PxP	Q-R2
42	QxP	BxP
43	Q-B6ch	K-B1
44	N-B5!	BxN
45	PxB	K-N2
46	Q-N6	R-R1
47	QxQ	RxQ
48	R-N6	K-B1
49	P-B6	R-R1
50	B-N4ch	K-Q1
51	B-K6	K-K1
52	BxNch	KxB
53	R(R2)xB	Resigns

21 Zürich 1934

A Strong Finish

The glorious Alekhin era was drawing to its close. After a few tournaments in which he was well ahead of the rest of the field—at San Remo he won by 3½ points and at Bled in 1931 by 5½, an unequalled feat in international tournaments—his rivals began to cause him more and more trouble.

At a tournament in Zürich from 14 to 29 July 1934, to celebrate the 125th anniversary of the Zürich Chess Society, there was an illustrious collection of players. Although Capablanca and Reshevsky as well as the Soviet contingent were missing (the latter only entering the international arena a year later), it was the strongest field that could be assembled at that time.

After the seventh round Lasker and Flohr were ahead with 5½ points, and from then until the eleventh round Flohr was in the sole lead. In the twelfth round he was caught by Alekhin, both of them having ten points, being half a point ahead of Euwe and a full point ahead of Bogolyubov. The others were already out of the running, Lasker, for example,

having lost in the eighth, tenth and twelfth rounds.

In the thirteenth round the main question was: Which of the two leaders would be able to forge ahead? Flohr came very close to doing so.

White can do nothing to hold the queen's side. Bogolyubov, however, uses his doubled rooks to mount a rescue action.

57	N-B5!	BxN
58	PxB	R-KN2
59	R-Q7	R-QB2
60	P-B6!	Q-B5!

Of course, not 60 . . . RxP? 61 RxRch KxR 62 Q-R7ch followed by 63 R-Q7. In answer to the text-move White must not be too aggressive, e.g. 61 RxR(B7) RxR 62 R-Q7ch? RxR 63 PxR Q-Q4!, when Black has the double threats of Q-R8 mate and QxP.

61	RxR(B7)	RxR
62	R-Q6!	RxP
63	R-Q7ch	K-N1
64	R-Q8ch	K-B2
65	Q-R7ch	R-B2
66	R-Q7ch	RxR
67	QxRch	
	Drawn	

Alekhin also had a strong opponent. However, he performed his task excellently in an instructive positional game.

Dutch Defence

Ståhlberg	Alekhin
1 P-Q4	P-K3
2 P-QB4	P-KB4

68. Bogolyubov–Flohr

Position after Black's 56th move

3	P-KN3	N-KB3
4	B-N2	B-N5ch
5	B-Q2	BxBch
6	QxB	0-0
7	N-QB3	P-Q4(?)

From the strategical point of view a doubtful move. The Stonewall System is playable if the black-squared bishops have not been exchanged (i.e. after 4 ... B-K2). In this case White often tries to force the exchange by P-QN3 and B-QR3. In the present game he does not need to go to such trouble. His opponent has already done it for him.

8	N-B3	N-B3!?

Operating with the threat of QPxP. The immediate 8 ... QPxP is not good on account of 9 N-K5.

9	PxP	PxP
10	N-K5	N-K2
11	0-0	P-B3
12	QR-B1	

A rather stereotyped move. The rook is better placed on QN1 to prepare the minority attack. A good move is 12 P-QN4,

69. Ståhlberg–Alekhin

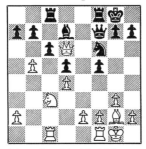

Position after Black's 17th move

which would have given White a definite advantage.

12	...	Q-K1
13	P-QN4	N-N3
14	NxN	QxN
15	P-N5	B-Q2

16	Q-B4	QR-B1
17	Q-Q6	Q-B2
18	PxP?	

This relieves Black of all his worries. Much stronger is 18 Q-N4.

18	...	BxP
19	Q-N4	Q-Q2
20	P-K3	N-K5
21	KR-K1(?)	

Another inaccuracy. Better is 21 KR-Q1 followed by B-B1.

21	...	P-QN3
22	P-B3	NxN
23	RxN	B-N4
24	B-B1?	

Yet another mistake. Now Black will be able to control the QB file and have a distinct advantage in the endgame. White should have preceded B-B1 by 24 R(K1)-QB1 B-B5 25 P-QR4.

24	...	BxB
25	KxB	RxR
26	QxR(B3)	R-B1
27	Q-Q3	P-N3
28	K-B2	

White has no way of getting active play. 28 P-K4, for example, is refuted by 28 ... QPxP 29 PxP PxP 30 QxP Q-KB2ch followed by QxP.

28	...	Q-R5
29	R-K2	R-B8
30	R-N2	K-N2
31	Q-N3	Q-B3

Black could get excellent chances in an endgame by 31 ... QxQ 32 PxQ P-QR4 and then playing his king to Q3. Alekhin assumes that he will still be able to force a rook ending at a later stage, and, for the time being, decides to tack.

32	Q-Q3	P-KR4
33	K-N2	R-B6
34	Q-K2	Q-R5

70. Ståhlberg–Alekhin

Position after Black's 34th move

Now White's position is suddenly critical; he is threatened with 35 ... Q-R6 36 K-B2 RxP! 37 QxR QxRch 38 K-N1 Q-N8ch 39 K-N2 QxPch 40 K-R3 K-B2. The best defence is 35 R-Q2.

35 P-N4?

White obviously expects the above-mentioned variation beginning with 35 ... Q-R6 and hopes to be able to get sufficient counter-play at the end (i.e. after 40 ... K-B2) by 41 PxBP PxP 42 Q-K5. The disadvantage of the text-move is that it seriously weakens the king.

35 ...	Q-K1!
36 R-N3	RxR
37 PxR	RPxP
38 PxP	Q-K5ch

Winning a pawn, for White must naturally avoid a pawn endgame: 39 Q-B3 QxNPch 40 QxQ PxQ 41 K-N3 P-R4.

| 39 K-B2 | PxP |

More precise than 39 ... QxNP 40 Q-N5.

40 Q-K1	Q-B7ch
41 K-N3	QxNP
42 K-R4	Q-B7
43 Q-N3	Q-KB4
44 Q-B7ch	K-R3
45 Resigns	

Zürich 1934

		1	2	3	4	5	6	7	8	9	10	11	12	13	14	15	16	Pts	Prize
1	Alekhin	–	0	½	½	1	1	1	1	1	1	1	1	1	1	1	1	13	I
2	Euwe	1	–	½	1	0	1	½	½	1	1	1	1	½	1	1	1	12	II, III
3	Flohr	½	½	–	½	½	½	½	1	1	1	1	1	1	1	1	1	12	II, III
4	Bogolyubov	½	0	½	–	1	½	½	½	1	1	1	1	1	1	1	1	11½	IV
5	Lasker	0	1	½	0	–	1	0	0	½	1	1	1	1	1	1	1	10	V
6	Bernstein	0	0	½	½	0	–	½	1	½	½	½	1	1	1	1	1	9	VI, VII
7	Nimzowitsch	0	½	½	½	1	½	–	½	0	0	1	1	½	1	1	1	9	VI, VII
8	Ståhlberg	0	½	0	½	1	0	½	–	½	1	0	1	1	½	1	½	8	VIII
9	Johner	0	0	0	0	½	½	1	½	–	0	1	1	1	1	½	½	7½	
10	Henneberger	0	0	0	0	0	½	1	0	1	–	0	0	1	0	1	1	5½	
11	Gygli	0	0	0	0	0	½	0	1	0	1	–	½	0	½	½	1	5	
12	Rosselli	0	0	0	0	0	0	0	0	0	1	½	–	½	1	1	½	4½	
13	Grob	0	½	0	0	0	0	½	0	0	0	1	½	–	0	½	1	4	
14	Müller	0	0	0	0	0	0	0	½	0	1	½	0	1	–	0	1	4	
15	Naegeli	0	0	0	0	0	0	0	0	½	0	½	0	½	1	–	½	3	
16	Joss	0	0	0	0	0	0	0	½	½	0	0	½	0	0	½	–	2	

22 Moscow 1935

Thirteen—Botvinnik's Unlucky Number

When Botvinnik blundered against me in the 1947 Moscow Tournament and lost the game (cf. page 129), he told me that he had always been afraid of the thirteenth round. I was quite surprised to hear that, for I had not expected the scientific brain of a future world champion to harbour such a superstition. Later I discovered that the thirteenth round really had been a critical point for Botvinnik in a number of tournaments and that he had on several such occasions suffered unexpected defeats at the hands of weaker players.

This series began in the second international tournament in Moscow, which took place from 15 February to 15 March. Botvinnik was twenty-four years old at the time and enjoyed an excellent reputation in the chess world; two years previously he had drawn a match with the renowned Czech grandmaster Salo Flohr. But what he really needed for his class to be fully recognized was success in tournaments, and Botvinnik saw Moscow 1935 as his real chance.

In the first round he slaughtered Spielmann in a famous twelve-move miniature. In the second, playing Black, he drew with Capablanca. Then there followed a series of victories against Miss Menshik, Romanovski, Löwenfisch, Rjumin and Ståhlberg, which left him with a lead of one point over Flohr at the end of the seventh round. He also had convincing wins in the ninth and eleventh rounds against Goglidse and Ragosin—both with Black. At the end of the twelfth round the leading scores were: Botvinnik 10, Flohr 9, Lasker and Löwenfisch 8, Capa-

blanca 7½, Spielmann, Lilienthal, Rabinowitsch, Ragosin 6½.

Among those he still had to face were Lasker, Lilienthal and Flohr, but he also had four Soviet opponents who were well known to him from home events. The tournament thus seemed to be virtually over and the press were already hailing the new star. However, there was to be a sudden and unexpected turn of events, for Botvinnik actually lost to two of his fellow-countrymen. His game in the thirteenth round was a real tragedy.

71. Kan–Botvinnik

Position after White's 20th move

White had played the opening weakly, losing a pawn. By developing quietly with 20 ... B-K2 Black could have maintained his advantage, for, on the one hand, 21 NxN PxN 22 B-K4 B-Q4 23 BxB QxB 24 Q-N4ch K-N1 25 QxP? is answered by 25 ... R(Q1)-N1, and, on the other, the attempt to attack on the QN file by doubling rooks comes to nothing because Black's knight can effectively join in the defence, e.g. 21 R-N3 K-N1 22 KR-N1 N-R4. For this latter reason, Black should not exchange off his knight.

| 20 ... | NxN? |
| 21 BxN | QxP?? |

This loses, for White gets an irresistible attack along two files. After the correct 21 ... B-K2, the doubling of his opponent's rooks would prove uncomfortable though Black would probably have an adequate defence in 22 R-N3 Q-R5! 23 KR-N1 P-QN4 24 B-QB2 Q-R4 25 P-QR4 P-QB3.

| 22 KR-B1 | Q-R4 |
| 23 Q-QB2! | P-QB3 |

Or 23 ... R-Q2 24 B-Q2 Q-R6 25 R-N3 followed by R(B1)-N1).

| 24 B-Q2 | Q-B2 |
| 25 Q-R4 | R-Q2 |

Apart from 26 BxQRP there was also the threat of 26 B-R5, e.g. 25 ... K-Q2 26 B-R5 Q-B1 27 BxR KxB 28 BxP! PxB 29 RxP.

| 26 BxQRP | Resigns |

In the same round Flohr's opponent, Capablanca, used all his resources to save an endgame with an isolated pawn. As a result Botvinnik was still in the lead, though only by half a point. The position was maintained in the next round, where Botvinnik drew with Lasker, and Flohr, unexpectedly, with Miss Menshik.

The fifteenth round had an important effect on the outcome of the tournament. Botvinnik was faced by Bogatyrtschuk, who was not in particularly good form

72. Bogatyrtschuk–Botvinnik

Position after White's 21st move

and who had only scored 4½ points from fourteen games.

Black is a little cramped but his position is firm enough. As a result of his advanced king-side pawns, his king is somewhat exposed, so he should try and prevent lines being opened. It is difficult to understand why Botvinnik now embarks on a plan that is quite contrary to the requirements of the situation.

| 21 ... | R-Q2(?) |

This is not accurate. He should instead play 21 ... N-R4 22 R-Q2 QR-K1! in order to maintain his KP at all costs.

| 22 R-Q2 | PxP? |

This exchange irreparably damages his position. Admittedly 22 ... R-K2 is not possible on account of 23 P-B5! KPxP 24 PxP, but he could still have prevented the opening of the game by playing 22 ... KR-Q1.

| 23 RxQP | R-K2 |
| 24 B-K1! | |

The bishop is heading for the long diagonal, which will be wide open after Black's "freeing" move P-KB4. Black, for his part, has no great choice, for he is faced by the threat of 25 P-KN4, which would make his KBP a permanent weakness.

24 ...	P-KB4
25 B-B3	R(B1)-K1
26 Q-Q3	B-B1
27 R-KB1!	

A simple, yet pretty pawn sacrifice. Black's best course is to decline it, though in that case, e.g. after the waiting move 27 ... K-R2, White would be able to strengthen his position by the manoeuvre B-N2, Q-B3, N-Q5, etc.

27 ...	PxP(?)
28 PxP	RxP
29 RxR	QxR
30 N-Q5!	

102

There is now no effective way of stopping the knight from moving on to KB6, for 30 ... N-R4? loses to 31 R-K1 QxQ 32 RxRch K-B2 33 R-K7ch followed by 34 PxQ.

30 ...	QxQ
31 N-B6ch	K-B2

After 31 ... K-R1 32 PxQ White threatens both NxR and N-R5.

32 PxQ	R-Q1

Black would also lose a piece by 32 ... R-K7 33 N-R5dis ch N-B4 34 N-N3 R-QB7 35 NxN BxN (35 ... RxB 36 NxQPdbl ch) 36 RxBch K-K3 37 R-B6ch K-K2 38 B-R1 R-B8ch 39 R-B1.

33 N-Q5dis ch	N-B4

If the king moves to N3 or N1, 34 N-K7ch followed by R-B7 is decisive.

34 P-KN4	R-K1
35 PxN	R-K7
36 R-B3	R-QB7
37 B-K1	P-N5
38 R-B1	Resigns

73. Flohr–Romanovski

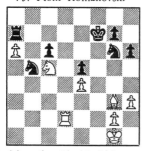

Position after Black's 46th move

This game is an example of precise positional play on Flohr's part. The way he now utilizes the advantage of the distant passed pawn is extremely instructive.

47 R-Q7ch!

It requires a fine positional feeling to realize that the endgame is won after an

exchange of rooks. 47 K-B2 would have given Black drawing chances.

47 ...	RxR
48 NxR	K-K3
49 N-B5ch	K-Q3
50 B-B2	N-B2

Black loses a piece by 50 ... N-B1? 51 P-R7! NxP 52 N-N3 N-N4 53 B-B5ch.

51 P-N3	N-QR1
52 K-N2	N-K2
53 K-B3	P-N3
54 N-Q3	

Threatening 55 B-B5ch followed by BxN and NxP.

54 ...	N-B1
55 B-B5ch	K-K3
56 N-N2!	N-Q3
57 BxN!	KxB
58 N-B4ch	K-B4

Otherwise the White king would get to QR5, when the passed QRP would cost Black a piece.

59 NxP	K-N3
60 NxNP	KxP
61 P-K5	K-N2
62 K-K4	K-B2
63 K-B5	K-Q2
64 P-K6ch	K-K1
65 N-K5	P-B4
66 N-Q7	P-B5
67 N-B6ch	K-B1
68 N-Q5	K-N2
69 K-K4!	Resigns

The position had thus changed completely. Flohr was now out ahead, closely followed by Botvinnik. In the last four rounds, however, Flohr appeared to have lost his previous energy and, more important, his sure touch in turning advantages into wins. He drew all four games, including one in the seventeenth round against Rjumin in which he was a pawn up in an easily won ending. Botvinnik, on the other hand, produced his best game of the tournament immediately after his second defeat.

Réti System

Botvinnik	Chekhover
1 N-KB3	P-Q4
2 P-B4	P-K3
3 P-QN3	N-KB3
4 B-N2	B-K2
5 P-K3	0-0
6 B-K2	P-B3(?)

Not a serious mistake, though a superfluous and passive move; it is also a potential loss of a tempo, for Black will sooner or later have to play P-QB4. Actually this latter move should have been played at once or after P-QN3 and B-N2.

7 0-0	QN-Q2
8 N-B3	P-QR3
9 N-Q4!?	

Black's eighth move signified that he was aiming for counter-play by advancing the QNP. Botvinnik nips this plan in the bud in an original manner. In view of the altered circumstances Black should change his plan and play 9 . . . P-B4 10 N-B3 P-QN3 followed by B-N2 with equality.

9 . . .	PxP?
10 PxP	N-B4(?)

Not really a good idea. Black now threatens to play P-K4 (which was not advisable on the tenth move because of 11 N-B5). However, this is easily countered by 11 P-KB4, which was in any case part of White's plan. Black's best course would have been 10 . . . P-B4 11 N-B3 P-QN3 12 P-Q4 PxP 13 PxP B-N2.

11 P-B4	Q-B2
12 N-B3	R-Q1
13 Q-B2	N(B4)-Q2
14 P-Q4	P-B4

At last Black resorts to this move. But the loss of tempo will make itself felt.

15 N-K5	P-QN3
16 B-Q3	PxP

In a way this lessens the force of a future P-Q5 by White, for such an advance leaves Black's knight on Q2 access to the square QB4. On the other hand, the situation has now been clarified in the centre, leaving White control of all the important central squares and enabling him to launch a king-side attack.

17 PxP	B-N2
18 Q-K2	N-B1

74. Botvinnik–Chekhover

19 N-Q1!

An excellent move, aimed not at protecting the QP, which was not really threatened (e.g. 19 QR-Q1 RxP? 20 N-Q5!), but at getting the knight into position for an attack on KB7. When making the move Botvinnik had to decide whether or not the long trek by the knight to KN5 via Q1, KB2 and KR3 could be rendered useless by the simple P-KR3 on the part of his opponent.

19 . . .   R-R2(?)

Such unusual moves are only good on the rarest of occasions, and this is not one of them. Black gets more chances by 19 . . . B-B3 with the intention of protecting KB2 by B-K1. In this case White could either press on with his plan or content himself with a smaller advantage, that of

Moscow 1935

	1	2	3	4	5	6	7	8	9	10	11	12	13	14	15	16	17	18	19	20	Pts	Prize
1 Botvinnik	–	½	½	½	1	0	1	½	1	1	½	1	½	1	½	0	1	½	1	1	13	I, II
2 Flohr	½	–	½	½	½	½	½	½	½	1	½	1	1	½	1	1	1	1	½	½	13	I, II
3 Lasker	½	½	–	1	½	1	½	½	½	½	½	1	½	½	½	½	½	1	1	1	12½	III
4 Capablanca	½	½	0	–	½	1	1	½	1	½	1	½	½	0	1	½	½	½	1	1	12	IV
5 Spielmann	0	½	½	½	–	½	½	½	0	1	1	½	0	½	½	½	1	1	1	1	11	V
6 Kan	1	½	0	0	½	–	½	0	1	0	½	½	1	1	0	1	1	½	½	1	10½	VI, VII
7 Löwenfisch	0	½	½	0	½	½	–	½	½	½	1	½	0	1	1	1	1	½	0	1	10½	VI, VII
8 Lilienthal	½	½	½	½	½	1	½	–	0	½	½	½	0	1	½	½	0	1	1	½	10	VIII–X
9 Ragosin	0	½	½	0	1	0	½	1	–	0	0	½	½	1	½	½	1	1	½	1	10	VIII–X
10 Romanovski	0	0	½	½	0	1	½	½	1	–	½	½	1	0	½	½	1	0	1	1	10	VIII–X
11 Alatorzev	½	½	½	0	0	½	0	½	1	½	–	0	0	1	1	½	½	½	1	1	9½	
12 Goglidse	0	0	0	½	½	½	½	½	½	½	1	–	½	½	½	½	0	1	1	1	9½	
13 Rabinowitsch	½	0	½	½	1	0	1	1	½	0	1	½	–	0	0	½	0	½	1	1	9½	
14 Rjumin	0	½	½	1	½	0	0	0	0	1	0	½	1	–	0	1	1	1	½	1	9½	
15 Lisizin	½	0	½	0	½	1	0	½	½	½	0	½	1	1	–	0	½	½	½	1	9	
16 Bogatyrtschuk	1	0	½	½	½	0	0	½	½	½	½	½	½	0	1	–	½	½	0	½	8	
17 Ståhlberg	0	0	½	½	0	0	0	1	0	0	½	1	1	0	½	½	–	½	1	1	8	
18 Pirc	½	0	0	½	0	½	½	0	0	1	½	0	½	0	½	½	½	–	1	1	7½	
19 Chekhover	0	½	0	0	0	½	1	0	½	0	0	0	0	½	½	1	0	0	–	1	5½	
20 Menshik	0	½	0	0	0	0	0	½	0	0	0	0	0	0	0	½	0	0	0	–	1½	

the two bishops, e.g. 20 NxB QxN 21
P-KB5.

| 20 N-B2 | Q-N1(?) |

Black misses the last opportunity to
play B-B3.

| 21 N-R3 | P-R3 |
| 22 N-N5! | |

A simple, yet effective, piece sacrifice,
which shows how faulty Black's whole
defensive set up is.

| 22 ... | PxN |
| 23 PxP | N(B1)-Q2 |

An attempt to keep the extra piece
would soon lead to disaster, e.g. 23 ...
N(B3)-Q2 24 NxP (threatening Q-R5) 24
... P-N3 25 BxP! NxB 26 Q-R5 N(Q2)-B1
27 N-R6ch K-R1 28 P-Q5dis ch P-K4
29 N-B5dis ch K-N1 30 NxBch NxN
31 Q-B7ch K-R1 32 Q-B6ch followed
by BxP. Or 23 ... N(B3)-R2 24 NxP
NxP (24 ... KBxP 25 BxNch NxB
26 QxP) 25 Q-R5 N(N4)-R2 26 P-Q5!
B-B4ch (26 ... PxP 27 N-R6ch K-R1 28
Q-B7) 27 K-R1 B-R1 28 BxP KxB (28 ...
R(Q1)-Q2 29 B-K5) 29 Q-N4ch, etc.

75. Botvinnik–Chekhover

24 NxP!?

This second impressive piece sacrifice
leads to a certain win, though not as
quickly as the simple 24 NxN RxN (24
... NxN 25 Q-R5) 25 PxN BxBP 26
RxB! PxR 27 Q-N4ch K-B1 28 B-R3ch
R-Q3 29 Q-N3 K-K2 30 P-B5, etc.

| 24 ... | KxN |
| 25 P-N6ch | K-N1 |

Other king moves do not help Black:

(*a*) 25 ... K-B1 26 QxP N-K4! 27 PxN
(or 27 RxNch PxR 28 Q-R3) 27 ...
B-B4ch 28 K-R1 B-B1 29 RxNch PxR 30
QxBPch K-K1 31 P-N7, etc.

(*b*) 25 ... K-K1 26 QxP N-B1 27
Q-B7ch K-Q2 28 B-R3 R-K1 29 RxN!
PxR 30 P-N7 and wins.

26 QxPch	K-R1
27 Q-R3ch	K-N1 .
28 B-B5	N-B1
29 B-K6ch!	NxB
30 QxNch	K-R1
31 Q-R3ch	K-N1
32 RxN!	BxR
33 Q-R7ch	K-B1
34 R-K1	B-K4
35 Q-R8ch	K-K2
36 QxPch	K-Q3
37 QxB(K5)ch	K-Q2
38 Q-KB5ch	K-B3
39 P-Q5ch	K-B4
40 B-R3ch	KxBP
41 Q-K4ch	K-B6
42 B-N4ch	K-N7
43 Q-N1 mate	

In the last three rounds Botvinnik, like
Flohr, only managed to draw his games,
so the two of them tied for top place,
having 13 points each. They were
followed by Lasker (12½), Capablanca
(12) and Spielmann (11).

23 World Championship Match 1935

The King is Dead? Long Live the King!

This was the title of an article in the magazine *Československy Šach* commenting on the result of the match between Alekhin and Euwe. Capablanca's renowned conquerer, the master who outclassed his rivals in a number of international tournaments, had lost his title in a match that should have been a clear-cut affair. The question mark in the headline was meant to indicate that the fall of the king was difficult to believe. As things turned out, it was not a permanent fall, for two years later Alekhin recovered his title by a great margin, and everything was in order again.

The result of the 1935 match was like a bomb going off and was the subject of numerous debates. The Russian master Snosko-Borovski, who had emigrated to Paris, explained it as the work of mysterious forces. "Euwe is not a great personality, because he is merely a tool in the hands of fate; and fate always finds some means of deposing a genius." Assertions of this kind were really unjust to the new world champion. Admittedly Euwe's tournament results were not up to those of Alekhin. On the other hand, Euwe was at the height of his chess career. In addition, he displayed a remarkably thorough knowledge of chess strategy and showed wonderful perseverance and great will-power. The main reason for Alekhin's defeat, however, was the hectic life he was leading at the time. Prior to the match he paid no attention to his physical condition. He took part in the Warsaw Olympiad in August before doing a tour of the Baltic states. Then he played in Paris on 15 September. This explains the uneven course of the match, which began on 3 October.

In the first seven rounds Alekhin won four times and his opponent only once. No one at the time believed that a reversal was possible. But that is what happened, the next seven games going exactly the other way, so that the match was all square at the end of the fourteenth round. After that the world champion used all his powers and won the sixteenth and nineteenth games. But then he dropped two, the second with White after an unbelievably poor performance. There followed three draws and then another defeat for Alekhin, again with White. He incorrectly sacrificed three pawns in the opening, but his attacking chances came to nothing as a result of a simple tactical counter on Euwe's part. The match was to be played over thirty games and it seemed clear that another defeat would really be the end for Alekhin when the two rivals met for the 26th game on 3 December.

Dutch Defence

Euwe	Alekhin
1 P-Q4	P-K3
2 P-QB4	P-KB4

In the situation Alekhin's choice of opening was tactically unwise. He still had two more games with White, so the usual match tactics were called for: playing solidly with Black and making the winning attempts with White. The world champion, however, had obviously underestimated his opponent right from the start and was now all out to get revenge for the reverses he had suffered. A single win leading to a drawn match was not enough for him.

3	P-KN3	B-N5ch
4	B-Q2	B-K2
5	B-N2	N-KB3
6	N-QB3	0-0
7	N-B3	N-K5

Alekhin was very fond of this knight sortie, adopting it also after a different order of moves. Today it is considered unfavourable, for White can continue with 8 P-Q5! followed by Q-B2, forcing the exchange of the knight and maintaining superiority in the centre.

8	0-0	P-QN3

In the 24th game Alekhin had played 8 . . . B-B3 and had attained an advantage as a result of faulty play by his opponent: 9 NxN? PxN 10 N-K1 BxP 11 BxP BxNP! 12 BxRPch KxB 13 Q-B2ch K-N1 14 QxB N-B3. Instead White should have replied with the quiet 9 Q-B2 or the more aggressive 9 P-Q5!, which is very strong in this position.

9	Q-B2	B-N2
10	N-K5	NxN!

This leads to full equality, since White dare not attempt to win the exchange: 11 BxB? NxKPch 12 K-R1 NxQP 13 Q-Q3 QN-B3 14 BxR QxB, etc.

11	BxN	BxB
12	KxB	Q-B1
13	P-Q5	P-Q3
14	N-Q3	P-K4
15	K-R1	P-B3

Threatening 16 . . . PxP 17 PxP Q-B5. White's delay in making the advance P-Q5 means that he fails to secure an advantage.

16	Q-N3	K-R1

More logical is 16 . . . P-B4 to avoid wasting time.

17	P-B4	P-K5
18	N-N4	P-B4
19	N-B2	N-Q2

The immediate B-B3 is safer, e.g. 19 . . . B-B3 20 BxB RxB 21 N-K3 R-B2 followed by N-Q2-B3.

20	N-K3	B-B3!?

If 20 . . . N-B3, White would have a positional advantage thanks to his strong bishop. Black therefore tries to exchange off this piece. There is, however, a snag: White is given the opportunity to make a dangerous piece sacrifice.

76. Euwe–Alekhin

21 NxP!

This sacrifice is no great risk. For the piece White gets three pawns, whose elimination will eventually cost Black material.

21	...	BxB
22	NxQP	Q-N1
23	NxP	B-B3
24	N-Q2	P-KN4!

An excellent move! To offset the advance of White's central pawns, Black requires counter-play, and this is only possible on the king's wing.

25	P-K4	PxP
26	PxP	B-Q5
27	P-K5	Q-K1
28	P-K6	R-KN1!

White must not take Black's counter-play on the KN file too lightly. The reply 29 PxN? is answered by 29 . . . Q-K7.

29 N-B3(?)

This should lead to a more or less forced draw. Instead 29 Q-KR3! would set Black an extremely difficult task in stopping the united passed pawns.

29 ...	Q-N3
30 R-KN1	BxR
31 RxB	

77. Euwe–Alekhin

| 31 ... | Q-B3? |

Why Alekhin made this losing move is difficult to explain. After the correct 31 ... Q-B4! 32 PxN RxRch 33 KxR QxP(Q2) 34 K-B2 Q-KN2 he would have had nothing to fear. The important difference between the two queen moves is that, after 31 ... Q-B4!, White cannot reply 32 N-N5? on account of 32 ... P-KR3! (32 ... RxN 33 PxR Q-K5ch would give Black a draw, but there is more than that in it for him) 33 N-B7ch K-R2, leaving Black a rook up. It is probable that Alekhin either failed to see White's reply or underestimated it and assumed that the position justified an attempt to play for a win. The reason for such a bad mistake is certainly a psychological one, for the tactical consequences of 31 ... Q-B4 are easy to see.

32 N-N5!   R-N2

If 32 ... P-KR3?, White can finish the game off prettily by 33 N-B7ch K-R2 34 Q-Q3ch R-N3 35 N-K5! NxN 36 PxN Q-N2 37 P-Q6 R-KN1 38 QxRch QxQ 39 RxQ KxR 40 P-Q7. The exchange sacri-

fice on KN4 does not save the game for Black either, e.g. 32 ... RxN? 33 PxR Q-K4 34 Q-QB3!, and White has an easily won endgame thanks to his united passed pawns.

| 33 PxN | RxP |
| 34 Q-K3 | |

Black has a difficult defence. He cannot, for example, take the QNP, for after 34 ... QxNP 35 Q-K5ch (better than 35 Q-K6 Q-N2 36 N-B7ch RxN! 37 RxQ RxR) 35 ... QxQ 36 PxQ White's united passed pawns cannot be stopped.

| 34 ... | R-K2 |
| 35 N-K6 | R-KB1 |

Again the QNP cannot be taken: 35 ... QxNP 36 P-Q6 R-Q2 37 N-N5, threatening 38 Q-K6 or 38 Q-K5ch. When the endgame is reached the QNP will not be of any great importance. The decisive factor will be whether Black will have enough time to stop the passed pawns.

36 Q-K5!

The clearest way to victory. If 36 P-N3 or 36 Q-KN3, White would have the better position, though the situation would be less clear cut.

| 36 ... | QxQ |
| 37 PxQ | R-B4 |

Here Black could have tried to save himself by going into a rook ending by 37 ... RxN 38 PxR R-B4 39 R-K1 K-N1 40 R-K3 K-B1. If White then continues with 41 R-QR3?, Black has drawing chances with 41 ... RxP 42 RxP R-K8ch 43 K-N2 R-K7ch 44 K-N3 RxNP.

However, White has a stronger line in 41 K-N2! K-K2 42 R-QR3 RxP 43 RxPch KxP 44 K-B3 R-R4 45 R-QN7, etc.

38 R-K1

There is also a win by 38 R-N5 RxR 39 NxR K-N2 40 P-K6 K-B3 41 N-K4ch K-K4 42 P-Q6! etc.

| 38 ... | P-KR3 |

Both sides were in dire time-trouble and did not even give RxN a thought. After 38 ... K-N1, the simplest way to win is 39 R-KN1ch K-R1 40 R-N5.

| 39 | N-Q8! | R-B7 |
| 40 | P-K6 | R-Q7 |

41	N-B6	R-K1
42	P-K7	P-N4
43	N-Q8!	K-N2
44	N-N7	K-B3
45	R-K6ch	K-N4
46	N-Q6	RxKP
47	N-K4ch!	Resigns

24 AVRO Tournament 1938

Fine's Poor Second Half

The idea of getting the world's greatest chess players together in a single tournament is an old one. Many tournament organizers have done their best to put it into effect. But whether it was St Petersburg 1909, San Sebastián 1911 or Semmering-Baden 1937, there were always some of the top stars missing. The first complete success was achieved by the AVRO broadcasting corporation, which organized a tournament that was played in several Dutch towns. All the top grandmasters, including the world champion, Alekhin, took part. The chess world saw it as the first candidates tournament for the world championship. It was generally expected that there would be a title match between the winner (or number two if Alekhin should win) and the world champion.

The tournament was a double-round one, and in the case of a tie the winner was to be determined by the Sonneborn-Berger System. The American grandmaster Fine had a brilliant start. He defeated Botvinnik in the first round and Reshevsky, with Black, in the second. Then, after drawing with Capablanca in a dramatic game, he produced a fine positional performance to defeat Euwe. He followed this up with victories over Flohr, in impressive combinational style, and Alekhin, against whom he had Black in the sixth round.

Keres started much more modestly, drawing his first three games. Then, however, he exploited an opening error to win against Reshevsky, and after a draw with Alekhin he won in excellent style against Capablanca. Nevertheless the position after the sixth round seemed fairly clear

cut: Fine 5½, Keres 4, Alekhin and Botvinnik 3. In the last round of the first half the two leaders came face to face. As Fine had White it was not expected that there would be any great change in the table.

Keres's great knowledge of opening theory—in this case the Ruy Lopez—proved to be an asset, and the game soon reached the endgame stage, where White's weakened pawns were compensated for by possession of the two bishops.

78. Fine–Keres

Position after White's 25th move

25 ...	NxQP

This leads to great complications, which White should avoid. Instead 26 NxQP BxN 27 BxN would give him a draw, for 27 ... NxP is not possible on account of 28 R-N2.

26 N-Q4?

Fine trusts that the threat 27 RxB KxR 28 N-B6ch will see him through, but Keres has calculated further.

26 ...	N-N5
27 B-Q2	

Not good is 27 NxP on account of 27
... B-B3 followed by P-Q4. After the
text-move it looks as if Black has no
adequate defence to 28 BxN RxB 29
N-B6. The point of Black's whole manoeuvre, however, rests on a pretty
exchange sacrifice.

27 ...	P-Q4!
28 BxN	RxB
29 N-B6	PxB
30 NxR	PxP
31 N-Q5	N-Q6!
32 R-Q2	P-N7
33 R-Q1	P-B4
34 R-QN1	P-B5
35 K-B1	B-B4

Winning the third pawn, which virtually decides the game.

36 K-K2	BxP
37 N-K3	P-B6!
38 N-B2	

If 38 KxN, then 38 ... BxN 39 KxP
B-B8.

38 ...	N-K8!
39 N-R3	

If 39 NxN, then 39 ... BxN 40 K-Q3
B-Q7.

39 ...	B-B4
40 KxN	BxN
41 K-Q1	B-Q3
42 K-B2	BxP
43 R-KR1	B-K4
44 RxP	K-B2
45 R-R1	P-N4
46 R-K1	K-B3
47 R-KN1	K-N3
48 R-K1	B-B3
49 R-KN1	P-N5!
50 PxP	P-B5
51 P-N5	B-Q5
52 R-Q1	B-K6
53 KxBP	B-B8
54 R-Q6ch	KxP
55 R-QN6	P-B6

56 K-Q3	K-B5
57 R-N8	K-N6
58 Resigns	

The second half produced some surprises. Keres played extremely cautiously
and drew all his games. The leader,
Fine, seemed to have lost his form
completely. After a draw against
Botvinnik in the ninth round he ran into
difficulties in a game where he had White
against Reshevsky. He also got into time-
trouble and had to make twelve moves in
three minutes. Although he succeeded in
reaching the time control, even improving
his position considerably into the bargain,
he again became very short of time before
the next time control and had to make
eight moves in one minute. On this
occasion he was not so successful and
exceeded the time in a drawn position on
his 55th move, with one more move to
go. He then had an interesting draw with
Capablanca, but in his game with Euwe
he suffered another unnecessary loss—
again with the White pieces—this time
owing to an error in the opening. As a
result he lost his lead. In the next round
he had a quick draw with Flohr, but only
managed to stay in second place because
Botvinnik, in a good position, blundered
against Euwe and lost. Two rounds before
the end the leading scores were Keres 7½,
Fine 7, Alekhin and Botvinnik 6½.

The dramatic penultimate round virtually decided the tournament. Here

79. Capablanca–Keres

Position after Black's 36th move

Keres was lucky to escape with half a point.

White can win here by 37 N-K8!, for Black cannot effectively defend his QP, e.g. 37 ... B-B8dis ch 38 K-B3 R-N4 39 R-Q8 or 37 ... B-R4dis ch 38 K-B3 R-N4 39 N-Q6. Capablanca, however, went after a less important pawn.

| 37 NxP? | PxP |
| 38 N-K5 | |

Or 38 PxP B-B8dis ch 39 K-B3 R-KR7.

38 ...	B-B8dis ch
39 K-Q3	R-Q7ch
40 K-B3	R-KN7
41 PxP	BxP
42 R-R7ch	

Drawn

This gift of half a point proved to be very valuable to Keres, for his rival Fine was in very aggressive form in the same round.

Ruy Lopez

Fine	Alekhin
1 P-K4	P-K4
2 N-KB3	N-QB3
3 B-N5	P-QR3
4 B-R4	P-Q3
5 0-0	

This natural developing move is now considered to be the best continuation. But first the theoreticians had to show that the reply 5 ... B-N5 6 P-KR3 P-KR4!? need not be feared on account of 7 P-Q4 or 7 P-B4.

| 5 ... | B-Q2 |
| 6 P-B3 | |

The gambit 6 P-Q4 is best replied to by the solid 6 ... N-B3, for 6 ... P-QN4 7 B-N3 NxP 8 NxN PxN 9 P-B3 PxP 10 Q-R5 or 9 ... P-Q6 10 P-QR4! is good for White.

| 6 ... | P-KN3 |
| 7 P-Q4 | B-N2 |

| 8 PxP | NxP(?) |

As a result of this game, taking by the knight is considered weaker than 8 ... PxP.

| 9 NxN | PxN |
| 10 P-KB4! | BxB |

In some books of instruction 10 ... B-N4 is recommended, but then 11 BxBch PxB 12 Q-N3 is unpleasant.

11 QxBch	Q-Q2
12 QxQch	KxQ
13 PxP	K-K3
14 B-B4	R-KB1

Black must not delay recapturing the pawn even if it involves this unnatural-looking move, for otherwise White could use the manoeuvre 15 N-Q2-B3, after which it is no easy matter to get the pawn back.

15 N-Q2	BxP
16 N-N3	BxB
17 RxB	P-N3

80. Fine–Alekhin

At first sight, Black's position appears to be quite sound and White's KP somewhat weak. However, White has pressure on the KB file and is ahead in development.

| 18 P-QR4! | K-K4? |

The king is more exposed here than on K3. Black should instead have prevented the threatened advance P-QR5 by playing

18 ... P-QR4. He gets his last suitable opportunity to do this on the next move.

19 P-N3   N-B3

By attacking the KP Black develops with a gain of tempo, but he combines this with a faulty plan.

20 N-Q2!   N-R4?

After this decentralization of the knight the game is lost. A much better continuation is 20 ... N-Q2, which enables Black to consolidate his position. It is possible that Alekhin was afraid of 21 QR-KB1 K-K3 22 N-B3 P-KB3 23 P-K5!?, though this would probably only lead to a draw: 23 ... NxP 24 NxN KxN 25 R-K1ch K-Q4 26 R-Q4ch K-B3 27 R-K7 P-QN4.

21 R-B2!

This quiet retreat is much better than 21 N-B3ch K-K3 22 N-N5ch K-K2.

21 ...	K-K3
22 P-R5	R-R1

Or 22 ... P-QN4 23 N-N3, threatening N-B5ch.

23 QR-KB1	KR-Q1
24 N-B3	K-K2

If 24 ... P-KB3, then 25 N-Q4ch K-Q2 (or B2) 26 P-KN4.

25 PxP	PxP
26 N-N5	P-R3

Black would lose even more quickly by 26 ... P-B3 27 NxRP R-Q3 28 P-K5! PxP 29 R-B7ch.

27 RxPch	K-Q3
28 N-B3	P-KN4
29 N-Q4	R-K1
30 R-KR7	R-R1
31 R(B1)-B7	RxR
32 RxR	R-KB1
33 RxPch	N-B3
34 N-B3	K-B4
35 N-Q2	P-N5
36 R-N6	N-Q2
37 RxKNP	N-K4
38 R-N5	K-Q3
39 R-B5	R-Q1
40 N-B3	N-Q6
41 R-Q5ch	K-K2
42 RxR	KxR
43 P-N3	K-K2
44 N-Q2	P-R4
45 K-B1	P-N4
46 K-K2	Resigns

The last round did not change the order in the table, for the game Keres–Fine ended in a draw on the nineteenth move. These two were thus equal in points, but Keres had the better Sonnenborn–Berger count and so emerged as victor. A short time later he challenged Alekhin to a world championship match, an event which never took place because of the war. In the post-war period Keres continued to strive for the highest trophy but without success. In the candidates tournaments he always played the role of a crown prince.

AVRO Tournament 1938

		1	2	3	4	5	6	7	8	Pts	Prize
1	Fine	– –	0 ½	1 ½	1 1	1 0	1 0	½ ½	1 ½	8½	I, II
2	Keres	1 ½	– –	½ ½	½ ½	½ ½	1 ½	1 ½	½ ½	8½	I, II
3	Botvinnik	0 ½	½ ½	– –	1 ½	½ 0	1 ½	½ 1	½ ½	7½	III
4	Alekhin	0 0	½ ½	0 ½	– –	1 ½	½ ½	½ 1	½ 1	7	IV
5	Euwe	0 1	½ ½	½ 1	0 ½	– –	0 ½	0 1	1 ½	7	IV
6	Reshevsky	0 1	0 ½	0 ½	½ ½	1 ½	– –	½ ½	1 ½	7	IV
7	Capablanca	½ ½	0 ½	½ 0	½ 0	1 0	½ ½	– –	½ 1	6	
8	Flohr	0 ½	½ ½	½ ½	½ 0	0 ½	0 ½	½ 0	– –	4½	

25 Prague 1942

Alekhin Announces Mate in Seven

The Duras Masters Tournament, played in Prague in December 1942, was the first big chess event I had ever watched. At that time I had no inkling of the fact that I myself would be taking part in a major tournament some four months later—and if I had, I wouldn't really have believed it. But to return to the matter in question. My visit to the tournament hall filled me with awe and a deep feeling of satisfaction, even though in my worn-out suit and experiencing pangs of hunger I did not quite feel at my best.

After a certain time the awe and the shyness of a person from the provinces visiting the capital were forgotten. In fact, at one stage I was so vociferous in expressing my feelings that I received a friendly, though energetic, warning from the chief organizer, Mr Kende. This occurred during a game which created an atmosphere of tense excitement in the hall and which, for all those present, had an importance going far beyond the field of chess.

Seated at the board were the world champion, A. Alekhin, and the nineteen-year-old German champion, Klaus Junge. At that time I had already heard some very unfavourable stories about Alekhin's past and present way of life. He drank a lot, he was difficult to get on with, he was irritable, he tortured the organizers in every tournament, and he was brusque to the spectators. His opponent, a tall, slender youth with sincere eyes who, at the age of nineteen, had already attained a higher level of play than many present-day grandmasters, was a modest and likeable person.

There can be no doubt on whose side

the public would have been in normal circumstances. But the circumstances were not normal. There was fighting going on near Stalingrad and the news from there was beginning to fill us with optimism. My brother was still in a concentration camp after three years, and I had already been subjected to interrogation by the Gestapo. For more than four hours I watched the slender youth, the feelings of a chess player attracting me to him. At the same time I knew he was the symbol of something I could never like. Such feelings were shared by the great majority of the spectators, feelings that expressed themselves in a rather naïve form of pan-Slavism. For us Alekhin was neither the world champion nor an emigré. Nor was he a person enjoying the protection of the rulers of this part of the world. He was first and foremost a Slav and therefore one of us.

It was a key game, played in the last round, Alekhin having White. Junge was in the lead with 8½ points from 12 games; Alekhin had one point less, so the scene had been wonderfully set for this last-round game, which was later awarded a brilliancy prize. When news got around that Alekhin had announced mate in seven, I forgot my awe of the masters and began to recite the mating variation to the spectators around me. Today I do not know whether I got it right or not, but in the excited atmosphere prevailing that was of no great importance.

Catalan System

Alekhin	Junge
1 P-Q4	P-Q4

2 P-QB4	P-K3
3 N-KB3	N-KB3
4 P-KN3	

In this form the Catalan System has now almost completely disappeared from tournament play. There are several ways of equalizing, one of which is used by Junge, who at that time was already an expert on theory. Black has a more difficult task after 1 P-QB4 P-K3 2 P-KN3 P-Q4 3 B-N2.

4 ...	PxP
5 Q-R4ch	QN-Q2

If White had played B-KN2 instead of N-KB3, he could continue 6 QxBP P-QR3 7 Q-B2, after which Black would have some difficulty in developing his bishop to QN2. His best course would then be 7 ... P-B4 8 N-KB3 P-QN3!

6 B-N2	P-QR3
7 QxBP	P-QN4
8 Q-B6	

It is part of Alekhin's plan to get his opponent's rook to QN1, though it is by no means certain that the rook is not better off there than on QR1. After the usual 8 Q-B2 B-N2 9 P-QR4, both 9 ... P-B4 and 9 ... P-QN5 are possible.

8 ...	R-QN1

At Nottingham in 1936 against Capablanca, Reshevsky played 8 ... R-R2, which is a less natural, though a quite satisfactory, move.

9 0-0	

The aggressive 9 B-B4 need not worry Black. In the game Szabó-Geller (Candidates Tournament 1953) the game was quickly equalized: 9 ... N-Q4 10 B-N5 B-K2 11 BxB QxB 12 0-0 B-N2 13 Q-B2 P-QB4.

9 ...	B-N2
10 Q-B2	P-B4
11 P-QR4!	

81. Alekhin–Junge

White's last move is the only way of trying to seize the initiative. It is interesting to read Alekhin's notes on it and White's eighth move, Q-B6: "White continues his plan. The fact that he thereby loses a pawn need not worry him for the following reasons: (1) From the positional point of view White has more than adequate compensation in the bishop pair, the weak white squares in the opponent's position and the open QR file. (2) From the psychological point of view it was certainly not wrong to tempt my opponent to pick up material in this decisive game. A disturbance of material equality often mentally upsets the 'fortunate' possessor of the extra material."

These are certainly interesting comments both from the strategical and psychological point of view. Alekhin, however, did not mention the possibility of his opponent declining the sacrifice. Four months later the same variation occurred in a game Thelen–Foltys, when the latter played 11 ... Q-N3! 12 PxNP PxNP and got a satisfactory position.

An experienced grandmaster would have declined the sacrifice in Junge's position. But the very talented youth had confidence in his ability and did not fear complications.

11 ...	BxN
12 BxB	PxQP
13 PxP	PxP
14 R-Q1	Q-N3

It would be bad to defend the pawn by 14 ... B-B4 on account of 15 B-B4!

P-K4 (15 ... R-QB1 16 B-N7 or 15 ...
R-N3 16 P-QN4 BxP 17 B-B7 and White
wins the exchange) 16 BxKP NxB 17
QxB NxBch 18 PxN, when Black has
nothing better than to let the pawn go by
18 ... Q-K2.

15 N-Q2	P-K4
16 N-N3	N-B4!?

Whether by design or oversight, Black
allows a dangerous exchange sacrifice.
However, it is unjust to call the move a
mistake, for normal development would
leave White with considerable pressure,
e.g. 16 ... B-K2 17 P-K3 PxP 18 BxP
Q-K3 19 B-R7 R-Q1 20 N-R5 or 16 ...
B-B4 17 B-N5! and Black cannot play 17
... QR-B1? on account of 18 R(Q1)-QB1
0-0 19 BxN followed by 20 B-N4.

17 NxN	BxN

If Black takes with the queen, White
can recover the pawn and retain the two
bishops: 17 ... QxN 18 B-B6ch K-Q1 19
QxQ BxQ 20 BxP. Alekhin, however, had
a different plan, involving a piece sacrifice: 17 ... QxN 18 B-B6ch K-Q1 19
Q-KB5! QxB 20 QxKP with a decisive
attack, e.g.
(i) 20 ... B-Q3 21 RxP R-N3 (21 ...
K-B2 22 RxB! QxR 23 R-R7ch) 22 B-B4
N-K1 (22 ... K-Q2 23 Q-KB5ch followed
by 24 RxB) 23 R-R7! K-B1 (23 ... R-N2
24 R-R8ch K-B2 25 RxB) 24 Q-KB5ch
and 25 QxBP.
(ii) 20 ... N-Q2 21 RxP R-B1 22
B-Q2! P-N5 (22 ... B-B4 23 B-R5ch
B-N3 24 RxNch KxR 25 R-Q1ch) 23
R-QB1 QxRch (23 ... Q-N2 24 RxRch
QxR 25 B-N5ch P-B3 26 BxPch) 24 BxQ
RxBch 25 K-N2 R-B2 26 Q-Q5 winning.

18 R-R6!	QxR
19 QxB	Q-K3!

The only move. 19 ... N-Q2 loses, e.g.
20 B-B6 P-B3 21 Q-Q6 or 20 ... QR-B1 21
QxKPch K-Q1 22 BxN KxB 23 RxPch.

20 B-B6ch	N-Q2
21 BxNch	KxB
22 Q-R7ch	

82. Alekhin–Junge

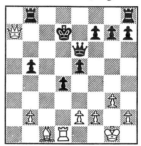

22 ...	K-B3?

22 ... K-B1 also loses at once, for
there is no defence to 23 B-N5!, threatening 24 R-QB1ch. But there is a stronger
move in 22 ... K-Q3!, which Junge
rejected because of 23 B-B4. However, as
Alekhin pointed out after the game, the
impressive 23 B-B4 only leads to a draw:
23 ... PxB 24 RxPch K-B3! 25 R-Q1
KR-QB1 (25 ... R-N3 26 R-QB1ch K-Q4
27 Q-B7!) 26 R-QB1ch K-Q4 27 R-Q1ch
with perpetual check. Nevertheless
Alekhin, in his annotations, called this
drawing variation White's best line,
though it can safely be assumed that in
the event he would have chosen something different, for a draw would have
been tantamount to failure. (Foltys, who
occupied third place, was 1½ points
behind). He would certainly have looked
for a way of strengthening his attack. The
continuation 23 B-Q2? Q-Q2! 24 B-N4ch
K-K3 25 Q-R6ch K-B4 is inadequate,
since the Black king, although in a strange
location, is quite safe. There is more to be
hoped for from 23 P-B4. Black then loses
if he continues with 23 ... P-B3? 24
PxPch PxP 25 B-B4! PxB 26 QxQPch!
K-K2 (without the moves 23 P-B4 P-B3?
Black's king would be quite safe on K2;
as it is Black is lost) 27 QxNPch Q-B2 28
R-Q7ch. In this line other king moves are

no better, e.g. 26 . . . K-B2 27 Q-R7ch K-B3 28 R-QB1ch or 26 . . . K-B3 27 R-QB1ch K-N2 28 QxNPch.

Going back a little, however, Black has another reply to 23 P-KB4, viz. 23 . . . Q-Q2!, e.g. 24 PxPch K-K3 25 Q-R6ch K-K2 26 B-N5ch K-K1, and the king is out of danger, though Black will still have difficulty in consolidating his position. This last line is probably the way the game would have gone if Junge had made the correct decision at the critical moment.

23 B-Q2 KR-QB1

Black had been relying on this, but had overlooked White's quiet reply. However, after the mistake on the previous move there is no way of saving the game, e.g.

(i) 23 . . . Q-Q2 24 R-QB1ch K-Q3 25 B-N4ch K-K3 26 R-B7 Q-Q4 27 RxP.

(ii) 23 . . . K-Q4 24 P-B3! Q-Q3 25 QxBPch K-B3 26 B-R5!

(iii) 23 . . . KR-Q1 24 R-QB1ch (or 24 P-K4) 24 . . . K-Q4 25 R-B5ch K-K5 26 P-B3ch K-B4 27 R-B6! QxR 28 QxBPch Q-KB3 29 P-KN4 mate.

Anyone who is interested can find a number of other mating patterns.

24 P-K4

Quite simple, but such simple moves are easily overlooked, especially when there are a number of threats to be parried. Black's king is prevented from retreating and there is the terrible threat of 25 R-B1ch. If now 24 . . . PxP e.p., then 25 BxP P-N5 26 Q-B5ch K-N2 27 R-Q7ch! QxR 28 Q-N6ch K-R1 29 Q-QR6ch, and if Black instead tries to escape by 24 . . . P-N5 there follows 25 R-R1! R-N3 26 P-N3! QxP 27 R-QB1ch K-N4 28 RxR Q-Q8ch 29 K-N2 QxB 30 Q-Q7ch, winning.

24 . . . Q-N6
25 R-R1 P-N5

There is no adequate defence to 26 R-R6ch. In his notes, Alekhin gives a pretty counter to 25 . . . R-N3, viz. 26 B-R5 R(N3)-N1 27 B-Q8! but does not mention the simple 26 R-QB1ch. After the text-move Alekhin announced mate in seven.

26 R-R6ch K-N4
27 R-R5ch K-B3
28 Q-B5ch K-Q2
29 R-R7ch Resigns

Prague 1942

	1	2	3	4	5	6	7	8	9	10	11	12	Pts	Prize
1 Alekhin	–	1	½	1	½	1	½	1	1	½	½	1	8½	I, II
2 Junge	0	–	½	½	1	1	1	1	½	1	1	1	8½	I, II
3 Foltys	½	½	–	0	½	1	½	1	½	1	½	1	7	III
4 Opočensky	0	½	1	–	0	0	1	1	1	½	½	1	6½	IV, V
5 Zita	½	0	½	1	–	½	0	½	½	1	1	1	6½	IV, V
6 Kottnauer	0	0	0	1	½	–	0	1	1	1	½	1	6	VI
7 Rejfir	½	0	½	0	1	1	–	0	1	½	1	0	5½	
8 Hromádka	0	0	0	0	½	0	1	–	½	½	½	1	4	
9 Podgorny	0	½	½	0	½	0	0	½	–	0	1	1	4	
10 Thelen	½	0	0	½	0	0	½	½	1	–	½	½	4	
11 Sämisch	½	0	½	½	0	½	0	½	0	½	–	0	3	
12 Prokop	0	0	0	0	0	0	1	0	0	½	1	–	2½	

26 Groningen 1946
Defeat of the Two Leaders

The chess world had been without a champion for about six months, the previous title-holder having died while still in possession of his title—the only world champion to do so. While his departure put an end to speculation about his chess future and his non-chess exploits, it left unsolved the question of who was to ascend the vacant throne. The Dutch Federation claimed the title for their representative, Dr Euwe, on the grounds that he had at least temporarily taken the title from Alekhin and that he had been the last to play a match with him. However, although Euwe was at the height of his chess powers, there were a number of others who were at least as well qualified as he was. The almost unanimous opinion of the chess world was, therefore, that the title should be fought for. The first tournament of the élite to help throw light on the question of determining the future champion took place at Groningen, Holland, in August and September 1946.

The tournament could not boast of the participation of all the top players, for the American grandmasters Reshevsky and Fine (the latter having virtually retired from active chess) were missing. So too was the winner of the 1938 AVRO Tournament, Keres, who at the time was not taking part in international tournaments.

The struggle for first place was confined to two players. After the thirteenth round Botvinnik was in the lead with 11½ points, one point ahead of Dr Euwe. Next came Smyslov and Szabó with 8½ points, but both of them were virtually out of the running. In the fourteenth round

Euwe had quite a bit of luck and as a result managed to win his game against the oldest competitor, the 65-year-old Dr Bernstein.

83. Bernstein–Euwe

Position after Black's 36th move

37 P-QR4??

One of those inexplicable psychological mysteries that influence the result of nearly every tournament. After a waiting move the game would be drawn. The following continuation would also lead to a draw: 37 N-B5ch K-Q4 38 N-N7 P-R5 39 PxP BxP 40 N-R5.

37 ...	BxN
38 KxB	K-Q4
39 P-QN4	

Bernstein had based his original calculations on 39 K-B3 K-B4? 40 P-QN4ch PxPch 41 K-N3 P-B4 42 P-R5 P-K5 43 PxP PxP 44 P-R6 K-N3 45 KxP, but then he realized that 39 K-B3 loses to 39 ... P-B4! 40 P-QN4 PxPch 41 KxP K-Q5!, for although White pushes his pawn through first, his opponent does so with check and then wins White's queen.

39 ...	PxP
40 P-R5	P-B4

41 P-R6	P-K5ch
42 PxP	PxPch
43 K-K3	K-B3
44 KxP	K-N3
45 K-Q3	KxP

and Black wins.

Botvinnik had White against Kotov and unexpectedly departed from his own system. After 1 P-Q4 N-KB3 2 P-QB4 P-K3 3 N-QB3 B-N5 4 P-QR3 BxNch 5 PxB P-Q4 6 PxP PxP he played 7 B-N5 instead of 7 P-K3, and later got into a strategically lost position.

84. Botvinnik–Kotov

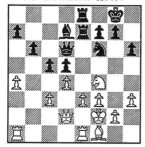

Position after White's 20th move

20 ...	P-B5!

This threatens P-KN4, winning the KP. Curiously enough White has no satisfactory defence; e.g. 21 P-N3 P-KN4 22 N-N2 N-R4! 23 P-B4 N-B3 followed by BxKRP.

21 P-N4	P-KN4
22 N-K2	

Or 22 N-N2 Q-R7 23 B-K2 RxP!

22 ...	RxP!
23 N-N3?	

White would lose even quicker by 23 N-N1 N-K5ch! 24 PxN Q-N6 mate. The relatively best defence is 23 QxR Q-R7ch 24 B-N2 RxQ 25 KxR QxB 26 R-R1, though in this case Black would have little difficulty in parrying the threatened QR-KN1, e.g. 26 ... N-K5! 27 PxN QxKPch.

23 ...	QxNch!
24 KxQ	N-K5ch
25 Resigns	

Euwe had thus caught up with Botvinnik. In the next round he even went ahead by a full point. He defeated Dr Vidmar in a well-played positional game, while his rival, Botvinnik lost his second consecutive game, and this time quite unnecessarily.

85. Yanofsky–Botvinnik

Position after White's 34th move

Black has a distinct positional advantage thanks to his opponent's weak QNP and QP. He should now continue with 34 ... R-N1 or B-QN4. Instead he unaccountably takes the QNP at once and allows his opponent to get a decisive pin on his knight.

34 ...	NxP?
35 R-K2!	B-R4?

This second mistake loses the game. The correct line is 35 ... R-B8ch! 36 QxR NxB, when Black's two bishops and consolidated position should ensure a draw.

36 R-N2	R-QN1

Black would get more practical chances by 36 ... Q-N3! 37 N-B2 R-QN1 38 N-Q2 NxB! 39 RxQ RxR (but not 39 ... BxR 40 N-K3! NxP? 41 N(Q2)-B4! B-R2 42 Q-B2 winning) 40 Q-Q1 BxN 41 QxB N-B5.

37	N-Q2!	Q-R2
38	N(Q2)-B4	Q-B4
39	NxB	QxN(R4)
40	N-B2	NxB

Now Black has to give up the exchange in much less favourable circumstances than on move 35.

41	RxRch	K-N2
42	N-K3	Q-Q7
43	Q-KB1	N-B4
44	Q-Q1	Q-B6?

In view of his weak QP Black's position is untenable. But he could have put up more resistance by exchanging queens. As it is, White gets a direct king-side attack.

45	R-N6	B-R5
46	Q-B3	Q-K8ch
47	K-R2	P-B4
48	RxP	

White could have gone in for a knight sacrifice here, e.g. 48 NxPch! PxN 49 Q-KN3ch K-B2 50 Q-R4!.

48	...	P-B5
49	N-B5ch!	

The knight sacrifice is even stronger now. If Black accepts he loses quickly: 49 ... PxN 50 Q-R5 N-Q2 51 Q-R6ch K-B2 52 Q-K6ch K-N2 53 Q-K7ch K-N1 54 R-QR6.

49	...	K-B2
50	Q-N4	N-K5

There is no defence to the threat of 51 Q-R4, e.g. 50 ... Q-K5 51 Q-R4! QxN 52 QxRPch K-K1 53 RxP.

51	Q-R4!	PxN
52	QxRPch	K-K1
53	Q-N8ch	Resigns

With four rounds to go Euwe was thus a full point ahead. This lead was reduced in the next round, however, when he drew with Stoltz after being on the verge of defeat and Botvinnik won against Kottnauer from a drawn position. As a result of two victories in the next two rounds (against Christoffel and Guimard) Botvinnik caught up with and overtook Euwe, who had in the meantime drawn with Flohr and Tartakower. When the last round began Botvinnik thus had a lead of half a point. Both players had equally difficult tasks; they both had Black and their opponents were of the same strength. That round, played on 7 September, proved to be the sensation of the whole tournament.

Nimzo-Indian

Najdorf	Botvinnik
1 P-Q4	P-K3
2 P-QB4	N-KB3
3 N-QB3	B-N5
4 Q-B2	P-Q4
5 PxP	PxP
6 P-QR3	

Najdorf's innovation, which should scarcely cause Black any real trouble. But the usual continuation, 6 B-N5 P-KR3 7 BxN (7 B-R4 P-B4) 7 ... QxB, only holds out a very slight chance of maintaining the initiative.

6	...	BxNch
7	PxB	P-B4
8	N-B3	Q-R4

A comfortable way of getting a satisfactory game is 8 ... Q-B2 9 Q-N2 P-QN3 followed by B-R3.

9	N-Q2	B-Q2
10	N-N3	Q-R5
11	Q-N2	N-R3
12	P-K3	P-B5

A double-edged move that leads to a strategically difficult position. It is surprising that Botvinnik should choose such a line in a game where, in all probability, a draw would have been sufficient to ensure first prize. In the tournament book Euwe recommended 12 ... PxP 13 BPxP P-QN3, when Black equalizes because he has recourse to the manoeuvre N-B2 and B-N4. Another way of equalizing is 12 ... P-QN3 13 BxN QxB 14 PxP 0-0 followed by KR-QB1. Here the pawn is of no importance, for Black is wonderfully developed. Both the above continuations are not only better, but also more logical, than the line chosen by Botvinnik.

13	N-Q2	0-0
14	B-K2	P-QN4
15	B-Q1	Q-R4
16	B-B2	KR-K1
17	0-0	QR-N1!

86. Najdorf–Botvinnik

18 N-B3

The natural plan for White is to push forward in the centre by P-KB3 and P-K4. One way of preparing the thrust is 18 R-K1, but this has the disadvantage that White gets behind in development; e.g. 18 ... R-K2 19 P-B3 QR-K1 20 P-K4 B-B4! 21 P-K5 BxB 22 QxB P-N5! and Black has an excellent game. An interesting line is 18 P-B3!? If Black replies 18 ... RxP, White must not continue 19 NxP? on account of 19 ... PxN! (made possible by Black's 17 ... QR-N1). He has, however, a much stronger continuation in 19 N-K4! NxN! 20 BxR NxP, when Black has two pawns for the exchange but has the disadvantage that his knight on QR3 is not particularly well placed. In this position White must not continue with 21 B-Q2? N-K7ch 22 K-R1 P-B6! (but not

22 ... QxB?? 23 BxPch!), which gives Black a second piece for his rook. (Deviating with 22 K-B2 would not help in this line, for 22 ... P-B6 23 Q-N1 NxP 24 BxRPch K-R1 25 B-K3 N-K3 followed by P-Q5 then leaves Black with united passed pawns, which should decide the game.) The best continuation for White is 21 KR-K1 (threatening 22 B-Q2) 21 ... N-R5 22 BxN QxB 23 B-B4, after which Black has some problems in view of the open king's file.

18 ...		Q-B2
19	N-K5	B-K3
20	P-B3	N-B4!
21	B-Q2	

Not 21 P-K4 N-R5 22 BxN PxB 23 Q-QB2 R-N6.

21 ...   N-R5?

Here the knight is out of play, which later leads to some difficulties. Much better is 21 ... N(B4)-Q2! 22 NxN BxN 23 QR-K1 B-B3 24 Q-N1 Q-N2 25 R-K2 R-K2 26 R(B1)-K1 R(N1)-K1. White would, it is true, maintain the initiative by either 27 Q-N4 followed by P-QR4 or the sharp advance 27 P-N4. But even so Black would have an easier task than in the game.

22	Q-N1	R-N3
23	Q-K1	N-Q2
24	Q-R4	N-B1

If 24 ... P-KR3, both 25 NxN QxN 26 P-K4 and 25 N-N4 are strong.

25	P-K4!	P-B3
26	N-N4	N-N3
27	Q-R5	Q-KB2
28	QR-K1	R(N3)-N1
29	N-K3	

Positionally the decisive move, for Black cannot hold the point Q4, e.g. 29 ... N-N3 30 P-B4! N-K2 31 QxQch BxQ (or 31 ... KxQ 32 P-B5 and 33 P-K5) 32 P-K5, and White gets a strong passed pawn. If instead 29 ... N-B5? 30 QxQch

BxQ 31 NxBP!, Black gets a poor position.

87. Najdorf–Botvinnik

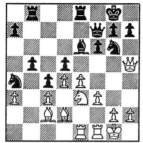

Position after White's 29th move

29 ...	N-K2
30 Q-R4	P-B4?

After 30 ... N-KN3! 31 Q-N3 N-K2 (31 ... N-N3 32 P-B4!), White has the unpleasant continuation 32 Q-B7, though Black could then put up a fight by 32 ... P-QR3. After the text-move, on the other hand, he is in dire straits.

31 P-N4!	P-B5

This loses material, but there is no hope of salvation from the alternative, 31 ... P-N3 32 KPxBP PxP 33 PxP NxKBP 34 BxN(B5) BxB 35 Q-N5ch B-N3 36 NxQP, after which White wins not so much owing to his pawn superiority but as a result of the weaknesses in his opponent's castled position.

32 PxP!	N-KN3

Or 32 ... PxN 33 PxB QxP 34 QxPch K-B1 35 RxP.

33 PxB	RxP
34 BxN(N6)	PxB
35 N-N2	R(N1)-K1
36 RxR	RxR
37 NxP	R-KB3
38 Q-N5	NxP
39 BxN	RxN
40 K-N2	Resigns

Euwe now had his great chance. But in this round, where nerves were showing, he did not fare any better.

Queen's Gambit

Kotov	Euwe
1 P-Q4	P-Q4
2 P-QB4	P-K3
3 N-KB3	N-KB3
4 N-B3	QN-Q2
5 PxP	PxP
6 B-B4	P-B3
7 P-K3(?)	

This makes the development of the bishop to KB4 a loss of tempo. Correct is 7 P-KR3.

7 ...	N-R4
8 B-KN5	B-K2
9 BxB	QxB
10 B-Q3	N-B5
11 0-0	NxB
12 QxN	0-0
13 KR-K1	

The plan to advance in the centre with P-K4 is only occasionally effective in this system. However, a minority attack does not offer much hope of success in view of the simplified material: 13 QR-N1 P-QR4 14 P-QR3 N-B3 15 P-QN4 PxP 16 PxP P-KN3.

13 ...	N-B3
14 N-K5	N-K1

In order to answer 15 P-KB4 by 15 ... P-KB3, driving the knight away from its strong position. At the same time Black's own knight heads for Q3, preparing the developing move B-B4.

15 P-K4	PxP
16 QxP	B-K3

Black could equalize quite simply by exchanging queens: 16 ... P-B3 17 N-Q3 QxQ 18 NxQ B-B4. Euwe was probably not much interested in simplifying so quickly, for a quick draw was not what

Groningen 1946

	1	2	3	4	5	6	7	8	9	10	11	12	13	14	15	16	17	18	19	20	Pts	Prize
1 Botvinnik	—	½	1	0	1	1	½	1	1	½	0	1	1	0	1	1	1	1	1	1	14½	I
2 Euwe	½	—	0	½	1	1	½	½	½	1	0	½	1	1	1	1	1	1	1	1	14	II
3 Smyslov	0	1	—	½	½	1	½	½	½	½	½	½	1	½	½	½	1	1	1	1	12½	III
4 Najdorf	1	½	½	—	1	1	½	0	½	½	½	½	0	1	½	½	½	1	½	1	11½	IV, V
5 Szabó	0	0	½	0	—	1	½	0	1	0	1	½	1	1	½	1	½	1	1	1	11½	IV, V
6 Boleslavski	0	0	0	0	0	—	½	1	1	1	1	1	½	½	½	½	½	1	1	1	11	VI, VII
7 Flohr	½	½	½	½	½	½	—	½	½	½	0	½	½	1	½	1	½	½	1	1	11	VI, VII
8 Lundin	0	½	½	1	1	0	½	—	½	0	½	1	0	1	0	½	½	1	1	1	10½	VIII, IX
9 Stoltz	0	½	½	½	0	0	½	½	—	1	½	½	1	½	1	1	0	½	1	1	10½	VIII, IX
10 Denker	½	0	½	½	1	0	½	1	0	—	0	½	0	½	1	½	½	1	1	½	9½	X
11 Kotov	1	1	½	½	0	0	1	½	½	1	—	½	0	½	0	1	½	0	1	0	9½	X
12 Tartakower	0	½	½	½	½	0	½	0	½	½	½	—	1	½	½	1	1	½	½	½	9½	X
13 Kottnauer	0	0	0	1	0	½	½	1	0	1	1	0	—	1	1	0	½	½	0	1	9	
14 Yanofsky	1	0	½	0	0	½	0	0	½	½	½	½	0	—	½	1	1	1	½	½	8½	
15 Bernstein	0	0	½	½	½	½	½	1	0	0	1	½	0	½	—	½	½	½	0	0	7	
16 Guidmard	0	0	½	½	0	½	0	½	0	½	0	0	1	0	½	—	1	½	½	1	7	
17 Vidmar	0	0	0	½	½	½	½	½	1	½	½	0	½	0	½	0	—	½	½	0	6½	
18 H. Steiner	0	0	0	0	0	0	½	0	½	0	1	½	½	0	½	½	½	—	1	½	6	
19 O'Kelly	0	0	0	½	0	0	0	0	0	0	0	½	1	½	1	½	½	0	—	1	5½	
20 Christoffel	0	0	0	0	0	0	0	0	0	½	1	½	0	½	1	0	1	½	0	—	5	

he was looking for. However, his opponent, if he had wished, could now have brought about a drawn position by 17 P-Q5 PxP 18 NxQP.

17	QR-Q1	R-Q1
18	N-Q3	N-B3
19	Q-K5	R-Q3
20	N-B4	R(B1)-Q1?

The first inaccuracy, which, however, does not lead to a lost game. On the other hand, 20 ... Q-Q2! would have given Black considerable pressure on the QP, leaving White to look for a way of equalizing.

21	Q-QR5	RxP

Again not the most accurate move. Correct is 21 ... P-QN3.

22	RxR	RxR
23	QxP	R-Q7
24	Q-R8ch	N-K1
25	NxB	

88. Kotov–Euwe

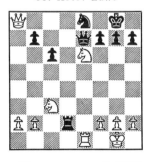

25 ...	RxNP??

One of those moves that cannot even be explained by the player making them. After 25 ... PxN Black would have had no trouble in holding the game; in fact, Kotov had intended to force a draw by

26 N-K4 RxNP 27 N-Q6! QxN 28 QxNch Q-B1 29 QxKPch. After the text-move, however, White has actually two ways of winning, that chosen by Kotov (26 Q-Q8) and the even quicker 26 Q-B8, e.g. 26 ... PxN 27 RxP or 26 ... R-B7 27 K-B1 RxN 28 N-B7!

26	Q-Q8	QxQ
27	NxQ	K-B1

The knight on Q8 is now trapped, so White is forced to play very accurately.

28	P-N3	P-KN3
29	N-K4!	P-R3

Or 29 ... K-K2 30 N-B6dis ch.

30	N-B5	N-Q3
31	R-Q1	K-K2
32	N(Q8)xNP	

This wins the exchange, which is more than sufficient for victory. (If Black takes the knight with his own knight, he will be a piece down after 33 R-Q7ch.)

32	...	RxN
33	NxR	NxN
34	K-N2	N-Q3
35	K-B3	K-Q2
36	K-B4	P-B3
37	P-KR4	P-QB4
38	R-QN1	K-B2
39	R-N2	N-N2
40	K-K4	K-B3
41	RxN!	P-B4ch
42	K-Q3	KxR
43	K-B4	

Now the issue is decided by a distant passed pawn.

43	...	K-N3
44	P-B4	K-B3
45	P-R4	Resigns

27 European Zonal 1947

Strategy not Supported by Tactics

At the first post-war congress, which took place in 1946, the International Chess Federation discussed a question that was of great interest to chess players throughout the world, namely, how the new world champion should be chosen; for A. A. Alekhin had died in Lisbon a few months previously under mysterious circumstances (suicide? accident?). The congress decided on a new solution: the new world champion was to be determined by a match tournament of the six strongest players of the time—Botvinnik, Smyslov and Keres from the USSR, Reshevsky and Fine from the USA and Dr Euwe from Holland. Fine declined the invitation to take part, so the tournament took the unusual form of a quintuple-round event with five competitors. At the same time a decision was taken on a system of qualifying tournaments, which would produce a challenger to the world champion two years after the match tournament.

The system was not very well thought out. For the whole of Europe, apart from the USSR, there was to be only one zonal tournament, which meant that the strongest chess nations were at a distinct disadvantage. However, any system was better than the arbitrary way in which the world champions had previously chosen their own opponents.

In July 1947 the champions of fourteen European countries assembled in the Dutch town of Hilversum for FIDE's first zonal tournament. The right to go on to the next stage was restricted to one player, the winner, though the number was later increased. In the case of a tie the Sonnenborn–Berger system was to decide.

When I arrived at Hilversum I did not have a great number of successes to my credit: victory in the Czechoslovak championship, a tie for first place in a small tournament in Arbon and a tie for 2nd–5th places in the Warsaw tournament. I therefore had everything to play for and nothing much to lose. I have rarely played with such élan, notching up six victories in the first six rounds. Then, in the next, where I had Black, I drew with O'Kelly after failing to press home my advantage. (At the time no one realized what a vital effect this game was to have on the final result.) I followed this up with a win in the eighth round, but then I slipped up and suffered two severe defeats, which seemed to put an end to all my hopes. However, in their youth people are inclined to fight on to the end, and against all expectations I managed to make up lost ground by winning against such strong opponents as Dr Trifunović and Szabó. Prior to the last round the leading scores were: O'Kelly (who had played calmly and consistently throughout the tournament without losing a game) and Pachman 9½, Scheltinga and Dr Trifunović 9. The next players in the table were 2½ points behind. O'Kelly had White against the tail-ender Doerner of Luxemburg, so I realized that I would have to win at all costs. My task, however, was much more difficult. I had Black against the Bulgarian champion Zvetkov, who was well known for his solid style of play. Admittedly he had been completely out of form throughout the tournament, so he did not by any means present an insurmountable obstacle. And if I were to win and tie with O'Kelly, the Sonnen-born–Berger would split the tie in my favour.

Four Knights

	Zvetkov	Pachman
1	P-K4	P-K4
2	N-KB3	N-QB3
3	N-B3	N-B3

At the time the game was played, the Keres System, 3 ... P-KN3, which has the advantage of avoiding drawing variations, was unknown.

4	B-N5	P-Q3

Two rounds previously I had won against Dr Trifunović using the variation 4 ... B-N5 5 0-0 0-0. In the present game I purposely avoided this line because White can get a quick draw by 6 BxN QPxB 7 NxP BxN 8 QPxB.

5	P-Q4	B-Q2
6	0-0	PxP

On the previous move I had waited full of anxiety, hoping that my opponent would not choose the simplifying 6 PxP. I did not want to give him a second chance, so I rejected the strongest move, 6 ... B-K2.

7	NxP	B-K2
8	BxN	PxB
9	P-B3?	

A colourless continuation which leaves Black without any opening problems.

9	...	0-0
10	B-K3	R-K1
11	Q-Q2	Q-N1!
12	P-QN3	P-QR4

Black's plan is to play P-QB4 and P-QR5 at a suitable moment.

13	N(Q4)-K2	Q-N5(?)

Not very accurate, as White's next move shows.

14	N-B4	

Now White is threatening N-Q3 followed by P-K5.

14	...	Q-N2
15	QR-Q1	KR-Q1(?)

This is not a good move either, for the rook will soon have to return to the king file. I was playing the Steinitz Defence for the first time in my life and did not feel at ease in the cramped position that arises from it.

16	Q-B2	B-KB1
17	R-Q3	P-B4
18	R(B1)-Q1	R-K1
19	P-KN4!?	

Psychologically my inaccurate play had a positive side to it. It induced Zvetkov to abandon his caution and initiate an attack that was not really justified. He should have played 19 N(B4)-Q5 instead.

19	...	B-B3
20	P-N5	N-Q2
21	Q-N3	

The position does not justify the queen moving to KN3. And yet, strangely enough, towards the end of the game it is from this very square that the queen is able to deliver the *coup de grâce*.

21	...	P-R5!
22	R(Q3)-Q2	PxP
23	RPxP	R-R6!

With the dangerous threat of 24 ... P-B5.

24	N(B4)-Q5	R-K3!

Eliminating any threats that White might generate by N-B6ch.

25	P-R4?	BxN!
26	NxB	P-B5!

At this stage I seemed to have a very real chance of winning the tournament. White loses a pawn, for he cannot play 27 PxP on account of 27 ... P-QB3 28 N-B4 RxB 29 NxR PxN 30 Q-N4 N-B4, leaving

89. Zvetkov–Pachman

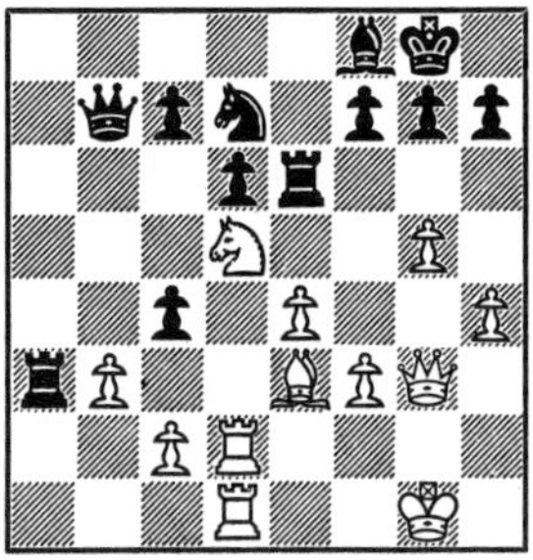

Position after Black's 26th move

him behind in material and with no compensating attack, e.g. 31 K-B2 R-B6 32 P-K5 P-Q4.

27 B-Q4	**PxP**
28 PxP	**RxNP**
29 P-R5!?	**N-K4??**

An inexplicable case of hallucinations. Prior to making this move I had analysed 29 . . . RxKP 30 N-B6ch NxN 31 PxN RxB! 32 RxR RxP 33 Q-N2 Q-N6, which leaves White hopelessly lost, for he is faced with the double threat of 34 . . . R-N6 and 34 . . . RxP. Then at the last moment–when I was beginning to run into time-trouble–I took fright at the possibility of my opponent deviating with 30 BxP? BxB? 31 N-B6ch, completely failing to see that the king can capture on KN2. If I had played the correct 29 . . . RxKP, I would have won the game and the tournament.

30 BxN	**RxB**
31 P-R6	

90. Zvetkov–Pachman

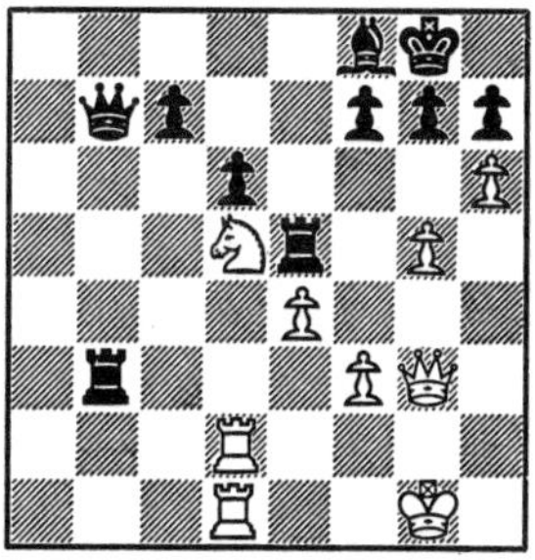

Now Black is suddenly confronted with a violent attack. He cannot take the KP (31 . . . RxKP 32 PxP KxP (32 . . . BxP 33 N-B6ch) 33 N-B6 R-K4(K3) 34 Q-R4, winning), and 31 . . . P-N3 is answered by 32 N-B6ch K-R1 33 Q-B4, e.g. 33 . . . Q-N3ch 34 K-R2 Q-K6 35 QxQ RxQ 36 R-QR1 followed by 37 R-R8. The only chance is 31 . . . R-K3! 32 PxP BxP 33 N-B6ch K-B1 34 NxPch K-K2, with a defensible position though with no winning chances.

31 . . .	**R-N8?**
32 PxP	**BxP??**

Hilversum 1947

		1	2	3	4	5	6	7	8	9	10	11	12	13	14	Pts	Prize
1	O'Kelly	—	½	½	½	1	1	½	1	1	½	1	1	1	1	10½	I
2	Pachman	½	—	1	1	0	1	1	1	0	0	1	1	1	1	9½	II, III
3	Trifunović	½	0	—	1	½	1	½	½	1	1	½	1	1	1	9½	II, III
4	v. Scheltinga	½	0	0	—	1	0	1	1	1	1	½	1	1	1	9	IV
5	Alexander	0	1	½	0	—	1	½	0	1	½	½	½	1	1	7½	V, VI
6	Szabó	0	0	0	1	0	—	½	1	½	1	½	1	1	1	7½	V, VI
7	Blau	½	0	½	0	½	½	—	0	0	1	½	1	1	1	6½	VII
8	Rossolimo	0	0	½	0	1	0	1	—	1	0	½	½	1	1	6½	VII
9	Castaldi	0	1	0	0	0	½	1	0	—	0	1	½	1	1	6	
10	Zvetkov	½	1	0	0	½	0	0	1	1	—	0	0	½	1	5½	
11	Foerder	0	0	½	½	½	½	½	½	0	1	—	0	0	1	5	
12	Plater	0	0	0	0	½	0	0	½	½	1	1	—	0	1	4½	
13	Doerner	0	0	0	0	0	0	0	0	0	½	1	1	—	½	3	
14	O'Sullivan	0	0	0	0	0	0	0	0	0	0	0	0	½	—	½	

Or 32 . . . KxP 33 Q-R4 RxRch 34 RxR
K-N3 35 P-B4, when Black has to give up
the exchange by 35 . . . RxN because 35
. . . RxKP loses to 36 N-B6. After Black's
blunder the game at least has a fine finish.

| 33 | N-B6ch | K-R1 |
| 34 | QxR!! | Resigns |

In view of 34 . . . PxQ 35 R-Q8ch
B-B1 36 RxBch K-N2 37 R-KN8 mate.

28 Chigorin Memorial, Moscow 1947

Depression Overcome

In 1947 Botvinnik was the odds-on favourite for the coming world championship. His victory in the tournament at Groningen, his excellent performance in the USSR championships and his modern style of play were really impressive. For him, as well as for two other leading players—Smyslov and Keres—the Chigorin Memorial, held in Moscow from 25 November to 23 December, was the final tournament appearance prior to the world championship. It was limited to players from eastern Europe—officially a tournament for Slavonic nations—but was nevertheless of a high level even by international standards.

Thanks to a series of victories between the sixth and the tenth round Botvinnik attained a lead of one point, which he increased to one and a half points in the eleventh round. After a draw in the twelfth he had 9½ points, one point more than his chief rivals, Keres and Kotov. In the following round he had White against me, a newcomer to big tournaments, and it was expected that he would increase his lead, for his rivals had Black against formidable opponents, Keres having to play Gligorić, Kotov and Bondarevski. That round, however, brought about an unexpected complication of the position. In the game between Botvinnik and myself, we both played the opening inaccurately; in fact I missed a chance to attain a clear advantage on move 12. Then the following position occurred.

Here I had expected 17 N-K4, to which I intended to reply with 17 ... Q-B4 (not 17 ... QxBP? 18 N-N5). Then after 18 NxB QxQ 19 BxQ PxN the game is even. Later it was discovered that White

91. Botvinnik–Pachman

Position after Black's 16th move

could deviate with 18 R-N4!, which would give him a very strong attack, e.g. 18 ... QxBP 19 R(R1)-N1 or 18 ... N-B5 19 Q-Q1.

17 R-N5??

This move came as a shock, for I had previously seen that it allowed 17 ... RxB. I was so excited that I was unable to think and I replied instantly, though secretly fearing that there was a hidden trap waiting to be sprung.

17 ...	RxB!

My opponent was quite upset over my reply and took a long time to recover and make his next move. As 18 QxR is answered by 18 ... B-B5, winning the queen, White has lost a piece.

18 RxPch	NxR
19 PxR	R-K1

This is better than 19 ... QxBP 20 R-B1 QxRP 21 N-K4.

20 N-Q5	Q-R3
21 K-N1	N-QR4
22 P-K4	NxB

23	QxN	P-QB3
24	N-B3	Q-K3

White resigned on move 45.

Kotov lost to Bondarevski, and Keres drew with Gligorić. As a result, two rounds before the end, Keres was within half a point of Botvinnik. In the next round the top two were drawn against each other. It was to be expected that Keres would make a great bid to gain first place, for he had two things in his favour. First he had White, and secondly it seemed likely that his opponent would be affected by a feeling of depression following his unexpected and unnecessary defeat.

Dutch Defence

	Keres	Botvinnik
1	P-Q4	P-K3
2	N-KB3	P-KB4
3	P-KN3	N-KB3
4	B-N2	B-K2
5	0-0	0-0
6	P-B4	P-Q4

At the time this game was played, the Stonewall System of the Dutch Defence was a favourite weapon of several Soviet grandmasters; apart from Botvinnik, it was employed among others by Bondarevski and Bronstein. The choice of this opening was an indication that, despite his defeat in the previous round, Botvinnik was not in a conciliatory mood. Keres was for him not only a contender for first prize in this tournament; he was also a personal rival of many years standing. In the AVRO Tournament he had tied for first place while Botvinnik had had to be content with third place. They had also measured swords with each other in the match tournament of 1941 for the "absolute champion of the USSR". On that occasion Botvinnik had come out 2½

points ahead. Since then they had not met in a tournament.

7	N-B3	P-B3
8	R-N1	

The purpose of this move is to prepare the advance P-QN4-QN5. The move was also played at Nottingham 1936 in a game Reshevsky–Botvinnik, which continued 8 ... Q-K1 9 P-B5! Q-R4 10 P-QN4 N-K5 11 Q-B2 N-Q2 12 P-N5 B-B3 13 B-B4, White having the better of it. An important factor for White is that his bishop can go to QB7 if Black should play P-KN4.

8	...	K-R1!

Botvinnik improves the system for Black by adopting a waiting move and keeping his queen on Q1. The move K-R1 is in any case useful in that it frees the square KN1 for the rook, thus enabling Black to launch an attack at a later stage by P-KN4. At first sight 8 ... QN-Q2 looks even better, though in that case White can continue 9 PxP KPxP 10 P-QN4.

9	PxP(?)

When Keres made this move he probably did not realize that Black, thanks to the fact that his knight is still on QN8, can now advantageously retake with the QBP and then develop the knight to QB3 without loss of time. White would have done better to reply to Black's waiting move with a waiting move of his own, e.g. 9 Q-B2.

9	...	BPxP
10	B-B4	N-B3
11	N-K5	

11 N-QN5 N-KR4 12 B-B7 Q-Q2 would be ineffective.

11	...	B-Q2
12	R-B1	R-B1
13	Q-Q3	N-KR4
14	B-Q2	B-Q3

92. Keres–Botvinnik

The opening has obviously ended in success for Black, who has succeeded in equalizing comfortably; if anything he has the more active position. If now 15 NxB QxN, White's two bishops are no advantage, for he has no good way of opening the game, e.g. 16 P-B3 B-N1 17 B-K1 P-B5. Nevertheless this would have been better than the continuation in the game, which gives Black the initiative.

| 15 NxN | BxN |
| 16 Q-B3(?) | |

Obviously expecting 16 ... N-B3, which White can answer by 17 B-B4, forcing an exchange of bishops. The queen manoeuvre is, however, merely a waste of time. White should instead double rooks on the QB file.

| 16 ... | Q-K1! |
| 17 Q-Q3 | N-B3(?) |

This deceptively simple position presents some difficult strategical problems, and both players commit inaccuracies in this phase of the game. Here Black should have played 17 ... P-KR3 as a precaution against White developing his bishop to KN5. White, for his part, should have made use of this omission and played 18 B-N5. After his failure to do so, Black ought to have made good his mistake and played 18 ... P-KR3, which would have given him a distinct positional advantage.

| 18 P-QR3(?) | R-QB2(?) |
| 19 B-N5! | |

Now White equalizes. If 19 ... P-KR3 20 BxN RxB 21 P-B4 P-KN4 22 P-K3, the two bishops are of no advantage to Black, while if 19 ... N-K5, White can reply 20 NxN followed by 21 Q-Q2. Should Black return to KR4 with his knight, White can continue 20 P-K3! P-KR3 21 B-B4.

19 ...	N-N5
20 Q-Q2	N-B3
21 B-B4	

This is even safer than 21 BxN.

21 ...	Q-Q2
22 BxB	QxB
23 Q-B4	

This unnecessarily nervous move does not actually ruin White's position, but a more logical continuation is 23 R-B2 followed by R(B1)-QB1 with a quick draw.

| 23 ... | QxQ |
| 24 PxQ | R(B1)-QB1 |

93. Keres–Botvinnik

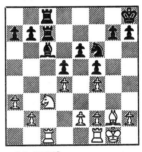

25 P-K3?

The first move in the endgame is a bad mistake and gives Black an opportunity of increasing his pressure on the QB file—his only chance of winning. White should have prevented this by 25 N-R2! Then 25 ... B-N4 26 RxR RxR 27 R-QB1 would have led to simplification and a draw.

25 ...	B-N4
26 KR-K1	K-N1
27 P-B3	

Not a particularly attractive move, but the necessary prerequisite for an exchange of bishops, for if White tries 27 B-B1 at once he loses a pawn, e.g. 27 . . . BxB 28 KxB N-K5 29 N-R2 R-B7 30 RxR RxR 31 R-K2 N-Q7ch 32 K-K1 (32 K-N2 RxP) 32 . . . N-B6ch.

27 . . .	**B-B5**
28 B-B1	**N-K1**
29 BxB	**RxB**
30 K-B2	

Of course, 30 N-R2 (or K2) is hopeless on account of 30 . . . R-B7. The text-move is an attempt to get the king to the centre, but he arrives one move too late.

30 . . .	**N-Q3**
31 K-K2	**P-QN4!**
32 K-Q3	**P-N5**

This wins a pawn, e.g. (i) 33 PxP RxNP 34 R-QN1 R(B1)-N1 35 K-B2 N-B5 (ii) 33 N-K2 RxR 34 NxR (34 RxR RxR 35 NxR PxP 36 PxP N-B5, etc.) 34 . . . PxP 35 PxP R-N1! (better than 35 . . . N-B5 36 N-N3 NxP 37 N-B5) 36 R-K2 N-B5 37 R-R2 R-N8 38 K-B2 R-N3 39 K-Q3 R-R3 40 P-QR4 RxP! etc.

33 N-R2	**PxP**
34 PxP	**R-R4**
35 RxRch	**NxR**
36 N-B3	**RxRP**
37 K-B2	**N-Q3**
38 R-QN1	**K-B2**
39 R-N4	**R-R8**
40 K-Q2	**R-R6**
41 K-B2	**R-R8**

The last few moves were played in time-trouble, which explains the repetition.

42 K-Q3	**R-K8!**
43 R-R4	**N-B5**
44 RxPch	**K-N3**
45 P-K4	**R-K6ch**
46 K-B2	**RxBP**
47 PxBPch	**KxP**
48 RxP	**R-B7ch**
49 K-N3	**R-QN7ch**
50 K-R4	**RxP**
51 R-KB7ch	**K-N3**
52 R-B8	**N-Q3**
53 N-N5	**N-B4**
54 N-B7	**R-K7**

Simpler than 54 . . . NxP 55 P-B5ch.

55 N-K8	**NxP**
56 R-B6ch	**K-R4**
57 R-B7	**N-B4**
58 RxPch	**K-N5**
59 R-Q7	**KxP**
60 N-B7	**K-K4**

There was a quicker win to be had by 60 . . . P-Q5

Moscow 1947

		1	2	3	4	5	6	7	8	9	10	11	12	13	14	15	16	Pts	Prize
1	Botvinnik	–	1	½	½	½	1	1	0	½	½	½	1	1	1	1	1	11	I
2	Ragosin	0	–	0	½	½	1	½	½	1	1	1	1	½	1	1	1	10½	II
3	Boleslavski	½	1	–	½	½	0	½	½	1	½	1	1	½	½	1	1	10	III, IV
4	Smyslov	½	½	½	–	0	½	½	1	½	½	1	½	1	1	1	1	10	III, IV
5	Kotov	½	½	½	1	–	0	1	½	½	1	0	½	½	1	1	1	9½	V
6	Keres	0	0	1	½	1	–	0	½	½	½	½	1	1	½	1	1	9	VI, VII
7	Novotelnov	0	½	½	½	0	1	–	½	0	1	½	1	1	1	½	1	9	VI, VII
8	Pachman	1	½	½	0	½	½	½	–	0	1	½	1	0	½	1	1	8½	VIII
9	Trifunović	½	0	0	½	½	½	1	1	–	½	½	½	½	½	1	½	8	
10	Gligorić	½	0	½	½	0	½	0	0	½	–	½	1	1	1	½	1	7½	
11	Bondarevski	½	0	0	0	1	½	½	½	½	½	–	0	½	1	0	1	6½	
12	Kholmov	0	0	0	½	½	0	0	0	½	0	1	–	½	1	½	1	5½	
13	Kottnauer	0	½	½	0	½	0	0	1	½	0	½	½	–	0	½	½	5	
14	Plater	0	0	½	0	0	½	0	½	½	0	0	0	1	–	½	½	4	
15	Sokolski	0	0	0	0	0	0	½	0	0	½	1	½	½	½	–	½	4	
16	Zvetkov	0	0	0	0	0	0	0	0	½	0	0	0	½	½	½	–	2	

61	K-N4	R-QB7
62	K-N3	N-Q5ch
63	K-N4	R-B5ch
64	K-R5	N-B4
65	K-N6	P-Q5
66	N-R6	N-Q3
67	N-B5	K-Q4
68	N-Q3	P-K4
69	R-KR7	R-B3ch
70	K-R5	N-B5ch
71	K-N5	R-QN3ch

72	K-R4	N-N7ch
73	K-R5	N-B5ch
74	K-R4	R-N1
75	N-N4ch	K-K3
76	N-B6	N-N7ch
77	K-R3	N-B5ch
78	K-R4	R-N8
79	R-R6ch	K-B4

White resigned after the second adjournment.

29 Interzonal 1948
Szabó's Wasted Chance

The 1948 Interzonal was held from 5 July to 15 August on the small island of Saltsjöbaden not far from Stockholm. The top five of the twenty competitors were to win the right to go on to the Candidates' Tournament. At that time the system of zonal tournaments had not been well thought out. As the Hilversum Tournament was the only one for Europe and as only the winner automatically went on to the Interzonal, the majority of competitors in the latter had to be appointed by the FIDE qualifying committee. This, of course, caused some ill-feeling, though it was generally agreed that the strongest players were all at the start—apart from the five grandmasters fighting for the world championship title in The Hague and Moscow (Botvinnik, Smyslov, Keres, Reshevsky, Euwe).

At the Interzonal, the Hungarian grandmaster Szabó took the lead in the sixth round and held it right up to near the end despite a defeat at the hands of one of his chief rivals, Bronstein. After the fourteenth round the position was Szabó 10½, Bronstein 10, Boleslavski and Lilienthal 9. In the next three rounds the two leaders drew their games, but still remained out in front. Then in the eighteenth round Bronstein, with Black, refuted an incorrect sacrifice by his opponent, L. Steiner, and scored an important point. Szabó was very near to winning his game, too, but he slipped up and only drew.

The QBP is an incurable weakness in White's position, and if Black continues correctly with 19 ... R(B1)-QB1, there is no satisfactory defence, e.g. 20 N-R3 RxQBP! 21 BxR BxB. Szabó, however,

94. Stoltz–Szabó

Position after White's 19th move

was in too much of a hurry to win material.

19 ...	RxNP?
20 PxR	BxR
21 N-B3	B-N7
22 R-N1	BxN

The exchange of the strong bishop is a direct consequence of Black's faulty nineteenth move. Now White has sufficient compensation for his pawn.

23 BxB	P-B3
24 R-K1	R-K1
25 P-R4!	Q-B3
26 P-R5!	PxP
27 Q-R3	R-K2
28 P-N5!	

Stoltz plays this phase of the game very energetically. If now 28 ... QxP 29 RxP RxR 30 QxRch, White should have no difficulty in getting a draw.

28 ...	Q-B4ch
29 K-R1	P-K4
30 PxP	PxP
31 P-N6!	

With this fourth pawn sacrifice White creates a passed rook pawn. In order to stop it Black will have to withdraw some of his forces from the defence of the king.

31	...	PxP
32	P-R6!	P-N4
33	R-R1	N-B3
34	P-R7!	RxP
35	Q-K6ch	K-N2
36	QxKP	RxRch
37	BxR	Q-KB7
38	Q-N5ch	K-B2
39	BxN	QxB
40	QxQPch	
	Drawn	

Going into the last round Szabó and Bronstein were thus equal in points. Both had White against opponents from the bottom half of the table, Bronstein having to play Tartakower, who was sharing fifteenth place, and Szabó, Lundin, who was sure to be bottom. Szabó's prospects were therefore slightly better than Bronstein's. The last round, however, turned everything upside down.

Caro-Kann

Bronstein	Tartakower
1 P-K4	P-QB3
2 N-KB3	P-Q3

Tartakower was always fond of experiments in the opening. Here, instead of the usual 2 ... P-Q4, he chooses the type of set-up found in the Pirc Defence (1 ... P-Q3).

| 3 P-Q4 | B-N5 |

More precise is first 3 ... N-KB3 and then (after 4 N-B3) 4 ... B-N5. This could be followed up with P-K3 and P-Q4, giving a sort of French set-up in which the problem of the development of the Queen's bishop has been solved. After the text-move White could have played 4 P-B4(!).

| 4 P-KR3 | B-R4 |

Also good is 4 ... BxN 5 QxB P-K3.

| 5 B-K3 | N-B3 |
| 6 QN-Q2 | QN-Q2 |

More accurate is 6 ... P-K3 followed by P-Q4. Thanks to his opponent's tame opening play, Black should not have any great difficulty in equalizing.

| 7 P-B3 | B-N3? |

Black underestimates the strength of his opponent's sacrifice on the next move. He should have played 7 ... P-K3, getting an elastic position in the centre and leaving himself free at a later stage to advance the QBP, the QP or the KP as required.

8 P-K5	N-Q4
9 P-K6!	PxP
10 B-K2	P-K4

This detracts from the value of Black's pawn majority and leaves White with lasting control over his K4 (e4). On the other hand, other moves would have caused Black great difficulty in completing his development.

11 PxP	NxKP
12 NxN	PxN
13 B-R5!	

The Black bishop controls Black's K5, so it is necessary to exchange it off. Black is now faced with a very unpleasant choice. If he allows White to exchange (14 BxBch PxB) he weakens his pawn structure, whereas if he exchanges himself (13 BxB 14 QxBch) he loses his extra pawn. And the third alternative (13 ... Q-Q3 14 N-K4) wastes time.

13	...	NxB
14	BxBch	PxB
15	PxN	Q-Q6
16	Q-B3	P-K3

17 Q-K4!	QxQ
18 NxQ	

95. Bronstein–Tartakower

The centrally posted knight is considerably stronger than the bishop, which means that White has a distinct and lasting advantage. Such a position is ideal in a decisive game, for as a result it is possible to play for a win without indulging in risks.

18 ...	B-K2
19 K-K2	R-Q1
20 QR-Q1	0-0
21 RxR	RxR
22 R-KB1	

This prevents the king moving towards the centre, for Black dare not oppose White's rook on the KB file, e.g. 22 ... R-KB1? 23 R-Q1 R-Q1 24 RxRch BxR 25 N-Q6 P-N3 26 K-Q3, and the White king enters the game with decisive effect.

22 ...	P-N3
23 N-B2	

This knight manoeuvre is crowned with unexpectedly speedy success. A good alternative is 23 P-QR4 possibly followed by R-QR1 and P-R5. If Black tries to hold up the pawn advance by P-QR4, White gets an excellent square on QB4 for his knight.

23 ...	R-Q4
24 N-Q3	B-B3
25 N-N4	R-N4?

The wrong square for the rook. Correct is 25 ... R-Q3, after which the

outcome is not so clear, e.g. 26 R-Q1 RxR 27 KxR P-B4 28 N-B6 P-R4 29 P-K4 K-B2 30 K-B2 K-K1 31 K-N3 K-Q2 32 N-R7.

26 P-QR4	R-B4
27 P-K4	

96. Bronstein–Tartakower

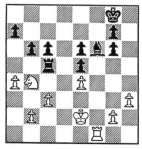

The game is won for White because the Black rook cannot escape. If 27 ... P-R4, then 28 K-Q3! PxN 29 PxP. Black probably overlooked this twist when making his 25th move.

27 ...	P-QN4
28 P-R5	B-Q1
29 R-QR1	R-B5
30 K-Q3	B-K2
31 N-R6	

This is even better than winning the exchange by 31 P-QN3 RxN 32 PxR BxP.

31 ...	R-R5
32 RxR	PxR
33 N-N8	P-R6
34 PxP	BxP
35 NxP	B-B4
36 K-B4	B-N8
37 K-N5	K-B2
38 K-R6	K-B3
39 NxRP	K-N4
40 P-N3	B-B7
41 P-B4	K-B3
42 N-B6	BxP
43 P-B5	K-B2
44 K-N6	K-K1
45 P-R6	Resigns

Hromádka System

Szabó	Lundin
1 P-Q4	N-KB3
2 P-QB4	P-QB4
3 P-Q5	P-QN4!?
4 PxP	P-QR3
5 PxP	

The move 5 P-K3 is also played in this position.

Black's pawn sacrifice, often called the Volga Gambit, is not quite correct, but gives considerable practical chances. Up to this point Lundin had only managed seven draws, and here he was all out to get a win irrespective of the state of the tournament and regardless of who his opponent was. Such tactics are often successful against someone fighting for first place and are in any case more promising than defending a strategically inferior position as Tartakower did.

5 ...	P-N3

More usual is 5 ... P-K3. Lundin prepares to transpose into the Hromádka System, in which the QNP is often sacrificed for tactical reasons. However, the fact that it has already been sacrificed (on the third move) gives White the opportunity to choose the most advantageous set-up.

6 N-QB3	BxP
7 P-K4	P-Q3

If instead 7 ... BxB 8 KxB, White can castle artificially by P-KN3 and K-N2. Nevertheless such a continuation would have been more promising for Black than that chosen in the game. In the Hromádka System Black does not usually sacrifice the QNP until his opponent has developed his bishop to K2, after which the exchange BxB involves a loss of tempo for White.

8 BxB	NxB
9 N-B3	B-N2

10 0-0	N-Q2
11 B-B4	0-0
12 Q-K2	

A more natural developing move is 12 Q-Q2, threatening B-R6. The probable reply is then 12 ... Q-N3 13 QR-N1 KR-N1, when Black's queen is not particularly well placed on QN3.

12 ...	Q-B2
13 KR-QB1	KR-N1
14 QR-N1	

97. Szabó–Lundin

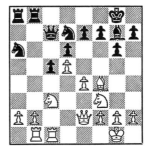

It is now apparent that Black has failed to obtain adequate compensation for his pawn. The most natural way of continuing is 14 ... R-N5 (or R-N2) followed by R(R1)-N1 in order to keep up the pressure on the QN file.

14 ...	BxN!?

A strange continuation, which, however, leads to unexpected success. The exchange is made for tactical reasons, for strategically the disappearance of the king's bishop is bad for Black.

15 RxB

The natural reply, but there is a stronger move in 15 PxB, threatening 16 P-K5 and forcing Black to waste an important tempo playing 15 ... P-B3.

15 ...	Q-R4!

Threatening both QxP and QxR. White, however, is able to parry both threats.

16 N-Q2!	N-B2

Not, of course, 16 ... QxP? 17 R-QR3, after which the queen is trapped.

17 R-QR3	Q-N3
18 RxR	RxR
19 P-QR3	N-N4
20 B-K3	R-R5!

Preventing the knight going to QB4, e.g. 21 N-B4 RxN 22 QxR NxP!

21 R-QB1	N-Q5
22 BxN	PxB
23 N-B3	

It is by no means easy to make use of the extra pawn. Pirc recommends 23 Q-Q1 R-R1 24 Q-N3 QxQ 25 NxQ, but then 25 ... R-N1 26 NxP RxP gives Black good prospects of saving the game. If, on the other hand, 23 N-B4, the pin 23 ... Q-N4 is unpleasant. The strongest line seems to be 23 Q-Q1 R-R1 24 N-B4. The text-move, however, does not throw the win away.

23 ...	N-B3
24 Q-B2!	R-R4
25 N-Q2!	

Black was threatening 25 ... R-B4 followed by RxR and NxKP.

98. Szabó–Lundin

25 ...	P-Q6!?
26 Q-B7?	

Capturing the QP would have led to a quick draw, e.g. 26 QxP QxNP 27 R-N1 RxRP 28 RxQ RxQ 29 P-B3. But the text-move is even worse, for Black wins two pawns. The correct move is 26 Q-B3!, e.g. 26 ... R-B4 27 N-B4 RxN!? 28 QxR QxNP 29 Q-B8ch! K-N2 30 Q-B3 and White, the exchange up, has good prospects of making use of his material advantage.

26 ...	QxNP
27 P-K5!?	QxN
28 PxN	PxP
29 P-KR4	K-N2
30 Q-B3	QxQ
31 RxQ	RxQP
32 R-B1	P-N4?

Black misses the win by 32 ... R-QR4 33 R-B3 P-Q7 34 R-Q3 RxP 35 RxP(Q2) R-R3.

33 K-B1	PxP
34 R-R1	P-B4
35 P-R4	K-B3
36 K-K1??	

This loses. There was a draw to be had by means of the simple continuation 36 P-R5 P-Q7 37 K-K2. Both players were in time-trouble, which explains the inaccuracies towards the end of the game.

36 ...	R-K4ch
37 K-Q2	R-K7ch
38 KxP	RxP
39 P-R5	RxP
40 P-R6	R-N1
41 K-B4	P-B5
42 K-Q5	K-B4
43 K-B6	P-B6
44 K-N7	R-K1
45 Resigns	

White has the choice between a lost queen ending (45 R-QB1 R-K2ch 46 R-B7 RxRch 47 KxR P-B7) and an even quicker defeat by 45 P-R7 K-N5 46 P-R8=Q RxQ followed by P-B7.

Saltsjöbaden 1948

	1	2	3	4	5	6	7	8	9	10	11	12	13	14	15	16	17	18	19	20	Pts	Prize
1 Bronstein	–	1	½	1	½	½	½	½	½	½	½	½	1	½	1	1	½	1	1	1	13½	I
2 Szabó	0	–	½	½	1	½	½	1	½	1	1	1	½	½	1	1	½	½	1	0	12½	II
3 Boleslavski	½	½	–	½	½	½	½	0	1	1	1	½	½	½	½	½	1	1	1	½	12	III
4 Kotov	0	½	½	–	½	½	½	½	½	½	½	½	1	½	½	1	1	1	1	½	11½	IV
5 Lilienthal	½	0	½	½	–	1	½	1	½	½	½	½	0	1	½	½	1	½	½	1	11	V
6 Bonderevski	½	½	½	½	0	–	1	½	½	0	½	1	½	½	0	½	1	½	1	1	10½	VI–IX
7 Flohr	½	½	½	½	½	0	–	½	½	½	½	½	½	½	½	½	1	½	1	1	10½	VI–IX
8 Najdorf	½	0	1	½	0	½	½	–	½	1	½	1	0	½	0	1	½	½	1	1	10½	VI–IX
9 Ståhlberg	½	½	0	½	½	½	½	½	–	0	1	1	½	½	½	½	½	1	½	1	10½	VI–IX
10 Trifunović	½	0	0	½	½	1	½	0	1	–	0	½	½	½	1	½	1	½	1	½	10	X
11 Böök	½	0	0	½	½	½	½	½	0	1	–	0	½	½	½	½	½	1	1	1	9½	
12 Gligorić	½	0	½	½	½	0	½	0	0	½	1	–	½	1	½	1	1	½	0	1	9½	
13 Pirc	0	½	½	0	1	½	½	1	½	½	½	½	–	1	0	0	½	1	½	½	9½	
14 Yanofsky	½	½	½	½	0	½	½	½	½	½	½	0	0	–	1	0	½	½	½	1	8½	
15 Ragosin	0	0	½	½	½	1	½	1	½	0	½	½	1	0	–	0	½	0	½	1	8½	
16 Tartakower	0	0	½	0	½	½	½	0	½	½	½	0	1	1	1	–	0	½	½	½	8	
17 Pachman	½	½	0	0	0	0	0	½	½	0	½	0	½	½	½	1	–	1	½	1	7½	
18 Stoltz	0	½	0	0	½	½	½	½	0	½	0	½	0	½	1	½	0	–	½	½	6½	
19 L. Steiner	0	0	0	0	½	0	0	0	½	0	0	1	½	½	½	½	½	½	–	½	5½	
20 Lundin	0	1	½	½	0	0	0	0	0	½	0	0	½	0	0	½	0	½	½	–	4½	

30 Candidates' Tournament 1950

A Drama in Instalments

The first Candidates' Tournament began in Budapest on 9 April 1950. Seven of the participating grandmasters were from the same country—the Soviet Union—and towards the end a duel unparalleled in the history of the Candidates' Tournament took place between two of them.

The tournament was a double-round affair, for it was only later that FIDE decided that eighteen games were not sufficient to determine the challenger to the world champion.

For most of the tournament the lead was held by Boleslavski, who was in excellent form. At the half-way stage the scores were: Boleslavski 6, Keres 5½, Bronstein and Ståhlberg 5, Kotov and Smyslov 4½, Lilienthal and Najdorf 4, Szabó 3½, Flohr 3. In the tenth round Boleslavski increased his lead to a full point and then continued to play solidly, not losing a single game. Nevertheless there gradually appeared a rival on the scene in the person of Bronstein. The latter had started badly, losing to Smyslov and Ståhlberg in the first half of the tournament, but then he had recovered and scored six points from eight games. Prior to the last round he was only half a point behind Boleslavski, who had 11½ points. In the last round Boleslavski had to play Ståhlberg, who, after an excellent start, had gradually slipped down the table; in the previous round he had lost with White to Bronstein. It therefore looked as if Boleslavski, at the time in excellent form, had everything in his favour, especially as he had White. Bronstein also had White in his game, though against a much more dangerous opponent, Keres.

The spectators who filled the great hall of the Budapest metal workers' cultural centre were very disappointed by what happened in the game between Boleslavski and Ståhlberg.

Sicilian Defence

Boleslavski	Ståhlberg
1 P-K4	P-QB4
2 N-KB3	P-Q3
3 P-Q4	PxP
4 NxP	N-KB3
5 N-QB3	P-QR3
6 B-K2	P-K4
7 N-N3	B-K3
8 0-0	B-K2
9 P-B4	PxP

Later the continuation 9 ... Q-B2 came into fashion.

10 BxBP	0-0
11 K-R1	N-B3
12 B-Q3	Q-N3
13 Q-K2	KR-K1
14 QR-K1	QR-B1
15 B-K3	Q-B2
16 N-Q4	

In this position, in which he has slightly the better of it, Boleslavski accepted a draw. Obviously he chose the tactics we have already mentioned, that is, with half a point lead in the last round try for a quick draw and thus put one's rival under the psychological pressure of having to play for a win. But every rule has its exception, and tactics which prove good a hundred times may fail to work on one occasion.

Boleslavski was thus only a spectator to the game that was to decide his fate.

Ruy Lopez

Bronstein	Keres
1 P-K4	P-K4
2 N-KB3	N-QB3
3 B-N5	P-QR3
4 B-R4	N-B3
5 0-0	B-K2
6 R-K1	P-QN4
7 B-N3	0-0
8 P-Q4	P-Q3
9 P-B3	B-N5
10 P-KR3	BxN
11 QxB!?	PxP
12 Q-Q1	PxP
13 NxP	

99. Bronstein–Keres

The gambit variation leading to this position was played in the present game for the first time. It did not, however, become very popular. White has the two bishops and the freer game for his pawn, but Black's position has no real weakness—unless the slightly loose queen's wing is regarded as one—and is therefore capable of being defended. An objective assessment of the position must therefore be that White has insufficient compensation for his pawn. In the situation in which the game was played, however, Bronstein's decision to adopt the gambit line was understandable and correct. A draw was of no use to him, so

he tried to get his opponent on to unexplored and complicated paths.

13 ...   N-QR4

A logical plan. Black needs to mobilize his queen-side majority by playing P-QB4. The fact that his QP will then become weak is not so important, for White is more or less obliged to concentrate on direct attack and not on the exploitation of small positional advantages.

14 B-B2   R-K1

Black could have played P-QB4 at once: e.g. 14 ... P-B4 15 P-B4 N-B3. Instead he prepares a manoeuvre which involves an exchange of minor pieces and which considerably reduces White's attacking chances.

15 P-B4   P-N5!
16 N-Q5

Playing the knight to K2 instead would be weak, for Black could continue with 16 ... P-Q4 17 P-K5 N-K5 and activate his pieces considerably. If White then tries 18 BxN PxB 19 N-N3, Black can reply with 19 ... B-R5!

16 ...   NxN
17 QxN

After 17 PxN B-B3 18 B-R4 RxRch 19 QxR P-B4! 20 PxPe.p. NxP 21 B-K3 N-Q5 Black would have a clear advantage (22 QxP R-N1 23 Q-Q2 RxP! or 23 Q-B4 N-B4 followed by RxP).

17 ...   P-QB3
18 Q-Q3   P-N3
19 K-R1

White intends to attack the QNP by means of B-Q2, but, with his king on KN1, his opponent could then reply with Q-N3ch. White therefore moves his king first.

19 ...   B-B1
20 R-B1

Preparing a king-side attack (P-KB5). The logical counter for Black is a push forward in the centre (20 ... P-Q4 21 P-K5 N-B5), after which he has the better game. In this case White would have only two ways of getting rid of the troublesome knight, neither of which is really satisfactory. The first (22 P-QN3 N-R6 23 BxN PxB) deprives him of all his attacking chances, after which Black's extra pawn is really worth something in spite of the bishop of opposite colours. The second (22 B-N3) gives Black the choice between a quick draw (22 ... N-R4 23 B-B2 N-B5 with repetition of moves) and the chance to mobilize his pawns by 22 ... N-N3 followed by P-QB4.

20 ...	B-N2(?)
21 B-Q2	P-QB4

Black gives up the idea of playing the freeing P-Q4 and instead starts making preparations to create a passed pawn on the queen-side at a later stage (P-QB5-QB6). A good alternative, however, is 21 ... BxP. Then, after 22 QR-N1 B-B6 23 BxB PxB 24 R(B1)-Q1 (24 QxBP Q-B2), he could continue with 24 ... P-Q4 25 PxP PxP 26 QxQP QxQ 27 RxQ N-B5 28 B-N3 N-Q7. The exchange sacrifice—22 BxP BxR 23 RxB—is, in this case, incorrect, for Black can play 23 ... P-Q4 24 PxP PxP.

22 B-R4	R-KB1
23 QR-N1	Q-N3

The immediate advance of the QBP would give White a very strong attack, e.g. 23 ... P-B5 24 Q-Q5 P-B6 (24 ... Q-N3 25 P-R3!) 25 PxP BxP (25 ... PxP 26 B-K3 threatening B-N6) 26 P-B5! The text-move threatens 24 ... P-B5 25 Q-Q5 Q-B4, though it has the slight disadvantage that it lessens Black's control over KB3, so making the advance of his opponent's KBP more effective.

24 P-B5	B-Q5

White was threatening 25 P-B6 B-R1 26 P-N4 followed by P-N5, shutting the bishop out of play and leaving Black virtually a piece down. Now the advance 25 P-B6 is completely harmless. There are, however, other attacking possibilities for White, revolving around the move B-R6, and the most logical course would be to play it at once. His opponent would in reply probably sacrifice the exchange: 25 ... P-B5 26 Q-KN3 N-N2! 27 BxR RxB. Black would then only have a single pawn for the exchange, though his minor pieces would be very active after a later N-QB4. White would in this case have to continue his king-side attack: 28 PxP RPxP 29 P-R4.

100. Bronstein–Keres

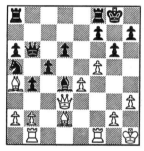

25 Q-KN3

From the psychological point of view, more promising than 25 B-R6. Black's whole counter-play is based on the advance P-QB5, which would now no longer be combined with a gain of tempo. As a result Black mistakenly departs from his original plan and seeks counter-play by other means. He should have played 25 ... P-B5 26 B-R6 N-N2! etc.

25 ...	N-B5?

Both players were in time-trouble, which explains the inaccuracies on this and White's next move as well as the blunder that decides the game.

| 26 B-R6? | |

26 B-B1! would be much better, for White would then be threatening to increase his pressure decisively by occupying the diagonal QR2-KN8 with a gain of tempo (27 B-N3 N-K4 28 B-Q5).

This hasty move should have deprived Bronstein of all chances of winning, for Black could have replied with the exchange sacrifice mentioned in a previous note: 26 . . . NxP! 27 BxR RxB. It is even stronger in this position, for Black has two pawns for the exchange, which in this case is more than sufficient compensation. White's only hope of holding the game would be 28 B-N3 P-B5 29 RxN! BxR 30 BxP, after which he would still have to fight hard, though a draw is probable in view of the unlike bishops.

26 . . .	B-N2??

At a point when White's attack should have been ended and with it Bronstein's hopes of winning the Candidates' Tournament, the game is decided by one of those inexplicable errors that are perpetrated even by top-ranking players.

27 BxB	KxB
28 P-B6ch	K-R1
29 Q-N5	P-N6?

Black could have held out longer, but not saved the game, by 29 . . . R-KN1 30 R-B4 Q-Q1 31 R-R4 (threatening 32 RxPch!) Q-KB1 32 R-R6 and White threatens 33 Q-R4. After Keres's move of despair White could have ended the game elegantly by 30 R-B4 PxP 31 Q-R6! PxP=Qch 32 K-R2 R-KN1 33 QxRPch! Bronstein discovers this combination a few moves later.

30 PxP	Q-N5

So as to reply to 31 R-B4 by 31 . . . Q-Q7.

31 PxN	QxB
32 R-B4	Q-B7
33 Q-R6!	Resigns

As a result of this dramatic encounter Bronstein caught up with Boleslavski, and on 31 July the two players started on a play-off of twelve games to decide who was to be the challenger to the world champion. In the first game Boleslavski was caught in a prepared variation and suffered a decisive loss of material as early as the 22nd move. This evidently upset him somewhat, for in the next two games he allowed his opponent to get an advantage, though in the end he did manage a draw in both. In the fourth game it was he who had the advantage, but he made a slip on the 28th move and as a result only drew. In the next game it was the other way round; Bronstein had a won position at the adjournment but threw away the win on move 52.

After a fairly quiet draw in the sixth game, Bronstein produced a fine positional performance in the seventh which led to victory. As a result he seemed to have the match in the bag, for he needed only two points from the remaining five games, which seemed a reasonably easy task in view of the fact that Boleslavski was not playing as well as he had done during the tournament. However, the position changed somewhat in the next game, where, in an interesting ending, Boleslavski chalked up his first victory—a fact which apparently gave a boost to his morale. He drew with Black in the ninth game and achieved a distinct superiority in the next. In fact he could have won a pawn and gone on to square the match, but he slipped up and allowed his opponent to get away with a draw.

Bronstein had White in the eleventh game, an Old Indian, but he played so passively that his opponent gradually gained the initiative and then won a pawn. At the adjournment the win was only a matter of technique. The match was thus all square again. As the twelfth game ended in a draw after a sharp struggle, excitement reached its peak. According to the rules the match was to be continued, victory going to the first player to win a game. A decisive result very nearly came about in the next encounter, in which the position in diagram 101 arose. Up to that point the game had not been without mistakes, and the dramatic complications that had occurred after the adjournment had got both players into time-trouble. With only two moves to make before the next time check, Boleslavski was very near to attaining the greatest success of his career. He only needed to play 55 ... K-B2!, after which there is a third queen on the way and White's attack is virtually at an end, e.g. 56 R-Q4 QxR 57 QxQ P-B8=Q 58 Q-Q5ch N-K3. Instead he played 55 ... QxN?? and the game ended in a draw by perpetual check after 56 PxQ P-B8=Q 57 PxN=Qch RxQ 58 Q-N5ch.

101. Bronstein–Boleslavski

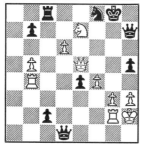

Position after White's 55th move

The next game proved decisive, victory being gained in a similar manner to the first—a surprise in the opening based on a prepared variation.

French Defence

Boleslavski	Bronstein
1 P-K4	P-K3
2 P-Q4	P-Q4
3 N-QB3	B-N5
4 B-Q2	PxP

In the twelfth game Bronstein had not been able to bring himself to play this move. Instead he had continued 4 ... P-QB4 5 P-QR3 BxN 6 BxB N-KB3 7 PxBP! NxP 8 BxP and come out of the opening very badly. Only later did he attain counter-play and secure a draw. This time he is much better prepared for the variation recommended by Alekhin. For Boleslavski it was therefore tactically unwise to try it again.

5 Q-N4   QxP

The position that later arises can also be reached by a different order of moves: 5 ... N-KB3 6 QxNP R-N1 7 Q-R6 QxP 8 0-0-0. In this case Black has an important alternative in 7 ... R-N3 8 Q-K3 N-B3 9 KN-K2 P-K4!.

6 0-0-0

In this position Alekhin recommended 6 N-B3, which is, however, completely innocuous on account of 6 ... N-KR3! 7 Q-B4 P-K4! According to Panov 6 KN-K2 is stronger. Keres gives the following analysis to this suggestion: 6 ... Q-K4 7 B-B4 Q-B3 8 0-0-0 Q-N3 9 QxQ RPxQ 10 BxP N-QB3 11 NxP N-B3 with an even game.

6 ...   N-KB3

The line 6 ... P-KB4 7 Q-N3 B-Q3 8 B-KB4 BxBch 9 QxB Q-B4 has been tried here several times, but White can continue with 10 P-KB3, getting active play with his pieces in return for the pawn. Another line for Black—and one, moreover, which proved its worth in several later games—is 6 ... P-KR4 7 Q-N3 B-Q3 8 B-KB4 P-R5!

7 QxNP   R-N1
8 Q-R6   B-B1!

The innovation prepared by Bronstein. Previously the usual continuation had been 8 ... R-N3 9 Q-R4 R-N5 10 Q-R3 QxP, which leads to a position similar to that reached in the game but with one important difference: the bishop is on QN5 and not KB1. The significance of this difference will become clear a few moves later.

9 Q-R4

If White is content with equality he can play 9 Q-B4, e.g. 9 ... R-N5 10 Q-K3! QxQ 11 BxQ, when the two bishops and the better development are adequate compensation for the pawn. Or 9 ... B-Q3 10 KN-K2! BxQ 11 NxQ BxBch 12 RxB, and White has equality in view of the weakness of the KP.

9 ...	R-N5
10 Q-R3	QxP!

102. Boleslavski–Bronstein

After the game, which on account of its importance aroused considerable interest, it was discovered that 11 B-K2 is the only satisfactory continuation. White then threatens both BxR and R-B1, and Black can hardly adopt the passive 11 ... R-N3, because of 12 P-KN4!, after which 12 ... P-K4? is answered by 13 B-K3. There are, however, two alternatives for Black:

(i) 11 . . . R-R5 12 QxR QxQ 13 P-KN3 Q-R3! (This shows the importance of the move 8 ... B-B1!) 14 BxQ BxBch, and Black has a satisfactory position: he has the two bishops and two pawns for the exchange, which is ample compensation for his doubled pawns.

(ii) 11 ... QxP 12 BxR QxB 13 QxQ NxQ 14 NxP. In this line the fact that the bishop is on KB1 and not QN5 is an advantage for Black, for otherwise he would have to exchange it, thus helping White's development, or waste time withdrawing it.

11 N-N5?	N-R3
12 K-N1	B-Q2
13 B-K3	

Or 13 B-B3 R-R5 14 B-Q4 RxQ 15 BxQ R-R4.

13 ...	Q-B4
14 N-Q4	

14 NxRP would lose quickly, e.g. 14 ... N-Q4 15 B-Q4 P-B4 or 15 N-N5 NxB 16 QxN BxN.

14 ...	Q-N3
15 N-N3	N-N5
16 N-K2	N(B3)-Q4
17 N-B3	

After 17 B-B1 P-K6! White would have difficulty in defending the pawn on QB2, e.g. 18 N(K2)-Q4 P-K4.

17 ...	NxN
18 PxN	N-Q4
19 B-Q4	R-N4!

Budapest 1950

	1	2	3	4	5	6	7	8	9	10	Pts	Prize
1 Boleslavski	— —	½ ½	1 ½	½ ½	½ ½	1 ½	½ ½	1 1	½ 1	½ 1	12	I, II
2 Bronstein	½ ½	— —	0 1	½ 1	1 1	1 ½	0 1	½ 1	½ ½	1 ½	12	I, II
3 Smyslov	0 ½	1 0	— —	½ ½	1 ½	½ 1	0 1	½ ½	½ 1	½ ½	10	III
4 Keres	½ ½	½ 0	½ ½	— —	½ ½	1 0	1 ½	½ ½	½ ½	½ 1	9½	IV
5 Najdorf	½ ½	0 0	0 ½	½ ½	— —	½ ½	½ ½	½ ½	1 1	½ 1	9	V
6 Kotov	0 ½	0 ½	½ 0	0 1	½ ½	— —	½ 1	1 ½	1 0	1 0	8½	
7 Ståhlberg	½ ½	1 0	1 0	0 ½	½ ½	½ 0	— —	½ ½	½ ½	½ ½	8	
8 Flohr	0 0	½ 0	½ ½	½ ½	½ ½	0 ½	½ ½	— —	½ ½	0 1	7	
9 Lilienthal	½ 0	½ ½	½ 0	½ ½	0 0	0 1	½ ½	½ ½	— —	1 0	7	
10 Szabó	½ 0	0 ½	½ ½	½ 0	½ 0	0 1	½ ½	1 0	0 1	— —	7	

With the irresistible threat of P-K4.
White's position is now in its last throes.

20	P-N4	P-K4
21	B-B2	BxP
22	RxN	BxQ
23	BxB	R-Q1

24	RxRch	KxR
25	R-Q1ch	B-Q3
26	B-K3	P-KB4
27	N-B5	P-B5
28	N-K6ch	K-K2
29	BxRP	R-R4
Resigns		

Saved at the Last Moment

The most dramatic chess event I have ever witnessed was without doubt the Botvinnik–Bronstein Match in 1951. Three years previously Botvinnik had won the match tournament by a large margin ((1) Botvinnik 14, (2) Smyslov 11, (3–4) Keres and Reshevsky 10½, (5) Euwe 4), and as a result of his clear-cut victory there were many pundits who forecast a long era dominated by this sole representative of the pre-war Soviet grandmasters. In the same year as his victory a new star had come to the fore—in the Interzonal—but the general view was that he lacked the experience to win against Botvinnik, who, for almost twenty years, had been measuring swords with such players as Alekhin, Capablanca, Flohr, Reshevsky and Euwe. Moreover, Bronstein had only won the Candidates' Tournament 1950 after a play-off with Boleslavski.

The world championship match began on 16 March in the Tchaikovsky Concert Hall in Moscow. In the first phase Bronstein gave the title-holder plenty to worry about, but by the time the match was adjourned for four days for the May celebrations everything seemed to be cut and dried. With twenty games played, Botvinnik had a lead of one point, and, as a tied match was enough for him to retain his title, he only needed 1½ points from the last four games—not, one would imagine, a particularly difficult task.

The position, however, soon became more complicated. On 4 May Bronstein used his favourite opening for the first time in the match, the Old Indian Defence, and won the game after the adjournment. This defeat with the White pieces was obviously a severe blow to Botvinnik, whose hopes of a peaceful finish to a match that had appeared to be over were now shattered. The 22nd game saw him produce one of his weakest performances, leading to a loss before the adjournment. The scales had thus tipped the other way; it was now Bronstein who only needed to draw the remaining games. His main task was to hold the 23rd game, for it was difficult to imagine that, if it did end in a draw, Botvinnik would win the last game, in which he had Black.

Grünfeld Indian

Botvinnik	Bronstein
1 P-Q4	N-KB3
2 P-QB4	P-KN3
3 P-KN3	P-B3

The opening moves often give an indication of the players' approach to the game in question. The variation beginning with 3 ... P-B3 is considered very solid, usually leading to a symmetrical position with marked drawing characteristics. That Bronstein should choose such a line is understandable in view of the state of the match. Why Botvinnik should have allowed it by playing 3 P-KN3 is at first sight less clear. The idea behind it is reminiscent of Lasker's way of handling his game against Capablanca at St Petersburg. In both cases a grandmaster did nothing to avoid a "drawing" variation in a vital game that had to be won at all costs, and the decision was based on an accurate assessment of the personality and mental state of the opponent. Lasker chose to bring about a position that demanded the sort of treatment that was opposed to Capablanca's preconceived aims; Botvinnik opted for a position that, in his opinion, did not suit his opponent. At the time the game was played Bronstein was at the height of his creative powers and was noted for his remarkable imaginative combinational play. His weak points were the imperfections in his endgame technique and his play when quiet positional manoeuvring was required.

The world champion staked everything on one card: his psychological assessment of his opponent. And that card finally turned up, although at various stages of the game it looked as if Botvinnik's chances were virtually nil.

4	B-N2	P-Q4
5	PxP	PxP
6	N-QB3	B-N2
7	N-R3	BxN

This helps Black with his development and is, objectively seen, the strongest continuation. And yet after the game Botvinnik told me that he had breathed a sigh of relief when his opponent made this move. The reason for such a reaction is that White gets at least one lasting asset—the two bishops—prior to the protracted positional manoeuvring that is now about to take place. An alternative for Black which also suffices for equality is 7 . . . 0-0 8 N-B4 P-K3 9 0-0 N-B3.

8	BxB	N-B3
9	B-N2	

White withdraws his bishop partly to ensure that his opponent does not play N-K5 and partly because, after Black's P-K3, it would have no great future on the diagonal KR3-QB8.

9	. . .	P-K3
10	P-K3	0-0

11	B-Q2	R-QB1
12	0-0	N-Q2
13	N-K2	Q-N3
14	B-QB3	

Botvinnik himself criticized this move, which merely wastes time. The immediate Q-N3 is stronger, for White will sooner or later have to exchange queens. Although such a decision is by no means easy in a game as vital as this one, it is, nevertheless, both from the psychological and strategical point of view, the logical course.

14	. . .	KR-Q1
15	N-B4	

Now 15 Q-N3 would be answered by 15 . . . B-B1! with the threat of B-N5 exchanging bishops. After the text-move White can reply to 15 . . . B-B1 by 16 N-Q3 or 16 P-QR3.

15	. . .	N-B3
16	Q-N3	

103. Botvinnik–Bronstein

An interesting question from the strategical point of view is whether it is better for Black to exchange queens himself and double his opponent's pawns or to allow his opponent to exchange. Bronstein chooses the latter course because his pieces thereby become very active. Objectively his decision is the right one; as we shall see later he gets several opportunities to equalize. On the other hand, it requires just a few inaccuracies for the doubled pawns to become a

decisive strategical factor. Exchanging
queens himself by 16 ... QxQ 17 PxQ
N-K5 18 B-K1 B-B3 19 N-Q3 N-Q3 would
also have equalized and been less complicated.

16 ...	N-K5
17 QxQ	PxQ
18 B-K1	

This retreat is necessary if White wants
to keep his bishop, which is essential if an
immediate draw is to be avoided.

| 18 ... | N-R4 |

I well remember that most commentators had a poor opinion of Botvinnik's
position at this point. What was he to do
about the threat 19 ... R-B7?

| 19 N-Q3 | B-B1(?) |

Playing the rook to the seventh would
not cause White much trouble, for after
19 ... R-B7 20 N-N4! Black cannot
continue with 20 ... RxNP? 21 BxN PxB
22 B-B3 R-K7 23 KR-QB1 followed by
24 K-B1, when his rook is trapped.
Nevertheless the text-move is an
inaccuracy, albeit a minor one. Better is
19 ... N-B5, making it difficult for White
to activate his pieces, e.g. 20 R-Q1 B-B1.
Botvinnik gives another possibility: 20
B-N4 B-B1 21 BxB KxB 22 KR-QB1, but
although White has a slight advantage it is
merely of a symbolic character.

| 20 P B3 | N-Q3 |
| 21 B-B2(?) | |

More accurate is 21 R-B2. After the
text-move Black is given a chance to get
active play by 21 ... R-B7.

21 ...	B-R3(?)
22 QR-B1	N(R4)-B5
23 KR-K1	

Bronstein's principal mistake is that he
largely conducts the game without a real
strategical plan, relying instead on tactical
manoeuvres. Strategically Black's main
task should be to force his opponent to

104. Botvinnik–Bronstein

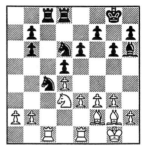

Position after White's 23rd move

play P-KB4 and thus prevent him from
pushing forward in the centre at a later
stage by P-K4. The simplest way of doing
this is 23 ... N-B4! In this case Black
would have to be prepared for 24
P-KN4!? N(B4)xKP 25 B-R3 (threatening
26 P-N3), though after 25 ... NxKNP!
26 BxN BxR 27 RxB N-Q3 he is quite
well placed.

23 ...	N-R4
24 K-B1	B-N2
25 P-KN4	N-B3
26 P-N3?	

In his subsequent analysis Botvinnik
expressed dissatisfaction with this move.
The weakening of the squares QB3 and
QR3 will soon become noticeable.

| 26 ... | N-N4! |
| 27 K-K2? | |

In Botvinnik's opinion the correct
move is 27 P-KR4. As a result of this
second inaccuracy White has lost all
winning chances. Black's simplest reply to
the text-move is 27 ... N-R6, and the
blockade of the queen's wing neutralizes
any advantage that the two bishops might
otherwise have for White. Bronstein, however, chooses another continuation,
which is also good.

| 27 ... | B-B1 |

This threatens B-R6 and thereby
forces White to play P-QR4, weakening
his QNP.

28 P-QR4	N-B2
29 B-N3	N-R3
30 B-B1	P-B3
31 KR-Q1	N-R4!
32 RxR	RxR
33 R-B1	RxR
34 NxR	B-R6
35 K-Q1	

105. Botvinnik–Bronstein

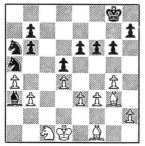

35 ...	BxN?

Bronstein's worst mistake in this game. Winning the QNP is of no real advantage to Black because of his own doubled pawns, and yet to do so he gives up his strongest defensive piece. Although it is possible that the game is not lost as a result, White does certainly get excellent practical chances.

36 KxB	NxPch
37 K-B2	N-R4
38 K-B3	K-B2
39 P-K4	P-B4?

Bronstein wanted to complicate the position in order to make the most of his opponent's time-trouble. But this advance, leading to a pawn exchange, is in complete contradiction to the demands of the situation. As a result the White bishops increase their power and Black's position will soon become untenable.

40 NPxP	NPxP
41 B-Q3	K-N3

The game was adjourned in this position with the world champion sealing his next move.

106. Botvinnik–Bronstein

Position after Black's 41st move

42 B-Q6

Sealed moves have a psychology of their own. The player making one does not always look for the strongest move, but chooses one that will give him a chance to find the best line at home. A move that brings about a repetition, thus leaving the options open, or a waiting move that does not alter the character of the position are ideal in this case. Often, too, a player chooses a move that his opponent does not expect, even though it may be objectively inferior.

There are, however, instances where too much importance should not be attached to the psychological side of the sealed move, namely, when the position demands a clear-cut procedure. The present is a case in question.

The majority of the spectators had expected the strong and logical continuation 42 B-N1!, with the intention of exchanging on Q5 and then winning the QP by B-R2. If White had actually sealed 42 B-N1, he would have had a win in all variations:

(i) 42 ... N-B5 43 PxQP PxP 44 B-B4 followed by 45 B-R2, winning a pawn.

(ii) 42 ... BPxP 43 PxP PxP 44 BxPch K-N2 45 BxNP!! (There is also a win by 45 B-Q6, as the white bishops are in complete command of the situation. The elegant piece sacrifice was discovered by Flohr immediately after the game was adjourned.) 45 ... NxB 46 K-B4 followed by 47 K-N5.

(iii) 42 ... N-B3 43 PxQP PxP 44 B-R2 N(R3)-N5 45 B-N3 K-B3 46 B-Q6 or 44 ... N-K2 45 B-R4, and Black loses a pawn.

Botvinnik purposely avoided the straightforward continuation 42 B-N1, choosing instead one that his opponent was unlikely to analyse. But this "psychological combination" very nearly lost him his title and caused him endless hours of anxiety devoted to analysing.

| 42 ... | N-B3 |
| 43 B-N1 | K-B3? |

The most natural move is not always the best. Black is concerned with the threat of 44 PxKP PxP 45 B-R2, which can now be answered by 45 ... K-K3. As a result he misses the last opportunity to get active play, viz. 43 ... N-R2! If White then continues with his plan (44 PxKP PxP 45 B-R2), Black can counter with 45 ... P-N4! Joint analysis after the game produced the following interesting variation: 46 P-R5 (46 BxP PxP 47 BxP N-N4ch, etc.) 46 ... P-N5ch! (but not 46 ... N-B3 47 BxP NxRP 48 P-B4 with advantage to White) 47 K-Q3 N-N4 48 B-K5 N(R3)-B2, and Black can defend himself.

44 B-N3!!

It is evident that Botvinnik devoted more time to the position at the adjournment than did his opponent who, in view of the expected continuation 42 B-N1, considered that the game was lost. The fine text-move brings about an interesting *zugzwang* position, the main idea being 44 ... N(R3)-N5 45 B-K5ch! K-N3 46 B-Q6 N-R3 47 PxKP PxP 48 B-R2, etc.

| 44 ... | BPxP |

This relieves the king of the duty of defending the KBP, but, on the negative side, it increases the scope of White's bishop and creates a new weakness, the KRP.

45 PxP	P-R3
46 B-B4	P-R4
47 PxP	PxP
48 P-R4	N(R3)-N1
49 B-N5ch	K-B2
50 B-B5	N-R2

Although this prevents the bishop going to QB8, Black would have greater practical chances with 50 ... N-K2. Then White dare not win the pawn immediately, for 51 BxN? KxB 52 B-N6 N-B3 53 BxP N-R2! 54 B-B3 K-K3 55 P-KR5 P-N4 56 P-R6 K-B3 57 BxP PxP 58 K-N4 P-R6! leads to a draw. According to Botvinnik's analysis, however, there is a win to be had against 50 ... N-K2 by 51 B-R3! N(N1)-B3 52 B-N2 K-N2 53 BxN NxB 54 K-N4 N-B3ch 55 K-N5 NxPch 56 KxP, when the passed rook pawn decides the issue.

51 B-B4	N(N1)-B3
52 B-Q3	N-B1
53 B-K2	K-N3
54 B-Q3ch	K-B3
55 B-K2	K-N3
56 B-B3	N(B3)-K2

There is no salvation in 56 ... N(B1)-K2 57 B-N5 (57 B-B7 is also strong) 57 ... N-B4 58 BxQP N(B4)xQP 59 B-K4ch K-B2 60 K-B4.

57 B-N5

107. Botvinnik–Bronstein

Bronstein thought over the position for fully forty minutes before deciding to resign. No matter what he moves he loses a pawn, and attempts to improve the situation on the queen's wing are fruitless, e.g. 57 ... N-B3 58 BxQP N-Q3 59 B-B3 K-B4 (threatening N-K5ch) 60 B-B1! P-N4 61 BxN PxB 62 P-R5 K-K3 63 P-R6 N-B1 64 B-B4, etc. The game was actually played to an end unofficially on the afternoon following the victory ceremony, the outcome being a symbolic confirmation of Bronstein's assessment of the position.

The last game of the match ended in a quick draw, and so the title remained in Botvinnik's hands.

32 Staunton Memorial Tournament 1951

Disaster in the Penultimate Round

In London's first international chess tournament, held in 1851, the world's leading players met in a knock-out competition of matches in which the first to win four games went on to the next round. The organizer of the tournament was the British master Howard Staunton, who, by virtue of a knowledge of positional play unequalled by any of his contemporaries, was the favourite. However, in the event, he was overshadowed by the rising German star Anderssen, who won the tournament.

Almost a hundred years later to the day, on 26 May 1951—the London tournament had begun on 27 May 1851—a tournament in memory of Staunton started in the town of Cheltenham, where the first six rounds were played. The next three took place in Leamington and the last six in Birmingham.

The tournament was dominated by the Yugoslav contingent. For most of the tournament three of them—Gligorić, Pirc and Trifunović—fought it out for first place, and with two rounds to go the leading scores were: Gligorić, 9, Trifunović 8½, Alexander, Matanović and Pirc 8.

In view of the position, Gligorić adopted a policy that has often helped the leader to victory in similar situations: he avoided every possible risk and quietly drew his games against Tartakower and Scheltinga. His tactics were all the wiser in that he had Black in the last two rounds. The fate of his chief rival, Dr Trifunović, was decided in the penultimate round.

Queen's Gambit

Trifunović	Bogolyubov
1 N-KB3	P-Q4
2 P-Q4	N-KB3
3 P-B4	P-B3
4 N-B3	P-K3
5 B-N5	

This move shows that Trifunović is resolved to play sharply for a win, for it gives his opponent a chance to adopt the very unclear Anti-Meran Gambit: 5 . . . PxP 6 P-K4 P-N4.

| 5 . . . | QN-Q2 |

But Bogolyubov would rather go into the Cambridge Springs, which is brought about by 6 P-K3 Q-R4. Then the best continuation for both sides is supposed to be 7 PxP NxP, whereas recapturing with the pawn (7 . . . KPxP) is not considered good for Black.

| 6 PxP | KPxP |
| 7 P-K3 | Q-R4? |

Black now gets into the weak variation mentioned above. The usual continuation is 7 . . . B-K2 8 Q-B2 0-0 9 B-Q3.

| 8 B-Q3 | N-K5 |
| 9 0-0! | |

This pawn sacrifice is considered to be the refutation of Black's play. If now 9 . . . NxN 10 PxN QxBP, then White gets a strong attack by 11 P-K4 PxP 12 R-K1! P-KB4 13 R-QB1 Q-R6 14 N-KR4.

| 9 . . . | NxB |
| 10 NxN | N-B3 |

In a game Janowski–Bogolyubov, New York 1924, White obtained the advantage after 10 . . . B-K2 11 P-B4 N-B3 12 Q-K1 Q-N3 13 R-N1 B-Q2 14 N-B3. By occupying the square K5 with his knight White gets good attacking chances on the king's wing.

11 R-K1?

White was probably preparing the advance P-K4, which, however, is not good in this position. He should have played 11 Q-B2, e.g. 11 . . . P-KR3 12 N-B3 B-K2 13 N-K5 followed by P-B4. The immediate 11 P-B4, on the other hand, would allow Black to simplify by 11 . . . P-KR3 12 N-B3 B-KN5.

11 . . .	B-K2
12 Q-B2	B-Q2
13 QR-QB1	R-Q1
14 P-QR3	

Instead of preparing the well-known minority attack, White should play 14 P-B4, though for an attack on the king's wing his rook would be better placed on KB1 than on K1. For two moves White is faced with the temptation of playing NxRP(?), which he resists. If he were to take the pawn, Black would be ill advised to play 14 . . . NxN 15 BxN P-KN3 16 BxP PxB 17 QxPch K-B1 18 P-K4, which gives White a dangerous attack. Much better is 14 . . . N-K5! 15 NxN PxN 16 BxP P-KB4 (or 16 . . . Q-KR4).

14 . . .	B-QB1
15 P-R3	Q-B2
16 N-R4	

Here 16 NxRP can be answered simply by 16 . . . NxN 17 BxN P-KN3, and although White gets three pawns for his piece (after 18 BxP), this is not sufficient compensation in view of Black's two bishops and the harmonious co-operation of his pieces.

| 16 . . . | B-Q3 |
| 17 N-B5 | P-KR3 |

| 18 N-B3 | 0-0 |
| 19 P-QN4 | Q-K2 |

Black is well developed and has nothing to fear from the minority attack. The most natural plan for him is KR-K1 and N-K5.

| 20 N-Q2 | B-N1 |

Now that the White knight has departed from KB3, Black intends to operate with the threat of Q-B2 or Q-Q3. However, 20 . . . KR-K1 is a more natural-looking move.

| 21 R-N1 | KR-K1 |
| 22 P-QR4 | P-QR4? |

This pawn sacrifice is incorrect and should have given White a clear advantage. The best move seems to be 22 . . . B-Q3!, making use of the tactical weakness of White's QN4. If then 23 P-N5, Black can continue 23 . . . P-QN3 24 N(B5)-N3 P-B4.

| 23 PxP | Q-B2 |
| 24 N-B3 | R-K2 |

108. Trifunović–Bogolyubov

| 25 B-B5! | N-K5!? |

Black has no good way of protecting the QNP, so he decides to go in for complications. This has the disadvantage that White could simply continue 26 NxN BxB 27 N-B6ch PxN 28 QxB, destroying Black's pawn position with fatal effects. At this stage of the game Dr Trifunović was very near to winning the tournament, for he had one of the less dangerous players as an opponent in the last round, a member of the home contingent, Klein.

26 BxB?	**QxB**
27 NxN	**PxN**
28 N-Q2	**Q-B2**
29 NxP!?	

More solid is 29 N-B1, though even in that case Black would have obtained a slight advantage by 29 . . . QxP.

29 . . .	**Q-R7ch**
30 K-B1	**Q-R8ch?**

Black fails to see a little tactical twist and as a result throws away his advantage. Instead 30 . . . R(Q1)-K1! is very strong, e.g. 31 P-B3 RxN! 32 PxR B-N6 33 KR-Q1 Q-R8ch 34 K-K2 QxNPch 35 K-Q3 QxKPch 36 K-B3 QxKPch and the White king has nowhere safe to go. In addition Black has a king-side pawn majority of 3:1. Both these facts would give him the much better game.

31 K-K2	**QxNP**
32 N-B6ch!	**K-B1**
33 R-KN1	

Now it is Black who appears to be lost, for 33 . . . QxRP allows the decisive reply 34 Q-R7. Unfortunately for Trifunović there is a tactical finesse in the position.

33 . . .	**RxKPch!**
34 KxR	**QxRPch**

109. Trifunović–Bogolyubov

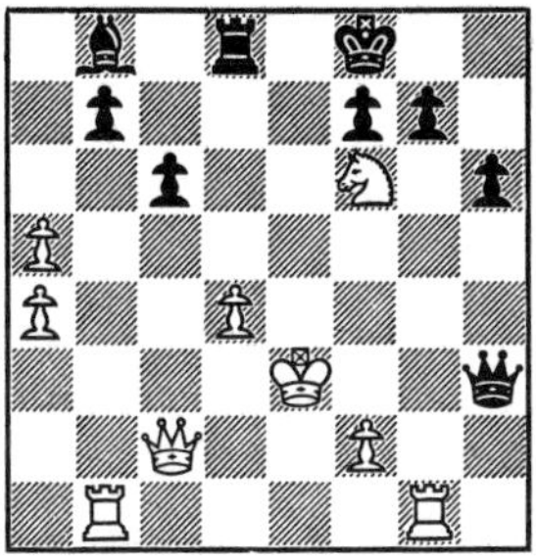

35 P-B3

This causes an irreparable weakness. Much stronger is 35 K-K2! PxN 36 Q-K4! P-KB4 (36 . . . R-K1? 37 R-N8ch) 37 Q-K3, when White should be able to draw the game in spite of the exposed position of his king.

35 . . .	**PxN**
36 Q-Q3	

If 36 Q-K4, the reply 36 . . . P-KB4 is strong, for White does not have access to K3.

36 . . .	**Q-R7**

Staunton Memorial 1951

		1	2	3	4	5	6	7	8	9	10	11	12	13	14	15	16	Pts	Prize
1	Gligorić	–	1	1	½	0	½	½	½	½	1	1	1	1	½	½	½	10	I
2	Pirc	0	–	½	0	½	0	1	1	½	½	1	1	1	1	1	½	9½	II–IV
3	Ståhlberg	0	½	–	½	1	½	½	½	½	1	1	½	1	½	½	1	9½	II–IV
4	Trifunović	½	1	½	–	½	½	½	½	½	1	0	½	½	1	1	1	9½	II–IV
5	Alexander	1	½	0	½	–	½	½	½	½	0	1	½	½	½	1	1	8½	V–VIII
6	Matanović	½	1	½	½	½	–	0	½	½	½	0	½	½	1	1	1	8½	V–VIII
7	Rossolimo	½	0	½	½	½	1	–	½	½	0	1	½	1	½	1	½	8½	V–VIII
8	Unzicker	½	0	½	½	½	½	½	–	0	1	1	½	½	½	1	1	8½	V–VIII
9	Donner	½	½	½	½	½	½	½	1	–	1	0	½	½	0	0	½	7	
10	Klein	0	½	0	0	1	½	1	0	0	–	1	½	1	1	½	0	7	
11	Bogolyubov	0	0	0	1	0	1	0	0	1	0	–	1	0	1	½	1	6½	
12	Golombek	0	0	½	½	½	½	½	½	½	½	0	–	0	1	½	½	6	
13	Broadbent	0	0	0	½	½	½	0	½	½	0	1	1	–	½	½	0	5½	
14	Tartakower	½	0	½	0	½	0	½	½	1	0	0	0	½	–	1	½	5½	
15	v. Scheltinga	½	0	½	0	0	0	0	0	1	½	½	½	½	0	–	1	5	
16	Wade	½	½	0	0	0	0	½	0	½	1	0	½	1	½	0	–	5	

| 37 | Q-K4 | P-KB4! |
| 38 | QxKBP | R-K1ch |

Now White is lost, for 39 K-Q3 is answered decisively by 39 . . . Q-K7ch 40 K-B3 R-K6ch 41 K-N4 B-Q3ch.

| 39 | Q-K4 | B-B5ch |

40	K-Q3	Q-Q7ch
41	K-B4	RxQ
42	PxR	Q-QB7ch

Confronted with mate on the next move, White resigned.

33 Maróczy Memorial, Budapest 1952

A Precise Positional Performance

From March to April 1952 an international tournament was held in Budapest in memory of the Hungarian grandmaster Geza Maróczy, in his day one of the strongest players in the world. The organizers succeeded in getting together a very powerful field, including the world champion, M. M. Botvinnik, who was at that time a rare participant in international events. Along with Keres and Smyslov, Botvinnik was one of the favourites for first place. All three grandmasters, however, suffered defeats within the first few rounds. In the second round Botvinnik with White lost to Geller, and Keres fell to Petrosian, who was just at the start of his international career; in the third round Smyslov was beaten by Keres. The latter then proceeded to make up lost ground with victories over Pilnik, Sliwa and Geller. Keres's important win over Geller was achieved in a pretty game.

110. Keres–Geller

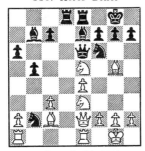

Position after Black's 17th move

18	NxP!	QxN
19	B-N3	N-B5
20	NxN	PxN
21	BxP	N-Q4
22	BxB	QxB

If 22 ... RxB, then 23 Q-Q2! R(Q1)-K1 24 BxN BxB 25 PxB RxRch 26 RxR RxRch 27 QxR, when 27 ... QxQP is not possible on account of 28 Q-K8 mate.

23	PxN	QxQ
24	RxQ	RxR
25	BxR	BxP
26	P-QR4!	

Not, of course, 26 R-Q1? R-K1 27 RxB RxB or 26 BxP R-R1 27 P-QB4? RxB 28 PxB R-R4, in both cases the ending being drawn.

26	...	R-Q3
27	R-Q1	K-B2
28	P-R5!	R-K3
29	B-B1	

If 29 BxP, then 29 ... B-N6.

29	...	B-N6
30	R-Q7ch	K-B1
31	RxBP	R-K4
32	R-B6	RxP
33	R-QN6!	

Not 33 RxP? R-QB4.

33	...	B-B7
34	RxP	R-QB4
35	R-R3	R-Q4
36	P-B3	R-Q8
37	K-B2	R-B8
38	P-R4	B-N3
39	B-B4	K-K2
40	P-N4	P-R3
41	B-Q5	Resigns

Botvinnik suffered a further, and even more unexpected, defeat in the seventh round. Instead of continuing with 39 ... Q-Q8ch 40 K-R2 Q-Q5, which would have led to a draw, he chose a losing move and the game continued **39 ... P-K5? 40 R-KB5! Q-N8ch 41 K-R2 Q-N5,** after which he resigned, for White has two ways of winning: 42 RxBch PxR 43 QxBPch K-K1 44 RxNch QxR 45 Q-QB6ch and 42 P-R6 R-K1 43 P-R7 Q-R6 44 R-N7 followed by 45 R-N8.

111. Szily–Botvinnik

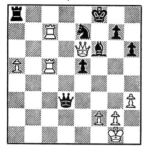

Position after White's 39th move

The least successful of the trio of favourites was Smyslov. After his defeat by Keres, he did admittedly win in the fourth round against Benkö, but then he lost the next two games, against Pilnik and, with White, against Kottnauer.

Keres lost a second time in the ninth round, to Szabó, but by the time the last round had been reached he had caught up with Geller, who had been in the lead the whole time. Both of them had 11½ points, Ståhlberg 11, Botvinnik and Smyslov 10. The last round proved to be very exciting. Smyslov and Botvinnik won against Gereben and Pilnik respectively, drawing level with Ståhlberg, who was a victim of the tense atmosphere. In the opening the latter unwisely allowed his opponent, Benkö, to open the KR file and as a result his king was badly exposed. After a while he lost two pawns and when the game was adjourned he was in a hopeless position.

The struggle for first prize was decided by the games of the leaders, Geller and Keres. Geller played the opening quietly, but then sought complications.

King's Indian

O'Kelly	Geller
1 P-Q4	N-KB3
2 N-KB3	P-KN3
3 B-B4	B-N2
4 QN-Q2	0-0
5 P-K4	P-Q3
6 B-Q3	QN-Q2
7 0-0	N-R4
8 B-KN5	P-KR3
9 B-R4	N-B5
10 B-B4	P-KN4
11 B-KN3	P-K4
12 P-B3	N-QN3
13 B-N3	B-N5
14 P-KR3	B-Q2
15 P-QR4	P-QR4
16 N-B4	NxN
17 BxN(QB4)	K-R1
18 R-K1	Q-K2
19 N-R2	QR-Q1
20 PxP	PxP
21 Q-N3	

112. O'Kelly–Geller

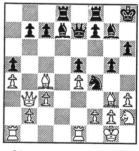

21 ...   P-KB4!?

If instead 21 ... P-N3, the game might well continue 22 N-N4 P-KB4 23 PxP BxBP 24 N-K3 B-K5 25 BxN NPxB (or 25 ... RxB but not 25 ... KPxB 26 N-Q5 Q-K4 27 P-B3) 26 N-Q5 BxN 27 BxB with a hopelessly drawn position.

Geller does not want to waste time defending the QNP and invites the variation 22 QxP R-QN1 23 Q-R7 RxP 24 QxRP, trusting that the fact that the queen is out of play will give him sufficient counter-play for the pawn. However, O'Kelly is not interested in such complications.

22	PxP	BxP
23	N-N4	Q-B4
24	N-K3	B-K5
25	QR-Q1	Q-B3
26	Q-N5!	Q-KB3!?

Taking the KNP is out of the question because White could then exchange off one of Black's attacking pieces, e.g. 26 . . . BxP? 27 BxN or 26 . . . NxP? 27 QxQ.

27	RxR	RxR
28	QxRP	P-N3

On his 26th move Geller avoided an exchange of queens by sacrificing a pawn. As O'Kelly did not decline the sacrifice, it was to be expected that a sharp struggle would ensue. Objectively seen, Black has insufficient compensation for the pawn, e.g. 29 Q-N5 B-B3 (29 . . . R-Q7? 30 N-N4 Q-B4 31 Q-K8ch B-B1 32 RxB!) 30 Q-N3 R-Q7 31 R-Q1 Q-Q3 32 BxN KPxB 33 N-Q5 RxRch 34 QxR. O'Kelly, however, offered a draw, which Geller understandably accepted, for the risks involved in playing on would have been very great indeed.

Queen's Gambit

	Barcza	Keres
1	N-KB3	P-Q4
2	P-Q4	

Barcza departs from his beloved 2 P-KN3. The reason is obviously psychological: he assumes, first, that Keres will have been prepared for 2 P-KN3 and, secondly, that he will not feel at home in the Queen's Gambit, which he normally avoids.

2	. . .	N-KB3
3	P-B4	PxP

At first sight, this looks a little surprising, for the Queen's Gambit accepted is a system in which White can get an easy draw if he wishes. However, Keres rightly concludes that 3 . . . P-K3 and 3 . . . P-B3 are no more promising and proceeds on the assumption that his opponent has a considerable interest in playing for a win—in the circumstances a reasonable assumption, for, at the time, a victory seemed likely to get Barcza among the prize winners, whereas a draw did not.

4	P-K3	P-K3
5	BxP	P-B4

When playing for a win, one can easily have a few anxious moments in such a position lest one's opponent might simplify by PxP on this or the next move.

6	0-0	P-QR3
7	Q-K2	P-QN4
8	B-Q3	

The usual move is 8 B-N3, but in his game with Smyslov, Keres, who had White, used the same retreat as in this game and got a slight advantage after 8 . . . N-B3 9 P-QR4 P-N5 (9 . . . PxRP 10 B-B2!) 10 PxP BxP 11 P-K4 P-K4 12 B-K3. Now Keres, with Black, finds a better defence.

8	. . .	PxP
9	PxP	B-N2?

The theoretical view of the variation 8 B-Q3 changed somewhat after the Budapest tournament, and a few years later it was discovered that this natural move is not good. Correct is 9 . . . B-K2! and then 10 P-QR4 PxP! After that 11 B-B2 is no longer dangerous, for Black can simply castle.

10 P-QR4   PxP!?

Strategically the right idea, though it has a tactical snag, for White can now get an advantage by 11 B-B2!, e.g. 11 . . . B-K2 12 BxQRPch B-B3 13 BxBch NxB 14 RxP NxP 15 NxN RxR 16 QxR QxN

17 B-K3 or 12 . . . QN-Q2? 13 N-K5 R-B1
14 P-Q5, with a strong attack (Spanjaard–
Devos, 1959). The best defence in this
line seems to be 12 . . . KN-Q2!

11 RxP?

Now the game goes into a position
that Black could have attained if he had
played 9 . . . B-K2.

11 ...	B-K2
12 QN-Q2	0-0
13 N-N3	

Neither on this square nor on QR5 will
the knight be well placed. A better move
is 13 N-B4, though in that case Black can
play 13 . . . N-B3 followed by N-QN5.

13 ...	B-B3
14 R-R1	Q-N3!
15 N-R5	B-N4

An excellent positional manoeuvre. An
exchange of white-squared bishops is
bound to help Black, for it eliminates the
danger of a king-side attack and allows
him to concentrate on his opponent's
isolated QP.

16 N-B4	Q-N2
17 KN-K5	N-B3

113. Barcza–Keres

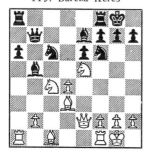

18 B-K3?

A bad positional mistake. White was
already worse off, and should have sought
to ease his position by exchanging
knights, e.g. 18 NxN QxN 19 B-K3.

18 ...	N-QN5!
19 B-N1	QR-B1
20 R-QB1	KR-Q1
21 P-QN3	P-N3

Black would like to finish regrouping
his pieces by N(B3)-Q4. However, he
cannot do it at once because of 22
BxPch.

22 P-B3?

Mistakes are easily made in difficult
situations. Now the weakness of the
square K3 will soon make itself felt. The
correct move is 22 N-Q3 in order to try
and exchange off a minor piece.

22 ...	N(B3)-Q4
23 B-K4?	

Strangely enough this move is bound
to lead to the loss of at least a pawn.
Barcza had probably intended to play 23
B-KB2 (which would explain his previous
move, P-KB3) but now realized that it
could be answered by 22 . . . B-N4. The
text-move is an attempt to meet the
threat of 23 . . . NxB 24 QxN RxP! (25
QxR? B-B4), but the best way of doing so
is 23 K-R1, when White at least maintains
material equality even though he has a
decidedly inferior position.

23 ...	P-B4!
24 BxN	

White cannot very well make good his
mistake by retreating with his Bishop (24
B-N1), for Black would go ahead and win
the QP in the way described in the
previous note.

24 ...	PxB
25 N-R5	RxRch!
26 BxR	

White would lose a piece by 26 RxR?
Q-N3.

26 ...	Q-N3
27 Q-Q1	

114. Barcza–Keres

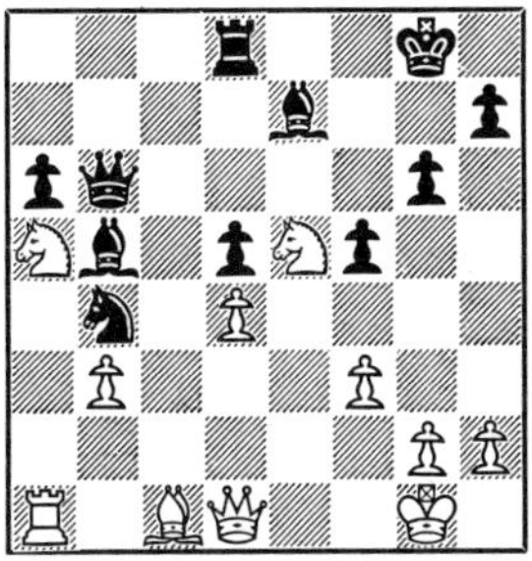

27 . . . R-QB1!

Black could instead win a pawn by 27 . . . N-B7 28 R-R2 QxPch 29 QxQ NxQ, but he is quite rightly not content with that. The text-move threatens 28 . . . RxB 29 RxR QxN and leaves White no way of avoiding loss of material.

28 K-R1

In order to reply to 28 . . . RxB? by 29 QxR.

28 . . . N-B7
29 N(R5)-B6

A last, despairing attempt to complicate matters. If, instead, 29 R-R2, the simple 29 . . . QxP is sufficient, and if 29 N(R5)-B4, Black can either capture the QP or win by 29 . . . PxN 30 QxN QxP 31 B-N2 P-B6.

29 . . .	**RxN**
30 NxR	**QxN**
31 R-R2	**N-N5**

Better than 31 . . . NxP 32 B-K3. Now White will not be able to get his rook into play.

32 R-KB2	**Q-B6**
33 B-N2	**N-Q6!**
34 R-QB2	**NxB**
35 Q-QB1	**QxNP**
36 RxN	**Q-B5**
37 R-QB2	**Q-B8ch**
38 Resigns	

Budapest 1952

		1	2	3	4	5	6	7	8	9	10	11	12	13	14	15	16	17	18	Pts	Prize
1	Keres	–	1	½	1	½	0	0	1	1	½	1	1	½	½	1	1	1	1	12½	I
2	Geller	0	–	1	½	½	1	½	1	½	½	1	½	½	½	1	1	1	1	12	II
3	Botvinnik	½	0	–	½	½	½	½	1	1	½	½	0	1	1	1	1	1	½	11	III–V
4	Smyslov	0	½	½	–	½	½	½	0	1	1	1	½	1	0	1	1	1	1	11	III–V
5	Ståhlberg	½	½	½	½	–	0	1	½	½	0	½	1	1	1	½	1	1	1	11	III–V
6	Szabó	1	0	½	½	1	–	1	½	½	1	1	1	1	0	½	0	0	1	10½	VI
7	Petrosian	1	½	½	½	0	0	–	0	½	0	1	½	1	½	½	1	1	1	9½	VII, VIII
8	Pilnik	0	0	0	1	½	½	1	–	½	½	0	1	½	½	½	1	1	1	9½	VII, VIII
9	O'Kelly	0	½	0	0	½	½	½	½	–	1	½	½	1	½	½	1	1	½	9	IX
10	Benkö	½	½	½	0	1	0	1	½	0	–	0	1	1	1	½	0	0	1	8½	
11	Barcza	0	0	½	0	½	0	0	1	½	1	–	½	½	1	1	0	½	1	8	
12	Szily	0	½	1	½	0	0	½	0	½	0	½	–	½	1	1	0	1	1	8	
13	Golombek	½	½	0	0	0	0	0	½	0	0	½	½	–	½	1	1	1	1	7	
14	Kottnauer	½	½	0	1	0	1	½	½	½	0	0	0	½	–	0	1	1	0	7	
15	Gereben	0	0	0	0	½	½	½	½	½	½	0	0	0	1	–	1	0	1	6	
16	Trolanescu	0	0	0	0	0	1	0	0	0	1	1	1	0	0	0	–	½	1	5½	
17	Sliwa	0	0	0	0	0	1	0	0	0	1	½	0	0	0	1	½	–	1	5	
18	Platz	0	0	½	0	0	0	0	0	½	0	0	0	0	1	0	0	0	–	2	

34 World Championship Match 1957

A Draw Worth its Weight in Gold

The match between Botvinnik and Smyslov played in 1957 is often compared to one that took place thirty years earlier, that between Alekhin and Capablanca. If we ignore the draws, then the challenger won by the same score, 6:3. Even more interesting is the fact that the order of the won games was the same, viz. 1:0, 1:1, 1:2, 2:2, 3:2, 4:2, 4:3, 5:3, 6:3. The bare figures might lead one to conclude that the decisive game was again that in which the challenger chalked up his fifth win to take a two-point lead, in this case the seventeenth game, in which Botvinnik had White. But a closer look at the game itself shows that Botvinnik hardly put up a real fight at all. He played well under his normal strength and at variance with his usual style. He conceded his opponent the two bishops in the opening; then he unnecessarily weakened his pawn structure. He lost a pawn in the ending and missed a drawing line after the second time control. This was, of course, virtually the end. After two quiet draws, the second of which lasted only fifteen moves, Smyslov won the twentieth game, and the next two games, drawn in thirteen and twenty-one moves respectively, were only a form of capitulation.

The real turning-point in the match occurred earlier, in the fifteenth round to be precise. But first let us go back a little. Smyslov managed to build up a lead of 7:5 in the first half of the match, and at that stage few observers gave Botvinnik much of a chance. His opponent, after all, was noted for his strong finishing powers, which had helped him in many a tournament to make up lost ground after an indifferent start. Nevertheless Botvinnik

came back into the match in the thirteenth game, which he conducted in his best style and won after making use of a small positional advantage in an exemplary manner. Two days later, in a game in which he had Black, he came very near to winning again, Smyslov only escaping by the skin of his teeth in an endgame in which he was virtually a pawn down. When the fifteenth game started, it was fairly clear that Botvinnik would make a big effort to win. And, in fact, he did have a clearly won game at the adjournment. But then he relaxed and allowed his opponent to draw.

Nimzo-Indian

	Botvinnik	Smyslov
1	P-QB4	N-KB3
2	N-QB3	P-K3
3	P-Q4	B-N5
4	P-K3	P-QN3
5	KN-K2	B-R3
6	P-QR3	

Prior to 1957 this continuation was considered strong, because Black usually replied by withdrawing his bishop to K2. Smyslov had made excellent preparation for the match and had discovered that Black has another move, and one, moreover, that equalizes. As a result, in later years 6 N-N3 was often seen. If the game then continues 6 ... BxNch (the sharp advance 6 ... P-R4!? is interesting) 7 PxP P-Q4 8 Q-B3 (the pawn sacrifice 8 B-R3 BxP 9 BxB PxB 10 0-0!? is less clear) 8 ... 0-0 9 PxP, the natural reply 9 ... PxP gives White an advantage, e.g. 10 BxB NxB 11 Q-K2 N-N1 12 P-B3. A better

line for Black is 9 ... QxP! 10 P-K4
Q-QR4.

	6 ...	BxNch!
	7 NxB	P-Q4

The idea behind the exchange. Black
gets an attack on the QBP in return for
the two bishops.

	8 P-QN3	0-0
	9 B-K2	

This whole variation occurred in the
match three times altogether. Two games
previously, Botvinnik had played the
immediate 9 P-QR4. If Smyslov had then
replied with 9 ... PxP followed by N-B3,
the same position as in the present game
would have been reached, for White
would certainly have developed his
bishop to K2. Smyslov, however, chose
a sharper continuation, 9 ... P-B4!? and
got a satisfactory position after 10 B-R3
QPxP 11 NPxP N-B3! 12 PxP PxP 13
QxQ R(B1)xQ 14 BxP N-QR4, though he
later lost the game.

	9 ...	PxP
	10 PxP	N-B3!

This, when followed by N-QR4, will
put increased pressure on the QBP. In the
seventh game, a draw was agreed after 11
N-N5 N-QR4 12 B-Q2 P-B3 13 BxN PxB!
14 N-B3 P-B4 15 N-R4 PxP 16 PxP Q-Q3
17 0-0 QR-Q1 18 Q-Q2 QxQP 19 QxP
Q-K5 20 N-B3 Q-B3 21 N-N5 Q-N3 22
QxQ PxQ 23 KR-Q1 N-K5. Match play
has its peculiarities. One of these is the
endeavour to discover weaknesses in the
opponent's theoretical armour and to
strengthen one's play in variations
specially prepared for the match by the
opponent. The next move is obviously a
result of Botvinnik's preparations.

	11 P-QR4(!)	Q-Q2(?)

Later analysis showed that this move,
which makes way for the rook, is superfluous. Black would have done better to
continue with 11 ... N-QR4 12 B-R3

R-K1 13 N-N5 P-B3! 14 N-Q6 R-K2,
which leads to equality.

	12 N-N5	KR-Q1
	13 B-N2	

Better than 13 B-R3. White keeps the
square QR3 free for his knight.

	13 ...	N-QR4
	14 Q-B2	P-B3
	15 N-R3	Q-K2
	16 0-0	P-B4
	17 N-N5	B-N2
	18 B-R3	

A natural-looking move, but probably
not the best. The bishop is better placed
on QN2, so the immediate 18 P-B3 is
preferable.

	18 ...	N-B3
	19 KR-Q1	P-QR3
	20 N-B3	N-QN5
	21 Q-N3	P-QR4
	22 N-N5	

Now the knight takes up a permanent
position on this strong post after having
previously occupied it twice. White's
pieces are all concentrated on the queen's
side, a fact which Smyslov quite rightly
exploits by preparing a dangerous king-
side attack.

	22 ...	P-R3
	23 B-N2	QR-B1
	24 P-B3	PxP
	25 PxP	N-R4
	26 B-KB1	Q-N4
	27 B-R3	

This wins a pawn, for the Black knight
cannot withdraw, e.g. 27 ... N-QB3 28
N-Q6 R-B2 29 P-Q5.

	27 ...	N-B5
	28 K-R1	

The first crisis in the game. It is fairly
clear that Black must pursue his king-side
action energetically. Strategically the
advance of the KRP to KR6 to weaken

115. Botvinnik–Smyslov

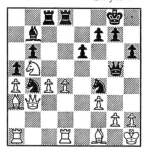

Position after White's 28th move

the opponent's pawns seems called for. But such a plan is too slow, so tactical measures are needed. The pretty rook sacrifice 28 . . . RxBP would have guaranteed at least a draw. Accepting it at once (29 QxR) would be very risky, for after 29 . . . R-QB1 White cannot continue 30 Q-N3 R-B7 31 BxN RxP! or 31 P-N3 Q-R4, which leads to a quick loss, but must give up his queen for the other rook by 30 QxRch BxQ, when Black has the advantage because his queen co-operates more harmoniously with the minor pieces than do White's rooks. A better continuation for White is 29 P-N3 N(B5)-Q6 30 QxR BxPch 31 B-N2 Q-K6 32 BxB QxBch with a draw. 30 RxN NxR 31 QxN Q-Q4!, on the other hand, is not particularly promising, since Black gets a second pawn and has excellent chances.

28 . . .	P-R4?
29 BxN	PxB
30 QxP	P-R5
31 R-R3	

It is necessary to overprotect the KBP and doing so with the rook is more logical than with the queen (Q-N3). Defence should always be economical, and the queen is very active where it is.

| 31 . . . | R-B4 |

A slight disadvantage of White's previous move is that Black is now able to transfer his rook to the king-side. How-

ever, the attack he gets there does not seriously endanger White.

| 32 R-K1 | R-KB4 |

116. Botvinnik–Smyslov

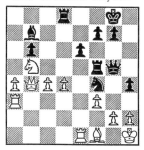

33 N-Q6?

Both players had used up a considerable amount of their time and it is not surprising that they make mistakes in this complicated position. Botvinnik's move not only gives away all White's advantage but even seriously endangers his position. Black should now reply energetically by advancing his RP; e.g. 33 . . . P-R6! 34 P-N3 N-N7 35 NxB (35 N-K4 BxN 36 PxB R-B7 37 R-N1 RxP or 37 BxN PxBch 38 K-N1 R-B8ch 39 KxP! RxR 40 QxR RxP with advantage to Black) 35 . . . NxR 36 NxR N-B7 37 Q-N2 (37 QxP? Q-B8!) 37 . . . NxR 38 QxN QxN 39 BxP R-QR4 and White loses a pawn.

The correct move for White in the above position is the strong 33 P-Q5!, which reduces the strength of Black's bishop. If Black then takes the pawn (33 . . . PxP) the reply 34 N-Q6 is decisive. And if 33 . . . R-K4 34 RxR QxR, White gets good winning chances, e.g. 35 Q-K7! Q-K8!? 36 QxRch K-R2 37 R-R1! (37 K-N1?? N-K7ch) 37 . . . QxR 38 QxRPch K-N1 39 K-N1 with a won game.

| 33 . . . | NxP? |

A faulty combination, which does not lose but returns the initiative to White.

34	BxN	P-R6
35	BxP	BxPch
36	RxB	RxR
37	NxP!	

Smyslov had been prepared for two replies, the first of which allows Black to draw: 37 B-N2 R-B7 38 R-KN1 Q-B5 39 N-N5 RxB 40 KxR Q-N5ch 41 K-B2 Q-B5ch with perpetual check. The second leads to a win: 37 N-K4? Q-R5 38 B-N2 R-QN6! 39 Q-Q2 RxP! 40 Q-K2 (40 Q-KB2 RxN!) 40 ... R-N7! 41 Q-B1 RxB! He failed to see this pretty counter and, what is more, he was so depressed that he did not find the relatively simple defence.

37	...	RxN

Not, of course, 37 ... KxN 38 BxPch K-B3 39 QxP, etc.

38	BxP	RxP?

This gets Black into a lost position, though it is not the last surprise in this interesting but nervously played game. The correct move is 38 ... Q-B3!, when Black can hold the game thanks to the weakened position of the White king, e.g. 39 BxRch KxB 40 P-Q5 Q-KB6ch 41 K-N1 Q-N5ch 42 K-B2 Q-B5ch 43 K-K2 R-K1ch 44 K-Q1 Q-N5ch! 45 K-Q2 Q-Q5ch 46 K-B2 RxR 47 QxR QxBPch, draw, or 39 Q-B3 RxP and the extra pawn is not sufficient to win in this position.

39	QxP	R(Q5)-B5
40	BxRch	RxB
41	Q-K6	

The game was adjourned at this stage, and some commentators thought Smyslov might resign without resuming play. Botvinnik himself was probably so influenced by the general feeling that he did not give his full attention to the adjournment analysis. His weak play on resumption was a rarity for him and in complete contrast to his normal fine

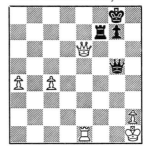

117. Botvinnik–Smyslov

Position after White's 41st move

precision in adjourned positions, which was the result of thorough and accurate analysis.

41	...	Q-B5
42	Q-QB6	R-B4

Meeting the main threat, 43 P-R5. White has now several ways of strengthening his position, e.g. 43 R-R1 or 43 R-KN1. Botvinnik opts for the simplest way of all, an exchange of queens, but in doing so has to give up one of his extra pawns.

43	Q-R8ch	K-R2
44	Q-K4	QxQ
45	RxQ	R-QR4
46	K-N2	K-N3
47	K-B3??	

On occasions even the greatest of players make quite elementary technical mistakes. In rook endings like this one, the most important thing is to keep the opposing king away from the pawn. There was a simple win by 47 R-B4!, e.g. 47 ... K-N4 48 K-B3 RxP 49 K-K3 R-R6ch 50 K-K4 R-KR6 (50 ... R-QB6 51 P-R4ch K-R4 52 K-Q4) 51 K-B2 or 49 ... P-N3 50 P-R4ch K-R4 51 K-Q4.

47	...	K-B4
48	R-B4ch	

Other moves are no better, e.g. 48 K-K3 RxP 49 P-R4 R-R8 or 49 K-Q4 R-R7, draw.

48	...	K-K4
49	R-K4ch	K-B4
50	R-B4ch	K-K4
51	K-N4	RxP
52	K-N5	R-R3!

53	P-R4	R-QB3
54	P-R5	K-K3
55	K-N6	K-K4dis ch
56	K-N5	K-K3
	Drawn	

Success for Tal, Catastrophe for Bronstein

The 1958 Interzonal was held at the charming Yugoslav seaside resort of Portoroz on the Adriatic coast. The unusual number of twenty-one contestants made it somewhat difficult to get a proper picture of the progress of this chess marathon. For a long time about half the competing masters and grandmasters—or, to be more exact, all the grandmasters and two of the masters, Fischer and Benkö—were in contention for the six places that would ensure promotion to the Candidates' Tournament.

The Soviet grandmaster Tal was in top form, which afterwards made him one of the favourites for the Candidates' Tournament. In the Interzonal he lost to Matanović in the fourth round, but then for a long time kept close behind the leader, Petrosian, before catching up with him by an impressive victory over Larsen in the fifteenth round. In the following round he took the sole lead when Larsen avenged himself on Petrosian for his defeat at the hands of Tal. After the sixteenth round the position was as follows: Tal 11, Petrosian 10½, Olafsson 10. None of these three had yet had the bye, unlike Averbach, Benkö, Fischer, Gligorić and Pachman, who, with nine points each, all had an extra game to play.

Tal's victory was decided in the seventeenth round. One cannot help admiring the way he risked so much in that decisive game despite the fact that a defeat would not only have cost him the first place but could even have endangered his chances of going on to the Candidates' Tournament.

Ruy Lopez

Tal	Panno
1 P-K4	P-K4
2 N-KB3	N-QB3
3 B-N5	P-QR3
4 B-R4	N-B3
5 O-O	B-K2
6 R-K1	P-QN4
7 B-N3	P-Q3
8 P-B3	O-O
9 P-KR3	N-Q2
10 P-Q4	N-N3

At the time the game was played, this move was considered better than 10 . . . B-B3 11 P-QR4.

11 B-K3

This was also the move recommended by theory. Later, Spasski in his match with Geller in 1965 produced a very strong improvement: 11 QN-Q2 B-B3 12 N-B1 R-K1 13 N(B1)-R2! followed by 14 N-N4. As a result, the variation beginning with 10 . . . N-N3 disappeared from major tournaments.

11 . . . PxP

Black must try and get in a counter-action in the centre to meet the threat of 12 PxP followed by BxN, for 11 . . . R-N1 would be a perceptible loss of time.

12 PxP   N-R4!

Bulgarian masters, who used to be fond of the move 10 . . . N-N3, recommended the advance 12 . . . P-Q4 with the idea of replying to 13 P-K5 by 13 . . . B-KB4, getting active play for Black's pieces. However, about a year before the

Portoroz tournament White deviated on move 13 in the game Tal–Antochin, in the Soviet Championship, and got a clear advantage: 13 N-B3! PxP 14 NxKP B-KB4 15 P-Q5 N-R4 16 P-Q6! PxP 17 BxN QxB 18 N-N3 B-K3 19 BxB PxB 20 RxP.

13 B-B2	P-QB4

118. Tal–Panno

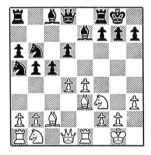

14 P-K5!?

At the first opportunity Tal complicates the game, though not in a way that is unfavourable to his opponent. However, the quiet continuation 14 PxP PxP 15 Q-K2 does not offer much hope of gaining an advantage and neither does 15 QxQ RxQ 16 P-QN4 N-N2.

14 ...	PxKP!

The strongest reply. If instead 14 ... PxQP 15 BxQP, Black cannot continue 15 ... N-B3 on account of 16 BxPch! KxB 17 Q-B2ch. Also weaker than the text-move is 14 ... N(R4)-B5 15 PxQP QxP, to which Tal intended the reply 16 B-N5! BxB 17 NxB with a piece attack on the king's side.

15 NxP	N(N3)-B5
16 Q-Q3	

If 16 Q-R5 P-N3, the double sacrifice on KN3 only leads to a draw: 17 NxNP BPxN 18 BxP PxB 19 QxNPch K-R1, and White cannot continue with 20 B-R6 on account of 20 ... R-KN1 21 Q-R5 Q-K1.

16 ...	P-B4
17 B-N3	P-B5

Black cannot sit back and wait, for 17 ... B-K3 18 PxP would cost him a pawn.

18 B-Q2	NxB(N6)!
19 N-B6!?	

If White were to play 19 QxN, Black would have a strong continuation in 19 ... B-B3! 20 NxN PxN 21 QxPch K-R1 22 QxBP BxQP with good counter-play.

19 ...	NxR!
20 NxQ	B-B4

This gains time for development and saves the knight on QR8, which would be lost by 20 ... BxN? 21 P-QN3.

21 Q-KB3	QRxN
22 RxB	BxN
23 BxP	

119. Tal–Panno

23 ...	RxP

After the game some commentators recommended 23 ... PxP and expressed the opinion that the passed queen pawn would decide the game in Black's favour. However, White has in that case sufficient attacking chances. Tal gives the continuation 24 P-QN3 B-N3 25 PxN P-Q6 26 Q-N4! P-Q7 27 R-Q7 or 26 ... RxB 27 QxR P-Q7 28 RxPch! etc.

24 Q-N4!

The move 24 Q-KN3 looks more natural, but as soon as Black plays B-N3 there is no future for the queen on KN3.

24 ... B-N3
25 Q-K6ch B-B2
26 Q-B5!

A nice trap: 26 ... B-N3? 27 RxPch! KxR 28 B-R6ch KxB 29 QxRch K-N4 30 QxPch followed by 31 QxR and White wins thanks to his superiority on the king's wing.

26 ... N-B7?

There was plenty of time for this move. Black should have continued 26 ... R-Q8ch 27 K-R2 N-Q7 28 BxN RxB and if White tries 29 QxBP, then 29 ... RxNP. This continuation would have given Black winning chances despite the active position of White's two pieces.

27 P-QN3 B-N3

This is possible because the rook on Q5 is protected by the knight on QB7. Black could also have tried 27 ... R-Q8ch 28 K-R2 N-Q7, for White must avoid 29 QxN? N-B8ch 30 K-N1 N-K6dis ch. However, 29 BxN RxB 30 QxP would leave White with the better chances in spite of the material disadvantage because Black's pieces lack co-ordination.

28 RxPch KxR
29 B-R6ch KxB
30 QxRch K-N4
31 PxN PxP!

It is imperative that the Black rook should remain active so that White does not have enough time to prepare a mating attack. The text-move has the added advantage that it leaves Black with an advanced passed pawn, which guarantees adequate counter-play.

32 P-N3 B-K5!
33 P-KR4ch!

Black would have an easier time with 33 P-B4ch K-N3 34 P-N4 P-R3. After the text-move, 33 ... K-N3 is no good on account of 34 P-B3 B-Q4, 35 P-N4 threatening 36 Q-B5ch.

33 ... K-N5!
34 K-R2

Threatening 35 Q-B4ch K-R4 36 Q-N5 mate. The reply 34 ... B-Q4 is inadequate because of 35 P-B3ch! BxP 36 Q-QB8ch K-R4 37 Q-KB5ch K-R3 38 Q-N5 mate. Panno, however, finds an excellent defence.

34 ... B-B4!

If White now continues 35 P-B3ch, it is Black who gets winning chances: 35 ... KxBP 36 QxBch K-K6!

35 Q-B6 P-R3
36 Q-K5 R-K5
37 Q-N7ch K-B6
38 Q-B3ch N-K6

This is not bad, but there is an immediate draw by 38 ... KxBP 39 QxNch K-B6.

39 K-N1! B-N5
40 PxN P-KR4

The active position of Black's pieces should ensure a draw. Up to this point Panno had defended with great ingenuity. Unfortunately for him his last move before the adjournment was a blunder.

41 Q-K1

120. Tal–Panno

41 ... RxP?

After putting up a stubborn fight for five hours, Black trips up shortly before the adjournment and throws away a well-earned draw. His most important pawn is that on QR3, which he should have covered with his rook by 41 ... R-K3! The position is then an interesting example of a positional draw, where White cannot win even if he captures the two bishop pawns.

42	Q-KB1ch	K-K5
43	QxPch	K-B6
44	Q-KB1ch	K-K5
45	QxP	K-Q5

Tal says that in his adjournment analysis he devoted most of his time to the continuation 45 ... RxPch 46 K-B2 R-Q6 and found the following win: 47 Q-B4ch R-Q5 48 Q-B2ch K-Q4 49 P-R4 K-B3 50 Q-N6ch K-N2 51 Q-K8 R-N5 52 K-K3. In the actual game his task was somewhat easier, for White's passed pawn is quicker than Black's.

46	Q-Q6ch	K-B5
47	P-R4	R-K8ch
48	K-B2	R-K7ch
49	K-B1	R-QR7
50	Q-QR6ch	K-Q5
51	P-R5	P-B5
52	Q-QN6ch	K-Q4
53	P-R6	R-R8ch
54	K-B2	P-B6
55	P-R7	P-B7
56	Q-N3ch	K-Q3
57	Q-Q3ch	Resigns

If 57 ... K-B4 or K-K4, then 58 Q-QB3ch. If 57 ... K-K2 then 58 QxP RxP 59 Q-R7ch. And if 57 ... K-K3 then 58 QxP RxP 59 Q-K4ch.

Prior to the last round the leading scores were Tal 13, Gligorić and Petrosian 12½, Benkö 12, Bronstein and Fischer 11½, Averbach, Olafsson, Pachman and Szabó 11. The struggle for the vital top six places was thus extremely interesting. Petrosian had a bye in the last round, so

he could not add to his score. The game between Gligorić and Fischer ended in a draw, which is what Tal had been relying on, for he played very solidly against Sherwin; in fact a draw was agreed before the first time control. Benkö drew with Nejkirch and so qualified for the Candidates' Tournament. Olafsson was the only one of those on 11 points to qualify; he defeated the Columbian player de Greiff in an ending that looked very drawn. I failed to beat Sanguinetti in a game in which I had White, and Szabó did not succeed in winning against Panno.

Going into the last round, Bronstein, who had 11½ points, seemed to be fairly certain of qualifying even though he had Black. First of all he was pitted against the weakest participant in the tournament, the Filipino Cardoso. Secondly it was highly likely that a draw would be sufficient, which meant that he would be able to play very solidly. In the event, however, a surprise was in store for him; his opponent played as if it were he who was trying to qualify.

Pirc Defence

Cardoso		Bronstein
1	P-K4	P-Q3
2	P-Q4	P-KN3
3	B-QB4	B-N2
4	N-K2	...

An original development of the knight instead of the usual 4 N-KB3. Cardoso combines the move B-QB4 with the set-up in the Sämisch variation of the King's Indian.

4	...	N-KB3
5	QN-B3	QN-Q2

More accurate is 5 ... P-B3, threatening P-Q4. If White then plays 6 B-N3 Black can reply 6 ... P-QN4.

6	P-B3	P-B3
7	P-QR4	P-QR4

The line 7 ... P-Q4 8 PxP N-N3 9 B-N3 QNxP deserves consideration.

| 8 | B-N3 | 0-0 |
| 9 | B-K3 | P-K3 |

It is obvious that Bronstein wants to keep the position strategically fluid. But here he allows his opponent too free a hand. A stronger continuation is the immediate 9 ... R-N1 followed by 10 ... P-QN4.

| 10 | Q-Q2 | R-N1 |
| 11 | N-Q1! | ... |

Nipping his opponent's queen-side counter-action in the bud, for 11 ... P-QN4? loses a pawn, e.g. 12 PxP PxP 13 QxP or 12 ... RxP 13 B-R4 R-N5 14 BxP

11	...	P-N3
12	N-B2	QB-R3
13	P-N4!	P-B4
14	P-R4	...

Cardoso was in nineteenth place in the tournament and had no hope of improving his position. The daring way in which he conducts the struggle with the renowned grandmaster therefore deserves our admiration.

| 14 | ... | P-R4 |

This does not stop the opening of lines on the king's side. Black has two better alternatives: 14 ... Q-K2 followed by KR-B1 and 14 ... BxN followed by P-R4.

121. Cardoso–Bronstein

15	N-N3	PxNP
16	BPxP	P-Q4
17	P-R5!	...

Not 17 P-K5 BPxP 18 B(K3)xP N-R2, which loses a pawn.

| 17 | ... | P-B5 |
| 18 | B-R2 | P-B6!? |

An attempt to put some activity into his position by means of a pawn sacrifice. Otherwise White obtains a very strong attack on the square KN6 by P-K5 followed by P-B3 and B-N1.

| 19 | NPxP | ... |

Better than 19 QxP QPxP followed by 20 ... N-Q4

19	...	Q-B2
20	P-K5	N-R2
21	N-Q3?	...

This move, which threatens 22 PxP PxP 23 N-B4, looks good. However, White thereby misses the chance of gaining a clear advantage. The modest 21 N-Q1 would have answered Black's threat of 21 ... NxP 22 PxN BxP (attacking both the knight on KN3 and the QBP) and at the same time have prepared the way for an attack on the KR file.

21	...	P-KN4!
22	P-R6	B-R1
23	N-R5	...

Only now does Cardoso realize that 23 BxNP is answered by 23 ... P-B3, for the KP is pinned.

| 23 | ... | QR-B1 |

The position has now changed completely. White's pawn on QB3 cannot be protected, and as soon as it falls the QRP and the other QBP will become weak. White is still unable to capture on KN5, e.g. 24 BxNP QxBP 25 QxQ RxQ 26 B-Q2 RxP, etc.

Portoroz 1958

	1	2	3	4	5	6	7	8	9	10	11	12	13	14	15	16	17	18	19	20	21	Pts	Prize
1 Tal	—	½	½	1	½	½	½	½	0	½	1	1	1	½	½	1	½	1	½	1	1	13½	I
2 Gligorić	½	—	½	½	0	½	½	½	½	1	½	1	½	½	1	1	0	1	1	1	1	13	II
3 Petrosian	½	½	—	½	½	½	½	½	1	½	1	½	½	½	½	0	1	1	1	½	1	12½	III, IV
4 Benkö	0	½	½	—	½	1	½	1	1	½	½	0	½	1	½	½	½	½	1	1	1	12½	III, IV
5 Olafsson	½	1	½	½	—	1	0	1	½	1	½	½	½	½	0	1	0	0	1	1	1	12	V, VI
6 Fischer	½	½	½	0	0	—	½	½	½	½	½	½	½	1	½	1	1	½	1	1	1	12	V, VI
7 Averbach	½	½	½	½	1	½	—	½	½	½	1	½	½	½	½	½	1	½	0	½	1	11½	
8 Bronstein	½	½	½	0	0	½	½	—	1	0	½	½	½	1	1	1	½	1	½	½	1	11½	
9 Mantović	1	½	0	0	½	½	½	0	—	1	½	½	½	½	½	1	1	½	1	½	1	11½	
10 Szabó	0	½	½	½	0	½	½	1	0	—	½	½	1	½	0	½	1	1	1	1	1	11½	
11 Pachman	½	0	0	½	½	½	0	½	½	½	—	½	½	½	1	1	1	½	1	1	1	11½	
12 Panno	0	0	½	1	½	½	½	½	½	½	½	—	½	1	½	½	1	½	1	½	½	11	
13 Filip	0	½	½	½	½	½	½	½	½	0	½	½	—	½	1	½	½	½	1	1	1	11	
14 Sanguinetti	½	½	½	0	½	0	½	0	½	½	½	0	½	—	1	½	1	1	½	1	½	10	
15 Nejkirch	½	0	½	½	1	½	½	0	½	1	0	½	0	0	—	0	½	1	1	½	1	9½	
16 Larsen	0	0	1	½	0	0	½	0	0	½	0	½	½	½	1	—	1	1	½	0	1	8½	
17 Sherwin	½	1	0	½	1	0	0	½	0	0	0	0	½	0	½	0	—	1	0	1	1	7½	
18 Rossetto	0	0	0	½	1	½	½	0	½	0	½	½	½	0	0	0	0	—	1	½	1	7	
19 Cardoso	½	0	0	0	0	0	1	½	0	0	0	0	0	½	0	½	1	0	—	1	1	6	
20 de Greiff	0	0	½	0	0	0	½	½	½	0	0	½	0	0	½	1	0	½	0	—	0	4½	
21 Füster	0	0	0	0	0	0	0	0	0	0	0	½	0	½	0	0	0	0	0	1	—	2	

24	R-QB1	QxBP
25	QxQ	RxQ
26	B-Q2?	...

This should have cost White the game. The correct line is 26 K-Q2 KR-B1 27 N-B2.

| 26 | ... | R-R6 |
| 27 | B-N1 | ... |

122. Cardoso–Bronstein

At this stage Bronstein was very near to qualifying. He could have done so by choosing the obvious continuation 27 ... BxN 28 PxB RxRP 29 R-B7 R-Q1. The difference between this variation and that in the game is that here White's bishop on QN1 is out of play, whereas it becomes a strong attacking piece in the actual game.

| 27 | ... | RxRP? |
| 28 | P-B3 | P-B3? |

Overlooking White's shrewd reply, which causes some difficulty. The correct move is 28 ... R-B5 followed by R-B2, which would, however, have led to nothing more than equality, for White can resort to the manoeuvre N-B2-R3.

| 29 | N-N7! | R-R8? |

Few positions can absorb three consecutive mistakes. Of course, neither 29 ... BxN(N2)? 30 PxB KxP 31 N-N2, with a typical double attack, nor 29 ...

BxN(Q6) 30 BxB, with the threat of 31 B-N5, would have saved the game, but 29 ... PxP! 30 NxP(K6) R-B3 would not have been too bad.

| 30 | N-B2! | ... |

Now Black's position is very bad. The threat of 31 BxNch forces him to give up the exchange

| 30 | ... | RxB |
| 31 | RxR | PxP? |

This eases White's task considerably. However, even after 31 ... BxN 32 PxB KxP 33 PxPch RxP, which gives him two pawns for the exchange, Black still has very much the worse of it, for his opponent can attack along the KR file after 34 B-K3 and 35 K-Q2.

32	NxP	R-B1
33	R-R3	PxP
34	NxQP	BxN
35	PxB	R-B3
36	QR-N3!	...

White's rooks enter the game in an interesting way—via the third rank. The strong pawn on KR6 prevents Black from making use of his only assets—the united passed pawns on the queen's wing.

| 36 | ... | K-B2 |
| 37 | R(N3)-K3 | N(Q2)-B3 |

Black is at a loss for a good move, for 37 ... P-R5 fails to 38 B-N4.

38	R-K5	R-K3
39	RxR	KxR
40	R-QN3	N-Q2
41	N-R3	K-B3
42	NxP	...

This was the sealed move. Black now resigned, for if he captures twice on KN4 he has no way of stopping the KRP.

36 Zürich 1959
Victory in the Balance

The first strong tournament in Switzerland for a considerable time took place in May and June 1959. Several of the world's leading players were present, among them Tal (who a year later became world champion by beating Botvinnik), Fischer, Keres, Larsen, Unzicker, Barcza, Olafsson and Donner—all well-known international grandmasters. As early as the first round there were signs that an exceptionally dramatic struggle was on the cards. The two main favourites were drawn against players from the host country, Switzerland, but the games were very far from being the walk-overs expected.

123. Walther–Fischer

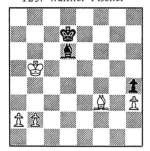

Position after Black's 53rd move

Black's chances of drawing rest in sacrificing his bishop for the two passed pawns, after which White cannot win, for his bishop is of a different colour from the queening square KR8. In order to carry out this plan, Black needs to get his king to QR2 and post his bishop on the diagonal QR2-KN8. White, however, can foil Black's attempts to achieve this set-up by 54 P-N4! K-B2 55 K-R5 K-N1 56 P-N5 and if 56 ... K-R2 then 57 P-N6ch

K-N1 58 P-R4 followed by K-R6 and P-R5, winning without difficulty in a few moves. Unfortunately for him the Swiss master succumbed to the temptation of advancing his passed pawns and allowed his opponent to draw the game.

54	P-R4?	K-B2
55	P-N4	K-N1
56	P-R5	K-R2
57	K-B4	B-N6
58	K-N3	B-K8
59	K-R4	B-Q7
60	B-R5	B-K8
61	P-N5	B-B7!
62	B-K2	B-K6
63	K-N3	B-Q7
64	P-N6ch	K-N2
65	K-R4	K-B3!
66	B-N5ch	K-B4
67	B-K8	B-K8
	Drawn	

The first round ended even worse for Tal.

124. Tal–Bhend

Position after Black's 21st move

With the logical continuation 22 N-B4 White could have got rid of his opponent's main asset—the bishop pair—and, after 22 ... BxB 23 RxB, secured a slight but distinct advantage. Tal instead allowed himself to be guided by his well-known temperament and sacrificed a piece.

22 BxP(?)   BxN!

Black cannot take the bishop because 22 ... PxB 23 N-K7 followed by 24 Q-R4ch would be decisive. But, strangely enough, the text-move saves him, for 23 Q-R5? is answered by 23 ... B-N1, and after 23 PxB Black can safely play 23 ... PxB.

23 R-K7   Q-Q1
24 R(B1)-K1 ...

After the game Tal said that he had originally intended to play 24 BxP but had then noticed that Black could beat off the attack with 24 ... B-B3! 25 Q-R6 QxR 26 B-K4dis ch K-N1 27 BxBch R-B2, etc.

24 ...   B-B2!

Tal could now have saved half a point by 25 B-R5! leaving Black with nothing better than a draw by repetition: 25 ... B-Q5! 26 Q-R6 B-N2 27 Q-N5, etc., for the line 25 ... R-N2? 26 BxB! RxB (26 ... RxR 27 QxR) 27 RxR(B7) QxQ 28 R-K8ch wins for White.

25 B-B2?   R-N2!

Black now simplifies the game and leaves White with insufficient attacking chances.

26	P-KR4	RxR
27	RxR	P-KR3
28	Q-B5	B-N1
29	Q-K4	P-Q4
30	PxP	QxP
31	Q-N6	Q-Q5
32	Q-N3	R-B2
33	R-K4	Q-N7
34	B-Q3	B-Q5
35	R-K2	Q-B8ch

36	K-R2	Q-KB4
37	R-K8	QxQch
38	PxQ	K-N2
39	B-B4	R-B1
40	R-K7ch	K-B3
41	RxP	BxB
42	PxB	K-B4
43	R-K7	R-QR1
44	R-K2	R-R6
45	K-R3	P-R4
Resigns		

This unpleasant and unnecessary defeat by no means upset Tal, who proceeded to win his next four games in a row. He gave clear evidence of his desire to fight when, in the second round, he went in for an unclear piece sacrifice against the Swiss master Kupper. He defeated Larsen in the third round in an interesting game and then Unzicker in the next, this time with Black. His victim in the fifth round was Nievergelt. At the end of the fifth and sixth rounds he shared the lead with Fischer but then went ahead. After the twelfth round the position was Tal 10, Fischer 9, Gligorić 8½, Keres 8, etc. Tal had White against Gligorić in the next round and he obviously wanted to increase his lead. But he played the game somewhat nervously and in the decisive phase too violently.

125. Tal–Gligorić

Position after Black's 20th move

Tal has given his opponent the bishop pair and has allowed his king-side pawns to be weakened—all for the sake of some nebulous attacking chances. Now he tries to renew his attack, but in so doing he compromises his position even further.

| 21 | P-KR4 | Q-Q2 |
| 22 | N-K3 | ... |

The advance 22 P-R5 would have been more consistent.

22	...	B-B2
23	K-B2	P-B3
24	P-R5!?	BxRP!
25	R-R1	Q-KB2!

When making his 24th move Tal had probably failed to see this simple defence. A weak continuation, on the other hand, would be 25 ... B-B2 26 RxPch KxR 27 R-KR1ch K-N1 28 N-N4 B-K2 29 Q-R4 K-B1 30 B-R6! B-N1 31 BxPch KxB 32 R-KN1 K-B2 (32 ... K-B1 33 Q-R6ch K-B2 33 N-K5ch) 33 N-R6ch K-K3 34 R-K1ch K-Q3 35 Q-B4ch K-Q4 36 Q-K4ch K-Q3 37 Q-B4ch, perpetual check.

26	Q-R3	B-N3
27	Q-N4	K-N1
28	Q-N1	Q-K3
29	Q-Q1	B-Q3
30	N-N2	R(B1)-Q1
31	BxB	QxB
32	N-B4	B-B2
33	Q-Q2	R-K2
34	QR-KN1	R(Q1)-K1
35	Q-Q3	P-N3
36	Q-B5	K-B1
37	Q-N4	P-N4
38	N-Q3	R-K7ch
39	K-B1	B-N3
40	N-B2	Q-K2
41	Q-N3	P-KR4
42	K-N2	P-R5
Resigns		

In the same round Fischer, playing Black, drew level with Tal by beating Donner. It was generally agreed that he thus had excellent chances of winning the tournament, for he was drawn against the Swiss player Keller in the next round and had, moreover, the White pieces, whereas his rival Tal had Black against Donner. In the final round they were due to play each other. The penultimate round, however, upset things considerably. First, Tal obtained a decisive advantage by means of an interesting positional manoeuvre in a position typical of the Hromádka System.

126. Donner–Tal

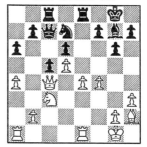

Position after White's 19th move

19	...	Q-N3
20	QR-N1	Q-N5
21	Q-B1	P-B5!
22	R-K2	P-QN4
23	PxP	PxP
24	K-R1	BxN!
25	PxB	QxP
26	RxP	Q-Q6
27	Q-K1	P-B6
28	R-N1	N-B4

White resigned at this stage in view of the continuation 29 Q-Q1 RxP 30 QxQ NxQ 31 RxR P-B7, etc.

Bobby Fischer is at the moment considered to be the number one expert on the Ruy Lopez, and this opening has won him many valuable points. In the decisive game in Zürich, however, his luck with it did not hold.

Ruy Lopez

Fischer	Keller
1 P-K4	P-K4
2 N-KB3	N-QB3

3	B-N5	P-QR3
4	B-R4	N-B3
5	0-0	B-K2
6	R-K1	P-QN4
7	B-N3	P-Q3
8	P-B3	0-0
9	P-KR3	N-Q2
10	P-Q4	N-N3

For some time this was considered better than 10 . . . B-B3 11 P-QR4, but in the sixth game of the Spasski–Geller match, 1965, White obtained a clear advantage by means of 11 QN-Q2 B-B3 12 N-B1 R-K1 13 N(B1)-R2! PxP 14 PxP N-R4 15 B-B2 P-B4 16 N-N4 BxN 17 PxB PxP 18 P-N5 B-K2 19 P-K5! etc.

11	PxP	. . .

Fischer had chosen this quiet continuation a year previously in his game against Tal in the 1958 Interzonal. After 11 . . . NxP 12 NxN PxN 13 Q-R5 Q-Q3 14 N-Q2 B-K3 15 N-B3 BxB 16 PxB N-Q2 17 P-QN4 KR-Q1 the game was equal. It is not easy to explain why Fischer should have adopted this quiet line in the present decisive game. Perhaps he simply underestimated his opponent.

11	. . .	NxP
12	NxN	PxN
13	Q-R5	B-B3

This continuation is adequate. The queen now has access to K2, and after the exchange of the white-squared bishops (following B-K3 by Black) White will have no real attacking chances.

14	N-Q2	Q-K2
15	N-B1	B-K3
16	N-K3	P-N3
17	Q-B3	BxB
18	PxB	B-N2
19	P-QN4	P-QB3

The game is now completely equal, for White has no way of exploiting his opponent's only weakness, the QRP. The logical result would have been a draw, but

127. Fischer–Keller

Position after Black's 19th move

that would understandably not have satisfied the American grandmaster. With his next move Fischer prepares the advance of his KRP, but, as things turn out, the whole manoeuvre merely weakens his own position.

20	P-KN3	Q-K3
21	P-R4	. . .

It would have been better to change his plan and play instead 21 P-KN4 to prevent his opponent from advancing his KBP. However, even in this case Black would have had a good game after 21 . . . KR-Q1.

21	. . .	P-KB4!
22	P-R5	P-B5
23	N-B1	NPxP
24	QxRP	R-B3!
25	N-R2?	R-N3
26	N-B3	. . .

White will get no compensation for the pawn, but as a result of the mistake on his previous move he had no satisfactory continuation. If instead 26 K-N2, Black could reply 26 . . . R-KB1 with the strong threat of R-R3, and if 26 P-KN4, there follows 26 . . . N-Q2 27 P-B3 N-B3 followed by P-KR4 and Black again wins a pawn.

26	. . .	PxP
27	PxP	RxPch
28	K-R2	Q-N5!

Forcing an exchange of queens, so that the game, notwithstanding certain technical difficulties, is already decided.

29	QxQ	RxQ
30	R-KN1	RxR
31	KxR	N-R5
32	K-B1	P-B4
33	P-N3!?	. . .

If 33 P-B4, Black has a strong reply in 33 . . . R-KB1!

33	. . .	NxP
34	PxP	NxP
35	P-B6	. . .

or 35 P-N4 NxP! 36 PxN P-K5

35	. . .	N-B4
36	B-K3	NxP
37	R-R2	P-QR4
38	R-KN2	K-R1
39	N-N5	R-KB1ch
40	K-K1	N-Q5
41	BxN	PxB
42	N-K6	R-K1
43	P-B7	B-K4
44	K-Q2	R-QB1
45	R-N5	BxP
46	RxP	B-Q3
47	K-Q3	R-R1
48	R-N6	B-N6
49	R-N7	P-R5
50	N-N5	P-R6
51	RxPch	K-N1
52	R-R1	P-R7
53	R-QR1	B-K4
54	N-K6	R-R6ch
55	K-K4	B-B3
56	K-B5	K-B2
57	N-N5ch	BxN

Resigns

Zürich 1959

	1	2	3	4	5	6	7	8	9	10	11	12	13	14	15	16	Pts	Prize
1 Tal	–	0	½	½	1	1	½	1	1	0	1	1	1	1	1	1	11½	I
2 Gligorić	1	–	1	0	1	½	0	1	½	1	½	1	½	1	1	1	11	II
3 Fischer	½	0	–	1	½	1	½	1	1	1	1	0	½	1	½	1	10½	III, IV
4 Keres	½	1	0	–	½	1	½	½	1	½	1	1	1	½	1	½	10½	III, IV
5 Larsen	0	0	½	½	–	½	0	1	½	½	1	1	1	1	1	1	9½	V, VI
6 Unzicker	0	½	0	0	½	–	½	½	1	1	1	½	1	1	1	1	9½	V, VI
7 Barcza	½	1	½	½	1	½	–	0	0	0	½	1	1	0	1	1	8½	VII
8 Olafsson	0	0	0	½	0	½	1	–	0	1	½	1	½	1	1	1	8	VIII
9 Kupper	0	½	0	0	½	0	1	1	–	½	0	½	1	½	½	1	7	
10 Bhend	1	0	0	½	½	0	1	0	½	–	1	1	0	0	½	½	6½	
11 Donner	0	½	0	0	0	0	½	½	1	0	–	0	1	1	1	1	6½	
12 Keller	0	0	1	0	0	½	0	0	½	0	1	–	1	1	1	0	6	
13 Walther	0	½	½	0	0	0	0	½	0	1	0	0	–	1	½	1	5	
14 Dückstein	0	0	0	½	0	0	1	0	½	1	0	0	0	–	1	1	5	
15 Blau	0	0	½	0	0	0	0	0	½	½	0	0	½	0	–	½	2½	
16 Nievergelt	0	0	0	½	0	0	0	0	0	½	0	1	0	0	½	–	2½	

37 Candidates' Tournament 1959

First Place Saved

The 1959 Candidates' Tournament was a four-leg marathon over twenty-eight rounds, played alternately in three Yugoslav towns—Veldes, Agram and Belgrade. After it FIDE discussed the possibility of changing the system, one of the reasons being that it was too exhausting.

The whole 1959 tournament revolved around a duel between Tal and Keres. At the half-way stage, Keres was in the lead by half a point, but he lost in the fifteenth round to Fischer as a result of a blunder, whereupon Tal drew level. In the course of the next six rounds the latter, partly helped by luck, built up a lead of 1½ points. This was due in great measure to the seventeenth round, which brought him up against Keres. The latter had White and achieved a distinct positional advantage in the opening, but he later faltered and lost it, and shortly before the end of the game he missed an opportunity of at least saving half a point.

The penultimate round was unexpectedly dramatic. Tal's lead had been reduced to one point and he was faced by a tough opponent, Fischer. The American grandmaster had lost in their previous three encounters, and it was safe to assume that he was bent on exacting his revenge. Although he had no chance of winning the tournament, he intended to use the advantage of having White to play for a win at all costs. Victory for him would have meant that Keres would be able to draw level with Tal before the last round.

Sicilian Defence

Fischer	Tal
1 P-K4	P-QB4
2 N-KB3	P-Q3
3 P-Q4	PxP
4 NxP	N-KB3
5 N-QB3	P-QR3

Tal really only needed two draws from the last two rounds, for it was unlikely that Keres would win against both Gligorić and Olafsson. Many players in Tal's position would have proceeded cautiously and aimed at attaining a safe position in the opening. For two reasons Tal adopted different tactics. First a quiet game does not suit his style, and second he apparently wanted to be instrumental in deciding the outcome of the tournament. He therefore chose one of the sharpest systems of the Sicilian Defence. His daring was crowned with success, but only after some nerve-racking moments.

6 B-QB4	P-K3
7 B-N3	P-QN4

A safer continuation is 7 ... B-K2 8 P-B4 0-0.

8 P-B4	P-N5!?

The risk that Black takes by accepting the pawn sacrifice would be too great even in normal circumstances, let alone in a game with so much at stake as the present one. Instead he could have had a good game by 8 ... B-N2 9 P-K5 PxP 10 PxP N-K5! (better than 10 ... N-Q4 11 Q-N4!).

9 N-R4	NxP!?
10 0-0	P-KN3

Black tries to hinder the advance 11 P-B5, but as things turn out he merely makes it more effective. A better reply is 10 ... N-KB3, inviting an extremely sharp continuation which Tal himself had already tried out, viz. 11 P-B5 P-K4 12 N-K6!?

11 P-B5!   NPxP
12 NxBP

128. Fischer–Tal

Within the first twelve moves Tal has got himself into a difficult situation. Now the knight cannot be taken because of 12 ... PxN 13 Q-Q5 R-R2 14 Q-Q4! winning the exchange.

12 ...   R-N1
13 B-Q5

White could also have obtained a dangerous attack for the pawn (e.g. 13 Q-R5 N-KB3 14 Q-B3 R-R2 15 N-N3 followed by 16 B-K3), but he chooses instead the simplest way. He recovers his pawn by force and remains with a positional advantage.

13 ...   R-R2
14 BxN   PxN
15 BxP

Both 15 B-Q5 and 15 B-B3 are good alternatives, for Black's pawn on KB4 is worth very little. Fischer, however, intends an attack along the KB file.

15 ...   R-K2
16 BxB   QxB

Black now has scattered pawns and, in addition, has lost the right to castle. Fischer's only problem is finding a good place for his knight, for Black is threatening Q-QB3. Players of a quiet disposition would be satisfied with 17 N-N6

Q-B3 18 N-Q5 R-K4 19 N-B4, for once the position has been consolidated White has a lasting advantage. This, however, was not enough for Fischer's temperament, especially when we remember that he was thirsting for revenge. He therefore opted for an interesting piece sacrifice.

17 B-B4!?   Q-B3
18 Q-B3   QxN!

The endgame after 18 ... QxQ 19 RxQ R-K7 20 R-B2 would be a sad affair for Black.

19 BxP   Q-B3

It is only this very shrewd counter which prevents Black's position from collapsing.

20 BxN   Q-QN3ch
21 K-R1   QxB

129. Fischer–Tal

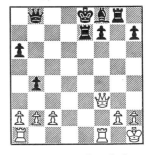

Fischer is apparently a little confused as a result of his opponent's manoeuvre and fails to find the right path. After the fairly obvious 22 QR-K1! White retains a certain advantage. His opponent can reply with neither 22 ... KR-N2?? 23 Q-QB6ch, which leads to a quick mate, nor 22 ... RxR? 23 QxPch K-Q1 24 RxR. There remains only 22 ... K-Q1 23 RxR BxR 24 QxP (threatening both QxRch and R-Q1ch) 24 ... R-N3 25 QxP Q-Q3. Black is then in no immediate danger, but White has three pawns for the piece and good prospects of making something of the somewhat exposed position of his opponent's king, e.g. 26 Q-R8ch K-B2 27 Q-K8 or 26 . . . K-Q2 27 Q-R3ch K-B2 28 Q-K3.

22	**Q-QB6ch?**	**R-Q2**
23	**QR-K1ch**	**B-K2**
24	**RxP**	**KxR**
25	**Q-K6ch**	**K-B1**

It is unbelievable that, in the course of a few moves, Black has miraculously overcome all his difficulties and attained a won position. White achieves nothing by 26 R-KB1ch K-N2 27 QxR Q-Q3 or 27 R-B7ch K-R1 28 QxR R-Q1! 29 Q-N4 Q-K4.

26	**QxQR**	**Q-Q3**
27	**Q-N7**	**R-N3**
28	**P-B3**	**P-QR4**
29	**Q-B8ch**	**K-N2**
30	**Q-B4**	**B-Q1**
31	**PxP**	**PxP**
32	**P-KN3**	**Q-QB3ch**
33	**R-K4**	**QxQ**
34	**RxQ**	**R-QN3**
35	**K-N2**	**K-B3**
36	**K-B3**	**K-K4**
37	**K-K3**	**B-N4ch**
38	**K-K2**	**K-Q4**
39	**K-Q3**	**B-B3**
40	**R-B2**	**B-K4**
41	**R-K2**	**R-KB3**
42	**R-QB2**	**R-B6ch**
43	**K-K2**	**R-B2**
44	**K-Q3**	**B-Q5**
45	**P-QR3**	

There is no way of saving the game. Against other moves Black can play 45 . . . R-B6ch followed by K-K5.

45	**. . .**	**P-N6**
46	**R-B8**	**BxP**
47	**R-Q8ch**	**K-B3**
48	**R-QN8**	**R-B6ch**
49	**K-B4**	**R-QB6ch**
50	**K-N4**	**K-B2**
51	**R-N5**	**B-R8**
52	**P-QR4**	**P-N7**

Resigns

Candidates' Tournament 1959

		1	2	3	4	5	6	7	8	Pts	Prize
1	Tal	– –	0 0	½ ½	0 1	1 ½	1 1	1 1	1 1	20	I
		– –	1 0	½ ½	½ 1	1 1	1 1	1 ½	1 ½		
2	Keres	1 1	– –	0 ½	1 ½	½ ½	0 1	1 1	1 1	18½	II
		0 1	– –	½ ½	½ 0	1 1	0 1	1 0	1 1		
3	Petrosian	½ ½	1 ½	– –	½ ½	0 ½	1 1	1 0	½ 1	15½	III
		½ ½	½ ½	– –	0 ½	½ 1	½ ½	0 ½	1 ½		
4	Smyslov	1 0	0 ½	½ ½	– –	0 ½	½ ½	½ 1	½ 0	15	IV
		½ 0	½ 1	1 ½	– –	1 0	1 0	½ 1	1 1		
5	Gligorić	0 ½	½ ½	1 ½	1 ½	– –	0 1	½ ½	½ 1	12½	
		0 0	0 0	½ 0	0 1	– –	½ ½	1 0	½ ½		
6	Fischer	0 0	1 0	0 0	½ ½	1 0	– –	0 1	½ 1	12½	
		0 0	1 0	½ ½	0 1	½ ½	– –	½ 1	½ 1		
7	Olafsson	0 0	0 0	0 1	½ 0	½ ½	1 0	– –	0 0	10	
		0 ½	0 1	1 ½	½ 0	0 1	½ 0	– –	½ 1		
8	Benkö	0 0	0 0	½ 0	½ 1	½ 0	½ 0	1 1	– –	8	
		0 ½	0 0	0 ½	0 0	½ ½	½ 0	½ 0	– –		

38 Candidates' Tournament 1962

The Tragedy of Paul Keres

There are few examples in the history of chess of a player producing top-class performances over such a lengthy period as Paul Keres has done. He was a world championship candidate in 1938, but his match with Alekhin never took place. At the world championship in 1948, after several years of below-average chess activity, he was not in particularly good form and shared third and fourth places. In the Candidates' Tournament of 1950 he was "only" fourth, but in 1953, 1956 and 1959 only one place separated him from the right to contest the highest title of all. He was second three times because Smyslov, on two occasions, and Tal, on one, played in their very best form. In 1959 Keres had the magnificent score of 15 (!) victories, six defeats and seven draws, i.e. 18½ points from 28 games, and still did not manage to win.

Three years later Keres again tried his luck in a candidates' tournament, the first to be played outside Europe. It was held in the exotic atmosphere of the island of Curaçao in the Dutch Antilles.

As early as the first round there were signs that the two favourites—Tal, victor over Botvinnik in 1960, and Fischer, who two months previously had had a scintillating victory in the Interzonal—were going to make heavy going of things. Tal lost in the first round to Petrosian, in the second, with White, to Keres, and in the third to Benkö. Three quarters of the way through the tournament his kidney trouble got worse and he had to give up. Fischer suffered an unexpected and depressing defeat in the first round against Benkö and lost the following day to Geller. After that he never got among the leaders.

At the half-way stage of the tournament, Geller and Petrosian had 9 points, Keres 8½ and Korchnoi 8. Later Petrosian went into the lead, thanks to a factor that distinguished him from all the other players in this extremely difficult chess marathon: he did not lose a single game. He advanced steadily by half a point or a full point, whereas his rivals suffered several severe defeats. In the 24th round, however, he was caught up by one of those at his heels. Unlike the previous tournaments, it looked as if fortune were dealing kindly with Keres this time, for he won a drawn ending against Fischer after prolonged tacking manoeuvres.

In the next two rounds both Petrosian and Keres had draws, the second against each other. Going into the final two rounds they not only had the same score but also opponents of similar strength: Petrosian was to play Fischer and Filip, while Keres had Benkö and Fischer.

Petrosian was obviously determined not to risk anything and to rely on the nervous atmosphere of the last round to see him through. He offered Fischer a draw in the opening, and obtained it on the 35th move.

Keres had Black against Benkö. In their previous games in the tournament Keres had won all three games. It was now a question of continuing the good work or at least not losing. Benkö, his opponent, had not the slightest chance of winning the tournament, so there was nothing at stake for him. But just that very fact was dangerous for Keres, who had unpleasant memories of a similar situation, when he played Filip in the penultimate round of the tournament in

1956. On that occasion he had had White, and a victory would have given him a good chance of winning the tournament. As it was, he had lost—likewise against an opponent for whom there was nothing at stake—and so was out of the running.

Barcza System

Benkö	Keres
1 N-KB3	P-Q4
2 P-KN3	B-N5
3 B-N2	N-Q2
4 0-0	P-QB3
5 P-Q3	P-K4

Such a natural move cannot be bad, and yet the more modest 5 . . . P-K3 is usually preferred.

6 P-KR3	B-R4

Also playable is 6 . . . BxN 7 BxB KN-B3 or 7 . . . B-Q3.

7 P-B4	PxP
8 PxP	KN-B3
9 B-K3	Q-B2

The psychological pressure of such a decisive game is beginning to make itself felt. Simplification by 9 . . . BxN 10 BxB B-B4 would lead to immediate equality and a probable draw. However, Keres had already beaten his opponent three times, and a victory here would have given him the chance of going into the lead in the tournament.

10 N-B3	B-QN5

Also possible is 10 . . . B-B4 11 BxB NxB 12 P-QN4 BxN 13 BxB N-K3 or 12 P-KN4 B-N3 13 P-QN4 QN-K5.

11 Q-N3	P-R4

For the third time Black has a chance to play B-B4; e.g. 11 . . . B-B4 12 BxB NxB 13 Q-R3 BxN 14 BxB Q-K2 with complete equality. The text-move threatens N-B4 but at the same time

weakens the queen's side, which will have its effect later.

12 QN-R4!	B-K2

Otherwise White plays 13 P-B5 with the threat of P-R3.

13 N-R4	

The well-known saying "A knight at the edge of the board brings bad luck" does not apply here. White has already obtained the initiative and does not need to worry about his pawns; e.g. 13 . . . BxP 14 KR-K1 B-R4 15 KN-B5 B-B1 16 P-B4, etc.

130. Benkö–Keres

13 . . .	0-0
14 P-N4	

White would certainly prefer to exchange off his opponent's other bishop but, after 14 KN-B5, Black can reply 14 . . . B-Q1, and the attack on his KP will prevent White from occupying Q6 (15 KR-K1 B-N3).

14 . . .	B-N3
15 NxB	RPxN
16 KR-Q1	R-N1

Without the weakness engendered by the move P-QR4 Black would naturally have no trouble in obtaining a draw. As it is, he cannot easily consolidate his position on the queen-side. True, he has the threat of P-QN3 or P-QN4, but White can easily stop both. A better move, therefore, than the one made was the immediate N-R2.

17 P-B5!   N-R2

The idea of exchanging off the passive bishop on K2 is strategically good; but it fails for tactical reasons. However, the threat of 18 Q-B3 was very unpleasant.

18 N-N6!   QR-Q1

If 18 ... NxP, White wins the exchange by 19 BxN BxB 20 N-Q7.

19 Q-B3   B-N4!?

Keres is aware of the critical state of his position and attempts to complicate matters. On 19 ... N(Q2)-B3, White would not take at once (20 QxRP N-Q4! with counter-play) but would continue to improve the position of his pieces; e.g. 20 QR-B1.

20 N-B4?

It is not quite clear why Benkö rejects 20 BxB NxB 21 QxRP N-K3 22 P-N4. The queen would, of course, be out of play, but a pawn is a pawn after all.

20 ...	BxB
21 QxB	KR-K1
22 Q-R3	R-R1

It would naturally be going a bit too far to say that Black's difficulties had entirely disappeared. However, his position is certainly in better shape now than a few moves previously.

23 R-Q2	KN-B1
24 QR-Q1	R(K1)-Q1

At last Black has a threat—N-K3 winning the QBP. A more natural continuation, however, is 24 ... R-K2 and then, if 25 N-N6, to refrain from capturing the knight and play 26 ... R-R3, after which he would have been out of danger. Keres was obviously afraid of 25 P-N4. However, he could have replied to that with N-K3! (26 NxRP N(Q2)xP!).

25 Q-K3   R-K1

Not 25 ... N-K3 26 N-N6! NxN 27 PxN RxR 28 RxR Q-N1 29 R-Q7, etc.

26 P-N3

White must now give up his plan to win the weak QRP and instead play a positional game. The possibility of advancing with his pawns on the queen's side combined with control of the square Q6 will enable him to maintain his clear advantage. It is unfortunate for Keres that his opponent feels wonderfully at home in positions such as this, where there are no tactical surprises.

26 ...	QR-N1
27 P-R3	R-R1
28 P-N4	PxP
29 PxP	R-R5
30 Q-QB3	R-R3
31 R-Q6	N-B3!?

Played for the same reason as his fifteenth move. Here Keres sacrifices a pawn to obtain at least a small amount of counter-play. Benkö, who is already in time-trouble, decides to avoid the complications arising from 32 NxP Q-K2 (32 ... R-R7 33 Q-B4 R-N7 34 R-Q7!) 33 P-B4 P-KN4 34 PxP QxN 35 QxQ RxQ 36 PxN RxKP 37 PxP KxP or 34 P-K3 PxP 35 PxP N-K3 36 N-Q3 R-R7 37 R-Q2. Although White comes out on top with correct play, it would have been easy to go wrong in time-trouble.

32 N-N6	P-K5
33 P-K3	P-N4
34 Q-Q2	Q-K2
35 R-Q8	R-R6
36 RxR	QxR
37 Q-N2	R-R2
38 N-B4?	

Just before the time-control neither player is aware of the consequences that could arise from the Black rook's inability to return to the first rank. A very strong continuation is 38 R-Q4 N-K3 39 R-Q6.

38 ...	Q-K3
39 B-B1	N-Q4
40 N-N6	NxN
41 PxN	

131. Benkö–Keres

41 ...	R-R5?

Even after the time-control Keres endeavours to keep the rook in an active position and thereby loses quickly on account of the weakness of the back rank. After the correct 41 ... R-R1 42 Q-Q4 Q-K2 43 Q-Q6 QxQ 44 RxQ R-K1, Black would have had a defensible, albeit difficult, position.

42 P-N5	R-R7?

Driving the queen to a better post, Black's only chance lay in 42 ... R—R1, accepting the loss of tempo this involves.

43 Q-N1!	PxP?

It is now too late for the rook to return to the back rank; e.g. 43 ... R-R1 44 PxP QxBP 45 R-Q4 R-K1 46 B-B4 N-Q2 47 B-Q5 QxP 48 BxBPch. Black could, however, have prolonged the game a little by 43 ... P-QB4 44 R-Q8 R-R4 45 Q-Q1 QxQNP 46 Q-Q7 Q-K3 47 QxNP.

44 R-Q8!

With the terrible threat of 45 Q-N4. If Black now plays 44 ... R-R5, there follows 45 QxNP and 46 Q-B5 or Q-N4.

44 ...	P-B4
45 PxP	Q-B2
46 BxP	P-N3
47 R-B8	Resigns

132. Geller–Benkö

Black to play

	1	2	3	4	5	6	7	8	Pts	Prize
1 Petrosian	— —	½ ½	½ ½	½ 1	½ ½	½ ½	1 1	½ 1	17½	I
	— —	½ ½	½ ½	½ ½	1 1	1 ½	½ —	1 ½		
2 Geller	½ ½	— —	½ ½	1 1	½ ½	½ ½	½ 1	½ 1	17	II, III
	½ ½	— —	½ ½	½ 0	1 ½	½ 1	1 —	1 ½		
3 Keres	½ ½	½ ½	— —	0 ½	½ ½	1 1	1 ½	½ 1	17	II, III
	½ ½	½ ½	— —	1 ½	1 ½	1 0	1 —	1 ½		
4 Fischer	½ 0	0 0	1 ½	— —	0 1	0 1	½ 1	1 ½	14	IV
	½ ½	½ 1	0 ½	— —	0 ½	½ 1	½ —	1 ½		
5 Korchnoi	½ ½	½ ½	½ ½	1 0	— —	½ ½	1 0	1 1	13½	
	0 0	0 ½	0 ½	1 ½	— —	½ 0	½ —	1 1		
6 Benkö	½ ½	½ ½	0 0	1 0	½ ½	— —	1 0	0 1	12	
	0 ½	½ 0	0 1	½ 0	½ 1	— —	½ —	1 ½		
7 Tal	0 0	½ 0	0 ½	½ 0	0 1	0 1	— —	1 0	7	
	½ —	0 —	0 —	½ —	½ —	½ —	— —	½ —		
8 Filip	½ 0	½ 0	½ 0	0 ½	0 0	1 0	0 1	— —	7	
	0 ½	0 ½	0 ½	0 ½	0 0	0 ½	½ —	— —		

For reasons of health Tal retired before the start of the last leg.

Keres was thus half a point behind Petrosian, and both drew their last round games. In the end Keres was caught up by Geller, whose opponent exceeded the time-limit on the 54th move in the won position shown in diagram 132.

Tartakower once came up with the following original aphorism: In a tournament the player who plays best ends up in second place; the winner is the one with the most luck. Keres was second in four consecutive candidates' tournaments and thereby had the best average performance of all the top players in the world. But he did not manage—or has not yet managed—to win the right to a world championship match.

39 Los Angeles 1963

How to Win with Black

The idea of playing a tournament with a small number of participants on a system of two or more rounds is by no means new. The famous AVRO Tournament in Holland in 1938, which was to determine Alekhin's opponent in a world championship match, was played on a double-round system with eight participants. A tournament that was organized in the same way took place in Los Angeles in 1963. The man behind this—or, rather, his wife, who was extremely keen on chess—was the famous cellist Piatigorsky, who provided the necessary funds.

It was a set-back for the organizers that they failed to persuade Bobby Fischer to take part, which meant that in the first major international tournament in America for years the home contingent was not at full strength. However, none of the competing eight grandmasters could have been considered an outsider, so there was an added interest to every game.

At the end there was only a difference of three points between the two winners (Keres and Petrosian) and the last two (Benkö and Panno).

After the tenth round Keres and Olafsson shared the lead with 6½ points in front of Petrosian (6), Najdorf and Gligorić (5 each). But the position changed in the next round. Keres, playing White, lost a second time to Reshevsky in a long positional struggle, and the misfortune that afflicted Olafsson was really a sensation.

Black is not threatened by anything, and he could play 35 ... K-B1 or Q-K2. It is almost unbelievable that a grandmaster as experienced as Olafsson should only last

133. Benkö–Olafsson

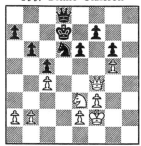

Position after White's 35th move

out another six moves from such a simple position.

35 ...	N-B4?
36 NxN	KPxN
37 P-K4	K-K3??

Despite his previous inaccuracy, Black could still have held the game by 37 ... Q-KR1.

38 PxPch	PxP
39 Q-K3ch	K-Q2
40 Q-Q2ch	K-K2
41 QxQch	KxQ
42 K-K3	Resigns

After 42 ... K-K2 43 K-B4 K-K3 44 P-N3 the tempo that White has saved on the queen's wing is decisive.

In the next round Olafsson, playing White, drew with Petrosian, while Keres, obviously suffering from depression following his defeat in the previous round, lost his third game of the tournament, this time against Najdorf. In the thirteenth round Keres won a pawn against Olafsson in the opening and then coasted safely to victory. In the meantime Petrosian had taken the lead by beating Panno.

Prior to the last round the position was as follows: Petrosian 8, Keres 7½, Najdorf and Olafsson 7. The top two players had Black, Petrosian against Reshevsky and Keres against Gligorić. The chances were that both games would be drawn, leaving the position unchanged, for it is an extremely difficult job to win a decisive game against a strong player with Black.

Petrosian did in fact draw in the last round, though the game was not without its exciting moments.

134. Reshevsky–Petrosian

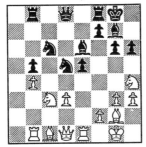

Position after Black's 17th move

In view of the endangered pawn on QN4, the most obvious line for White is 18 NxN BxN 19 B-K3 with equality. Reshevsky, however, managed to find a way of complicating the game to his advantage.

18 N-K4!	N(Q4)xP?

This leads to great difficulties. The move 18 . . . Q-K2 looks stronger.

19 B-R3	Q-R4
20 R-R1!	Q-Q1

Black now decides to give up the exchange and to rely on his passed pawn to see him through. He would also have suffered material loss after 20 . . . KR-Q1 21 N-QB5!, e.g. 21 . . . B-Q4 22 BxN QxB 23 N-R6.

21 Q-Q2	N-Q4

It is probable that the world champion had only just realized that 21 . . . NxP is not good on account of 22 R-K3 B-B5 23 B-KB1, after which the knight cannot escape.

22 BxR	QxB
23 R(K1)-QB1	N-Q5
24 N-QB5	Q-K2
25 K-R2?	

After this unnecessary loss of time, Black can equalize by advancing his passed pawn. White had two promising lines which would have given him good prospects of making use of his material advantage: 25 N-KB3 to eliminate the unpleasant Black knight, and 25 NxB QxN 26 Q-R2.

25 . . .	P-N5!
26 R-R6	N-QB6
27 NxB	NxN
28 R(B1)-R1	N-B2
29 R-B6	N(B2)-N4
30 R-K1	R-Q1
31 R-B4	N-R6
32 RxN	PxR
33 QxBP	Q-Q3
34 Q-R5	N-B7

Not 34 . . . QxP? 35 R-K3

35 R-QN1	N-Q5

Now 35 . . . QxP is answered by 36 B-K4.

36 R-N6	Drawn

Keres won his last round game and so managed to catch up with the world champion. In a much-analysed opening he found an important theoretical innovation—always a great help when victory is so important.

Nimzo-Indian

Gligorić	Keres
1 P-Q4	N-KB3
2 P-QB4	P-K3

3	N-QB3	B-N5
4	P-K3	0-0
5	B-Q3	P-Q4
6	N-B3	P-B4
7	0-0	QPxP
8	BxBP	QN-Q2
9	Q-Q3	

Until this game the move 9 Q-Q3 was considered to be the most active continuation. Subsequently it was replaced by the less ambitious 9 Q-K2

9	...	P-QR3
10	P-QR4	

This was the move previously recommended by theory. The continuation 10 P-QR3 B-R4 11 PxP NxP 12 QxQ BxQ leads to equality.

10	...	Q-B2!

As we shall see, the queen is well placed here, quite unlike White's queen, which will be in a rather vulnerable position after Black's next move—a fact that will impede the development of an active plan for White. Gligorić decides to transfer his bishop to QB2 and aim at attacking the castled king. However, the conditions are not ripe for such an undertaking, so the modest 11 B-Q2 followed by QR-B1 would have been better. The move 11 P-Q5 is answered by 11 . . . PxP 12 NxP NxN 13 BxN N-B3.

11	B-N3	R-Q1
12	B-B2?	P-QN3
13	N-R2	P-QR4
14	NxB	RPxN
15	R-K1	P-K4

Also good is 15 . . . P-QN4. With the text-move Black starts operating on the king's side. He now threatens P-K5, and the preventive 16 PxKP NxP would be to his advantage.

16	Q-N3	B-N2
17	PxBP	P-K5!

Much stronger than 17 . . . PxP 18 P-K4. If White now replies 18 PxP there follows 18 . . . Q-B4!, and the Black queen is ready to transfer to the king's wing.

18	P-B6	BxP
19	N-Q4	

135. Gligorić–Keres

19	...	N-N5!

A typical attack on the king's wing, where Black's pawn on K5 guarantees him an advantage in space. Now 20 NxB fails to 20 . . . QxPch 21 K-B1 Q-R5! etc. After White's best reply, 20 P-N3, Black maintains the upper hand by 20 . . . N(Q2)-K4! with the threat of RxN and N-B6ch. The continuation chosen by Gligorić loses quickly.

20	P-R3?	Q-R7ch
21	K-B1	N(Q2)-K4!

The decisive tactical blow, which threatens not only Q-R8ch but also B-Q4. After 22 NxB Black could win by either 22 . . . Q-R8ch 23 K-K2 QxNP or 22 . . . N-B6!

22	PxN	B-Q4!

Threatening B-B5ch, thus forcing White to give up his queen.

23	QxB	RxQ
24	BxP	R(R1)-Q1
25	P-B3	

Or 25 BxR RxB 26 P-B3 N-Q6.

25	...	R(Q4)-Q3	31 P-QN3	N-Q7ch
26	P-R5	PxP	32 K-B2	PxN
27	RxP	R-K1	33 BxP	Q-R5ch
28	N-B5	R(Q3)-Q1	34 K-K2	RxPch
29	B-N1	N-B5	35 KxR	QxRch
30	R-R1	P-N3	36 Resigns	

Los Angeles 1963

	1	2	3	4	5	6	7	8	Pts	Prize
1 Keres	– –	½ ½	½ 0	1 1	0 0	½ 1	1 1	½ 1	8½	I, II
2 Petrosian	½ ½	– –	½ ½	½ ½	½ ½	0 1	1 1	½ 1	8½	I, II
3 Najdorf	½ 1	½ ½	– –	½ 0	1 ½	½ ½	0 ½	1 ½	7½	III, IV
4 Olafsson	0 0	½ ½	½ 1	– –	½ 1	½ 1	1 0	½ ½	7½	III, IV
5 Reshevsky	1 1	½ ½	0 ½	½ 0	– –	½ ½	1 ½	0 ½	7	
6 Gligorić	½ 0	1 0	½ ½	½ 0	½ ½	– –	½ 0	1 ½	6	
7 Benkö	0 0	0 0	1 ½	0 1	0 ½	½ 1	– –	1 0	5½	
8 Panno	½ 0	½ 0	0 ½	½ ½	1 ½	0 ½	0 1	– –	5½	

40 Havana 1963

Curious Positions

The six years from 1962 to 1967 marked a glorious era for chess on the island of Cuba. In 1966 there was the chess olympiad, which in spite of certain technical difficulties produced a record entry of teams. In the other years there were category A international tournaments to commemorate the former world champion J. R. Capablanca. I played in all of these tournaments until 1967, being absent for the first time at the 1968 Capablanca Memorial Tournament, which was only a poor image of the previous ones.

The atmosphere on Cuba, brimming over as it was with enthusiasm for chess, certainly appealed to me. On two occasions in Havana I again reached grandmaster level, and on one of these I was within an ace of occupying first place. This occurred in the second of the tournaments, in August and September 1963.

It was the second year of the tournament. In view of the competition it seemed hopeless to entertain thoughts of gaining first place, for there were entries from three top-notch Russian grandmasters—Tal, Korchnoi and Geller—as well as eight other grandmasters—Ivkov, Trifunović, Uhlmann, Robatsch, Barcza, O'Kelly and Darga. This seemed too tough an assignment, and, as I personally was partly involved in the organizing of the tournament, I occasionally blamed myself in my unguarded moments for setting up such a hurdle as that field of abnormally gifted players. Yet one never knows when success is just around the corner.

The draw was very favourable for me,

giving me White against my strongest opponents, so that I managed to go through the tournament undefeated. Among my wins were two against such formidable adversaries as Korchnoi and Ivkov.

Korchnoi also lost to his fellow-countryman Geller, but unlike the latter, who lost to the Cuban Garcia as well as Tal and the tail-ender Calero, he was merciless with all his opponents from the bottom half of the table. His good record there, however, was not completely obtained without luck. His victory against the English champion Wade in the decisive phase of the tournament—round 15—came at the end of a very strange game.

136. Korchnoi–Wade

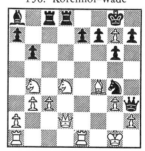

Position after White's 23rd move

A few moves previously Wade had sacrificed a piece, which he now recovers in an ingenious manner.

23 ...   P-KN4!

If now 24 BxP Black replies 24 ... P-B3 followed by P-K4. Then, in spite of the equality of material, the long diagonal QR1-KR8 controlled by Black would confront his opponent with a hopeless task.

24	R-K2	PxB
25	QxP	P-K4
26	Q-B5	

Korchnoi was now in severe time-trouble, and no one realized what he was trying to do. However, it soon became clear that he was resolved to risk everything, including material loss, in an endeavour to gain counter-play. Such tactics are suitable for lightning games, but it seems unbelievable that they should bear fruit in an international tournament of masters. But the mysteries of chess are unfathomable.

26	...	PxN

Winning a piece is without doubt sound strategy. But here Black had something better. After 26 ... RxP! threatening RxPch! White could well have resigned.

27	R-KB1	R-B2
28	PxP	

After the game Korchnoi admitted that his own time-trouble had saved him, for he hadn't had time to resign. Now Black can win without any unnecessary delays by 28 ... R-Q3 followed by KxP (which is also decisive after 29 R-K8ch because of the mate threat on KR7).

28	...	R-K2

Wade goes in for a combination, which is really unnecessary when a piece up.

29	N-Q3	

Neither rook can be taken because of the mate. Black's next move illustrates the *motif* of decoying.

29	...	B-K5
30	Q-KN5	P-B3
31	RxP!	

There would be no point in doing things by halves. Now at least the mate threat on KR2 has been eliminated.

31	...	NxR
32	QxN	Q-K3
33	Q-B4	R(Q1)-K1

Black can now win very much as he wants. But the wisest course would be to get rid of the troublesome pawn by KxP, depriving White of his last hope.

34	N-K5	B-N3??

The miracle has happened. White has now got a draw. Black missed an easy win by 34 ... B-R1 35 N-N6! PxN 36 RxQ RxR.

35	NxB	PxN??

Now the game is won for White. If Black had instead taken with his queen he would have had a perpetual check after 36 RxR Q-N8ch 37 K-N2 Q-B7ch, for the White king cannot go to KR3 because of Q-B1ch, which stops the mating threat and allows the rook to be taken.

36	RxQ	RxR

Unfortunately for Wade, Korchnoi was not affected by his time-trouble and went on to convert his advantage in the endgame.

37	K-N2	KxP
38	P-Q5	R-K5
39	Q-QB7ch	R(K1)-K2
40	Q-B6	R-K7ch
41	K-R3	K-R2

Or 41 ... RxQRP 42 P-Q6 R(K2)-K7 43 P-Q7 winning, e.g. 43 ... RxPch 44 K-N4 R(KR7)-Q7 45 P-Q8=Q! RxQ 46 Q-B7ch.

42	P-Q6	R-KN2
43	Q-Q5	R-K1
44	K-N4	R-Q1
45	K-N5	R(N2)-Q2
46	P-KN4	P-R4
47	Q-K6	RxP
48	Q-B7ch	K-R1

49	K-R6	P-KN4dis ch
50	KxP	R-KN1ch
51	K-R5	R(N1)-Q1
52	P-N5	R(Q1)-Q2
53	Q-K8ch	K-N2
54	P-QR4	R-Q7
55	Q-K5ch	K-N1
56	Q-K6ch	K-R1
57	Q-K8ch	K-N2
58	P-R4	R(Q7)-Q3
59	Q-QB8	R-Q5
60	Q-QN8	R(Q2)-Q3
61	Q-B7ch	K-N1
62	Q-QN7	K-R1
63	Q-KB7!	

Black resigned at this stage because he was in *zugzwang*, e.g. 63 ... R(Q5)-Q4 64 K-N4 R-Q5ch 65 K-B5 R(Q5)-Q4ch 66 K-K4 R-Q5ch 67 K-K5 winning or 63 ... R(Q3)-Q4 64 Q-B6ch K-N1 65 QxP etc.

At this moment it seemed almost certain to experienced tournament players that Korchnoi was going to win the tournament. It is well known that where the players are evenly matched it always takes a bit of luck to win first prize. And you either have luck or you don't. It is rare for Mother Fortune to move from one board to the next.

Before the last round the position was: Korchnoi 16, Pachman 15½, Barcza, Geller and Tal 15, Ivkov 14½, etc. Korchnoi had White against Bobozov, and to everyone's surprise the game ended in a quick draw. In similar situations, such tactics are generally good, for one's main rival, who has thus been given new hope, often becomes so nervous that he plays below his usual strength. The same tactics were adopted by my rival Ståhlberg in a similar situation at Trentschin-Teplitz. I then played my game with Golombek in a completely inexplicable manner—and lost.

But to return to the present tournament. As expected, Geller, with White,

defeated Letelier, and Tal, Broderman. The fate of the first five places therefore depended on the result of the following game.

English Opening

	Barcza	Pachman
1	P-KN3	P-KN3
2	B-N2	B-N2
3	P-QB4	P-K4
4	N-QB3	N-K2
5	P-Q3	0-0
6	R-N1	P-QR4(?)

Not a particularly good continuation, for it helps White to open the QR file, thus increasing his chances on the queen's wing. Besides the normal 6 ... P-Q3, there is also the interesting 6 ... P-QB3 7 P-K4 (preventing P-Q4), after which Black can either play 7 ... P-Q3 followed by B-K3 or sacrifice a pawn. In the latter case (7 ... P-Q4!? 8 KPxP PxP 9 NxP QN-B3 followed by B-K3), Black gets active play for his pieces in return for the pawn.

| 7 | P-QR3 | P-Q3 |

In view of the previous weakening of his queen's wing, 7 ... P-QB3 would not be particularly good, for White could reply with 8 P-B5!, e.g. 8 ... P-Q4 9 PxP e.p. QxP 10 P-QN4 with a very good game.

| 8 | P-K3 | QN-B3 |
| 9 | KN-K2 | B-N5 |

A good manoeuvre, which makes it difficult for White to castle.

10	P-R3	B-K3
11	N-Q5	Q-Q2
12	Q-R4	B-B4

As a rule it is unwise to move a piece several times before development has been completed. Yet there is an exception to every rule, and in the present case the third move with the bishop is not a mistake, for it answers White's threat of 13 NxNch winning a pawn. But there was a better move for Black: he could simply have ignored the threat and played 12 . . . K-R1! Then White would have had to think twice about winning the pawn, for after 13 NxN QxN 14 BxN PxB 15 QxBP he would have had considerable weaknesses on the king's side. After other replies to 12 . . . K-R1 Black could have continued with N-KN1 and P-B4, preparing an action on the king's wing.

13	Q-B2	K-R1
14	P-KR4	

Otherwise he cannot castle. But now his king-side position is weakened, and that is exactly where Black is planning to get active.

14	. . .	P-R4
15	N(K2)-B3	N(K2)-N1
16	0-0	N-B3

This transfer of the knight has cost several tempi, but on KB3 it is much more active than on K2. At a suitable moment it can go to KN5, for White would only block his king's bishop on KN2 if he were to drive it off with P-KB3.

17	P-QN4	PxP
18	PxP	N-Q1

Objectively the best move is 18 . . . R(R1)-N1 followed by N-K2. But in this

137. Barcza–Pachman

Position after Black's 18th move

case Black cannot hope for more than simplification and equality. At this stage of the game it had become clear that the encounter between Korchnoi and Bobozov was heading for a draw, so I decided to chance my arm and prepare a king-side attack. But first it was necessary to exchange off White's king's bishop.

19	B-N2	R-B1
20	R-R1	B-R6
21	Q-K2	BxB
22	KxB	N-K3?

A bad mistake; the correct move is 22 . . . N-N5.

23 R-R7!

I had been prepared for 23 NxN BxN 24 Q-B3 B-N2, after which White cannot win a pawn: 25 QxNP R-QN1. But the intermediary move 23 R-R7 changes the situation. I could not bring myself to withdraw the knight to Q1, and so I embarked on the following dubious pawn sacrifice.

23	. . .	R-QN1!?
24	P-N5?	

Barcza misses his way. He should have continued with 24 NxN BxN 25 Q-B3 B-N2 26 RxP RxR 27 QxR, when the attacking chances I had hoped to obtain with 27 . . . P-KB4 are inadequate. It is interesting to note that Barcza rejected this line for quite a different reason. He thought that Black could deviate with 26 RxP P-K5 27 QxKP P-Q4, which is a hallucination, for 28 PxP RxR 29 PxN Q-B1 30 PxP would give White too many pawns for the exchange.

24	. . .	N-N5
25	N-K4	Q-Q1
26	P-B3	N-R3
27	P-B4	P-KB4
28	N-N5	NxN
29	RPxN	N-N5

The game is now virtually level. It is true that the White rook on R7 is unpleasant for Black, as it prevents him from playing P-QB3 driving the knight away from its dominating position. But Black's own knight on KN5 is by no means badly placed. And his position has no weaknesses.

30	B-B3	R-B2
31	P-K4	K-N1
32	PxBP	RxP
33	R-B3	Q-Q2
34	PxP	PxP
35	RxR	PxR
36	Q-B3	

138. Barcza–Pachman

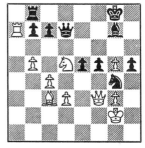

From the psychological point of view a very interesting position. We were both in time-trouble, and I had the impression that White intended to play 37 QxP, expecting 37 . . . QxQ? 38 N-K7ch. This, of course, would have been a grave mistake, for Black also has a knight fork at the ready, so that he could reply to 37 QxP? by 37 . . . QxNch! Such traps are the ideal tactical weapon in the time-scramble. Unfortunately I could not find a reasonable move that would leave the trap open. Moreover, I was not particularly happy with the position as it was, so I decided to go in for a freeing manoeuvre.

36	. . .	P-K5!
37	PxP	PxP
38	QxP	BxB
39	NxB	Q-Q7ch
40	N-K2	QxP

Before making the last move prior to the time-control I also considered the

continuation 40 . . . N-K6ch 41 K-B3 R-KB1ch 42 N-B4 Q-KN7ch 43 KxN QxPch 44 K-Q2! Two things, however, were not quite clear. First, was the rook ending after 44 . . . QxNch 45 QxQ RxQ 46 K-Q3 actually drawn? And, second, should I give up all chances of playing for a win? The answer to the first question is that 46 . . . P-R5 does actually ensure a draw. As regards the second, the move I chose left me in a slightly inferior position, so that I should not really have been thinking in terms of a win.

In fact, when analysing the game in the adjournment, I even rebuked myself for playing QxP on my 40th move. But as things worked out the pendulum swung back and the game again took a dramatic turn.

41 R-R3(?)

The sealed move, after which I breathed a sigh of relief. Although my analysis had shown there was nothing to be feared from 41 RxP RxR 42 QxR Q-QB4, after which White has nothing better than a drawing continuation 43 Q-Q5ch QxQ 44 PxQ N-K6ch, my position would have been more difficult after 41 N-B4. I had worked out that Black could only hold the game in this case by 41 . . . P-R5!

Another continuation, 41 Q-K6ch K-R1 42 N-B4, can be answered by 42 . . . P-R5 or 42 . . . R-KN1. An important factor here is that Black gets immediate counter-play on the king's wing.

41	. . .	R-KB1
42	N-B4	P-R5!
43	Q-Q5ch	

Or 43 Q-N6ch QxQ 44 NxQ R-K1 45 NxP N-K6ch, draw.

43	. . .	QxQ
44	PxQ	R-B4!

The only good defence to 45 N-K6. At this point it was really time to offer and

accept a draw. But we both wanted to
play on to the bitter end.

45	R-R7	PxP
46	KxP	N-B3
47	P-Q6??	N-K5ch
48	K-N4	NxP
49	N-K6	RxP
50	NxP	R-K4
51	K-B4	R-K5ch
52	K-B3	R-K4
53	K-B4	R-B4ch
54	K-K3?	

Even after the almost unbelievable loss
of a pawn several moves previously when
Barcza had simply overlooked a pawn
fork, the position was still drawn. It
would have sufficed for White to play 54
K-N4! R-QB4 55 N-K6. But this present,
and less obvious, mistake allows White's
knight to be driven into the corner. It is
only a miracle that Black cannot force a
win.

54 ...	R-QB4!
55 N-R8	R-B3
56 R-R1	K-B2
57 K-Q4	K-K3
58 R-QN1	P-N4
59 R-K1ch	K-Q2
60 K-Q5	N-B1!

Answering the threat of 61 R-K7ch.
At the same time Black prepares to
regroup his pieces, thus preventing the
unfortunate knight from escaping.

139. Barcza–Pachman

Position after Black's 64th move

61	R-QR1	N-K2ch
62	K-Q4	R-B5ch
63	K-Q3	N-Q4
64	R-R7ch	K-B3

At first sight White appears to be lost,
for Black is threatening 65 ... R-QR5!
66 RxR PxR 67 K-B4 K-N2 winning.

65 R-KN7!

A study-like move that saves the game.
If White were instead to play 65 R-KR7,
he would lose, as will soon become clear.

| 65 ... | R-QR5 |
| 66 R-N8 | K-N2 |

Or 66 ... K-B4 67 R-QB8ch K-N5 68
R-Q8! draw, but not 68 N-B7? NxN 69
RxN R-R7!

67 R-N5!

The subtlety of White's 65th move is
now apparent. If the rook had been on
KR8 White might as well have resigned
(67 R-R5 N-B5ch). As it is there is
nothing Black can do. The position is one
of those exceptions where the result does
not accord with chess logic. If now 67 ...
K-B3, the reply 68 RxN! draws.

67 ...	R-R6ch
68 K-Q4	N-B6
69 R-QB5	P-N5
70 N-B7	K-N3
71 K-B4	P-N6
72 N-Q5ch	NxN
73 RxN	K-B3
74 R-QB5ch	
Drawn	

Thanks to the present FIDE rules it
can happen that even games which do not
affect the final placings can have a
dramatic character. International grandmaster and master titles are obtained by
reaching a standard, that is attaining a
certain score, which is determined according to the strength of the tournament. In
the final round of the Havana Tournament, Klaus Darga had no chance of
ending up in one of the first five places.

Yet his game was of enormous importance, for in the event of victory he would have reached the grandmaster standard. That is not just a mere matter of a title. The fact is grandmasters are more often invited to international tournaments and are given better conditions. For that reason the last few years have witnessed a hunt for titles which is not always in the ethical and aesthetic interest of chess.

In this case, however, it was an honourable struggle and an example of how to solve the not too easy task of beating an admittedly weaker opponent in a decisive game when one has Black.

King's Indian

De Greiff	Darga
1 P-Q4	N-KB3
2 P-QB4	P-KN3
3 N-QB3	B-N2
4 P-K4	P-Q3
5 B-K2	0-0
6 N-B3	P-K4
7 0-0	QN-Q2

On his previous move Darga had been afraid of the simplifying 7 PxP PxP 8 QxQ. He does not want to risk it a second time.

8 R-K1	P-B3
9 R-N1	

I consider 9 B-B1 R-K1 10 P-Q5 P-B4 11 P-KN3 to be stronger, though that is a purely subjective assessment. Those who prefer open games like to retain the tension in the centre, but in that case 9 B-B1 R-K1 10 R-N1 is better.

9 ...	PxP
10 NxP	R-K1

Black can equalize at once by 10 ... P-Q4 11 KPxP PxP 12 PxP N-N3 or 12 N(Q4)-N5 PxP 13 BxP N-N3 followed by B-B4. For Darga, of course, such a continuation with prospects of an early draw was out of the question.

11 B-B1	P-QR4
12 P-B3	N-B4
13 B-K3	KN-Q2
14 Q-Q2	B-K4

There is no question that such positions in the King's Indian or Old Indian are more comfortable for White, who has a clear-cut plan: placing his pieces so that they exert the maximum pressure on Q6 and, possibly, preparation of an action on the queen's wing (P-QN3, P-QR3, P-QN4, etc.). Black, for his part, has no real strategical plan. He must more or less play a waiting game, at the same time trying to keep his opponent occupied answering small tactical threats, even merely apparent ones. Black's last move belongs to this latter category. Black threatens a queen sally to KR5 and induces his opponent to make a weakening move on the king's side. In actual fact White had no need to worry about the threat. He should have played 16 P-QN3, which is in any case a useful move. If his opponent had then gone in for Q-R5 there was still time for 16 P-KN3.

15 P-KN3(?)	B-N2

Now that the bishop has done its job of provoking a king-side weakness, it returns home, thus preventing 16 P-B4 followed by B-N2.

16 QR-Q1(?)	

There was still time for P-N3.

16 ...	P-R5!
17 Q-QB2	Q-R4
18 K-N2	N-K4

A good continuation is 18 ... P-R6 19 P-N3 N-R3 followed by N-N5. However, although blockading the queen's wing gives Black a satisfactory game, there is little scope for introducing complications, which is what Darga needs. For that reason he decides to keep his opponent occupied in the centre and on the king's wing, holding back the advance P-R6 for a more favourable occasion.

19	P-B4	N-N5
20	B-N1	N-B3
21	N-B3	

140. De Greiff–Darga

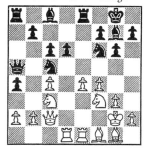

Black's QP is under attack and direct protection (R-Q1, B-B1 or Q-B2) would lessen the effectiveness of Black's pieces. There now follows an exciting tactical duel revolving around the pawn in question.

	21 ...	P-R6!

At first sight not a very impressive move. In fact it looks as if White can simply take the QP. But there is something else beneath the surface: 22 RxP? KNxP! 23 NxN NxN 24 RxN RxR 25 QxR B-B4 followed by PxP winning material.

22	P-N3	B-N5!

Another interesting indirect defence of the pawn, e.g. 23 RxP? KNxP 24 NxN BxNch 25 KxB QxR or 24 RxN BxQN.

23	P-R3	BxNch
24	KxB	

Psychologically a very interesting position. Darga realizes that White still ought not to take the pawn but would like to induce him to do so. For that reason he resorts to a "neutral" move.

	24 ...	P-R4!?

Viewed from the point of view of the above-mentioned psychological factor this move is very logical. In fact, it even

has its positive sides—it can if necessary threaten P-R5. On the other hand, it has the drawback that it does change the position, for White can now take the QP and the complications that ensue should lead to a draw.

25	RxP!	KNxP
26	RxN	BxN
27	RxRch	RxR
28	RxNPch!	

An unpleasant surprise for Black, who now seems to be lost. If he plays 28 . . . PxR there follows 29 QxPch K-B1 30 Q-B5ch K-N1 31 BxN B-N2 32 B-Q3 winning.

	28 ...	B-N2!

Luckily for Darga there is still this resource. In view of the threat Q-K8 White is forced to sacrifice the exchange, for after 29 R-N5? Q-K8 30 BxN QxBch 31 Q-B2 Q-Q6ch 32 B-K3 Q-K5ch 33 K-K2 K-B1 (threatening B-Q5) 34 K-Q2 R-Q1ch 35 K-K2 R-Q6 Black's threat of B-Q5 cannot be answered by 36 Q-B3 on account of the elegant rejoinder 36 . . . R-Q7ch! And after the alternative 29 B-Q4 Black does not have to be content with a draw (29 . . . PxR 30 QxP R-K2 31 BxB RxB 32 Q-K8ch, perpetual check), but can play 29 . . . N-K3!

29	RxBch!	KxR
30	B-Q4ch	K-N1
31	Q-B5!	

De Greiff obviously overlooked Darga's reply, but it was one of those oversights that improve one's chances. In spite of the apparent power of his position, White actually lacks a satisfactory attacking continuation, e.g. 31 B-B3 Q-Q1!, and neither 32 Q-B5 Q-Q8ch nor 32 B-R1 N-K5 33 B-Q3 NxP! 34 Q-B3 P-B3 35 B-N6 N-K7 can save him.

	31 ...	NxP!
32	QxQ!	NxQ
33	B-B3	

Havana 1963

	1	2	3	4	5	6	7	8	9	10	11	12	13	14	15	16	17	18	19	20	21	22	Pts	Prize
1 Korchnoi	—	0	0	½	1	½	½	1	1	½	½	1	1	1	1	1	1	1	1	1	1	1	16½	I
2 Geller	1	—	½	0	½	1	½	1	½	1	1	½	1	½	1	1	1	0	1	1	1	1	16	II–IV
3 Pachman	1	½	—	½	½	1	½	½	½	½	1	½	1	1	½	1	½	1	1	1	1	1	16	II–IV
4 Tal	½	1	½	—	1	0	1	1	0	1	½	1	1	1	½	1	1	1	1	1	1	0	16	II–IV
5 Barcza	0	½	½	0	—	½	1	1	½	1	½	½	1	1	½	1	1	1	1	1	1	1	15½	V, VI
6 Ivkov	½	0	0	1	½	—	½	1	½	½	1	1	1	1	1	½	½	1	1	1	1	1	15½	V, VI
7 Darga	½	½	½	0	0	½	—	½	½	½	½	½	1	1	1	½	1	0	1	1	1	1	13	VII
8 Uhlmann	0	0	½	0	0	0	½	—	½	½	½	1	1	½	1	1	1	1	1	1	1	½	12½	VIII
9 Trifunović	0	½	½	1	½	½	½	½	—	½	½	½	½	½	½	½	½	1	½	½	½	1	11½	IX
10 Bobozov	½	0	½	0	0	½	½	½	½	—	½	1	1	1	½	0	½	1	½	½	1	½	11	X
11 O'Kelly	½	0	0	½	½	0	½	½	½	½	—	½	1	½	½	½	½	1	1	½	½	1	11	X
12 Robatsch	0	½	½	0	½	0	½	0	½	0	½	—	½	½	1	½	1	1	½	1	1	1	11	X
13 Letelier	0	0	0	0	0	0	0	0	½	0	0	½	—	½	½	1	1	1	1	1	1	1	9	
14 Wade	0	½	0	0	0	0	0	½	½	0	½	½	½	—	½	0	½	1	1	½	1	1	8½	
15 Cobo	0	0	½	½	½	0	0	0	½	½	½	0	½	½	—	½	½	0	1	½	½	1	8	
16 Jiménez	0	0	0	0	0	½	½	0	½	1	½	½	0	1	½	—	½	0	½	½	½	½	7½	
17 Pérez	0	0	½	0	0	½	0	0	½	½	½	0	0	½	½	½	—	0	½	1	1	1	7½	
18 Garcia	0	1	0	0	0	0	1	0	0	0	0	0	0	0	1	1	1	—	0	1	0	1	7	
19 Ortega	0	0	0	0	0	0	0	0	½	½	0	½	0	0	0	½	½	1	—	1	½	1	6	
20 de Greiff	0	0	0	0	0	0	0	0	½	½	½	0	0	½	½	½	0	0	0	—	1	½	4½	
21 Broderman	0	0	0	0	0	0	0	0	½	0	½	0	0	0	½	½	0	1	½	0	—	½	4	
22 Calero	0	0	0	1	0	0	0	½	0	½	0	0	0	0	0	½	0	0	0	½	½	—	3½	

141. De Greiff–Darga

Position after White's 33rd move

It is hard to believe that Black cannot win even though he is the exchange up. However, his knight is out of play, and attempts to protect it by R-R1 or P-N3 lead to a draw after 34 P-QB5. But Darga finds a last chance, and it is that which gains him the grandmaster title.

| 33 ... | R-Q1! |
| 34 BxN? | |

Just one precise move and White would have had his draw, for after 34 B-K2! the Black rook cannot attack the QRP. And there is no other winning plan for Black, the continuation 34 ... NxP 35 BxN P-N4 36 B-K2 offering him no chance, but rather the reverse.

34 ...	R-Q8
35 B-K2	R-QR8
36 B-B3	RxP
37 P-QB5	R-B7
38 B-K5	P-R7
39 K-K3	RxP
40 B-Q4	

White resigned without waiting for his opponent's reply. The most accurate reply is 40 ... P-R5 and if 41 P-N4 then R-B8.

41 Candidates' Tournament 1965

Unsuccessful Surprise in the Opening

Since 1965 the former candidates' tournaments have been replaced by a knock-out system of matches of ten games each. In the first round eight grandmasters take part. The four successful contestants then play a second match of ten games, the winners meeting in the final, where victory determines the challenger to the world champion. In the first of these new candidates' tournaments, the draw brought two of the favourites together in the first round. One of these, the 49-year-old Estonian grandmaster, Paul Keres, had won the 1938 AVRO Tournament, which had been regarded as the qualifying tournament for a world championship title match against the world champion, Alekhin. This tournament was thus virtually the first candidates' tournament, being like those regular three-yearly tournaments which were started after World War II. The title match between Alekhin and Keres never took place. During the war the front moved twice over Tallin, where Keres lived.

In the candidates' tournaments since the war Keres had achieved the best overall result, but had lacked that last little piece of luck necessary for victory. It was clear that 1965 would be the last chance for Keres, who was now nearly fifty years old. His opponent in the first round was Boris Spasski, a thirty-year-old master with an all-round style, who was excellently equipped both physically and mentally.

Keres won the first encounter with Black, a very sharply played game, and managed to scrape a draw in the second in a very difficult endgame in which there was at one stage a forced win for his opponent. But then Spasski convincingly won a series of three games and it looked as if the match had lost all its drama. However, after two draws Keres hit back, winning a great game and reducing his opponent's lead to one point with two rounds to go. In the ninth game the match might well have come to a conclusion, for Spasski overlooked a simple manoeuvre that would have gained a piece. This bad mistake, which cost him half a point, heightened the drama. The score was now 5:4 in Spasski's favour, but Keres had White, and by winning the next game could have squared the match and forced a continuation.

On 23 August 1965 the officers' mess in Riga was full of spectators, most of whom were interested in which of the two contestants would emerge as the chief rival to their chess idol, Michael Tal.

King's Indian

Keres	Spasski
1 P-Q4	N-KB3
2 P-QB4	P-KN3
3 N-QB3	B-N2

The opening set-up chosen by both players is highly surprising, for it was the first tournament game between Keres and Spasski in which the King's Indian Defence had occurred. The Estonian grandmaster almost always opens with 1 P-K4. However, in the second game he nearly lost and in the fourth game he actually did lose, in both cases in a Ruy Lopez. So his change of repertoire is understandable.

It is less clear why Spasski in such an important game should choose a defence that he only occasionally adopts. His usual defences to 1 P-Q4 are the Nimzo-Indian and, more often, the Tartakower variation of the Queen's Gambit. The choice of the King's Indian seems to be tactically wrong in view of the fact that Black only needed a draw. Why should he risk getting into a complicated position?

The explanation of Spasski's psychological approach to the final game can be found by looking at the eighth. In that, a Nimzo-Indian, Keres had sacrificed two pawns and shattered his opponent in twenty-five moves. This time Spasski decides not to play for a draw. He calculates that sharp play will upset Keres, who in any case faces a stiff mental test. His decision, which very few present-day grandmasters would have taken, pays off handsomely in the end.

4 P-K4	P-Q3
5 P-B4	

With his choice of this two-edged system, Keres returns to a favourite line of his in his youth—as played, for example, in a game against Hromádka in 1937. Here he has prepared a little surprise in a modern variation.

5 . . .	P-B4
6 P-Q5	0-0
7 N-B3	P-K3
8 B-K2	PxP
9 BPxP	P-QN4!?

At this stage I feel I have to make a confession. This move, in place of the older and sound 9 . . . R-K1 10 N-Q2 N-N5 11 BxN Q-R5ch, etc., is known as my improvement to the whole variation, because I recommended it many years ago. When doing so, I had overlooked that White wins a pawn by 10 BxP NxKP 11 NxN Q-R4ch 12 K-B2 QxB 13 NxQP. Subsequent analysis by others, however, showed that Black has adequate compensation for the pawn, e.g. 13 . . . Q-N3 14

NxB RxN or 14 N-B4 Q-R3 15 N-K3 N-Q2, etc. Theorists began to write about a pawn sacrifice advocated by Pachman. Actually, it happens quite frequently that a mistake later turns out to be a combination. Of course, the reverse is by no means less common.

10 P-K5!	PxP
11 PxP	N-N5
12 B-KB4	

Several games have shown that after 12 BxP NxKP 13 0-0 the passed pawn gives White no advantage. On the contrary, it is Black with his active bishop on KN2 and the open QN file who has the initiative.

An interesting variation is 12 B-KN5 Q-N3 13 0-0 P-B5dis ch 14 K-R1 NxKP (not 14 . . . N-B7ch? 15 RxN QxR 16 NxP with a won position for White) 15 B-K7 QN-Q2 or better 15 NxN BxN 16 B-K7. It is, however, understandable that in this game Keres did not want to choose a line that at the time enjoyed widespread interest. Instead, he hoped to spring a surprise on his opponent.

12 . . .	N-Q2
13 P-K6!	

142. Keres–Spasski

13 . . .	PxP!?

With this move Spasski shows that he has no intention of avoiding risks. He could have by-passed all complications by 13 . . . N(Q2)-K4, e.g. 14 NxN NxN 15

0-0 PxP 16 BxP PxP 17 QxPch QxQ 18 NxQ B-N2, etc.

14 PxP   RxB

Now the exchange sacrifice is necessary, for if Black moves away his knight on Q2, his opponent gets a better game: 14 ... N-N3 15 QxQ RxQ 16 NxP BxNP 17 P-K7 R-K1 18 R-QN1 winning the exchange, or 14 ... N(Q2)-B3 15 QxQ RxQ 16 P-K7 R-K1 17 B-Q6, etc.

15 Q-Q5

This move caused great excitement among the otherwise disciplined spectators, who for the most part were hoping for a victory by Keres—either because of the nearness of Riga and Tallin or for the more selfish reason that they assumed Keres would be an easier opponent for their darling, Tal. By threatening 16 P-K7 dis ch White wins the exchange, and Black apparently gets no adequate compensation.

15 ...	K-R1
16 QxR	N-N3
17 QxP	

The first debatable point. Is the pawn worth the removal of the queen from the scene of action? The move 17 Q-N8 looks more logical, for the enemy rook apparently has to waste a tempo moving away. If Black tries to keep the White king in the middle by 17 ... BxNch 18 PxB R-K5, there follows 19 0-0! RxB 20 QR-K1, and Black's position is critical. However, Black has a good alternative, which is more effective in preventing White from castling and, what is more, does not give up the two bishops, viz. (17 Q-N8) N-K6! If White replies 18 K-B2, Black plays 18 ... N-N5ch, after which White cannot continue 19 K-N3 RxNch 20 KxR Q-B3ch 21 K-N3 (21 KxN Q-B4ch) 21 ... Q-N4, which loses the queen or allows a quick mate, but must be content with a draw by repetition (19

K-K1 N-K6), which is tantamount to defeat.

The reason for Keres's seventeenth move (QxP) was not therefore to win a pawn but to gain time for castling by threatening 18 P-K7.

17 ...	BxP
18 0-0	N-K6

143. Keres–Spasski

In the course of the last few moves Black's pieces have become quite active, and there is now the constant threat of P-N5. Under normal circumstances Keres would almost certainly have given back the exchange either by 19 BxP NxR 20 RxN R-B2 21 Q-R5, which gives him a slightly better game, though Black's two bishops should ensure a draw, or by 19 QR-Q1 NxQR 20 RxN B-Q5ch 21 K-R1 P-N5 22 N-QN5 B-Q4!, after which Black threatens BxN with complete equality. Being forced to play for a win, however, Keres understandably decides to hold on to the extra material.

19 R-B2   P-N5

Now Black can no longer think of recovering the exchange, for 19 ... N-N5? 20 R-Q1 B-Q5 21 NxB would lose at once.

20 QN-N5?

On its new post the knight will soon get into danger, and that is one of the main reasons for White's defeat. The correct move is 20 N-Q1!, which Black should not answer by 20 ... N-N5? hoping for 21 R(B2)-B1? B-Q5ch 22 K-R1 Q-Q3 (threatening 23 ... RxN) 23 P-KN3 B-Q4!, because White has a much stronger reply in 21 N-KN5 RxR (21 ... QxKN 22 Q-N8ch) 22 NxP! (not, of course 22 NxB RxPch 23 KxR Q-Q4ch, etc.). After 20 N-Q1 Black would have to play 20 ... N(K6)-Q4, after which the game is quite open. For the exchange Black would have considerable pressure, though no immediate threats.

> 20 ...   R-B2
> 21 Q-R5

If the queen were to withdraw to R6 Black would simply continue with 21 ... BxNP 22 R-K1 N-N5 23 R-Q1 B-Q4. After the text-move, however, the Black knight is pinned, and if Black were to play as in the note, White could continue with 24 RxB! QxR 25 QxN NxR 26 KxN, which gains him two pieces for a rook.

> 21 ...   Q-QN1
> 22 R-K1

The promising-looking reply 22 ... N-N5 can now be answered by 23 B-B1! with advantage to White.

> 22 ...   B-Q4
> 23 B-B1

Or 23 B-Q3 QN-B5 24 BxN (but not 24 Q-R6 NxKNP! 25 KxN Q-B5 with a mating attack by Black) 24 ... NxB 25 Q-R6 R-B3 26 Q-R4 (or 26 Q-R7 QxN 27 R-K7 N-Q3! 28 RxB N-B2 29 R-Q2 Q-B3, etc.), and now Black must not play 26 ... B-B3? on account of 27 Q-R7 QxN 28 R-K7, but 26 ... R-B1! threatening NxP and B-QB3.

> 23 ...   NxB
> 24 KRxN   N-B5
> 25 Q-R6   R-B3
> 26 Q-R4

In the same way as in the note to move 23, a counter-attack by 26 Q-R7 QxN 27 R-K7 fails on account of 28 ... N-Q3, and giving up a piece by 27 N-N5 RxRch 28 RxR B-Q5ch 29 K-R1 B-KNPch 30 KxB N-K6ch is no good either.

> 26 ...   NxP

144. Keres–Spasski

27 Q-B2?

Prematurely resigning himself to his fate. Keres probably rejected 27 Q-R5 on account of 27 ... N-B5 28 Q-R4 B-B3, overlooking the fact that 28 Q-B7 would have kept him out of danger, for 28 ... QxN 29 Q-Q8ch B-N1 30 R-K8 would actually lose for Black.

After the game Spasski said he had intended to reply to 27 Q-R5 by 27 ... N-Q6, which would have given him excellent chances, though the win would still have had to be demonstrated.

> 27 ...   QxN
> 28 R-K7   N-Q6
> 29 Q-K2   P-B5
> 30 R-K8ch   R-B1
> 31 RxRch   BxR
> 32 N-N5   B-B4ch
> 33 K-R1   Q-Q2
> 34 Q-Q2   Q-K2
> 35 N-B3   Q-K6

White lost by exceeding the time-limit.

42 Candidates' Tournament 1965

Two Years' Analysis

The Danish grandmaster Larsen was one of the most successful chess players of the second half of the 1960s. He is by nature a great optimist. Twice before candidates' tournaments he has publicly expressed his conviction that he would emerge victorious and then go on to win the match for the world's highest title.

In the semi-final of the 1965 tournament Larsen's opponent was Tal, who at that time was already past his peak and who was physically not in the best of condition. Larsen was the favourite by a short head. He took the lead after the first and fifth games, but each time Tal subsequently managed to catch up, and after the ninth game, in which Larsen failed to make use of his chances in the ending, they were still all square. The tenth game, in which Tal had White, began on 8 August in Bled, the venue for many a great chess contest, but the post-mortem lasted two full years. The analyses of the critical position filled many handwritten and printed pages, for Tal made a piece sacrifice on intuition rather than exact calculation, something which few grandmasters would have dared in such a vital game. However, in this match the two players had one thing in common—they were both great optimists who had their fair share of "healthy impudence", as it is called in sports jargon.

Sicilian Defence

Tal	Larsen
1 P-K4	P-QB4
2 N-KB3	N-QB3
3 P-Q4	PxP
4 NxP	P-K3
5 N-QB3	P-Q3

The Scheveningen System was at one time characterized by the moves 4 ... N-B3 5 N-QB3 P-Q3 6 B-K2 P-K3. Nowadays this line rarely occurs in the games of strong players, for the move 6 ... P-K4 is so good that no one allows it. Instead it is prevented by the Richter-Rauser Attack (6 B-KN5) or the developing move 6 B-QB4.

The order of moves chosen by Larsen in this game has, on the one hand, the advantage of preventing 6 B-KN5. On the other, it has the disadvantage that White has not yet played his king's bishop to K2 and can post it more aggressively on Q3 or QB4. Tal decides to adopt the sharpest continuation, which is characterized by queen-side castling.

6 B-K3	N-B3
7 P-B4	B-K2
8 Q-B3	0-0!?

More peacefully disposed players prefer 8 ... P-K4, preventing the typical classical Sicilian attack, characterized by an advance of White's king-side pawns. If White then replies 9 N-B5, Black gets an excellent game by 9 ... BxN 10 PxB N-Q5! Therefore White would do better with 9 PxP PxP 10 NxN PxN 11 B-QB4 0-0 12 P-KR3 (more promising than 12 0-0 N-N5 13 QR-Q1 NxB!).

| 9 0-0-0 | Q-B2 |

The continuation 9 ... NxN 10 BxN Q-R4 11 P-K5 has proved to be less good.

| 10 N(Q4)-N5!? | |

With this move Tal decides to go along unexplored and unfathomable paths. 10 P-KN4 is premature on account of 10 . . . NxN 11 RxN P-K4!, but in a number of games 10 R-N1 has been played, preparing the advance of the KNP.

10	. . .	Q-N1
11	P-KN4!?	P-QR3
12	N-Q4	NxN
13	BxN	P-QN4?

Larsen does nothing to stop the typical pawn advance—a testament to his exaggerated optimism. Here 13 . . . P-K4 was necessary, which is almost always the natural reaction to P-KN4. After this and White's best reply, 14 P-N5, Black, in view of the position of his queen on QN1, should avoid the immediate 14 . . . PxB 15 PxN PxN 16 PxB PxPch 17 K-N1 R-K1 18 P-B5! RxP 19 R-N1, which gives White a strong attack, and insert the intermediary move 14 . . . B-N5!, which more or less leads to equality, e.g. 15 Q-N3 PxB 16 PxN PxN 17 PxB PxPch 18 K-N1 BxR 19 B-B4 B-R4.

14	P-N5	N-Q2
15	B-Q3!?	

Preparing the sacrifice of a piece. The preventive 15 P-QR3 is not particularly good, for Black gets strong counter-play on the open QN file (15 . . . P-N5 16 PxP QxP). However, it would have been possible to build up an attacking position without any undue risks by 15 P-KR4, which enables White to reply to 15 . . . P-N5 with 16 N-K2.

15	. . .	P-N5
16	N-Q5!	

That is the controversial sacrifice that kept chess annotators and editors busy for such a long time. However, in view of White's previous move, the sacrifice is practically forced, for if instead White withdraws the knight by 16 N-K2, Black can exploit the weakness of the KNP

145. Tal–Larsen

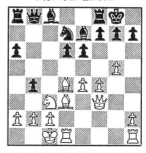

Position after Black's 15th move

(which because of White's decision not to play P-KR4 is inadequately protected) to attack in the centre: 16 . . . P-K4 17 B-K3 PxP 18 BxP (If White had already played P-KR4 he could instead continue with NxP followed by N-Q5.) 18 . . . N-K4.

16	. . .	PxN

Declining the sacrifice would give White a decisive attack: 16 . . . B-Q1 17 N-B6ch PxN 18 PxP BxP (18 . . . NxP 19 QR-N1ch K-R1 20 Q-N3) 19 QR-N1ch K-R1 20 P-K5 with the irresistible threat of 21 Q-R5.

17	PxP	P-B4?

White was threatening 18 Q-K4, which could not have been adequately parried by 17 . . . B-Q1 because of the multiple piece sacrifice 18 BxRPch KxB 19 Q-R5ch K-N1 20 BxP! KxB (20 . . . P-B4 21 Q-N6 R-B2 22 B-R6dis ch) 21 Q-R6ch K-N1 22 P-N6 PxP (22 . . . N-B3 23 P-N7) 23 QxPch K-R1 24 QR-N1 followed by mate in two moves.

The greatest controversy centred around the position that would have arisen after Black's strongest defence, 17 . . . P-N3! A number of analysts voiced the opinion that, although in this case White would have very good chances in practice, objectively seen Black should win with precise defence. Larsen was of the same opinion after the game, maintaining that his faulty choice of defence had robbed him of victory in this important game and with it the chance of contesting the world championship title.

The result of considerable analysis points to the fact that Black's defence would in this case have been extremely difficult. It seems most likely that the position was an example of dynamic equilibrium, where even the slightest inaccuracy on Black's part would have led to an immediate loss. In practice the attacker tends to have an advantage in such situations, for defence in tactically complicated positions is more difficult, and more time-consuming, than attack.

From the array of possible variations arising after 17 . . . P-N3, we shall consider a few of the most typical. White has clearly two basic plans of attack: he can do his best to attain the maximum effectiveness of his pieces or he can try to weaken Black's king's side by advancing his KRP.

The most suitable way of initiating the first plan is to play 18 QR-K1 and after 18 . . . B-Q1 adopt the queen manoeuvre 19 Q-R3 N-K4! (not 19 . . . B-N3? 20 BxNP!! BPxB 21 R-K7 R-B2 22 Q-K6 N-K4 23 QxRch NxQ 24 R-K8 mate) 20 Q-R6 B-N3 (much weaker is the continuation 20 . . . NxBch 21 PxN Q-B2ch 22 K-N1 P-B3 23 PxP Q-KB2, when White can win the exchange by 24 Q-N7ch or, even better play for attack by 24 R-K6!) 21 PxN BxB 22 R-K4 B-B7! (preventing 23 R-R4) 23 P-K6. The resulting position deserves further analysis. Schamkowitsch gives the following interesting line, which leads to an equal endgame: 23 . . . PxP 24 PxP P-Q4 25 R-K2 Q-B5ch 26 K-N1 Q-R5 27 BxNP! QxQ (not 27 . . . PxB 28 QxPch K-R1 29 P-K7, etc.) 28 B-B7ch K-R1 29 PxQ BxP 30 BxB.

Just as complicated is Black's defence if White adopts the other plan: 18 P-KR4 N-B4 19 B-B4! (better than 19 P-R5 NxB 20 RxN B-B4) 19 . . . B-B4 20 P-R5! Now Black can hardly continue with 20 . . . B-K5? 21 Q-K3 BxR 22 QxB or 21 . . .

R-K1 22 PxP B(K5)xNP 23 P-B5! BxBP 24 P-N6! BxNP 25 RxP!! BxR 26 R-N1ch B-N3 27 Q-R6 winning.

18 QR-K1   R-B2

Black must not only cover his bishop but also the point KN2. In reply to 18 . . . B-Q1, Tal had planned the following interesting continuation, which he demonstrated after the game: 19 Q-R5 N-B4 20 BxNP NxBch 21 K-N1 NxR 22 P-N6 KxB 23 QxRPch K-B3 24 P-N7 R-B2 (24 . . . R-K1 25 Q-R6ch K-B2 26 Q-R5ch) 25 P-N8=N mate. This is a typical Tal combination. However, this time there is a flaw in it, for, instead of 21 . . . NxR, Black can withstand the attack by 21 . . . Q-B2 22 BxR NxR 23 RxN Q-KB2!.

In later analysis Grandmaster Schamkowitsch improved on Tal's idea by 19 BxNP!! KxB 20 Q-R5, after which Black, in spite of his two extra pieces, has no adequate defence to the threat of 21 Q-R6ch followed by P-N6; e.g. 20 . . . K-R1 21 R-K8! (threatening BxBP) RxR 22 QxRch K-N2 23 QxB with the fatal threat of BxBP or R-K1. Likewise 20 . . . N-B5 21 Q-R6ch K-N1 22 P-N6 NxBch 23 K-N1! Q-B2 24 KR-N1 loses for Black as does 20 . . . Q-B2 21 Q-R6ch K-N1 22 P-N6 N-B3 23 KR-N1. Black's best chance is to return one of the extra pieces by 20 . . . N-K4!, though even in this case White secures an advantage by 21 PxN R-R2 22 P-K6 followed by Q-R6ch and P-N6.

19 P-KR4!

At the moment there is no way the attack with pieces can be reinforced. White must therefore try to break open his opponent's castled position by advancing his own pawns. After the text-move White threatens P-R5 followed by P-KN6. The strength of this threat can be seen from the following variation: 19 . . . N-B1 20 P-R5 Q-B2 21 P-N6 R-B3! 22

P-R6! and White achieves a decisive opening of the files, e.g. 22 ... RxP 23 PxP RxP 24 BxR KxB 25 QR-N1ch N-N3 26 RxPch!, winning. The defence 19 ... N-B1 20 P-R5 P-N3 is not very good either, for the opening of the KR file backed up by the bishop on Q4 is deadly, as the following combination shows: 21 QR-N1! Q-B2 (or 21 ... B-Q1) 22 PxP NxP 23 Q-R5 (threatening QxNch!) NxP 24 P-N6!! NxQ 25 PxPdbl ch KxP 26 RxN mate.

19 ...   B-N2!

146. Tal–Larsen

Larsen quite rightly opts for active defence. If White now continues with his plan (20 P-R5? N-K4! 21 PxN BxPch 22 K-N1 PxP 23 BxKP Q-Q1), Black gets a good game, thanks to his attack on the QP.

20 BxBP

After the game Tal expressed dissatisfaction over this decision, which was taken after considerable thought. His comments on it are very interesting: "That is the cost of calculation in sport. If this game had not been played in the last round I should certainly have chosen the sharper 20 P-N6! PxP 21 P-R5!" A very interesting comment, which shows something of Tal's views on chess. For him chess is not only a game that has to be won but also something aesthetic. And in his case the two components were in conflict.

Tal rejected the continuation he later

suggested because of the defence 21 ... P-N4! 22 BxBP B-KB3! He felt sure there must be a way of forcing a win for White. But with limited time for thought he was unable to find it; so he chose what was probably the weaker continuation, objectively seen, because it was safer. If he had chosen the sharper line, he could not have played 23 B-K6 (intending to answer 23 ... BxB by 24 PxP) because Black can insert the move 23 ... P-N5 before taking the bishop. However, things are different if White inverts moves, e.g. 23 PxP BxB? 24 B-K6 N-K4 25 RxN! BxR 26 QxRch K-R1 27 P-R6 P-N3 28 P-R7, winning. For that reason a better defence for Black is 23 ... BxNPch 24 K-N1, though White also maintains his advantage, e.g. 24 ... K-B1 25 Q-N4 B-KB3 26 BxN BxB 27 B-K6 B-KB3 28 BxR KxB 29 Q-K6ch K-B1 30 P-R6, winning, or 24 ... B-KB3 25 B-K6 Q-KB8 26 P-R6! etc.

Tal's assessment of the situation was therefore correct. Nevertheless his continuation, 20 BxBP, does not deserve a question-mark, for it also leaves White in an attacking position, and, what is more, with a reduced material disadvantage and consequently less risk. Moreover, the calculation of all the possible variations arising from 20 P-KN6 was probably too much for the human brain.

20 ... RxB!?

Larsen had obviously had enough of being pinned down to dour defence and decided, with this and the next move, to initiate a desperate counter-attack. After the game he was of the opinion that continuing to defend by 20 ... N-B1 would have offered him better chances. However, in that case the game might have continued 21 Q-K4 (threatening to sacrifice the queen by 22 QxB!) 21 ... Q-K1 (if 21 ... Q-B2, White can also continue quietly with 22 P-R5 and 23 P-N6) 22 BxPch! (better than the line given by Larsen: 22 P-R5 RxB! 23 QxR

Q-B2) 22 ... NxB 23 P-N6 N-B3 24 PxRch KxP 25 Q-B5!, after which White, who has more or less recovered the material sacrificed, maintains a strong attack. The situation is similar if Black deviates with 21 ... P-N3 22 B-N4 (not 22 QxB PxB!) followed by P-R5.

21 RxB	**N-K4!**

The reason for Black's previous move. If, instead, 21 ... R-B2 22 RxR KxR, White wins quickly by 23 P-N6ch! PxP (23 ... K-N1 24 PxPch K-R1 25 R-N1) 24 P-R5, e.g.

(i) 24 ... N-B3 25 PxPch KxP 26 Q-N3ch K-B2 27 BxN KxB 28 Q-N5ch K-B2 29 Q-B5ch, etc.

(ii) 24 ... P-N4 25 PxPdis ch K-N1 26 P-R6 Q-KB1 27 QxQch NxQ 28 PxP N-N3 29 R-R8ch K-B2 30 P-N8=Qch! RxQ 31 R-R7ch, etc.

(iii) 24 ... Q-KB1 25 PxPch K-K1 26 R-R7 N-B3 27 Q-K3ch K-Q1 (27 ... Q-K2 28 QxQch KxQ 29 RxPch or 27 ... K-Q2 28 Q-K6ch) 28 BxNch QxB 29 Q-N6ch winning.

22 Q-K4	**Q-KB1**
23 PxN!	

Naturally not 23 RxB?? RxBP 24 Q-K3 R-B8ch, which wins for Black!

23 ...	**R-B5**
24 Q-K3	**R-B6?**

The only way of strengthening the defence was 24 ... BxP! 25 PxP! RxB 26 QxR BxR, though White can then continue with 27 P-N3!, when his positional superiority should lead to a win, e.g. 27 ... P-QR4 28 P-R5! followed by 29 P-R6 or 27 ... B-B6 28 Q-QB4ch K-R1 29 R-KB7 QxP 30 RxB. In this last variation White has an even better line in 28 QxQNP K-R1 29 Q-Q4, with an easily won game.

25 Q-K2	**QxR**
26 QxR	**PxP**
27 R-K1	**R-Q1**
28 RxP	**Q-Q3**
29 Q-B4!	**R-KB1**

If 29 ... BxP?, then 30 R-K8ch! winning the queen.

30 Q-K4	**P-N6**

In the time-scramble, Black makes a last attempt to complicate the position.

31 RPxP	**R-B8ch**
32 K-Q2	**Q-N5ch**
33 P-B3	**Q-Q3**
34 B-B5!	**QxB**
35 R-K8ch	**R-B1**
36 Q-K6ch	**K-R1**
37 Q-B7	**Resigns**

43 Candidates' Tournament 1965

The Advantage of the Black Pieces

The final of the candidates' tournament, at Tbilisi in November 1965, brought Tal and Spasski together. Their match had one strange aspect: contrary to the usual run of things, most of the games not drawn were won by Black. Tal took the lead in the second game, a Sicilian Defence, when his opponent attacked too vigorously on the king-side and got a lost ending after twelve moves. In the next game it was Spasski who got the better endgame, which he managed to win after Tal had missed excellent drawing chances. After five drawn games Spasski was victorious in the ninth, again with the black pieces. In the following game he used a remarkable method to thwart his opponent's bid to equal matters. Playing White, he deployed his forces in such a passive manner that, a short time after the opening, it looked as if he were playing with the black pieces; but these strange tactics paid off and he won the game. He also won the next, in which he really did have Black, and with it the match. Afterwards the commentators had the difficult task of explaining the strange superiority of the black pieces.

It is probable that Spasski, after his early defeat, thought out his tactics for the future games very carefully. His opponent is well known for his powers of imagination, which sometimes run to excess, and for his aggressive style of play. Spasski therefore decided to adopt a waiting policy, using the opportunities that would arise when Tal, throwing caution to the wind, plunged into risky adventures. These tactics paid off in the end.

The real decision in the match was reached in the ninth game, when Tal tried to force a win by going on the offensive. After his loss there he failed to recover.

Ruy Lopez

Tal	Spasski
1 P-K4	P-K4
2 N-KB3	N-QB3
3 B-N5	P-QR3
4 B-R4	N-KB3
5 0-0	B-K2
6 R-K1	P-QN4
7 B-N3	0-0
8 P-QR4	

In the first, fifth and seventh games Tal had played 8 P-QB3, whereupon Spasski opted for the Marshall Attack: 8 ... P-Q4 9 PxP NxP 10 NxP NxN 11 RxN P-QB3. At one time this was considered to be a very sharp attacking line, but today it tends to be looked upon as a reliable way of drawing. All three games did in fact end in a draw, and for that reason Tal decided to try something else towards the end of the match.

8 ...		P-N5!

For a long time the move 8 ... B-N2 was customary in this position. However, after White's reply 9 P-Q3 the bishop is confined to playing a passive role.

9 P-B3	P-Q3
10 P-R5	

By no means new, but at the time a continuation that had almost been forgotten. After the better-known 10 P-Q4 the best line is 10 ... PxP 11 NxP (11

PxP B-N5) 11 ... B-Q2 and Black has a good game.

10 ...   PxP(?)

The lesson to be drawn from the present game is that this exchange is not advantageous, mainly because it helps White to develop and obtain good chances on the queen's wing. According to my analysis the immediate 10 ... B-K3! is much stronger. Black need not worry about his pawn, for the line 11 BxB PxB 12 Q-N3 Q-Q2 13 PxP QR-N1 14 R-R4 N-KR4 is obviously good for him.

11 QPxP!   B-K3
12 QN-Q2   R-N1

The disadvantage of this move is that it weakens Black's QNP and allows White to retain his bishop, which can later be used to attack the pawn. In March 1966 Jansa played the superior 12 ... BxB against Tal in the tournament at Sarajevo, but White maintained a slight, though distinct, positional advantage after 13 QxB and Q-R4. The game ended in a sensational loss for Tal, which, however, was not due to the opening.

13 B-B2   N-KR4

Black is at a disadvantage on the queen's wing, so he must try something on the other side. A beginner might easily overlook the typical trap 14 NxP?? NxN 15 QxN B-N5 leading to the loss of the White queen.

14 N-B1	P-N3
15 N-K3	B-B3
16 N-Q5	B-N2
17 B-Q3	R-R1
18 N-N5	B-B1
19 B-QB4	P-R3
20 N-B3	B-K3

Black wants to neutralize his opponent's pressure on the long white diagonal KN1-QR7 and is prepared to allow his bishop to be passively placed for the next few moves. A more logical continuation is 20 ... N-K2 21 N-R4 K-R2 (not 21 ... NxN? 22 NxP) 22 N-B5! NxN(B4) 23 PxN N-B3 24 PxPch PxP and Black has almost equalized.

21 Q-Q3   N-N1?

In the opinion of the former world champion Petrosian Black could have sacrificed a pawn here by 21 ... K-R2 22 BxQRP P-KB4.

22 B-K3   N-KB3

147. Tal–Spasski

23 KR-Q1?

The first critical moment in the game. With this indecisive move Tal does not quite throw away all of his advantage. On the other hand, the continuation 23 NxN QxN 24 B-Q5 BxB 25 QxB (also good is 25 PxB Q-K2 26 N-Q2 P-KB4 27 P-B3) 25 ... P-B3 26 Q-Q2 K-R2 27 B-N6 with the threat of 28 KR-Q1 is much more energetic. If Black deviates on move 24 with P-B3 White gains an advantage by 25 BxB QxB 26 B-N6!

23 ...   BxN
24 BxB   NxB
25 QxN   N-Q2

Black has eased his situation by exchanging two minor pieces; in addition his pieces are no longer tied to the defence of the QRP. Nevertheless White still has a distinct advantage. He only needs to keep an eye on Black's king-side attack, initiated by K-R2 and P-KB4, and at the same time prepare the creation and conversion of a passed-pawn on the queen's wing. A strong continuation is 26 P-QN4 K-R2 27 N-Q2 P-KB4 28 P-B3 or 27 ... N-B3 28 Q-Q3 N-N5 29 N-B4, etc.

Instead Tal opts for a complicated and not very logical plan. He intends to transfer his pieces to the king's side to meet Black's attack there.

26 Q-B4	K-R2
27 R-R4(?)	P-KB4
28 P-N3	Q-B1!

A very fine move, which threatens 29 ... P-B5 30 PxP PxP 31 B-Q4 N-K4 followed by Q-N5ch. In addition the Black queen is ready to move to QN2.

148. Tal–Spasski

29 Q-K2?

The decisive mistake, after which White loses a pawn. Tal obviously realized this, but was of the opinion that he would then attain a king-side attack, the reasoning behind the moves 26 Q-QB4 and 27 R-QR4. The correct continuation was 29 PxP PxP 30 N-R4!, preventing the enemy pawn advance, e.g. 30 ... P-B5? 31 Q-K4ch K-N1 32 Q-Q5ch R-B2 33 N-N6 threatening 34 N-K7ch, or 30 ... P-K5 31 B-Q4, etc. In view of this Black would probably have played 30 ... N-B3.

29 ...	PxP
30 RxKP	Q-N2!
31 N-Q2	

Tal obviously thinks that taking the QNP will cost Black too much time. A

bad line for White is 31 B-B1 N-B4 32 R-K3 N-N6, when Black wins a pawn with impunity.

31 ...	QxP!

The pawn on QN2 is often said to be poisoned, which does not, of course, mean that it should never be captured. There is only one rule that has any validity: it is correct to take the pawn when doing so is advantageous.

32 Q-Q3	Q-N1

White was threatening not only 33 R-KN4 but also 33 R-QN4 Q-R7 34 N-N3. The latter threat, however, could have been ignored, e.g. 32 ... N-B3! 33 R-QN4 Q-R7 34 N-N3 (34 R-N7 R-B2!), for Black can easily free his queen by the manoeuvre 34 ... P-K5 35 Q-B4 N-N5. The text-move allows White a certain initiative.

33 R-KR4	N-B3

Black can cover all his endangered points without any undue difficulty— KN3 with the queen and if necessary KR3 with the knight. The extra pawn is quite sound, so White must endeavour to complicate the game as best he can.

34 N-B3	Q-K1

Not 34 ... Q-B1 35 N-N5ch K-N1 36 Q-B4ch P-Q4 37 RxQP. With the Black queen on K1, however, White's device is not possible, for the square KB2 is covered after 37 ... NxR 38 QxNch K-R1. Even 37 ... PxN 38 R-Q8dis ch Q-B2 (or 38 R-Q7dis ch R-B2) is possible.

35 R-K1	

An indirect attack on the queen, thus preventing a Black pawn advance in the centre, e.g. 35 ... P-Q4? 36 BxP! BxB 37 RxP followed by 38 N-N5ch.

A continuation that is not as strong as it looks is 35 Q-B4 (threatening 36 N-N5ch). Black replies with 35 ... N-R4!

gaining a tempo by attacking the knight on KB6.

| 35 ... | Q-Q2! |
| 36 P-N4! | |

White's attack has now reached its climax. The line 36 N-N5ch K-N1 37 QxNP is not good because of 37 ... PxN. Black cannot take the KNP, e.g. 36 ... NxP? 37 N-N5ch K-N1 38 QxNP! PxN 39 Q-R7ch K-B2 40 Q-R5ch, etc. Tal's misfortune in this position is that he does not really threaten anything, for 37 P-KN5 can be answered by 38 ... N-R4! and 39 RxN by Q-N5ch.

| 36 ... | QR-K1! |

Now Black has a threat, P-K5, and if White takes the QRP, Black can capture the KNP.

| 37 BxP!? | BxB |
| 38 P-N5 | N-R4 |

One of the commonest characteristics of important games is that the player with a distinct advantage usually chooses the safest, rather than the shortest, way to win. With this move and the next one, Spasski forces an exchange of queens, which leaves him with a won ending. There was, however, a quicker, though more complicated, win, viz. 38 ... P-K5 39 RxBch K-N2 40 PxNch RxP 41 RxKP RxR 42 QxR KxR 43 Q-R4ch K-N2 44 N-N5 Q-B4! etc.

39 PxB	Q-B4!
40 QxQ	RxQ
41 N-Q2	N-B5

The game was adjourned at this stage, and the great surprise was that Tal was able to hold out for another thirty moves from a position that looked hopeless.

42 N-K4	R-QN1
43 N-N3	R(B4)-B1
44 N-K4	N-K3
45 P-QB4	R-N7
46 R-Q1	R-B4
47 P-B5!?	

149. Tal–Spasski

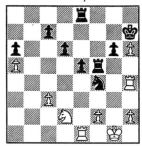

Position after Black's 41st move

An interesting try. Tal realizes that he will have to give up the exchange; but it is nevertheless his best chance.

47 ...	P-Q4!
48 RxP	R-N8ch
49 K-N2	N-B5ch
50 RxN	RxR
51 RxP	KxP

White has a pawn for the exchange and an active position as well. However, his pawn structure has so many weaknesses that he will not be able to defend all of them.

52 R-K6	R-K8
53 P-B3	R-K6
54 RxRP	R(K6)xP
55 R-B6	R-QR6
56 N-N3	R-R7ch
57 K-N1	

Not 57 K-R3? K-N4, and White loses at once.

57 ...	R(B5)-B7
58 N-B1	R-B2
59 N-K3	K-N4
60 P-R6	R-K2
61 N-B1	K-R3!

Bringing about an interesting *zugzwang* position. After 62 R-KB6 R-K8 63 R-QB6 R(R2)-R8 64 R-KB6 R(K1)-B1 the QBP is lost.

| 62 P-R3 | K-N2 |
| 63 P-R4 | K-B2 |

64	P-R5	PxP	68	K-R1	R-R8
65	R-R6	R-K4	69	P-R7	RxNch
66	R-R7ch	K-N3	70	K-R2	R-QR8
67	RxBP	R-N4ch		Resigns	

44 Capablanca Memorial Tournament, Havana 1965

Boris Ivkov's Misfortune

The fourth Capablanca Memorial Tournament, which took place from August to September 1965, was responsible for quite a sensation. Bobby Fischer had been invited to the tournament, but did not receive the necessary permission to travel; so the organizers arranged for him to participate in an extraordinary way. A teleprinter was installed in the tournament hall in the Havana hotel, establishing communication for seven hours a day with the Manhattan Chess Club in New York. At the same time a telephone line was reserved. In this rather expensive way Fischer was enabled to compete with the stars gathered together at this tournament. Of course, the American player was handicapped by the longer playing session resulting from the time wasted in transmitting the moves, and that is one reason why he lost to three of his chief rivals.

The only players to remain undefeated were the Soviet representatives Geller and Kolmov, whereas Smyslov, the winner, and the Yugoslav grandmaster Ivkov, who shared second to fourth places with Fischer and Geller, both suffered three losses.

For Ivkov, who shared second place in such a strong field, the tournament was certainly a fine success. However, he will always remember it as one of the black spots in his career, for he was within an ace of an even greater success. Right from the start he went into the lead, which he maintained even after his loss to Kolmov in the fourteenth round. Two rounds before the finish everything seemed to be cut and dried, the position being Ivkov 15, Geller and Smyslov 14, Fischer and Kolmov 13, etc. Moreover, Ivkov had

easier opponents than his rivals, having to face Garcia from Cuba and Robatsch from Austria, whereas Smyslov and Geller had to play each other in the penultimate round. For Ivkov to win the tournament it looked as though two draws would suffice, which no one considered particularly difficult.

In the penultimate round, however, the situation took a turn for the worse. Ivkov's opponent played the opening very weakly, and it looked as if everything would be over within two hours. Although Garcia then defended stubbornly, Ivkov was the exchange and three pawns up shortly before the first time-check, so that victory seemed imminent. There remained only one hurdle, that of completing the required forty moves before the time-check. In time-trouble he threw away the game, which from the position in Diagram 150 continued 36 . . . P-Q6?? 37 B-B3 Resigns.

150. Garcia–Ivkov

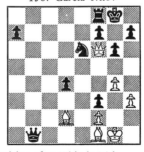

Position after White's 36th move

Instead of the terrible blunder 36 . . . P-Q6, Ivkov could have won with almost any move. His best course, tactically, would have been to move his rook backwards and forwards along the back rank and wait for the adjournment.

In Smyslov's game with Geller, both players exchanged one piece after the other, so that at the end of the round the ex-world-champion had reduced Ivkov's lead to half a point. Then he went on to defeat the Polish player Doda by means of some accurate positional play.

151. Smyslov–Doda

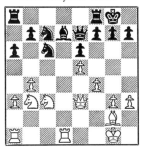

24 Q-B5!	QxQ
25 NxQ	B-B1
26 N(B3)-R4	P-QR4

There was no way of avoiding the loss of a pawn, e.g. 26 ... R-K1 27 N-N6 R-N1 28 N(N6)-Q7 BxN 29 RxB R(K1)-QB1 30 NxNP.

27 N-N6	R-R2
28 NxB	RxN
29 NxNP!	RxN
30 BxN	R-N3
31 B-Q7	R(B1)-N1
32 QR-B1	N-Q4
33 P-N5	P-N3
34 P-QR4	P-R4
35 B-B6	P-R5
36 BxN	PxB
37 RxP	PxP
38 K-N2	P-B3
39 KxP	PxP
40 PxP	K-B2
41 R-B7ch	K-K3
42 R(Q5)-B5	K-B4
43 R-B7ch	K-K5
44 R-KB4ch	Resigns

Ivkov also had White in the last round and it was expected that he would try to make the most of this advantage. However, it soon became clear that he was suffering from depression following his defeat in the previous game. In addition, his opponent had done some excellent preparation for the game and played the opening both accurately and in an original manner.

Ruy Lopez

Ivkov	Robatsch
1 P-K4	P-K4
2 N-KB3	N-QB3
3 B-N5	P-QR3
4 B-R4	N-B3
5 0-0	B-K2
6 R-K1	P-QN4
7 B-N3	P-Q3
8 P-B3	0-0
9 P-KR3	N-QR4
10 B-B2	P-B4
11 P-Q4	Q-B2
12 QN-Q2	N-B3

The assessment of the individual opening variations often changes. The manoeuvre with the knight is one of the oldest defences to the closed system of the Ruy Lopez. Later it went out of fashion, but now it is again considered to be the best way of achieving equality.

13 PxBP	PxP
14 N-B1	B-K3
15 N-K3	QR-Q1
16 Q-K2	P-B5

The revival of the move 12 ... N-QB3 is associated with this advance. Black gives his bishop access to the square QB4, confident that he has nothing to fear from 17 N-N5 P-R3 18 NxB PxN, after which his active pieces make up for his weakened pawns. In the game Kolmov–Fischer, play continued 19 P-QN4? N-Q5 20 PxN PxP 21 P-R3 P-Q6 22 BxP RxB, and Black soon had a considerable advantage.

17 N-B5   BxN

Later games showed that 17 . . . KR-K1! 18 B-N5 N-Q2 is a more precise way of attaining equality.

18 PxB   KR-K1

So far the continuation 18 . . . P-R3 19 NxP NxN 20 QxN B-Q3 21 Q-K2 KR-K1, with chances of achieving equality, has hardly been tried out in practice. After the text-move White can retain the upper hand by 19 B-N5, e.g. 19 . . . N-Q4 20 B-Q2 or 19 . . . P-R3 20 BxN BxB 21 B-K4.

19 N-N5(?)

152. Ivkov–Robatsch

White's last move looks quite logical, and indeed if he can manage to occupy the square K4 permanently he will have a clear advantage. Black, however, has an interesting manoeuvre, which he obviously worked out before the game.

19 . . .	N-N1!
20 B-K3	QN-Q2
21 P-QR4	N-B4
22 BxN	

Otherwise White fails to gain control over K4. However, there are now bishops of opposite colours, which soon gives the game a drawish character.

| 22 . . . | BxB |
| 23 PxP | PxP |

| 24 P-QN4 | B-N3 |
| 25 KR-Q1? | |

White's whole strategy was based on the occupation of K4, which Ivkov now neglects. The correct continuation was 25 N-K4 NxN 26 BxN, after which White would still have had a slight advantage, though probably not one that would have sufficed for victory.

| 25 . . . | RxRch |
| 26 QxR | |

If 26 RxR, there follows 26 . . . P-K5! 27 NxKP NxN 28 BxN Q-K4.

| 26 . . . | Q-B3! |

Threatening to cut off White's line of retreat by 27 . . . P-K5.

27 N-B3	P-K5
28 N-Q4	Q-Q4
29 R-R6	BxN
30 QxB	QxQ
31 PxQ	R-N1
32 K-B1	N-Q4

153. Ivkov–Robatsch

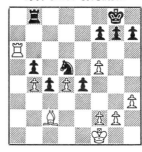

In the endgame White's pieces are so unfavourably placed that he cannot save his pawn on QN4, which means that his opponent will get two united passed pawns. The active position of his rook will not be enough to save him.

33 BxP	NxP
34 R-R7	K-B1
35 P-Q5	R-Q1
36 P-B6	PxP
37 P-B3	NxP

Havana 1965

	1	2	3	4	5	6	7	8	9	10	11	12	13	14	15	16	17	18	19	20	21	22	Pts	Prize
1 Smyslov	–	0	½	0	½	½	1	½	1	½	1	1	1	1	0	1	1	1	1	1	1	1	15½	I
2 Ivkov	1	–	½	1	0	½	1	0	1	½	½	½	1	1	1	½	1	1	1	1	1	0	15	II–IV
3 Geller	½	½	–	1	½	½	½	½	1	1	½	½	½	½	1	½	1	1	½	1	1	1	15	II–IV
4 Fischer	1	0	0	–	0	½	1	1	1	½	1	1	½	1	½	½	1	1	½	1	1	1	15	II–IV
5 Kholmov	½	1	½	1	–	½	½	½	½	½	½	½	½	1	1	1	½	½	½	1	1	1	14½	V
6 Pachman	½	½	½	½	½	–	1	0	½	½	½	½	½	½	½	½	1	½	1	1	1	1	13	VI
7 Donner	0	0	½	0	½	0	–	1	1	½	1	1	1	½	1	½	½	½	½	½	1	1	12½	VII
8 Robatsch	½	1	½	0	½	1	0	–	½	½	1	0	½	½	½	½	½	½	½	1	1	1	12	VIII
9 Bilek	0	0	0	0	½	½	0	½	–	½	½	½	½	½	½	1	1	1	1	1	1	1	11½	IX
10 Parma	½	½	0	½	½	½	½	½	½	–	0	1	½	½	1	½	½	½	1	½	½	½	11	X
11 Szabó	0	½	½	0	½	½	0	0	½	1	–	1	½	½	½	1	0	½	1	1	0	1	10½	XI
12 Pietzsch	0	½	½	0	½	½	0	1	½	0	0	–	½	1	½	½	½	½	½	1	1	1	10½	XI
13 O'Kelly	0	0	½	½	½	½	0	½	½	½	½	½	–	½	½	0	1	½	½	½	1	1	10	
14 Tringov	0	0	½	0	0	½	½	½	½	½	½	0	½	–	0	½	1	1	1	1	½	1	10	
15 Jiménez	1	0	0	½	0	½	0	½	½	0	½	½	½	1	–	½	½	½	½	½	½	1	9½	
16 Ciocaltea	0	½	½	½	0	½	½	½	0	½	0	½	1	½	½	–	½	0	1	0	½	1	9	
17 Doda	0	0	0	0	½	0	½	½	0	½	1	½	0	0	½	½	–	1	0	1	½	1	8	
18 Lehmann	0	0	0	0	½	½	½	½	0	½	½	½	½	0	½	1	0	–	1	½	½	0	7½	
19 Wade	0	0	½	½	½	0	½	½	0	0	0	½	½	0	½	0	1	0	–	½	1	1	7½	
20 Cobo	0	0	0	0	0	0	½	0	0	½	0	0	½	0	½	1	0	½	½	–	1	½	5½	
21 Pérez	0	0	0	0	0	0	0	0	0	½	1	0	0	½	½	½	½	½	0	0	–	0	4	
22 Garcia	0	1	0	0	0	0	0	0	0	½	0	0	0	0	0	0	0	1	0	½	1	–	4	

38	R-N7	P-B4
39	B-N1	P-N5
40	K-B2	P-B5
41	BxP	P-N6
42	P-N4	N-B6
43	R-N4	R-Q7ch
44	K-K1	R-Q8ch
45	K-B2	R-QB8!

Now Black's QBP is indirectly protected (46 RxBP? N-Q8ch), which means the end of all White's hopes.

46	P-R4	K-N2

47	B-B5	P-N7!
48	P-R5	P-N8=Q
49	BxQ	NxB
50	K-K2	R-B7ch
51	K-Q1	N-R6
52	R-R4	R-QR7
53	P-N5	P-B6
54	P-R6ch	K-R1
55	R-R8ch	K-R2
56	R-KB8	P-B7ch
57	K-Q2	R-R8
58	RxPch	K-N1
Resigns		

45 Santa Monica 1966

Contest between Two Aspirants for the Chess Crown

Three years after the first Piatigorsky tournament, which was financed from an endowment made by Piatigorsky's wife, the second one took place—at Santa Monica in July and August 1966. This time the participants, whose number had been increased to ten, included Bobby Fischer, who thus had an opportunity to cross swords with the world champion, Petrosian, and the challenger, Spasski. At the start all three were regarded as favourites, but soon Petrosian, who was in poor form, dropped behind, losing three times and finally sharing sixth and seventh places. His two defeats at the hands of Larsen were a bitter pill for him. Larsen himself dropped out of the running after losing in the tenth, twelfth and thirteenth rounds. The struggle for first prize gradually developed into an exciting contest between two players, Spasski and Fischer.

Fischer suffered three defeats in the sixth, seventh and eighth rounds, and it looked for a while as if he was out of the running, for Spasski was 2½ points ahead of him. However, the American grandmaster regained lost ground by four straight victories in rounds 10 to 13 and two more in rounds 15 and 16. Two rounds before the end Fischer and Spasski shared the lead with 10 points each, 1½ points ahead of Larsen, Portisch and Unzicker. In the last round but one the two leaders met for the second time, and it was to be expected that Fischer, playing White, would make a big effort to win, for he knew that he would have a difficult job with Black against Petrosian in the last round, whereas Spasski would have White against Donner.

Ruy Lopez

Fischer	Spasski
1 P-K4	P-K4
2 N-KB3	N-QB3
3 B-N5	P-QR3
4 B-R4	N-B3
5 0-0	B-K2
6 R-K1	P-QN4
7 B-N3	0-0
8 P-QB3	P-Q4

In view of the state of the tournament, it must have been clear to Spasski that a draw here would suffice. His choice of opening may therefore appear surprising. For some time, however, the Marshall Attack has lost its reputation of being a two-edged counter-attack. It is now customary for Black to handle it in a decidedly positional manner. As a rule his attack on the king's wing is held up, but as compensation he obtains active play for his pieces and generally also secures the advantage of the two bishops. Spasski quite rightly reasons that, against an opponent of Fischer's type, the best policy is to have the initiative. From this point of view the choice of opening is correct. It is interesting to note that, in the 1965 Capablanca Memorial Tournament, Fischer did not succeed in winning against either Wade or O'Kelly when they played the Marshall Attack.

9 PxP	NxP
10 NxP	NxN
11 RxN	P-QB3
12 P-N3	

With this move White prevents the usual development of the Black pieces

(12 P-Q4 B-Q3 13 R-K1 Q-R5). The system was adopted for the first time in the game Fischer–O'Kelly, mentioned above, which continued 12 ... B-B3 13 R-K1 R-R2 14 P-Q4 R-K2 15 RxR QxR 16 BxN PxB 17 B-K3 R-K1 18 N-Q2 B-R6 19 Q-B3 Q-K3 20 R-K1 B-N5 21 Q-N2 B-R6 22 Q-B3 B-N5 23 Q-R1 P-KR4. Black later got the upper hand thanks to his two bishops.

The disadvantage of the move 12 P-N3 is that it wastes an important tempo and also weakens the king's side.

12 ...	N-B3

Preparing P-B4. According to Spasski 12 ... B-Q3 13 R-K1 Q-Q2 followed by 14 ... Q-R6 is also possible, with the intention of reaching a position akin to that arising from the variation 12 P-Q4 B-Q3.

13 P-Q4	B-Q3

Spasski originally intended to play 13 ... P-B4 at once, but then rejected it on account of the reply 14 B-N5.

14 R-K1	B-KN5
15 Q-Q3	

White does not want to weaken his king's side any further by 15 P-B3. By moving his queen, however, he loses another tempo and allows Black to get active without fear of an exchange of queens.

154. Fischer–Spasski

15 ...	P-B4!
16 PxP	BxBP
17 QxQ	QRxQ
18 B(B1)-B4	P-R3
19 N-R3	P-N4
20 B-K3	

If 20 B-K5, Black can occupy the seventh rank with a rook (20 ... R-Q7), which guarantees him adequate counterplay.

20 ...	BxB
21 RxB	R-Q7
22 N-B2	R-K1
23 RxRch	NxR
24 N-K3	B-B6
25 B-B2	N-Q3

Threatening 25 ... N-B5.

26 P-N3	K-B1
27 P-QR4	N-K5
28 BxN	BxB
29 PxP	PxP
30 P-QN4	R-N7
31 P-N4	K-N2
32 K-B1	K-B3
33 R-R5	

Now Black can force a draw by repetition. There is no way White can improve his position, for the enemy rook can thwart all attempts to win.

33 ...	R-N8ch
34 K-K2	R-N7ch
35 K-B1	
Drawn	

As expected the game in the final round between Petrosian and Fischer ended in a straightforward draw. Spasski, on the other hand, made the most of his chances and thus won first prize in the tournament.

Ruy Lopez

Spasski	Donner
1 P-K4	P-K4
2 N-KB3	N-QB3
3 B-N5	P-QR3

| 4 B-R4 | N-B3 |
| 5 Q-K2 | |

At the beginning of his career Spasski was very fond of this move. Now, in this important match, he returned to his "first love", as he called it.

5 ...	P-QN4
6 B-N3	B-K2
7 0-0	0-0
8 P-B3	P-Q4

This push forward in the centre seems to give White greater chances than the quiet 8 ... P-Q3. After the text-move, however, White should avoid 9 PxP P-K5 10 PxN B-KN5, which gives Black excellent counter-play.

| 9 P-Q3! | P-Q5 |
| 10 R-Q1! | |

An innovation. Until this game the usual continuation was 10 PxP NxQP 11 NxN QxN 12 B-K3, which allowed Black to equalize by 12 ... Q-Q3 13 R-Q1 B-K3.

| 10 ... | B-K3 |

Spasski considers this move to be wrong, because it allows White to occupy QN3 with his knight, and recommends 10 ... B-Q2 instead. However, the bishop is not well placed on Q2. The fact is, Black's position lacks elasticity.

11 QN-Q2	R-K1
12 BxB	PxB
13 N-N3	PxP

This allows White to obtain a strong centre, but it is difficult for Black to hit upon a suitable plan. If, for example, he tries to attain superiority on the queen's wing by 13 ... P-QR4, White can reply with 14 PxP NxQP 15 N(N3)xN PxN 16 P-QR4!

14 PxP	B-Q3
15 P-Q4	N-Q2
16 B-N5	

Here Spasski rejected 16 PxP N(Q2)xP 17 NxN NxN 18 N-B5 in view of the queen sacrifice by 18 ... BxN! 19 RxQ R(R1)xR, which gives Black active play with his pieces.

16 ...	Q-B1
17 P-B4	NxP
18 N(N3)xN	PxN
19 P-K5	B-B1?

It is well known that exchanging pieces often eases a cramped position. For that reason 19 ... B-K2 was called for. Black does indeed adopt this idea two moves later, though only after wasting an important tempo.

| 20 RxP | P-B3 |
| 21 R-R4 | B-K2 |

155. Spasski–Donner

22 BxB(?)

With this move White loses a large part of his advantage. The correct continuation, subsequently pointed out by Spasski, is 22 Q-B2! N-B1 (22 ... P-R3? 23 RxP) 23 BxB RxB 24 N-N5 P-R3 25 N-K4.

| 22 ... | RxB |
| 23 N-N5 | P-R3 |

The difference between this and the variation mentioned in the previous note is that Black is not forced to play the passive N-KB1. As a result White's penetration to Q6 with his knight will lose much of its force.

| 24 N-K4 | Q-B2 |
| 25 N-Q6 | R-Q1? |

This is an irreparable mistake, after which Black's resistance will soon be broken down. It would have been much better to re-group by means of 25 ... Q-N3! followed by Q-B4 and N-N3.

26 R-Q1   Q-N3
27 KR-Q4   R-KB1

A clear indication that Black's rook was badly placed on Q1. The continuation 27 ... Q-B4 is not possible because of 28 N-N7.

28 K-R1   Q-B4
29 P-B4   N-N3
30 N-K4!   Q-R6
31 Q-N4!

156. Spasski–Donner

Strangely enough Black has no adequate defence to the coming attack.

According to Spasski's analysis in the tournament book the following lines are possible:

(i) 31 ... K-R1 32 R-Q8 R(K2)-K1 (32 ... R(K2)-KB2? 33 N-Q6!) 33 RxR RxR 34 N-Q6 R-KB1 35 P-KB5! PxP (35 ... NxP 36 PxKP NxN 37 P-K7) 36 NxBP R-KN1 37 Q-N6 Q-R5 38 R-Q8, etc.

(ii) 31 ... K-R2! 32 R(Q4)-Q3! Q-N5 33 R-KN3 R-Q2 34 R-KN1 Q-K2 35 Q-N6ch K-R1 36 N-B6! RxN 37 PxR QxP 38 QxQ PxQ 39 PxP RPxP 40 R-K3 with a won ending. The alternative 32 ... Q-N7 33 R-Q8! R(K2)-KB2 (33 ... RxR 34 N-N5ch PxN 35 Q-R5ch) 34 Q-R5! R-B4 35 N-N5ch K-R1 36 RxRch RxR 37 NxP is also won for White.

31 ...   PxP
32 N-B6ch   K-R1
33 R-Q8   R-QB2

The penetration of the White queen is also decisive after 33 ... R(K2)-KB2.

34 Q-N6   PxN
35 QxBPch   Resigns

There is no way of saving the queen, e.g. 35 ... K-N1 36 RxRch QxR 37 R-Q8, etc.

Santa Monica 1966

		1	2	3	4	5	6	7	8	9	10	Pts	Prize
1	Spasski	– –	1 ½	½ 1	½ ½	1 ½	½ ½	½ ½	½ ½	1 ½	½ 1	11½	I
2	Fischer	0 ½	– –	0 1	½ 1	½ ½	½ ½	½ 1	0 1	1 1	½ 1	11	II
3	Larsen	½ 0	1 0	– –	1 ½	½ 0	1 1	½ 1	1 ½	0 1	½ 0	10	III
4	Portisch	½ ½	½ 0	0 ½	– –	½ ½	1 ½	½ ½	½ ½	½ 1	½ 1	9½	IV, V
5	Unzicker	0 ½	½ ½	½ 1	½ ½	– –	½ ½	½ ½	½ ½	1 ½	½ ½	9½	IV, V
6	Petrosian	½ ½	½ ½	0 0	0 ½	½ ½	– –	½ ½	1 1	½ ½	½ 1	9	
7	Reshevsky	½ ½	½ 0	½ 0	½ ½	½ ½	½ ½	– –	½ 1	½ ½	1 ½	9	
8	Najdorf	½ ½	1 0	0 ½	½ ½	½ ½	0 0	½ 0	– –	1 ½	½ 1	8	
9	Ivkov	0 ½	0 0	1 0	½ 0	0 ½	½ ½	½ ½	0 ½	– –	½ 1	6½	
10	Donner	½ 0	½ 0	½ 1	½ 0	½ ½	½ 0	0 ½	½ 0	½ 0	– –	6	

A Cool Defence

The Spanish island resort of Palma de Mallorca, one of the main centres of European tourism, has in the last few years become well known for its strong international tournaments. The second of the now traditional tournaments began on 25 November 1967 after a rather dramatic series of events. The Russian players originally announced for the tournament, Botvinnik and Suetin, were changed to Smyslov and Spasski just a week before the tournament was due to begin. Then Spasski withdrew, and the organizers hurriedly called in Tatai and Dr Lehmann. On the first day of the tournament a telegram was received saying that Botvinnik, together with Smyslov, would be arriving two days later. Thus at the last moment the tournament gained in interest, for a tough struggle was expected between Larsen and the two Soviet representatives. The group of favourites also included the Yugoslav grandmasters Gligorić and Ivkov as well as the Hungarian Portisch.

For a long time it looked as if there were not going to be a real struggle for first place. Larsen began with a series of five wins, and after the fifth round he had a lead of one point over Ivkov and 1½ points over Botvinnik and Smyslov. Smyslov lost his first game in the fourth round—with White against Donner—and Botvinnik his first in the next game—against Damjanović. Gligorić, playing White, was the victim of an energetic attack conducted by Larsen in the fifth round. Ivkov dropped out of the leading group after seven consecutive draws followed by a defeat at the hands of Larsen in the thirteenth round. At the end of

this round the position was as follows: Larsen 11½, Botvinnik and Smyslov 10, Gligorić 8½, Portisch 8, etc. In the next round, two of the top favourites met in the following dramatic game.

Catalan System

	Botvinnik	Larsen
1	P-QB4	N-KB3
2	N-KB3	P-K3
3	P-KN3	P-Q4
4	B-N2	B-K2
5	0-0	0-0
6	P-N3	

Up to a short time ago this was not considered to be a particularly active continuation. A number of games have shown, however, that the system gives White good chances. His plan consists in delaying the advance P-Q4 and the opening of the game until he has completed his development.

6	...	P-B4
7	B-N2	N-B3

After 7 ... P-Q5, both 8 P-K3 and 8 P-QN4 are good.

8	P-K3	P-QN3

Advancing the pawn to Q5 is not good at this stage either, e.g. 8 ... P-Q5 9 PxP PxP 10 R-K1, and Black has difficulty with the development of his queen's side.

9	N-B3	B-N2
10	P-Q3	

Another possibility is 10 PxP NxP 11 NxN QxN 12 P-Q4.

10 ...	R-B1
11 R-B1	R-B2

Larsen is generally reluctant to resolve the tension in the centre, for that is the kind of position he likes. Here, however, 11 ... PxP 12 NPxP Q-B2 seems to be the better continuation, though not, of course, 12 ... N-QN5 13 Q-N3! (13 ... QxP 14 N-K5 or 13 ... NxP 14 QR-Q1).

12 Q-K2	R-Q2
13 KR-Q1	R-K1

Black should again have exchanged pawns.

14 PxP	NxP

Retaking with the pawn would not be so good, for White could then continue with 15 P-Q4, threatening 16 PxP PxP 17 N-QR4.

15 NxN	RxN
16 P-Q4	

With this move White achieves some initiative. Black cannot reply 16 ... PxP because of 17 NxP NxN 18 BxN R-Q2 19 BxB RxB 20 BxKNP.

16 ...	Q-R1

The Black queen would not be particularly well placed on the QB or Q files. However, Black now gives up control of the square Q2, thus enabling the White rook to penetrate to the seventh rank.

17 PxP	RxRch
18 RxR	BxP
19 N-N5!	P-KR3
20 N-K4	B-KB1?

This natural-looking retreat, which defends the square KN2, should have led to a quick loss. The correct move is 20 ... B-K2, after which Black can reply to 21 Q-N4 by P-K4.

21 R-Q7

This is sufficient to achieve a winning superiority. There was, however, a more

157. Botvinnik–Larsen

Position after Black's 20th move

elegant, and quicker, win by means of the following combination: 21 N-B6ch PxN 22 Q-N4ch K-R2 23 B-K4ch P-B4 24 R-Q7! (stronger than 24 BxPch PxB 25 QxPch K-N1 26 Q-B6 N-K4) 24 ... N-Q1 25 RxPch! NxR 26 BxPch PxB 27 QxPch K-N1 28 Q-N6ch or 24 ... N-K2 25 RxN! RxR 26 BxPch PxB 27 QxPch K-N1 28 Q-B6 K-R2 29 P-KN4, and there is no way of preventing mate by 30 Q-R8ch K-N3 31 Q-N8ch, etc.

21 ...	P-B4

After 21 ... R-K2, White wins by 22 N-B6ch K-R1 (22 ... PxN 23 Q-N4ch) 23 Q-B2 PxN 24 BxPch K-N1 25 Q-Q1.

22 N-Q6?

The attempt to do everything in this game by positional means could well have cost Botvinnik an important half point. The knight sacrifice on KB6 would again have won: 22 N-B6ch! PxN 23 Q-R5 R-K2 24 Q-N6ch R-N2 25 RxR BxR 26 BxN BxB 27 BxP Q-KB1 28 BxB Q-B2 (28 ... QxB 29 QxKPch) 29 QxRP winning or 24 ... B-N2 25 BxN RxR 26 BxR B-R8 27 BxPch K-R1 28 P-B3 BxP 29 B(K6)xP, etc.

22 ...	BxN
23 RxB(Q6)	N-Q5!

Larsen answers the unpleasant threat of 24 Q-B4 by simplifying. This loses a pawn, though not necessarily the game, for there are bishops of opposite colours.

24	RxN	BxB
25	R-Q7	B-R6

Not, of course, 25 . . . P-K4 26 Q-B4ch
K-R1 (or R2) 27 Q-KB7, etc.

26	P-B3	R-Q1
27	RxNPch	K-B1
28	R-R7	Q-Q4

158. Botvinnik–Larsen

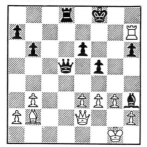

Now White has his problems, for if he
wins a second pawn by 29 RxKRP Black
replies 29 . . . Q-Q8ch 30 K-B2 Q-KR8 31
RxB R-Q8. Botvinnik therefore opts for
an exchange of rooks. This, however,
eliminates the mating threats, so that
Black has good drawing chances in view
of the bishops of opposite colours.

29	K-B2	Q-Q8
30	R-R8ch	K-B2
31	RxR	QxR
32	Q-B2	Q-Q4!
33	Q-B7ch	K-K1
34	Q-N8ch?	

White would have some practical
chances with 34 B-Q4. After the text-
move, Black could have forced an
exchange of queens by the natural Q-Q1,
leaving an endgame that could not have
been won, despite the fact that Black's
bishop is temporarily out of play.

| 34 | . . . | K-Q2? |

In the time-scramble, Larsen makes a
mistake that loses.

35	QxRPch	K-B1
36	Q-R6ch	K-B2

37	Q-B4ch	QxQ
38	PxQ	K-B3
39	B-Q4	P-R4
40	P-R4	K-B2

Black is in *zugzwang*. As his bishop is
immobile he is forced to move his king,
which allows his opponent to create a
passed pawn on the queen's side.

41	P-B5	PxP
42	BxP	K-B3
43	B-N4	K-N3
44	P-N4!	

White needs another passed pawn,
which he can only obtain by means of
this tactical break-through.

| 44 | . . . | RPxP |

Or 44 . . . BPxP 45 K-N3 K-R3 46
P-K4 K-N3 47 P-B4, etc.

| 45 | K-N3 | P-K4 |

This eases White's task, though there
was also a win after 45 . . . K-B3 46 P-R5
K-N4 47 B-B3 K-R3 48 PxP PxP (48 . . .
BxP 49 P-R4) 49 K-B4 K-N4 50 K-N5
K-R3 51 B-K1 K-N4 52 P-K4 K-R3 53
P-K5 K-N4 54 K-B6 K-R3 55 B-N3.

46	P-K4!	PxKP
47	PxNP	Resigns

Larsen was obviously depressed by this
defeat. He drew with White against Toran
in the fifteenth round in 26 moves and
lost to another Spanish master, Medina,
in the next.

159. Medina–Larsen

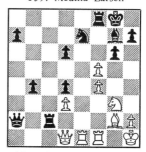

Position after Black's 24th move

It looks almost as if White could resign. Medina, however, finds a line which gives him some chances.

25 QxR!	**QxQ**
26 RxN	**P-QR4?**

Black obviously underestimates his opponent's threats. There were two ways of winning in this position:

(i) 26 . . . P-N6 27 PxP PxP 28 B-Q5ch K-R1 29 R-B3 P-N7 30 N-B1 R-B4! In this line the move 27 . . . P-N7 (instead of 27 . . . PxP) is not good on account of 28 N-R5 PxP 29 RxBch K-R1 30 R-QN7 PxN 31 B-K4.

(ii) 26 . . . PxP 27 B-R3 (27 N-R5 B-R3) 27 . . . QxP, etc.

27 PxP	**PxP**
28 B-Q5ch	**K-R1**
29 R-B3!	

White has suddenly got some strong threats. If now 29 . . . P-N6, the reply is 30 N-K4 R-B4 31 R-R3ch R-R4 32 RxRch PxR 33 R-K8ch K-R2 34 N-N5ch, etc.

29 . . .	**Q-B4**
30 B-K6	**B-B3**
31 R-Q7	**Q-B8ch**
32 K-N2	**Q-Q7ch**
33 K-R3?	

The right move was 33 K-B1, leaving the square KR3 free for the rook. Black would then have had nothing better than repetition of moves.

33 . . .	**Q-Q8?**

This loses. The correct move was 33 . . . P-R5, and if 34 P-B5 then 34 . . . P-N4.

34 B-Q5!	**P-R5**
35 P-B5!	**B-K4**

Or 35 . . . P-N4 36 K-N4, followed by K-R5-N6, to which there is no defence.

36 PxP	**Resigns**

Before the final round the position was exciting: Botvinnik, Larsen and Smyslov 12, Portisch 11, Gligorić 10, etc. Larsen's two rivals for first place had difficult opponents—Smyslov was to play Gligorić and Botvinnik, Ivkov. Moreover, they both had Black. As expected, the two games ended in a draw (Botvinnik's after a mere ten moves), so that victory in the tournament hinged on the following game.

King's Indian

Larsen	Diez Corral
1 N-KB3	N-KB3
2 P-QB4	P-KN3
3 N-B3	B-N2
4 P-K4	P-Q3
5 P-Q4	0-0
6 B-N5	B-N5

Whereas the development of White's bishop on KN5 is quite common, the same move by Black is not recommended by theory. The reason is that after the exchange BxKN Black gives up an active bishop which could later play a useful role on the king's side.

7 B-K2	**P-B3**

7 . . . N-B3 followed by N-Q2 would have been more in the spirit of the set-up chosen by Black.

8 0-0	**QN-Q2**
9 R-K1	

White has better chances with 9 N-Q2, for the knight is more active than the bishop once the centre is blocked.

9 . . .	**BxN**
10 BxB	**P-K4**
11 P-Q5	**P-KR3**
12 B-K3	**P-B4**
13 P-QR3	**Q-K2**
14 R-N1	**KR-QB1**

It is not quite logical to remove the rook from the king's wing. Stronger is 14 . . . QR-QB1 or 14 . . . N-K1 followed by P-B4.

15 Q-Q3

White could instead have developed his queen to K2, thus preventing Black's subsequent manoeuvre with his knight. Larsen, however, sees no reason for avoiding the exchange of his bishop for a knight, since he will then have a "good" bishop on K3 while his opponent remains with a passive one on KN2.

15 ...	P-KR4
16 P-QN4	N-N5
17 BxN	PxB
18 Q-K2	

It is not quite clear why Larsen forces his opponent to play P-KB4, which was in any case part of the latter's strategical plan. However, in doing so he does not weaken his position, for Black has no real chances on the king's wing.

18 ...	PxP
19 RxP	P-N3
20 P-QR4	P-B4
21 P-R5	K-B2!?
22 RPxP	RPxP

160. Larsen–Diez Corral

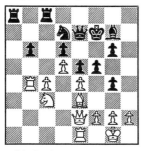

23 P-B3

With his 21st move Black offered a pawn to speed up his king-side play. Larsen, however, decides to proceed carefully and play positionally, in order not to give his opponent any tactical chances in such an important game, though it looks as if he could have taken the pawn without any danger: 23 BxP R-R1 24

P-B3 NxB 25 RxN Q-R2 26 Q-KB2 or 25 ... RxP? 26 KxR Q-R5ch 27 K-N1 P-N6 28 Q-K3! P-B5 29 R-N7ch, etc., or 24 ... RxP? 25 KxR Q-R5ch 26 K-N1 P-N6 27 K-B1! NxB 28 Q-K3! winning.

23 ...	P-B5
24 B-Q2	

Now the pawn can no longer be taken: 24 BxP? NxB 25 RxN Q-R2 26 Q-B2 P-N6.

24 ...	R-R1(?)

A much better line is 24 ... PxP 25 PxP R-R3, after which Black would have had some drawing chances despite the difficulties of defending his QNP.

25 PxP	Q-R5
26 P-N3!	

The Spanish master had obviously only reckoned with 26 P-R3? Q-N6! 27 K-B1 (27 K-R1 RxPch! 28 PxR R-R1) 27 ... QR-R6 28 R-QB1 (28 N-N5? RxP!) 28 ... N-B4, after which Black has the threat of N-Q6 or N-N6.

26 ...	PxP
27 Q-B3ch	K-K2
28 QxP	QxQch
29 PxQ	KR-R6
30 K-N2	QR-R1
31 B-N5ch	B-B3
32 B-K3	RxPch

Or 32 ... R-R7ch 33 K-B3 R-QB7 34 N-R4 and Black cannot save his QNP.

33 KxR	B-R5ch
34 K-N2	BxR

If White now had to protect his knight (35 R-N3) he would have to give up all thoughts of winning. As it is, the exposed position of Black's king soon decides the game.

35 B-N5ch	K-B2

Or 35 ... N-B3 36 RxP.

36	R-R4!	BxN		44	P-N5	R-KB8ch
37	R-R7	R-QB1		45	K-N2	R-K8
38	RxNch	K-K1		46	K-B2	K-B2
39	RxP	RxP		47	R-N7ch	K-N3
40	K-B3	P-N4		48	P-Q6	R-Q8
41	RxP	P-N5		49	P-Q7	K-R4
42	R-QN6	R-Q5		50	K-K2	Resigns
43	B-K3	R-Q8				

Palma de Mallorca 1967

		1	2	3	4	5	6	7	8	9	10	11	12	13	14	15	16	17	18	Pts	Prize
1	Larsen	–	0	½	1	1	1	½	½	1	½	1	1	0	1	1	1	1	1	13	I
2	Botvinnik	1	–	½	½	1	½	1	1	½	1	1	½	1	0	½	1	½	1	12½	II, III
3	Smyslov	½	½	–	½	½	½	1	1	1	0	½	1	1	1	1	½	1	1	12½	II, III
4	Portisch	0	½	½	–	½	½	½	1	½	½	1	½	1	1	½	1	1	1	11½	IV
5	Gligorić	0	0	½	½	–	½	1	½	½	½	½	½	1	1	1	½	1	1	10½	V
6	Ivkov	0	½	½	½	½	–	½	1	1	½	½	½	½	1	1	½	½	½	10	VI
7	Matulović	½	0	0	½	0	½	–	0	½	½	1	½	0	1	1	1	1	1	9	VII
8	Torán	½	0	0	0	½	0	1	–	½	1	1	1	½	½	½	½	½	½	8½	VIII, IX
9	Lehmann	0	½	0	½	½	0	½	½	–	½	½	½	1	½	1	1	½	½	8½	VIII, IX
10	Donner	½	0	1	½	½	½	½	0	½	–	½	1	1	½	½	0	0	½	8	
11	Diez Corral	0	0	½	0	½	½	0	0	½	½	–	0	1	1	1	½	1	1	8	
12	O'Kelly	0	½	0	½	½	½	½	0	½	0	1	–	½	½	1	½	0	0	6½	
13	Medina	1	0	0	0	0	½	1	½	0	0	0	½	–	½	½	½	1	½	6½	
14	Damjanović	0	1	0	0	0	0	0	½	½	½	0	½	½	–	½	1	1	0	6	
15	Tatal	0	½	0	½	0	0	0	½	0	½	0	0	½	½	–	1	1	1	6	
16	Bednarski	0	0	½	0	½	½	0	½	0	1	½	½	½	0	0	–	0	1	5½	
17	Calvo	0	½	0	0	0	½	0	½	½	1	0	1	0	0	0	1	–	½	5½	
18	Jiménez	0	0	0	0	0	½	0	½	½	½	0	1	½	1	0	0	½	–	5	

47 Candidates' Tournament 1968

A Hard Struggle and an Easy Victory

Two of the contestants in the first round of the 1968 Candidates' Tournament were players of completely different styles. The Danish player Larsen simply abounds in self-confidence and optimism; he avoids no risk and plays for a win even in bad positions. The Hungarian player Portisch, on the other hand, is noted for the cool and objective way he assesses his chances; he likes clear and tidy positions, especially favourable endings. He is very strong in defence; he goes on the attack, however, only after a thorough positional assessment of the situation.

The match took place in the Yugoslav coastal town of Poreci on the Adriatic. Larsen was an odds-on favourite, and he did nothing to hide the fact that he was determined to win his way to the world championship title. His forecast for the match was 5½ to 2½ in his favour. However, he soon found himself facing tough resistance, and after the eighth game the match was all square, he having won the second and third games, Portisch the fourth and seventh.

In the ninth game Larsen very nearly paid a high price for his tremendous optimism. In an even position he declined his opponent's offer of a draw and then went on incautiously to weaken his pawn position, with the result that he got into a lost ending. After the adjournment Portisch could have pressed home his advantage in several ways. However, fortunately for Larsen he played irresolutely and gradually let the win slip away. The game lasted 77 moves and played havoc with Portisch's nerves. It is reported that he was unable to sleep after

it and spent the night analysing the game and looking for wins he had missed.

Thus when the final and decisive game took place Portisch's nerves were in a very bad state. That is the reason why a match that up to then had been even was ended by a game that looked as if it had been conducted by players of completely different playing strengths.

Vienna Game

Larsen	Portisch
1 P-K4	P-K4
2 N-QB3	N-QB3
3 B-B4	N-B3
4 P-Q3	N-QR4

Theory recommends 4 ... B-N5 5 B-KN5 P-KR3 or 5 KN-K2 P-Q4. Portisch, however, had done well in the eighth game with 4 ... N-QR4 5 B-N3? NxB 6 RPxN P-Q4! 7 PxP B-QN5 8 N-B3 NxP 9 B-Q2 NxN 10 PxN B-Q3, which gave him an advantage thanks to his two bishops.

5 KN-K2!

After the game some annotators referred to this move as an innovation. However, the move had already occurred in the game Schlechter–Steinitz in 1898, which continued 5 ... NxB 6 PxN P-Q3 7 O-O B-K3 8 P-QN3 P-B3 9 Q-Q3 B-K2 10 B-N5 P-KR3 11 BxN BxB 12 QR-Q1 B-K2 13 P-B5! PxP 14 Q-N3 with advantage to White. In that game Black would have done better with 9 ... P-Q4! 10 BPxP PxP 11 PxP NxP 12 Q-N5ch Q-Q2 13 QxQch KxQ 14 R-Q1 K-B3 and if

White had played 12 R-Q1 then 12 ...
NxN, etc.

Larsen was obviously familiar with this
game—it often pays to study old books—
and hit on the idea of fianchettoing his
queen's bishop to prevent his opponent
from freeing himself by P-Q4.

| 5 ... | NxB |
| 6 PxN | B-K2 |

The system of development adopted
by Steinitz—P-Q3, B-K3 and P-QB3—is
more logical, for it threatens P-Q4. By
first playing his bishop to K2 Black loses
an important tempo.

| 7 0-0 | P-Q3 |
| 8 P-QN3 | 0-0 |

If 8 ... B-K3 9 Q-Q3 P-B3, White has
a good reply in 10 B-N5 transposing into
the Schlechter–Steinitz game mentioned
above. Now, however, White must look
for another way, for 9 Q-Q3 can be
answered by the manoeuvre 9 ... N-Q2
followed by N-B4 and P-KB4.

| 9 N-N3 | P-B3 |
| 10 B-N2 | |

That is the set-up prepared by Larsen.
The bishop on QN2 is not brilliantly
placed. On the other hand, it stops Black
from freeing himself and thus gives White
time to manoeuvre.

161. Larsen–Portisch

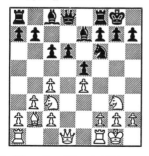

Position after White's 10th move

| 10 ... | Q-R4 |

This is not a loss of tempo, as some
annotators critical of the move maintained. It is true that after 11 Q-K1
Black's queen is forced to retreat on
account of the threat 12 N-Q5. On the
other hand, White's queen is no better
placed on K1 than on Q1.

| 11 Q-K1 | Q-B2 |
| 12 P-QR4 | B-K3 |

12 ... B-Q2 looks better, with the
intention of aiming at P-QN4.

13 R-Q1	P-QR3
14 Q-K2	B-N5
15 P-B3	B-Q2

After this manoeuvre Black threatens
16 ... P-QN4! 17 RPxP RPxP 18 PxP
PxP, for 19 NxP?? is answered by 19 ...
Q-N3ch. However, such a threat is easily
countered.

| 16 K-R1 | QR-N1(?) |

It is not always good to stick stubbornly to one's plan—here the preparation of the advance of the QNP. After 16
... KR-Q1! White would only have a
slight advantage, for the manoeuvre 17
N-B5 has been deprived of a lot of its
force: 17 ... BxN 18 PxB P-Q4, etc. If
White instead plays 17 B-R3, the reply 17
... P-QN4 is strong. Larsen would therefore probably have opted for 17 KR-K1,
preventing the freeing 17 ... P-Q4.

| 17 N-B5! | BxN |
| 18 PxB | KR-K1 |

This move, which only makes sense if
Black has prospects of forcing P-Q4, was
universally condemned. Some annotators
recommended 18 ... P-KN3, but this is
only a good plan if White is forced to
play PxP. As it is, the move would simply
weaken the long black diagonal
KR1-QR8; e.g. 19 N-K4 PxP 20 NxNch
BxN 21 P-B4 KR-K1 22 Q-R5 or 19 ...
NxN 20 QxN with the threat of 21 P-B4.
A better plan for Black is 18 ... KR-Q1
followed by R-Q2 and QR-Q1.

| 19 R-Q2 | QR-Q1 |
| 20 KR-Q1 | N-R4? |

A strange manoeuvre, after which Black gets into a hopeless position. The knight is heading for KB5, a square on which it will be very much exposed to attack. White can easily counter the tactical threat of 21 ... B-N4 by attacking the QP.

| 21 B-R3! | N-B5 |
| 22 Q-B2 | Q-R4? |

162. Larsen–Portisch

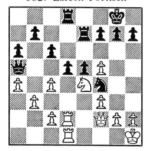

Position after Black's 24th move

A tactical blunder, which loses material. Necessary was 22 ... R-Q2 followed by R(K1)-Q1.

23 N-K4	P-Q4
24 BxB	RxB
25 Q-R4!	R(K2)-Q2
26 P-N3	N-K7

When making his 22nd move Portisch had overlooked the fact that 26 ... PxN fails to 27 QxRch! QxQ 28 RxR, etc.

For the time being Black has succeeded in avoiding the loss of a piece (e.g. 27 RxN? PxN), but the knight on K7 cannot escape. Moreover, the Black king will soon come under fire.

| 27 P-B6! | Q-N5 |

In order to answer 28 Q-N5 by 28 ... Q-B1.

| 28 Q-N4! |

But now Black loses a whole piece: 28 ... P-KN3 29 RxN and the reply 29 ... PxN is not possible because the rook on Q2 is subjected to a double attack. Black therefore resigned.

An Untitled Player Outstrips Ten Grandmasters

In a grandmaster tournament it is natural to look for the favourites among the well-known title-holders. It is quite a surprise for several grandmasters to be edged out by an international master, though there are a number of examples of such an occurrence. But can it happen that a player without a title at all can win a strong tournament and beat several grandmasters? In the last few decades there is only one case I know of.

For the first Dr Vidmar Memorial Tournament, which took place in Ljubljana from 2 to 20 June 1969, the organizers managed to arrange a tournament that, according to the FIDE rules, was classified as 1A, the highest category. Taking part were no less than ten grandmasters (of whom only one had not yet had his qualification confirmed) and three international masters. Names like Gligorić, Unzicker, Matanović and Gheorghiu are an indication that the high classification was not merely a matter of form. And it was from among these four that the victor was to be expected. But things turned out completely differently. Also taking part was a real amateur. A young man by the name of Albin Planinc, a turner by trade, who worked in the bicycle factory in Ljubljana, was probably the only competitor who was unable to take a day off to prepare for the tournament. Right up until the start he worked busily in the factory. He did not possess an international title, although he was known as an attacking player who often used the King's Gambit and sought complicated combinations of the sort that had made Tal famous a few years previously. His results, however, were inconsistent; so a place half-way down the tournament table would have been quite a success for him in view of the strong field. But at the age of twenty-five one is ambitious!

In the first round he adopted his favourite opening, the King's Gambit, against Matanović and won in 28 moves by means of a king-side attack. Then, with the Black pieces, he defeated Barcza, who admittedly helped him to his victory by under-estimating him and trying to force the pace. After that there soon followed a defeat at the hands of Gligorić, who played in his relentless positional style. This set-back, however, did not seem to affect Planinc. In the tenth round he won a pretty game against Unzicker, and in the next he attained the necessary number of points for the title of international master. But he had his eyes fixed on higher goals.

With one round to go Planinc was half a point ahead of Gligorić, though a tie seemed to be the most likely result, for Gligorić was to play the tail-ender, Stupica, while Planinc had a much more dangerous opponent in grandmaster Gheorghiu. Many players in Planinc's place would have been content with a tie and have used the advantage of the White pieces to obtain the necessary half point. As things turned out this would have been easy to achieve, for Gheorghiu offered him a draw twice during the game. The young player, however, had other ideas and first sacrificed a pawn in an unclear position and then later made a perfectly correct rook sacrifice. The game, which turned out to be one of the most beautiful of the tournament, gave

Planinc the final point, which caused a great sensation in the world of chess. An unknown player had won first prize and had satisfied the standard for the award of the grandmaster title—a title which he could not receive because the FIDE rules do not permit such jumps. A player first has to be a master before he can become a grandmaster.

Sicilian

Planinc	Gheorghiu
1 P-K4	P-QB4
2 N-KB3	P-Q3
3 P-Q4	PxP
4 NxP	N-KB3
5 N-QB3	P-QR3
6 B-KN5	N-B3

Black probably wants to avoid the sharp main variation (6 . . . P-K3 7 P-B4) and transposes into the Rauser System (1 P-K4 P-QB4 2 N-KB3 N-QB3 3 P-Q4 PxP 4 NxP N-B3 5 N-QB3 P-Q3 6 B-KN5), in which a set-up where Black avoids 6 . . . P-K3 has become popular lately. However, the usual continuation is then 6 . . . B-Q2 followed by R-B1, NxN and Q-R4. The fact that Gheorghiu has already played P-QR3 is a disadvantage in this set-up.

| 7 Q-Q2 | B-Q2 |
| 8 0-0-0 | |

The usual continuation at the time was 8 P-B4, but the text-move is more accurate. As we shall soon see, Black will have difficulty in developing his king-side pieces.

8 . . .	P-N4
9 NxN	BxN
10 Q-K1	

This prevents 10 . . . P-K3 because of 11 P-K5 P-R3 12 B-R4 P-N4 13 B-N3 N-R4 14 PxP NxB 15 RPxN BxQP 16 N-K4 with a clear advantage to White.

| 10 . . . | Q-R4 |
| 11 K-N1 | P-R3 |

The move P-K3 is still not good for Black; e.g. 11 . ,. P-K3 12 BxN PxB 13 N-Q5! QxQ 14 RxQ BxN 15 PxB P-K4 16 B-Q3, and White should win the endgame despite the bishops of opposite colours.

12 BxN	NPxB
13 P-B4	0-0-0
14 P-KR4!	

Proof that the Black king has not found a safe retreat on the queen's wing. White intends to get his rook into play against the king via KR3.

| 14 . . . | P-K3 |

163. Planinc–Gheorghiu

Here Gheorghiu made his first offer of a draw—we have not been able to find out when he made his second. It now looks as if Black is threatening to win a pawn by 15 . . . P-N5, and the natural defence, 15 B-Q3, would stop the intended rook manoeuvre.

| 15 R-R3! | |

This looks almost like an oversight, but the pawn sacrifice is quite sound.

15 . . .	P-N5
16 N-K2	BxP
17 N-Q4	P-B4?

The first mistake, which White does not properly exploit. Black's best move is 17 . . . B-Q4!, meeting the main threat of

18 R-QN3. White can, of course, then win back his pawn by 18 R-QR3 as in the game, but he gets nothing more than equality.

18 R-QR3?

Immediately after the game Planinc pointed out that 18 R-QN3! was much stronger. If then 18 . . . P-Q4, White replies with 19 P-QR3 and Black's queen-side falls to pieces. A more interesting line is 18 . . . B-Q4 19 RxP QxPch 20 K-B1, when Black, despite his extra pawn, is in a poor position for his opponent threatens Q-B3ch. If Black then plays 20 . . . K-Q2, there follows the surprising continuation 21 Q-B3 R-B1 22 N-B6! R-R2 23 R-N7ch K-K1 24 R-N8 RxR 25 NxR, and if 20 . . . Q-R8ch, then 21 K-Q2 Q-R4 22 K-K3, threatening to win the queen by 23 R-N8ch.

18 . . .	**Q-B4**
19 BxPch	**K-Q2**
20 R-QN3	**B-KN2?**

Gheorghiu does not want to waste time on defensive moves and relies on his counter-attack against QB7. The correct move, however, was 20 . . . R-QN1!, after which Black is quite safe, e.g. 21 P-R3 B-KN2 22 PxP Q-Q4 23 Q-Q2 BxN 24 QxB QxQ 25 RxQ BxNP with an even endgame.

164. Planinc–Gheorghiu

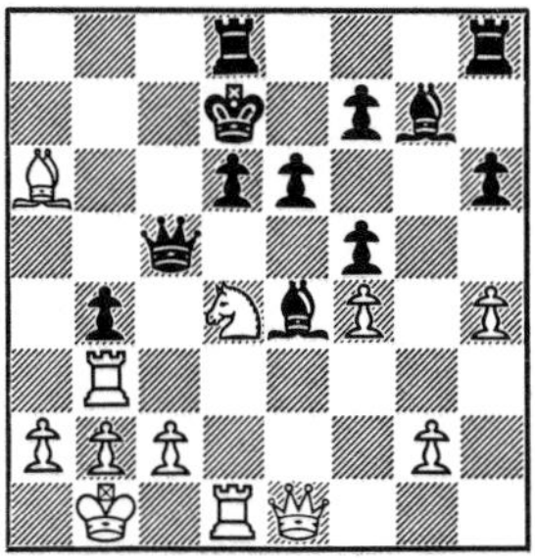

Position after Black's 20th move

21 QxP!	**BxN?**

Again Black thinks his opponent has overlooked something. The combination, however, has been accurately calculated. Black's only chance of salvation lay in 21 . . . QxQ 22 RxQ BxNP.

22 QxB	**BxBPch**
23 K-R1	**BxR(Q8)**

Black has to go ahead, for trans-position into an endgame would not help him, e.g. 23 . . . QxQ 24 R-N7ch K-B3 25 RxQ P-Q4 (answering the threat of 26 R-B4ch) 26 RxBP or 24 . . . K-K1 25 RxQ R-KN1 26 P-R4.

Ljubljana 1969

		1	2	3	4	5	6	7	8	9	10	11	12	13	14	15	16	Pts	Prize
1	Planinc	—	0	1	½	½	1	1	½	1	½	½	1	½	½	1	1	10½	I
2	Gligorić	1	—	½	½	½	½	½	1	1	½	½	½	½	1	½	1	10	II
3	Unzicker	0	½	—	½	½	½	½	1	½	½	1	1	½	½	1	1	9½	III
4	Tringov	½	½	½	—	½	½	½	0	1	1	½	½	½	1	½	1	9	IV
5	R. Byrne	½	½	½	½	—	½	½	½	½	½	½	½	½	½	1	1	8½	V, VI
6	Matanović	0	½	½	½	½	—	½	½	1	½	½	1	1	½	½	½	8½	V, VI
7	Gheorghiu	0	½	½	½	½	½	—	0	½	½	1	½	½	½	1	1	8	VII, VIII
8	Puc	½	0	0	1	½	½	1	—	½	1	0	½	½	½	½	1	8	VII, VIII
9	Barcza	0	0	½	0	½	0	½	½	—	½	½	½	1	½	1	1	7	
10	Damjanović	½	½	½	0	½	½	½	0	½	—	½	0	½	1	1	½	7	
11	Parma	½	½	0	½	½	½	0	1	½	½	—	½	½	½	½	½	7	
12	Musil	0	½	0	½	½	0	½	½	½	1	½	—	½	½	½	½	6½	
13	Robatsch	½	½	½	½	½	0	½	½	0	½	½	½	—	½	½	½	6½	
14	Bajec	½	0	½	0	½	½	½	½	½	0	½	½	½	—	0	½	5½	
15	Forintos	0	½	0	½	0	½	0	½	0	0	½	½	½	1	—	1	5½	
16	Stupica	0	0	0	0	0	½	0	0	0	½	½	½	½	½	0	—	3	

24	R-N7ch	K-B3
25	QxB	R-QN1

The unfortunate position of the Black king makes an adequate defence impossible. There was the threat of 26 Q-R4ch K-Q4 27 R-N5, and if 25 . . . P-Q4, then 26 Q-R4ch K-Q3 27 B-Q3 Q-B8ch 28 B-N1 Q-B5 29 Q-R7, etc.

26	Q-R4ch	K-Q4
27	Q-N3ch	K-B3
28	P-R3!	

A pretty conclusion. The Black rook cannot leave the square QN1 because of 29 Q-R4ch K-Q4 30 R-N5, while 28 . . .

RxR leads to mate in one. Preceding the exchange of rooks by checking does not help either, for Black then loses his queen, e.g. 28 . . . Q-B8ch 29 K-R2 RxR 30 QxRch K-B4 31 Q-B7ch or 28 . . . Q-N8ch 29 K-R2 RxR 30 QxRch K-B4 31 Q-R7ch, etc.

28 . . .	Q-R4

White does not have to take the rook at once. A typical queen manoeuvre wins the decisive tempo.

29	Q-B2ch	Q-B4
30	Q-R4ch	K-Q4
31	Q-N3ch	Resigns

49 Skopje 1970

Are Combinations Justified in the Last Round?

We have already mentioned that the last round is enveloped in a special type of atmosphere which tends to produce bad mistakes rather than good games. I personally have ruined my chances in the last round of many a tournament, mainly through going in for complications and trying to bring off combinations that were incorrect. I can recall the international tournament at Trencianske Teplica in 1949, where I was in the lead up until near the end. Then in the last round but one I lost with White to Rossolimo through trying too hard for a win, so that I was caught by Ståhlberg. In the last round the latter wisely went in for a quick draw, whereas I, because of my youth, played in a wild fashion against Golombek, even sacrificing a piece. As a result of losing the game I ended up half a point behind Ståhlberg. At the time, a friend of mine said to me, "Never go in for a combination in the last round." This advice, of course, goes too far, as several of the games in this book, including the next one, show. The question posed at the head of this chapter can therefore be answered in the affirmative. It is all right to go in for a combination in the last round, provided the combination is sound.

Our next drama is again set in Yugoslavia. The Macedonian capital, Skopje, has been the venue of several important tournaments in recent years. They are called "tournaments of solidarity" to commemorate the great earthquake. The fourth such tournament, which took place in June 1970, brought together ten grandmasters, four international masters and two national masters.

The Soviet grandmaster Taimanov played in great style, going through the tournament undefeated and chalking up wins against such redoubtable opponents as Gligorić and Gheorghiu. His fellow-countryman Vasjukov dropped back after losing to Gligorić but then brought off a series of victories against players in the lower half of the table. Nevertheless with 10 points he was still half a point behind Taimanov at the start of the last round. The race was between these two, for Gheorghiu with 9½ points was virtually out of the running. In the last round Taimanov was pitted against Browne, whereas Vasjukov had a tough opponent in Matanović, a player who very rarely loses. In these circumstances the wisest course for Taimanov seemed to be to take no risks and be content with a draw, for the encounter Vasjukov–Matanović would probably end the same way. But it did not turn out like that, for Vasjukov produced one of the finest games of the tournament.

Ruy Lopez

	Vasjukov	Matanović
1	P-K4	P-K4
2	N-KB3	N-QB3
3	B-N5	P-QR3
4	B-R4	N-B3
5	0-0	B-K2
6	R-K1	P-QN4
7	B-N3	P-Q3
8	P-B3	0-0
9	P-Q4	

This variation has not been subjected to the same amount of analysis as 9

P-KR3. As this game shows it can therefore produce innovations.

9 ...	B-N5
10 P-Q5	N-QR4
11 P-KR3	

And here we have one. It is not always
necessary to prevent the "Spanish"
bishop from being exchanged. After the
logical reply 11 ... NxB 12 PxN B-Q2 13
P-B4 Black's two bishops are of no real
importance, which, of course, does not
mean that he would be unable to attain
equality.

11 ...	B-R4

This involves a slight concession, for
the bishop is rarely well placed on KR4 in
this variation.

12 B-B2	P-B3
13 PxP	Q-B2

Better than 13 ... NxBP, 14 B-N5, by
which Black loses control of the square
Q4. After the text-move 14 B-N5 is not
good on account of 14 ... N-B5.

14 QN-Q2	QxP(?)

This move is only good when White
has delayed P-KR3, so that Black can
play B-K3; e.g. 11 B-B2 P-B3 12 PxP
Q-B2 13 P-KR3 B-K3! 14 QN-Q2 QxP!
The game then resembles a Sicilian in
which Black has good prospects on the
open QB file. In such a set-up it is not
good to have the bishop on KR4 as is the
case here. Black therefore should have
played 14 ... NxP and then aimed at
P-Q4, e.g. 15 N-B1 QR-Q1 16 N-N3 (16
N-K3 P-Q4! 17 NxQP NxN 18 PxN
P-B4!) 16 ... B-N3 17 Q-K2 P-Q4!? 18
PxP BxB 19 PxN B-Q6 20 QxP B-Q3 and
Black has considerable pressure for the
pawn sacrificed.

15 N-B1	KR-K1

The freeing advance is no longer
feasible because the pawn on K4 is
unprotected. Black is thus forced into a
passive position in which his bishop on
KR4 is a strategical weakness.

16 N-N3	B-N3
17 N-R4!	B-B1
18 P-R4	

The move P-QR4 occurs quite frequently in the Ruy Lopez and is generally
given an exclamation mark by annotators
—even in this case. Here, however, it is
doubtful whether such an assessment is
correct, for the opening of the game on
the queen's wing gives Black some
counter-play. A more consistent, and
stronger continuation is 18 N(R4)-B5
followed by 19 P-KR4.

18 ...	N-Q2
19 N(R4)-B5	N-N3

This removes an important piece from
the defence of the king's side. The
immediate 19 ... P-B3 followed by B-B2
was worthy of consideration.

20 PxP	PxP
21 P-R4	P-B3
22 P-R5	B-B2
23 Q-N4	K-R1
24 N-R4!	N-N6
25 BxN	BxB

165. Vasjukov–Matanović

26 N-N6ch!

Now White's plan is clear. One knight
on KN6, the other on KB5.

26 ...	K-N1
27 N-B5!	

White does not even need to bother about his rook on QR1, for after 27 . . . RxR 28 N-R6ch! PxN 29 NxPdis ch the Black queen is lost.

27 . . . Q-B2

For the time being everything is covered. White should now avoid 28 N-R6ch? PxN, for none of the discovered checks can harm Black.

28 B-K3 RxR
29 RxR N-R5

The position still does not look too bad for Black, for all his weak points are covered and White has no more pieces to throw into his king-side attack. But now there comes an ingenious sacrifice of two pawns.

30 P-QB4 BxP

It is understandable that Black is reluctant to have his bishop on QN6 cut off from the defence of the king's side. Nevertheless 30 . . . PxP would have been better, to which White would have replied 31 P-KN3 followed by K-N2, R-KR1 and P-R6!

31 R-QB1!

The bishop is now pinned and there is the threat of 32 P-QN3. Unpinning by 31

166. Vasjukov–Matanović

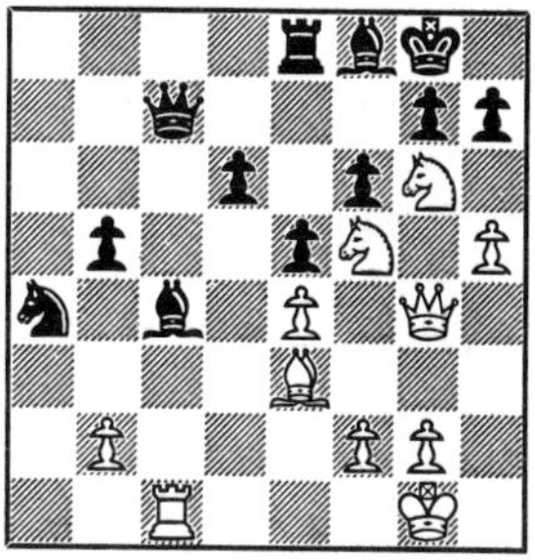

Position after White's 31st move

. . . Q-N2 allows the combination that occurs later in the game, viz. 32 RxB! PxR 33 N-R6ch! PxN 34 N-K7dbl ch. Apart from the move played the only other plausible alternative is 31 . . . N-B4 32 P-QN3! BxP 33 NxB RxN (33 . . . KxN? 34 NxQP) 34 BxN PxB 35 RxP! Q-R2 (35 . . . Q-N2 36 RxNP or 35 . . . Q-Q2? or Q-KB2? 36 N-R6ch) 36 N-R6ch K-R1 37 R-B8 Q-R6 (37 . . . Q-K2? 38 Q-Q7!) 38 R-B7 winning.

31 . . . NxP
32 B-N6!!

The culmination of a combination which resembles a study. If now 32 . . . QxB, White wins by 33 NxB Q-B2 34 N-Q7! QxN 35 N-R6ch.

Skopje 1970

		1	2	3	4	5	6	7	8	9	10	11	12	13	14	15	16	Pts	Prize
1	Taimanov	–	½	1	1	½	1	1	½	½	½	½	½	½	1	1	1	11	I, II
2	Vasjukov	½	–	½	½	½	½	0	1	1	1	1	1	½	1	1	1	11	I, II
3	Gheorghiu	0	½	–	½	½	0	½	1	½	½	1	1	1	1	1	1	10	III
4	Marović	0	½	½	–	½	½	½	½	½	½	½	1	1	1	½	1	9	IV
5	Balaschow	½	½	½	½	–	½	0	½	½	1	1	½	½	0	1	1	8½	V
6	Forintos	0	½	1	½	½	–	½	½	1	½	½	1	½	½	0	½	8	VI–VIII
7	Gligorić	0	1	½	½	1	½	–	½	½	½	½	½	½	½	½	½	8	VI–VIII
8	Matulović	½	0	0	½	½	½	½	–	1	½	½	½	½	½	1	1	8	VI–VIII
9	Browne	½	0	½	½	½	0	½	0	–	½	1	0	½	1	1	1	7½	
10	Matanović	½	0	½	½	0	½	½	½	½	–	½	½	½	½	1	1	7½	
11	Reshevsky	½	0	0	½	0	½	½	½	0	½	–	1	1	½	1	½	7	
12	Janosević	½	0	0	0	½	0	½	½	1	½	0	–	½	½	½	½	5½	
13	Sofrevski	½	½	0	0	½	½	½	½	½	½	0	½	–	0	½	½	5½	
14	Barczay	0	0	0	0	1	½	½	½	0	½	½	½	1	–	0	0	5	
15	Nicebski	0	0	0	½	0	1	½	0	0	0	0	½	½	1	–	½	4½	
16	Panov	0	0	0	0	0	½	½	0	0	0	½	½	½	1	½	–	4	

32 ...	Q-N2
33 RxB!	

White has carried out his plan. The bishop must now be eliminated to prevent it going to KB2.

33 ...	NxR
34 NxR6ch!	PxN
35 N-K7dbl ch	K-B2
36 Q-N8ch	KxN

37 QxPch	K-K3
38 QxQ	NxB
39 QxN	P-B4
40 QxNP	R-Q1
41 Q-Q5ch	K-B3
42 PxP	KxP
43 Q-B7ch	K-K5
44 Q-QB7	

Now the rook is caught. Black therefore resigned.

50 Candidates' Tournament 1971

Bobby on the Way to the World Championship

Many a strong player of world class has started his career inconspicuously, then by diligence and perseverance slowly increased his list of successes until he finally reached chess maturity.

True chess geniuses, however, travel along a different path. They are admired while still young boys and within a short time they demonstrate their ability to the whole chess world. So it was with Paul Morphy on his trip to Europe in 1858 and 1859 and also with José Raoul Capablanca at San Sebastián in 1911.

It was the same with Fischer. He played in the USA Championship for the first time in 1957, winning the title a full point ahead of the great Sammy Reshevsky. At the age of fifteen he played in the Interzonal in 1958 for the first time and qualified for the strongest of all chess competitions, the Candidates' Tournament. He played in the Candidates' Tournament for the first time in 1959 and . . . . No, it was not quite as simple as that. The world championship title is not so easily gained in the twentieth century as it was at the time of Bobby's fellow-countryman Morphy.

In 1967 Bobby was mature enough to accomplish the task. In the Interzonal he annihilated one opponent after the other. True, out of obstinacy he lost a game by default in the tenth round, but he won the next two games and kept well in the lead. Then in his antipathy towards the organizers he pushed matters to a head and hurriedly departed from Sousse, throwing away a great chance of becoming world champion. After this episode he criticized the organizers, FIDE, and everyone else, but in his heart of hearts he must have been extremely annoyed with himself.

Three years later he was again in the Interzonal—though only after certain difficulties had been overcome, for he had refused to take part in the US Championship. This time he was determined to achieve his aim. His opponents in Palma de Mallorca were no real problem for him; he outdistanced them by the unbelievable margin of 3½ points. A remarkable fact is that he won his last six games in a row.

The first of the elimination matches began in Vancouver on 16 May 1971. His opponent was Taimanov, who in the Interzonal had shared fifth and sixth places and who, objectively seen, was no real danger. Interest in this match was world wide. In these topsy-turvy times, everything is elevated to the realm of politics. We cannot really say that mankind is conquering space but rather that two super-powers are in a race one against the other to do so. Nor do individual athletes compete against each other at the Olympic Games; there are the national flags in the background waiting for the victory ceremonies. It is no different in chess. The first twenty-five years after the war were dominated by Soviet masters, the world championship matches being a purely domestic affair. Then for the first time Soviet dominance seemed to be threatened, and, what is more, by a representative of the other super-power. Taimanov was therefore playing not as Taimanov but as the first Soviet barrier to the invader.

This additional psychological burden played its part in Taimanov's tragedy.

Although he is a very sound player he lost all six games. The reporters were naturally cock-a-hoop, for, after winning his last six games in Palma, Fischer had now won a further six, and, what is more, against an opponent with a grandmaster title.

Fischer's match in Denver in July looked to be a much tougher proposition. In the course of the previous few years Larsen had chalked up several excellent victories in tournaments, often against competition from Soviet grandmasters. Just like Fischer he declared at the start of the Candidates' Tournament that he intended to become world champion and that he was not afraid of any player. But only one of these two optimists could survive the match at Denver and go on to compete for the world title; so a bitter struggle was expected. The result is well known, and it may surprise the reader to hear us talk of a decisive game. The score was again 6:0, so that the excited reporters were able to write down for Fischer's last eighteen games the unbelievable result, won: 18; drawn: 0; lost: 0. As Larsen, however, is a player of stature, there must have been a reason for his 6:0 defeat. And it is evident that it can only have been a psychological reason. We can spot it by playing over the first game of the match.

French Defence

Fischer	Larsen
1 P-K4	P-K3
2 P-Q4	P-Q4
3 N-QB3	B-N5

Such variations are not chosen by anyone playing for a draw. One sensible approach to matches is to play for a win with White and a draw with Black. But such tactics do not suit Larsen. He never plays for a draw, and in fact he cannot play for a draw. That is why he wins, and

loses, as many games with Black as with White.

4 P-K5	N-K2
5 P-QR3	BxNch
6 PxB	P-QB4
7 P-QR4	

If Larsen had had White he would probably have chosen the sharper continuation 7 Q-N4, which leads to great tactical complications. Quieter moves like 7 P-QR4 or 7 N-B3 are favoured by players who prefer clear strategical ideas to tactical complexities, such as Smyslov, who has been called Capablanca's successor. Fischer has something of Capablanca's style, but gives it more dynamism in accord with the general tendency in the second half of the twentieth century.

7 ...	QN-B3
8 N-B3	B-Q2

The general opinion is that the best post for the Black queen is QR4, and consequently Black's best defence the immediate 8 ... Q-R4. In the game Fischer–Uhlmann from the 1962 Olympiad Black attained equality after 8 ... Q-R4 9 Q-Q2 B-Q2 10 B-Q3 P-B3 11 0-0 PxKP 12 NxP NxN 13 PxN 0-0 14 P-QB4 QxQ 15 BxQ B-B3. An improvement, however, was found by Stein in his game with Doroshkevich in the 1970 Soviet Championship, when he played 11 KPxP! PxBP 12 PxP P-K4 13 P-B4 PxP 14 BxBP 0-0-0 15 0-0 QxBP 16 B-N3 B-N5 17 Q-R6, retaining a slight advantage. Larsen has a different idea: he will post his queen on QB2 and thus increase his control over K4. It is unlikely that Fischer was prepared for this plan; nevertheless he found an excellent tactical refutation over the board.

9 B-Q3	Q-B2
10 0-0	P-B5
11 B-K2	P-B3

Now if 12 PxP, Black gets a strong centre by 12 ... PxP followed by P-K4.

12 R-K1!	**N-N3?**

This shows that Larsen intends to take the KP. A more prudent continuation is 12 ... 0-0 13 B-R3 R-B2, after which Black's position is fairly sound. Larsen, however, is not fond of such precautionary measures; his self-confidence does not let him think of danger. He always wants to gain something right from the very first game, and here he is given an opportunity. He can have the KP.

13 B-R3!	**PxP**

It would have been difficult to change his plan, for short castling is no longer possible and long castling would be rather dangerous in view of B-Q6.

14 PxP	**QNxP**
15 NxN	**NxN**
16 Q-Q4!	

167. Fischer–Larsen

This diagram has appeared in many chess magazines. Black is in some difficulty because of his exposed king. He can castle neither short nor long (the latter owing to QxRP). And if 16 ... N-B3, White naturally avoids 17 QxNP? 0-0-0 and plays 17 B-R5ch K-Q1 18 QxNP. In any case, Black is faced by the very unpleasant threat of 17 B-R5ch.

16 ...	**N-N3**

17 B-R5	**K-B2**
18 P-B4	**KR-K1**

There is no time to defend Q4, e.g. 18 ... B-B3? 19 P-B5 PxP 20 R-K7ch QxR 21 BxQ KxB 22 QxNPch winning.

19 P-B5	**PxP**
20 QxQPch	**K-B3**

Perhaps it was only at this point that Larsen realized that 20 ... B-K3 loses to 21 RxB! RxR 22 QxBPch R-KB3 23 Q-Q5ch R-K3 24 R-KB1ch.

21 B-B3	

It is strange that White has no direct way of winning and has to be satisfied with this fairly modest move. If, for example, he tries 21 B-Q6 there follows 21 ... Q-N3ch 22 B-B5 Q-B3 23 Q-Q4ch K-N4 24 B-B3 Q-B2, and he has no decisive attacking continuation, while after 21 P-N4 Black can reply 21 ... N-K4! 22 BxR RxB.

21 ...	**N-K4?**

This losing move was considered by some commentators to be the best practical chance. Larsen sets his hopes on a sharp counter-attack, which, however, is refuted by a fine tactical finesse. It is true that before the text-move Black's position was rather uncomfortable, but whether it was already lost is an open question. Black should have continued quietly with 21 ... B-B3, allowing his opponent to recover his pawn with check, viz. 22 Q-Q4ch K-B2 23 QxBPch K-B3. Or he could have played 21 ... B-K3. In either case, White would have had a difficult job to strengthen his attack, whereas in the game he gains a material advantage by force.

22 Q-Q4!	

The main threat is 23 B-Q6 Q-R4 24 BxNch, winning a piece, though White is also threatening 23 Q-R4ch. Larsen was prepared for White's move, to which he replies with a sacrifice that looks as if it offers him some chances.

22 ...	K-N3!?
23 RxN!	QxR

Of course, not 23 ... RxR? 24 B-Q6, etc.

24 QxB	QR-Q1
25 QxQNP	Q-K6ch

After 25 ... QxBP the continuation 26 Q-N1 R-Q7 27 B-B5 is adequate, whereas 26 Q-B6ch? K-N4 would be quite wrong.

26 K-B1	R-Q7
27 Q-B6ch	R-K3

168. Fischer–Larsen

In working out the line he had chosen Larsen had seen 28 Q-B5? R-B7ch 29 K-N1 RxBdis ch, winning, which would have been a fine start to the fulfilment of the claim he had made before the match ("I am going to be the challenger to world champion Spasski, and I'm not afraid of Fischer"). But the next move, which Fischer had seen several moves previously, put an end to his dreams.

28 B-B5!	R-B7ch

Winning the queen, but at too high a price. However, 28 ... Q-K4 29 B-Q4 is even worse.

29 K-N1	RxNPdbl ch
30 KxR	Q-Q7ch

31 K-R1	RxQ
32 BxR	QxP(B6)

This eases White's task, as it gives him a passed pawn. A better continuation is 32 ... P-QR4, although even in this case White's superiority after 33 R-KN1ch K-B2 (33 ... K-R3 34 B-B8) 34 B-Q4 P-N3 35 B-Q5ch followed by BxP is sufficient to win. An important factor is that White's king, unlike Black's, is quite safe.

33 R-KN1ch	K-B3
34 BxP	P-B5
35 B-N6	QxP
36 P-R5	

A pretty example of the co-operation of pieces and pawns. Both bishops support the passed pawn in its march forward, while the rook holds Black's passed pawns.

36 ...	Q-QN7
37 B-Q8ch	K-K3
38 P-R6	Q-R6
39 B-N7	Q-B4

Otherwise White's bishop returns to QN6.

40 R-QN1!	P-QB6
41 B-N6	

Black resigned after the adjournment.

Larsen is a do-or-die player who often suffers defeats but who has the ability to overcome their psychological effects. This time, however, it was to be different. His hopes had been set too high and the way he lost had been too humiliating. In the second game he inexplicably failed to hold a drawn endgame, and in the third he was in a hopeless position after a mere fifteen moves—and that in a system of the Sicilian he could almost certainly have expected. Of the other three games he had drawing chances in only two at the most.

Whereas Fischer disposed of both opponents in an almost unbelievable manner, the ex-world-champion Petrosian played rather modestly. He defeated his first opponent Hübner in a match that gave rise to quite a heated discussion. Following six drawn games, Petrosian won the seventh after coming out of the opening in an almost lost position. His opponent thereupon resigned the match and protested at the unacceptable playing conditions in the tournament room in Seville.

In his match with Korchnoi, Petrosian again only succeeded in winning one game—the ninth—but that was enough for victory, for the others were all drawn.

Expressed mathematically in terms of wins the relationship was thus 12:2 in Fischer's favour. However, they were not competing in a tournament but in a match, where such mathematical relationships do not apply.

The first game was won, on 30 September, by Fischer, his nineteenth win in succession. In the opening his opponent came out with an innovation, but Fischer then transposed into an endgame in which Petrosian failed to find the best defence. The second round brought a surprise. In his favourite opening—Grünfeld-Indian—Fischer was in a lost position after only twenty moves and resigned twelve moves later. The great question was: Would this mean the psychological turning-point for Fischer? At any rate his run of wins had been broken.

The next three games were drawn although Fischer had White in two of them. Petrosian even had winning chances in the third game. In the sixth game Petrosian had White. Would he attempt to seize the initiative? Those who expected such a course must have been very disappointed. The decisive game of the whole Candidates' Tournament was one of those psychological mysteries that keep cropping up in chess and which give the game an irrational element.

Nimzowitsch Attack

Petrosian	Fischer
1 N-KB3	P-QB4
2 P-QN3	P-Q4
3 B-N2?	

Nimzowitsch knew why 3 P-K3 should precede B-N2. Every book on theory has a note such as: 3 B-N2? is bad on account of 3 . . . P-B3 followed by P-K4. And that is certainly true.

3 . . .	P-B3!
4 P-B4	

It is interesting to compare the first few moves with a rarely played opening, in which the colours are reversed, viz. 1 P-Q4 N-KB3 2 P-QB4 P-QN3 3 N-QB3 B-N2 4 P-B3 P-Q4 5 PxP NxP 6 P-K4 NxN 7 PxN. In this, Black was able to play 4 . . . P-Q4 and then exchange knights, going into a form of the Grünfeld. In the present game White cannot do the same, for Black's knight has not been developed. If he tries 4 P-Q4 PxP 5 NxP P-K4 he gets the worst of it. So instead he must look for other ways of attacking his opponent's centre.

4 . . .	P-Q5
5 P-Q3	P-K4
6 P-K3	N-K2!

A good manoeuvre. Black intends to post his king's knight on QB3 and his queen's knight on Q2. He has, of course, to be prepared for White's pieces getting active on the queen's wing by 7 PxP BPxP 8 P-QN4, but he has a good counter in 8 . . . P-QR4 9 P-QN5 N-Q2 10 P-N3 P-QN3 11 B-N2 B-N2 12 B-QR3 N-N3 13 BxB N(N3)xB followed by N-K3 or 9 P-QR3 PxP 10 PxP RxR 11 BxR KN-B3 12 P-N5 B-N5ch 13 QN-Q2 N-K2, in both cases with control of the strategically important square QB4.

| 7 B-K2? | |

Petrosian's tactics after his success in the second game are to goad his spirited opponent into impatience by a series of draws. These are actually very wise tactics and probably his only chance. But in putting them into effect he goes astray. It just cannot be right for him when playing with White to present Fischer with the initiative and confine himself to passive defence. A better line was 7 PxP followed by 8 P-N3, after which his queen's bishop is, admittedly, by no means well placed. The disadvantage this entails is, however, bearable.

7 ...	KN-B3
8 QN-Q2	B-K2
9 0-0	0-0
10 P-K4	

As the bishop is passive on K2, opening the centre by PxP would no longer be good. One might well ask why White did not play 6 P-K4 at once. Now he has lost a tempo in an Old Indian set-up, and in addition his queen's bishop is badly placed.

10 ...	P-QR3
11 N-K1	P-QN4
12 B-N4	BxB
13 QxB	Q-B1!

A positional manoeuvre typical of the American. He does not necessarily want to exploit his space advantage in the middle-game, but would be content to

169. Petrosian–Fischer

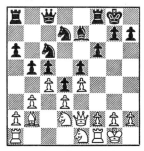

Position after Black's 14th move

transpose into an endgame. As he has the initiative on the queen's wing, he could, after an exchange of queens, quietly strengthen his position by N-Q2, N-N3 and PxP without having to fear a counterattack on the king's wing.

| 14 Q-K2 | N-Q2 |
| 15 N-B2? | |

Petrosian loses this game, and consequently the match, because he plays completely planlessly. He should have started operating on the king's side, and that called for 15 P-N3 followed by P-KB4. There is nothing to be achieved on the queen's wing.

15 ...	R-N1
16 KR-B1	Q-K1
17 B-R3?	B-Q3
18 N-K1	P-N3

Black is not subjected to any threats and can safely start operations on the opposite wing. He now prepares P-KB4. White's position is still fairly sound and he could continue with 19 P-N3 followed by N-N2. Instead he chooses to open up the game on the queen's wing, which is strategically wrong, for his pieces are less well posted than his opponent's.

19 PxP?	PxP
20 B-N2	N-N3
21 N(K1)-B3	R-R1
22 P-QR3	N-R4
23 Q-Q1	Q-B2
24 P-QR4?	PxP
25 PxP	P-B5!
26 PxP	N(N3)xP
27 NxN	NxN
28 Q-K2	NxB
29 QxN	KR-N1

It is now apparent that White's action has failed. A protected passed pawn is stronger than an unprotected one, and Black's rooks can operate effectively on the QR and QN files.

30 Q-R2

An endgame is not good for White, but it is difficult to find another move. 30 Q-K2 is answered by 30 ... B-N5 followed by B-B6, after which White loses his QRP.

30 ...	**B-N5!**
31 QxQch	**KxQ**
32 R-B7ch	**K-K3!**

This had to be seen two moves in advance. White has no time to capture the KRP, e.g. 33 RxP B-B6 34 R-Q1 RxP 35 P-R4 R-R7 36 P-N4 R(N1)-N7 37 R-KB1 R-K7 or 34 R-KB1 RxP 35 N-R4 P-Q6 36 P-B3 P-Q7 followed by R-R8.

33 P-N4	**B-B6**
34 R-R2	

170. Petrosian–Fischer

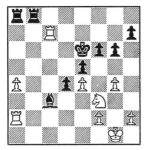

The first critical stage of this endgame. Black could now have won by 34 ... R-N5! e.g. 35 R-B6ch K-Q2! 36 RxP P-Q6, etc.

34 ...	**R-QB1?**

After the game this move had a great deal of praise heaped on it. In my opinion, however, it throws away the win. White must, it is true, again refrain from capturing the KRP, though the ensuing variations are admittedly quite complicated, e.g. 35 RxP? R-B5 36 R-QN7 R(R1)xP 37 RxR RxR 38 R-N6ch K-Q2! 39 RxP P-Q6 40 RxP RxP followed by R-K7 or 39 P-N5 P-Q6! 40 PxP R-R8ch 41 K-N2 P-Q7 42 R-N7ch

K-K1 43 P-B7ch K-B1 44 N-N5 R-KN8ch! By exchanging rooks, however, he can obtain good drawing chances.

35 RxR!	**RxR**
36 P-R5	**R-QR1**
37 P-R6	**R-R2**
38 K-B1	

At the moment the advance 38 P-N5 is not good on account of the reply 38 ... P-B4, but it would be strong if Black's king were to leave its central position in order to go after the QRP.

38 ...	**P-N4**

But Black stops it once and for all, after which he can proceed to win the QRP. The game, however, is by no means over.

39 K-K2	**K-Q3**
40 K-Q3	**K-B4** ·
41 N-N1	**K-N4**

171. Petrosian–Fischer

And here we have the second critical position. It is obvious that Black must win the QRP without allowing an exchange of rooks, for an endgame bishop versus knight would be dead drawn in spite of the extra pawn. Black has two ways of proceeding, the first B-R4 followed by R(or K)xP, the second K-N5-N6, driving the rook away. In view of this White ought to have sought counter-play, which he could have had with the surprising 42 P-B4!!, which gives rise to the following possibilities:

(i) 42 ... KPxP 43 N-B3 RxP (43 ...

K-N5 44 NxQP? BxN 45 KxB leads to the pretty mate R-Q2, but White has a stronger line in 44 P-R4!, e.g. 44 ... P-R3 45 RPxP RPxP 46 P-K5 or 44 ... K-N6 45 R-KR2 and the game is drawn) 44 RxR KxR 45 P-K5! PxP 46 NxKP K-N4 47 N-B7 with equality.

(ii) 42 ... NPxP 43 N-B3 RxP 44 RxR KxR 45 P-N5 PxP 46 NxNP B-R4 (46 ... B-N5 47 N-B7) 47 NxP B-Q1 48 N-B8 K-N4 49 N-Q7 B-B2 50 P-R4 K-B3 51 N-B6 B-Q1 52 N-N4 K-Q3 53 P-R5 K-K3 54 K-K2 with equality, or 43 ... B-R4 44 P-N5 B-Q1 45 P-R4! RxP 46 RxR KxR 47 P-R5! PxP 48 NxKP K-N4 49 N-B3 P-N5 50 NxPch K-N3 51 P-K5 with equality, or 43 ... K-N5 44 P-N5 PxP (44 ... K-N6 45 R-KN2) 45 NxKP K-N6 46 N-B6 R-R1 47 R-KN2 RxP 48 NxPch BxN 49 KxB and Black cannot win.

Petrosian would certainly have found this hidden chance if he could have made his 42nd move after the adjournment. As it was he had to seal it, so it is no wonder that he made a natural, and losing, move.

42	N-K2?	B-R4
43	R-N2ch	KxP
44	R-N1	R-QB2
45	R-N2	B-K8
46	P-B3	

This eases Black's task a little. After 46 R-N1, Black could not have taken the pawn (46 R-N1 BxP? 47 R-KB1 followed by RxPch drawing), so the bishop would have had to retreat and Black would have had a harder job to strengthen the position of his king. He would have had to resort to the manoeuvre B-N3 followed by K-N2.

| 46 | ... | K-R4! |
| 47 | R-B2 | |

Otherwise 47 ... B-N5 followed by K-N4 with the threat of R-R2.

47	...	R-QN2
48	R-R2ch	K-N4
49	R-N2ch	B-N5
50	R-R2	R-QB2

| 51 | R-R1 | R-B1 |
| 52 | R-R7? | |

This attempt to get play only speeds up defeat. White should have embarked on active measures much earlier. The waiting move 52 R-R2, however, does not save the game, e.g. 52 ... B-B5 53 R-R1 K-B3 54 K-B4 B-N3 55 K-Q3 K-N2 followed by R-B4, and Black's rook gets into White's position via the QN or QR file.

| 52 | ... | B-R4! |
| 53 | R-Q7 | |

Or 53 RxP B-N3 followed by R-QR1.

53	...	B-N3
54	R-Q5ch	B-B4
55	N-B1	K-R5!
56	R-Q7	B-N5
57	N-K2	K-N6
58	R-QN7	

Otherwise 58 ... R-B7 wins at once.

58	...	R-QR1
59	RxP	R-R8
60	NxP	PxN
61	KxP	R-Q8ch
62	K-K3	B-B4ch
63	K-K2	R-KR8
64	P-R4	

The last hope: 64 ... RxP? 65 RxR PxR 66 P-B4 drawn.

64	...	K-B5!
65	P-R5	R-R7ch
66	K-K1	K-Q6
Resigns		

This defeat broke down Petrosian's resistance. In the next game he failed to hold an ending in which he had the slightly worse position. He also lost the eighth game after giving a very colourless performance. And he did not even manage to save the ninth, from a symmetrical position. But by then the fight was virtually over.

Fischer was thus very close to his goal.

In chess ability alone he had no equal and it seemed unlikely that Spasski's well-known sporting qualities—his will to fight, his staying power and his calmness—would cause the precise, machine-like play of Fischer any real trouble.

Whether Bobby would win the world championship in 1972 or at a later date, one thing was certain. He had opened up a new era in the development of chess, just as Morphy and Capablanca had done in their time.

51 World Championship 1972

World Champion of the 1970s

Straight wins in the last seven games of the 1970 Interzonal, a clean score of 6:0 against Taimanov, a similar crushing 6:0 victory against his great rival Larsen, then a 6½:2½ result against Petrosian in a match where the latter's much stiffer resistance had to be broken down—that was Fischer's glorious path to the 1972 world championship title match.

In the spring of 1972 the chess world was buzzing with excitement. For the first time since the war the world championship was not to be decided by Soviet grandmasters alone. As a result a chess event was transferred to the sphere of politics because it echoed the rivalry of the two mightiest countries on our planet. The present century has become so crazy that not only space flight but also sporting or chess events are treated by one or the other of the great powers as matters of the utmost importance.

Most of the pundits naturally favoured Fischer, though there were not surprisingly some who thought Spasski had good chances. The former world champion Botvinnik, for example, unequivocally tipped Spasski to win, maintaining that Fischer's previous successes were by no means convincing proof of his superiority. That, however, was probably wishful thinking, for Spasski had not been playing particularly well, as witness his failure in the Alekhin Memorial Tournament in the autumn of 1971.

In an article from a series that appeared in *Schach-Echo* in the spring of 1972 I voiced the following opinion: Fischer is very much superior to all his opponents and will certainly become world champion if he does not fall victim to the only opponent who can endanger him. That single dangerous opponent is called Bobby Fischer.

Those words almost proved prophetic. The match in Reykjavik had a sensational prelude and a dramatic first act, with the result that the whole chess world was kept in breathless excitement. The story has been told so fully—though not always accurately—and is so recent that it hardly needs retelling. To recapitulate, however, Fischer began by adopting the risky ploy of demanding that the already fantastically high purse for both winner and loser should be raised by an enormous amount. This was risky because it could well have jeopardized all his chances of becoming world champion. That it worked wonderfully was due to the fact that there was in London one of those strange people who are prepared to spend any amount of money on their hobby and at the same time to expose themselves to the possibility of ridicule from the rest of the world and even to open themselves to the suspicion of acting in such a way simply to gain popularity.

Contrary to the rules, the match in Reykjavik began on 11 July, that is nine days late. The reigning world champion had White in the first game, but treated the opening so placidly that the contestants would have been justified in agreeing to a draw after about fifteen moves. Each game, however, was being played for more than ten thousand dollars, and it is possible that professional honour forbade the acceptance of such a high sum for so little work. At any rate the game continued, and the following position was reached after the 28th move.

172. Spasski–Fischer

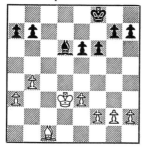

Position after Black's 28th move

29 P-N5!

This prevents White from slipping into an inferior position, which is what would happen if Black were allowed to play P-QN4, locking the White pawn on squares of the same colour as the bishops. The text-move involves a minor combination, though it is no great problem for a strong amateur, let along a grandmaster, to see that 29 ... BxKRP loses the bishop.

29 ...   BxKRP?

Black nevertheless takes the pawn, a course which, while not quite losing, is completely inexplicable. The following can really only be answered by Fischer himself, who, however, is not in the habit of answering such questions:

(i) Did Black fail to see that the bishop could not be freed by the advance of the KRP? It is almost inconceivable; and yet over the years chess has produced other cases of the famous "chess blindness". Such an error is perhaps understandable in view of the tactical twist mentioned in the note to Black's 32nd move.

(ii) Did Black sacrifice his bishop in the hope of getting two pawns and an active king-side position as compensation? Did Fischer even believe that he would thereby have winning chances? This explanation sounds more likely, for Fischer tends to over-estimate his chances and under-estimate his opponent.

(iii) Was Fischer, thinking that the position was still a dead draw after the loss of the bishop, simply playing to the gallery? It is possible, though irresponsible.

30 P-N3	P-KR4
31 K-K2	P-R5
32 K-B3!	K-K2

The bishop cannot be saved by 32 ... P-R6, e.g. 33 K-N4 B-N8 34 KxP BxP 35 B-Q2! followed by 36 K-N2, and White has reached a position better than the one in the game, for the bishop on Q2 means a gain of a valuable tempo.

33 K-N2	PxP
34 PxP	BxP
35 KxB	K-Q3
36 P-R4	

After 36 P-K4 K-B4 37 B-K3ch KxP 38 BxP P-KN3 followed by P-K4 and P-B4 the game is drawn, for White only retains his QRP, which in conjunction with the black-squared bishop is insufficient to win.

36 ...   K-Q4

Now 36 ... K-B4 would be bad on account of 37 B-R3ch, e.g. 37 ... K-B5 38 B-B8 P-KN3 39 B-K7 P-B4 40 K-B4 winning.

37 B-R3   K-K5?

In normal positions such moves are made automatically. Where the position is not normal, however, every move requires special thought, which is the case here. The king ought to remain near the queen's wing until the pawn structure there has been fixed. The correct move is therefore 37 ... P-R3!, which leads to a draw, for after 38 P-N6 K-B3 39 P-R5 K-Q4, Black can sacrifice all his king-side pawns to get rid of White's KP and then play his king to QB1 or QR1, from where it cannot be dislodged. That White cannot win in spite of his material superiority of a whole piece can be seen by setting up the following position: White K on Q5, B on K5, pawns on QR5 and QN6, Black K on QB1, pawns on QR3 and QN2. This position is a dead draw. If, however, White's QRP were on QR4 instead of QR5, it would be an easy win. White simply gets the enemy king into a *zugzwang* position, thus forcing Black to play P-QR4. This pawn can then be won by the bishop.

Returning to the move 37 ... P-R3! an examination of White's alternative replies shows that there is no win in the position, e.g. 38 PxP PxP or 38 B-B8 PxP 39 PxP K-K5 40 BxP (40 K-B2 P-B4 41 BxP P-K4 followed by P-B5) 40 ... KxP 41 BxP P-N3 42 B-Q8 K-Q6 43 BxP K-B5.

38 B-B5   P-R3

Of course, not 38 ... P-QN3? because of 39 BxP PxB 40 P-R5 K-Q4 41 P-R6 winning.

39 P-N6!

Now White has a won game. His plan is to get in among Black's king-side pawns with his king, winning at least one of them. Then he can transfer his king to QB7. To achieve his ends he will force his opponent into *zugzwang*. For that reason he must not play P-QR5.

39 ...   P-B4

Other defences are:
(i) 39 ... K-Q4 40 B-B8 P-N3 41 B-K7 P-B4 42 K-B4 or 41 ... K-K4 42 K-N4, etc.
(ii) 39 ... P-K4 40 K-N4 P-N3 41 K-N3! P-B4 42 K-R4 P-B5 43 PxP KxP (43 ... PxP 44 K-N5) 44 B-K7! P-K5 45 B-N5ch K-B6 46 B-B1! P-K6 47 K-N5 P-K7 48 B-Q2 K-B7 49 KxP or 45 ... K-B4 46 B-Q2.

40 K-R4   P-B5

After the game a widely held view was that Black could have saved the game by

40 ... K-Q4. This is incorrect, e.g. 41 B-N4! (not, however, 41 B-R3? K-B3 42 B-N2 KxP 43 BxP K-B4 44 K-N5 K-Q4 45 K-B4 P-N4 46 P-R5 P-N5 47 B-N2 K-B5 48 K-K5 K-Q6 49 KxKP KxP draw) 41 ... K-B3 42 B-R5! K-B4 43 K-N5 K-B5 44 K-N6 K-Q6 45 KxNP KxP 46 K-B6 or 41 ... K-K5 42 B-Q2 K-Q6 43 B-B1 K-B7 44 B-R3 K-N6 45 B-B8 KxP 46 BxP K-N4 47 K-N5, etc.

41 PxP

The sealed move, which Spasski made before the end of the session, so that the time remaining was added to his clock. This left him with only fifteen minutes for his next twenty-five moves. In spite of this handicap, however, the win was no great problem, for Black was soon forced into *zugzwang* and had to give way to his opponent's king.

41 ...	KxP
42 K-R5	K-B4
43 B-K3	K-K5

Or 43 ... P-N3ch 44 K-R6 K-B3 45 B-Q2 K-B4 46 B-N5 P-K4 47 B-Q2 K-B3 48 B-K3 K-B4 49 B-N5, etc.

44 B-B2	K-B4
45 B-R4!	P-K4
46 B-N5	

Black has only one more move with his KP, after which he will be virtually in *zugzwang*.

46 ...	P-K5
47 B-K3	K-B3
48 K-N4!	K-K4
49 K-N5	K-Q4
50 K-B4	P-R4
51 B-B2	P-N4
52 KxNP	K-B5
53 K-B5	K-N5
54 KxP	KxP
55 K-Q5	K-N4
56 K-Q6	**Resigns**

The next game was due to be played on 13 July. Fischer protested about the television cameras, and because of his lack of success in carrying his point with the organizers he did not show up for the second game. At 5 p.m. his clock was started and one hour later Spasski was declared the winner of the second game. The American protested, but it did not change the result, so that Spasski was in the lead by 2:0. Moreover, the latter had the advantage of only having to tie the match, which meant that, mathematically, he was really 2½ points ahead. Fischer's most dangerous opponent had thus done his work. Spasski was given a chance he could hardly even have dreamed of.

Would Fischer break off the match? Apparently there was some danger of this, but then President Nixon's foreign-policy adviser is supposed to have phoned him, saying that such a step would be harmful to the interests of the United States. Whatever it was, something happened that gave the world new hope that the great chess battle would be continued.

The third game took place as planned, though not in the tournament hall but in another room. According to eye-witnesses Fischer looked tired and haggard. The great question was: Would he stand up to the mental strain? Spasski was certainly of the opinion that his great moment had come and that he must act energetically to finish off his opponent once and for all. It was like a boxing match. The opponent was groggy and the time had come to deliver the *coup de grâce*.

Was this calculation correct? No, it was not. It was a terrible miscalculation on the part of Spasski and probably also on the part of his advisers. With the score at 2:0 in his favour Spasski was still in the match with a chance—albeit a small one—but to make use of it he needed to choose super-safe openings and aim at simplification and a draw in every game. That

would have been the best way of upsetting his ambitious but somewhat unstable opponent and of making up for the distinct difference in pure chess ability. When, however, Spasski instead chose a sharp opening in the third game and one, moreover, that belonged to Fischer's specialities—the American pulled himself together and produced a great game. That virtually decided the match, the remaining games going as was to have been expected. They merely showed up the difference in playing strength of the two players. Spasski was not given another chance. "The damage done in one second cannot be made good in a life-time."

In the normal course of events there is not another player with a chance against Fischer. And now that he has the title there is no reason why he should not play his normal game. The world champion of the 1970s is therefore Robert James Fischer.

Benoni Defence: Hromádka System

	Spasski	Fischer
1	P-Q4	N-KB3
2	P-QB4	P-K3
3	N-KB3	P-B4
4	P-Q5	PxP
5	PxP	P-Q3
6	N-QB3	P-KN3
7	N-Q2	QN-Q2
8	P-K4	B-N2
9	B-K2	0-0
10	0-0	R-K1

This position from the Hromádka System is usually reached by the sequence 1 P-Q4 N-KB3 2 P-QB4 P-B4 3 P-Q5 P-K3 4 N-QB3 PxP 5 PxP P-Q3 6 P-K4 P-KN3 7 N-B3 B-N2 8 B-K2 0-0 9 0-0 R-K1 10 N-Q2 QN-Q2. From the theoretical point of view it is worth while making a few comments on the order of the moves played.

(i) In the normal Hromádka System the set-up 7 P-B4 B-N2 8 B-N5ch is quite

173. Spasski–Fischer

Position after Black's 10th move

dangerous for Black. In the present game, of course, it is not possible.

(ii) On move 7 of the variation occurring in the game, Black usually plays 7 ... B-N2, which allows him the choice of developing his knight on QR3 or Q2. He need not fear 8 N-B4 0-0 9 B-B4 N-K1 10 N-N5 P-N3!, for he can adequately counter the threat to his QP.

(iii) After 7 ... QN-Q2 White can attain an advantage by 8 N-B4 N-N3 9 P-K4! NxN 10 BxN. For that reason I consider 7 ... B-N2 to be more accurate.

A more important factor for a general assessment of the whole opening system is that it leads to a strategically and tactically complicated game. Black has many ways of seizing the initiative and is by no means confined to passive defence. Fischer understands the system better than anyone else and is more familiar with the position arising from it than Spasski. The choice of opening was therefore a mistake for the defending world champion. With a lead of 2:0 he ought to have adopted a quieter set-up, such as 4 P-K3, which would have been much more unpleasant for his opponent.

11 Q-B2?

An innovation, though an unfortunate one. The usual continuation is 11 P-QR4 (preventing the advance P-QN4!) 11 ... N-K4 12 Q-B2, which could be met by 12 ... P-KN4!?, an interesting though risky

move introduced by Fischer.

11 ...   N-R4!

This manoeuvre occurs in several variations of the King's Indian. It is true that Black's pawns can now be weakened considerably, but to achieve this White has to give up a bishop and at the same time allow his opponent's pieces to gain in activity.

12 BxN(?)

Black was threatening N-B5 as well as Q-R5, and 12 N-B4 could have been answered by 12 ... N-K4, after which 13 N-K3 is not good on account of 13 ... N-KB5. Nevertheless, taking the bishop is suspect. White ought to have played 12 P-B4, which, though it does not look good, would have prevented him from slipping into a bad game despite his weak eleventh move. If play had then continued 12 ... B-Q5ch (12 ... Q-R5? 13 N-B3) 13 K-R1 Q-R5, White would have had the reply 14 R-B3!, after which Black has nothing better than 14 ... Q-K8ch 15 R-B1 Q-R5 with repetition of moves, for if 14 ... N(Q2)-B3, there follows 15 P-KN3, which is good for White. This concealed twist would have been unwelcome to Fischer, who, it is safe to assume, would not have been happy with a draw.

12 ...	PxB
13 N-B4	N-K4
14 N-K3	Q-R5
15 B-Q2?	

This move shows that Spasski has under-estimated the dangers facing him. The correct continuation is 15 P-B3!, after which his pawns remain intact and mobile. Black would admittedly be actively placed, though he would not find it easy to strengthen his position.

The seemingly active 15 P-B4 would, on the other hand, be weak, because of 15 ... N-N5 16 P-KR3? NxN 17 BxN BxP!, winning for Black, while the immediate 15 P-KR3, to be followed by P-KB4, is answered by the dangerous piece sacrifice 15 . . . BxP! 16 PxB QxRP; e.g. 17 P-B4 N-B6ch 18 K-B2 N-R5 19 K-K1 P-B4 or 18 RxN QxR 19 Q-N2 QxQch 20 KxQ BxN followed by RxP.

15 . . .	N-N5!
16 NxN	

This undoubling of Black's pawns is forced, because, after 16 P-KR3 NxN 17 BxN, Black wins a pawn by BxN followed by QxKP. Now, however, Black's pawn structure is in order again and White's majority in the centre will be hindered by Black's KNP.

16 . . .	PxN
17 B-B4	Q-B3!

The move 17 . . . B-K4 is not so strong as it looks because of 18 BxB RxB 19 P-B4! with advantage to White! Fischer finds the right plan: pressure against the KP.

18 P-KN3

White's desire to maintain the bishop on its active post means compromising his king-side pawn majority. On the other hand, 18 B-N3 could have been answered

174. Spasski–Fischer

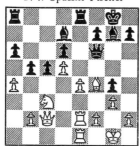

Position after White's 22nd move

by 18 . . . B-Q2 followed by P-KR4, after which Black again has the better chances.

18 . . .	B-Q2
19 P-QR4	P-N3

20 KR-K1	P-QR3
21 R-K2	P-N4
22 QR-K1	

Now White has his first threat in the game—the breakthrough P-K5, which, if successful, would be a great achievement. Unfortunately for him, the threat is easily countered.

22 . . .	Q-N3!
23 P-N3	

Otherwise Black pushes on his queen-side pawns by P-QB5 and P-QN5.

23 . . .	R-K2
24 Q-Q3	R-N1
25 PxP	PxP

Black now has a strong threat on the queen's wing: 26 . . . P-B5! 27 PxP PxP 28 Q-B2 (28 QxP R-QB1) 28 . . . R-N6, etc. White finds a counter to it, but only at the cost of conceding a protected passed pawn.

26 P-N4	P-B5!

Of course, not 26 . . . PxP? 27 N-R2 followed by NxP, when the knight goes to QB6.

27 Q-Q2	R(N1)-K1
28 R-K3	P-R4
29 R(K3)-K2	

White has no way of improving his position and is condemned to waiting for his opponent to act. Fischer now decides to repeat a few moves to gain time to solve a vital question, viz: Will the game be won if he captures the KP by BxN followed by RxKP, or will White have drawing chances thanks to the unlike bishops.

29 . . .	K-R2
30 R-K3	K-N1
31 R(K1)-K2	BxN!
32 QxB	RxP
33 RxR	RxR
34 RxR	QxR
35 B-R6	

White's second threat in the game, and this time quite a strong one, though again it can be easily countered. Now that the KP has fallen Black has a won game, for White's king is no less exposed than Black's.

Black was threatening 41 ... Q-KB6ch 42 K-K1 Q-R8ch 43 K-K2 B-Q6ch 44 K-K3 Q-K5mate, and 41 Q-N5ch B-N3 does not save the game. Now, however, it is all over.

35 ...	Q-N3
36 B-B1	Q-N8
37 K-B1	B-B4
38 K-K2	Q-K5ch
39 Q-K3	Q-B7ch
40 Q-Q2	Q-N6
41 Q-Q4	

41 ...	B-Q6ch
Resigns	

If 42 K-K3, Black plays 42 ... Q-Q8 with the double threat of Q-B6ch and QxBch.

Index of Games and Positions

Index of Openings

A CATALOG OF SELECTED
DOVER BOOKS
IN ALL FIELDS OF INTEREST

A CATALOG OF SELECTED DOVER
BOOKS IN ALL FIELDS OF INTEREST

CONCERNING THE SPIRITUAL IN ART, Wassily Kandinsky. Pioneering work by father of abstract art. Thoughts on color theory, nature of art. Analysis of earlier masters. 12 illustrations. 80pp. of text. 5⅜ × 8½.   23411-8 Pa. $3.95

ANIMALS: 1,419 Copyright-Free Illustrations of Mammals, Birds, Fish, Insects, etc., Jim Harter (ed.). Clear wood engravings present, in extremely lifelike poses, over 1,000 species of animals. One of the most extensive pictorial sourcebooks of its kind. Captions. Index. 284pp. 9 × 12.   23766-4 Pa. $11.95

CELTIC ART: The Methods of Construction, George Bain. Simple geometric techniques for making Celtic interlacements, spirals, Kells-type initials, animals, humans, etc. Over 500 illustrations. 160pp. 9 × 12. (USO)   22923-8 Pa. $9.95

AN ATLAS OF ANATOMY FOR ARTISTS, Fritz Schider. Most thorough reference work on art anatomy in the world. Hundreds of illustrations, including selections from works by Vesalius, Leonardo, Goya, Ingres, Michelangelo, others. 593 illustrations. 192pp. 7⅛ × 10¼.   20241-0 Pa. $8.95

CELTIC HAND STROKE-BY-STROKE (Irish Half-Uncial from "The Book of Kells"): An Arthur Baker Calligraphy Manual, Arthur Baker. Complete guide to creating each letter of the alphabet in distinctive Celtic manner. Covers hand position, strokes, pens, inks, paper, more. Illustrated. 48pp. 8¼ × 11.
          24336-2 Pa. $3.95

EASY ORIGAMI, John Montroll. Charming collection of 32 projects (hat, cup, pelican, piano, swan, many more) specially designed for the novice origami hobbyist. Clearly illustrated easy-to-follow instructions insure that even beginning papercrafters will achieve successful results. 48pp. 8¼ × 11.   27298-2 Pa. $2.95

THE COMPLETE BOOK OF BIRDHOUSE CONSTRUCTION FOR WOOD-WORKERS, Scott D. Campbell. Detailed instructions, illustrations, tables. Also data on bird habitat and instinct patterns. Bibliography. 3 tables. 63 illustrations in 15 figures. 48pp. 5¼ × 8½.   24407-5 Pa. $1.95

BLOOMINGDALE'S ILLUSTRATED 1886 CATALOG: Fashions, Dry Goods and Housewares, Bloomingdale Brothers. Famed merchants' extremely rare catalog depicting about 1,700 products: clothing, housewares, firearms, dry goods, jewelry, more. Invaluable for dating, identifying vintage items. Also, copyright-free graphics for artists, designers. Co-published with Henry Ford Museum & Green-field Village. 160pp. 8¼ × 11.   25780-0 Pa. $9.95

HISTORIC COSTUME IN PICTURES, Braun & Schneider. Over 1,450 costumed figures in clearly detailed engravings—from dawn of civilization to end of 19th century. Captions. Many folk costumes. 256pp. 8⅜ × 11¾.   23150-X Pa. $11.95

STICKLEY CRAFTSMAN FURNITURE CATALOGS, Gustav Stickley and L. & J. G. Stickley. Beautiful, functional furniture in two authentic catalogs from 1910. 594 illustrations, including 277 photos, show settles, rockers, armchairs, reclining chairs, bookcases, desks, tables. 183pp. 6½ × 9¼.   23838-5 Pa. $8.95

AMERICAN LOCOMOTIVES IN HISTORIC PHOTOGRAPHS: 1858 to 1949, Ron Ziel (ed.). A rare collection of 126 meticulously detailed official photographs, called "builder portraits," of American locomotives that majestically chronicle the rise of steam locomotive power in America. Introduction. Detailed captions. xi + 129pp. 9 × 12.   27393-8 Pa. $12.95

AMERICA'S LIGHTHOUSES: An Illustrated History, Francis Ross Holland, Jr. Delightfully written, profusely illustrated fact-filled survey of over 200 American lighthouses since 1716. History, anecdotes, technological advances, more. 240pp. 8 × 10¾.   25576-X Pa. $11.95

TOWARDS A NEW ARCHITECTURE, Le Corbusier. Pioneering manifesto by founder of "International School." Technical and aesthetic theories, views of industry, economics, relation of form to function, "mass-production split" and much more. Profusely illustrated. 320pp. 6⅛ × 9¼. (USO)   25023-7 Pa. $8.95

HOW THE OTHER HALF LIVES, Jacob Riis. Famous journalistic record, exposing poverty and degradation of New York slums around 1900, by major social reformer. 100 striking and influential photographs. 233pp. 10 × 7⅞.

22012-5 Pa $10.95

FRUIT KEY AND TWIG KEY TO TREES AND SHRUBS, William M. Harlow. One of the handiest and most widely used identification aids. Fruit key covers 120 deciduous and evergreen species; twig key 160 deciduous species. Easily used. Over 300 photographs. 126pp. 5⅜ × 8½.   20511-8 Pa. $3.95

COMMON BIRD SONGS, Dr. Donald J. Borror. Songs of 60 most common U.S. birds: robins, sparrows, cardinals, bluejays, finches, more—arranged in order of increasing complexity. Up to 9 variations of songs of each species.

Cassette and manual 99911-4 $8.95

ORCHIDS AS HOUSE PLANTS, Rebecca Tyson Northen. Grow cattleyas and many other kinds of orchids—in a window, in a case, or under artificial light. 63 illustrations. 148pp. 5⅜ × 8½.   23261-1 Pa. $3.95

MONSTER MAZES, Dave Phillips. Masterful mazes at four levels of difficulty. Avoid deadly perils and evil creatures to find magical treasures. Solutions for all 32 exciting illustrated puzzles. 48pp. 8¼ × 11.   26005-4 Pa. $2.95

MOZART'S DON GIOVANNI (DOVER OPERA LIBRETTO SERIES), Wolfgang Amadeus Mozart. Introduced and translated by Ellen H. Bleiler. Standard Italian libretto, with complete English translation. Convenient and thoroughly portable—an ideal companion for reading along with a recording or the performance itself. Introduction. List of characters. Plot summary. 121pp. 5¼ × 8½.

24944-1 Pa. $2.95

TECHNICAL MANUAL AND DICTIONARY OF CLASSICAL BALLET, Gail Grant. Defines, explains, comments on steps, movements, poses and concepts. 15-page pictorial section. Basic book for student, viewer. 127pp. 5⅜ × 8½.

21843-0 Pa. $3.95

BRASS INSTRUMENTS: Their History and Development, Anthony Baines. Authoritative, updated survey of the evolution of trumpets, trombones, bugles, cornets, French horns, tubas and other brass wind instruments. Over 140 illustrations and 48 music examples. Corrected and updated by author. New preface. Bibliography. 320pp. 5⅜ × 8½. 27574-4 Pa. $9.95

HOLLYWOOD GLAMOR PORTRAITS, John Kobal (ed.). 145 photos from 1926–49. Harlow, Gable, Bogart, Bacall; 94 stars in all. Full background on photographers, technical aspects. 160pp. 8⅜ × 11¼. 23352-9 Pa. $11.95

MAX AND MORITZ, Wilhelm Busch. Great humor classic in both German and English. Also 10 other works: "Cat and Mouse," "Plisch and Plumm," etc. 216pp. 5⅜ × 8½. 20181-3 Pa. $5.95

THE RAVEN AND OTHER FAVORITE POEMS, Edgar Allan Poe. Over 40 of the author's most memorable poems: "The Bells," "Ulalume," "Israfel," "To Helen," "The Conqueror Worm," "Eldorado," "Annabel Lee," many more. Alphabetic lists of titles and first lines. 64pp. 5³⁄₁₆ × 8¼. 26685-0 Pa. $1.00

SEVEN SCIENCE FICTION NOVELS, H. G. Wells. The standard collection of the great novels. Complete, unabridged. First Men in the Moon, Island of Dr. Moreau, War of the Worlds, Food of the Gods, Invisible Man, Time Machine, In the Days of the Comet. Total of 1,015pp. 5⅜ × 8½. (USO) 20264-X Clothbd. $29.95

AMULETS AND SUPERSTITIONS, E. A. Wallis Budge. Comprehensive discourse on origin, powers of amulets in many ancient cultures: Arab, Persian, Babylonian, Assyrian, Egyptian, Gnostic, Hebrew, Phoenician, Syriac, etc. Covers cross, swastika, crucifix, seals, rings, stones, etc. 584pp. 5⅜ × 8½. 23573-4 Pa. $12.95

RUSSIAN STORIES/PYCCKNE PACCKA3bl: A Dual-Language Book, edited by Gleb Struve. Twelve tales by such masters as Chekhov, Tolstoy, Dostoevsky, Pushkin, others. Excellent word-for-word English translations on facing pages, plus teaching and study aids, Russian/English vocabulary, biographical/critical introductions, more. 416pp. 5⅜ × 8½. 26244-8 Pa. $8.95

PHILADELPHIA THEN AND NOW: 60 Sites Photographed in the Past and Present, Kenneth Finkel and Susan Oyama. Rare photographs of City Hall, Logan Square, Independence Hall, Betsy Ross House, other landmarks juxtaposed with contemporary views. Captures changing face of historic city. Introduction. Captions. 128pp. 8¼ × 11. 25790-8 Pa. $9.95

AIA ARCHITECTURAL GUIDE TO NASSAU AND SUFFOLK COUNTIES, LONG ISLAND, The American Institute of Architects, Long Island Chapter, and the Society for the Preservation of Long Island Antiquities. Comprehensive, well-researched and generously illustrated volume brings to life over three centuries of Long Island's great architectural heritage. More than 240 photographs with authoritative, extensively detailed captions. 176pp. 8¼ × 11. 26946-9 Pa. $14.95

NORTH AMERICAN INDIAN LIFE: Customs and Traditions of 23 Tribes, Elsie Clews Parsons (ed.). 27 fictionalized essays by noted anthropologists examine religion, customs, government, additional facets of life among the Winnebago, Crow, Zuni, Eskimo, other tribes. 480pp. 6⅛ × 9¼. 27377-6 Pa. $10.95

FRANK LLOYD WRIGHT'S HOLLYHOCK HOUSE, Donald Hoffmann. Lavishly illustrated, carefully documented study of one of Wright's most controversial residential designs. Over 120 photographs, floor plans, elevations, etc. Detailed perceptive text by noted Wright scholar. Index. 128pp. 9¼ × 10¾.
27133-1 Pa. $11.95

THE MALE AND FEMALE FIGURE IN MOTION: 60 Classic Photographic Sequences, Eadweard Muybridge. 60 true-action photographs of men and women walking, running, climbing, bending, turning, etc., reproduced from rare 19th-century masterpiece. vi + 121pp. 9 × 12.
24745-7 Pa. $10.95

1001 QUESTIONS ANSWERED ABOUT THE SEASHORE, N. J. Berrill and Jacquelyn Berrill. Queries answered about dolphins, sea snails, sponges, starfish, fishes, shore birds, many others. Covers appearance, breeding, growth, feeding, much more. 305pp. 5¼ × 8¼.
23366-9 Pa. $7.95

GUIDE TO OWL WATCHING IN NORTH AMERICA, Donald S. Heintzelman. Superb guide offers complete data and descriptions of 19 species: barn owl, screech owl, snowy owl, many more. Expert coverage of owl-watching equipment, conservation, migrations and invasions, etc. Guide to observing sites. 84 illustrations. xiii + 193pp. 5⅜ × 8½.
27344-X Pa. $7.95

MEDICINAL AND OTHER USES OF NORTH AMERICAN PLANTS: A Historical Survey with Special Reference to the Eastern Indian Tribes, Charlotte Erichsen-Brown. Chronological historical citations document 500 years of usage of plants, trees, shrubs native to eastern Canada, northeastern U.S. Also complete identifying information. 343 illustrations. 544pp. 6½ × 9¼.
25951-X Pa. $12.95

STORYBOOK MAZES, Dave Phillips. 23 stories and mazes on two-page spreads: Wizard of Oz, Treasure Island, Robin Hood, etc. Solutions. 64pp. 8¼ × 11.
23628-5 Pa. $2.95

NEGRO FOLK MUSIC, U.S.A., Harold Courlander. Noted folklorist's scholarly yet readable analysis of rich and varied musical tradition. Includes authentic versions of over 40 folk songs. Valuable bibliography and discography. xi + 324pp. 5⅜ × 8½.
27350-4 Pa. $7.95

MOVIE-STAR PORTRAITS OF THE FORTIES, John Kobal (ed.). 163 glamor, studio photos of 106 stars of the 1940s: Rita Hayworth, Ava Gardner, Marlon Brando, Clark Gable, many more. 176pp. 8⅜ × 11¼.
23546-7 Pa. $10.95

BENCHLEY LOST AND FOUND, Robert Benchley. Finest humor from early 30s, about pet peeves, child psychologists, post office and others. Mostly unavailable elsewhere. 73 illustrations by Peter Arno and others. 183pp. 5⅜ × 8½.
22410-4 Pa. $5.95

YEKL and THE IMPORTED BRIDEGROOM AND OTHER STORIES OF YIDDISH NEW YORK, Abraham Cahan. Film Hester Street based on Yekl (1896). Novel, other stories among first about Jewish immigrants on N.Y.'s East Side. 240pp. 5⅜ × 8½.
22427-9 Pa. $6.95

SELECTED POEMS, Walt Whitman. Generous sampling from *Leaves of Grass*. Twenty-four poems include "I Hear America Singing," "Song of the Open Road," "I Sing the Body Electric," "When Lilacs Last in the Dooryard Bloom'd," "O Captain! My Captain!"—all reprinted from an authoritative edition. Lists of titles and first lines. 128pp. 5³⁄₁₆ × 8¼.
26878-0 Pa. $1.00

THE BEST TALES OF HOFFMANN, E. T. A. Hoffmann. 10 of Hoffmann's most important stories: "Nutcracker and the King of Mice," "The Golden Flowerpot," etc. 458pp. 5⅜ × 8½. 21793-0 Pa. $8.95

FROM FETISH TO GOD IN ANCIENT EGYPT, E. A. Wallis Budge. Rich detailed survey of Egyptian conception of "God" and gods, magic, cult of animals, Osiris, more. Also, superb English translations of hymns and legends. 240 illustrations. 545pp. 5⅜ × 8½. 25803-3 Pa. $11.95

FRENCH STORIES/CONTES FRANÇAIS: A Dual-Language Book, Wallace Fowlie. Ten stories by French masters, Voltaire to Camus: "Micromegas" by Voltaire; "The Atheist's Mass" by Balzac; "Minuet" by de Maupassant; "The Guest" by Camus, six more. Excellent English translations on facing pages. Also French-English vocabulary list, exercises, more. 352pp. 5⅜ × 8½. 26443-2 Pa. $8.95

CHICAGO AT THE TURN OF THE CENTURY IN PHOTOGRAPHS: 122 Historic Views from the Collections of the Chicago Historical Society, Larry A. Viskochil. Rare large-format prints offer detailed views of City Hall, State Street, the Loop, Hull House, Union Station, many other landmarks, circa 1904-1913. Introduction. Captions. Maps. 144pp. 9⅜ × 12¼. 24656-6 Pa. $12.95

OLD BROOKLYN IN EARLY PHOTOGRAPHS, 1865-1929, William Lee Younger. Luna Park, Gravesend race track, construction of Grand Army Plaza, moving of Hotel Brighton, etc. 157 previously unpublished photographs. 165pp. 8⅞ × 11¾. 23587-4 Pa. $13.95

THE MYTHS OF THE NORTH AMERICAN INDIANS, Lewis Spence. Rich anthology of the myths and legends of the Algonquins, Iroquois, Pawnees and Sioux, prefaced by an extensive historical and ethnological commentary. 36 illustrations. 480pp. 5⅜ × 8½. 25967-6 Pa. $8.95

AN ENCYCLOPEDIA OF BATTLES: Accounts of Over 1,560 Battles from 1479 B.C. to the Present, David Eggenberger. Essential details of every major battle in recorded history from the first battle of Megiddo in 1479 B.C. to Grenada in 1984. List of Battle Maps. New Appendix covering the years 1967-1984. Index. 99 illustrations. 544pp. 6½ × 9¼. 24913-1 Pa. $14.95

SAILING ALONE AROUND THE WORLD, Captain Joshua Slocum. First man to sail around the world, alone, in small boat. One of great feats of seamanship told in delightful manner. 67 illustrations. 294pp. 5⅜ × 8½. 20326-3 Pa. $5.95

ANARCHISM AND OTHER ESSAYS, Emma Goldman. Powerful, penetrating, prophetic essays on direct action, role of minorities, prison reform, puritan hypocrisy, violence, etc. 271pp. 5⅜ × 8½. 22484-8 Pa. $5.95

MYTHS OF THE HINDUS AND BUDDHISTS, Ananda K. Coomaraswamy and Sister Nivedita. Great stories of the epics; deeds of Krishna, Shiva, taken from puranas, Vedas, folk tales; etc. 32 illustrations. 400pp. 5⅜ × 8½. 21759-0 Pa. $9.95

BEYOND PSYCHOLOGY, Otto Rank. Fear of death, desire of immortality, nature of sexuality, social organization, creativity, according to Rankian system. 291pp. 5⅜ × 8½. 20485-5 Pa. $7.95

A THEOLOGICO-POLITICAL TREATISE, Benedict Spinoza. Also contains unfinished Political Treatise. Great classic on religious liberty, theory of government on common consent. R. Elwes translation. Total of 421pp. 5⅜ × 8½.
20249-6 Pa. $8.95

MY BONDAGE AND MY FREEDOM, Frederick Douglass. Born a slave, Douglass became outspoken force in antislavery movement. The best of Douglass' autobiographies. Graphic description of slave life. 464pp. 5⅜ × 8½. 22457-0 Pa. $8.95

FOLLOWING THE EQUATOR: A Journey Around the World, Mark Twain. Fascinating humorous account of 1897 voyage to Hawaii, Australia, India, New Zealand, etc. Ironic, bemused reports on peoples, customs, climate, flora and fauna, politics, much more. 197 illustrations. 720pp. 5⅜ × 8½. 26113-1 Pa. $15.95

THE PEOPLE CALLED SHAKERS, Edward D. Andrews. Definitive study of Shakers: origins, beliefs, practices, dances, social organization, furniture and crafts, etc. 33 illustrations. 351pp. 5⅜ × 8½. 21081-2 Pa. $8.95

THE MYTHS OF GREECE AND ROME, H. A. Guerber. A classic of mythology, generously illustrated, long prized for its simple, graphic, accurate retelling of the principal myths of Greece and Rome, and for its commentary on their origins and significance. With 64 illustrations by Michelangelo, Raphael, Titian, Rubens, Canova, Bernini and others. 480pp. 5⅜ × 8½. 27584-1 Pa. $9.95

PSYCHOLOGY OF MUSIC, Carl E. Seashore. Classic work discusses music as a medium from psychological viewpoint. Clear treatment of physical acoustics, auditory apparatus, sound perception, development of musical skills, nature of musical feeling, host of other topics. 88 figures. 408pp. 5⅜ × 8½. 21851-1 Pa. $9.95

THE PHILOSOPHY OF HISTORY, Georg W. Hegel. Great classic of Western thought develops concept that history is not chance but rational process, the evolution of freedom. 457pp. 5⅜ × 8½. 20112-0 Pa. $9.95

THE BOOK OF TEA, Kakuzo Okakura. Minor classic of the Orient: entertaining, charming explanation, interpretation of traditional Japanese culture in terms of tea ceremony. 94pp. 5⅜ × 8½. 20070-1 Pa. $2.95

LIFE IN ANCIENT EGYPT, Adolf Erman. Fullest, most thorough, detailed older account with much not in more recent books, domestic life, religion, magic, medicine, commerce, much more. Many illustrations reproduce tomb paintings, carvings, hieroglyphs, etc. 597pp. 5⅜ × 8½. 22632-8 Pa. $10.95

SUNDIALS, Their Theory and Construction, Albert Waugh. Far and away the best, most thorough coverage of ideas, mathematics concerned, types, construction, adjusting anywhere. Simple, nontechnical treatment allows even children to build several of these dials. Over 100 illustrations. 230pp. 5⅜ × 8½. 22947-5 Pa. $7.95

DYNAMICS OF FLUIDS IN POROUS MEDIA, Jacob Bear. For advanced students of ground water hydrology, soil mechanics and physics, drainage and irrigation engineering, and more. 335 illustrations. Exercises, with answers. 784pp. 6⅛ × 9¼. 65675-6 Pa. $19.95

SONGS OF EXPERIENCE: Facsimile Reproduction with 26 Plates in Full Color, William Blake. 26 full-color plates from a rare 1826 edition. Includes "The Tyger," "London," "Holy Thursday," and other poems. Printed text of poems. 48pp. 5¼ × 7. 24636-1 Pa. $4.95

OLD-TIME VIGNETTES IN FULL COLOR, Carol Belanger Grafton (ed.). Over 390 charming, often sentimental illustrations, selected from archives of Victorian graphics—pretty women posing, children playing, food, flowers, kittens and puppies, smiling cherubs, birds and butterflies, much more. All copyright-free. 48pp. 9¼ × 12¼. 27269-9 Pa. $5.95

PERSPECTIVE FOR ARTISTS, Rex Vicat Cole. Depth, perspective of sky and sea, shadows, much more, not usually covered. 391 diagrams, 81 reproductions of drawings and paintings. 279pp. 5⅜ × 8½. 22487-2 Pa. $6.95

DRAWING THE LIVING FIGURE, Joseph Sheppard. Innovative approach to artistic anatomy focuses on specifics of surface anatomy, rather than muscles and bones. Over 170 drawings of live models in front, back and side views, and in widely varying poses. Accompanying diagrams. 177 illustrations. Introduction. Index. 144pp. 8⅜ × 11¼. 26723-7 Pa. $7.95

GOTHIC AND OLD ENGLISH ALPHABETS: 100 Complete Fonts, Dan X. Solo. Add power, elegance to posters, signs, other graphics with 100 stunning copyright-free alphabets: Blackstone, Dolbey, Germania, 97 more—including many lower-case, numerals, punctuation marks. 104pp. 8⅛ × 11. 24695-7 Pa. $7.95

HOW TO DO BEADWORK, Mary White. Fundamental book on craft from simple projects to five-bead chains and woven works. 106 illustrations. 142pp. 5⅜ × 8.
20697-1 Pa. $4.95

THE BOOK OF WOOD CARVING, Charles Marshall Sayers. Finest book for beginners discusses fundamentals and offers 34 designs. "Absolutely first rate . . . well thought out and well executed."—E. J. Tangerman. 118pp. 7¾ × 10⅝.
23654-4 Pa. $5.95

ILLUSTRATED CATALOG OF CIVIL WAR MILITARY GOODS: Union Army Weapons, Insignia, Uniform Accessories, and Other Equipment, Schuyler, Hartley, and Graham. Rare, profusely illustrated 1846 catalog includes Union Army uniform and dress regulations, arms and ammunition, coats, insignia, flags, swords, rifles, etc. 226 illustrations. 160pp. 9 × 12. 24939-5 Pa. $10.95

WOMEN'S FASHIONS OF THE EARLY 1900s: An Unabridged Republication of "New York Fashions, 1909," National Cloak & Suit Co. Rare catalog of mail-order fashions documents women's and children's clothing styles shortly after the turn of the century. Captions offer full descriptions, prices. Invaluable resource for fashion, costume historians. Approximately 725 illustrations. 128pp. 8⅜ × 11¼.
27276-1 Pa. $11.95

THE 1912 AND 1915 GUSTAV STICKLEY FURNITURE CATALOGS, Gustav Stickley. With over 200 detailed illustrations and descriptions, these two catalogs are essential reading and reference materials and identification guides for Stickley furniture. Captions cite materials, dimensions and prices. 112pp. 6½ × 9¼.
26676-1 Pa. $9.95

EARLY AMERICAN LOCOMOTIVES, John H. White, Jr. Finest locomotive engravings from early 19th century: historical (1804–74), main-line (after 1870), special, foreign, etc. 147 plates. 142pp. 11⅜ × 8¼. 22772-3 Pa. $8.95

THE TALL SHIPS OF TODAY IN PHOTOGRAPHS, Frank O. Braynard. Lavishly illustrated tribute to nearly 100 majestic contemporary sailing vessels: Amerigo Vespucci, Clearwater, Constitution, Eagle, Mayflower, Sea Cloud, Victory, many more. Authoritative captions provide statistics, background on each ship. 190 black-and-white photographs and illustrations. Introduction. 128pp. 8⅞ × 11¾. 27163-3 Pa. $13.95

EARLY NINETEENTH-CENTURY CRAFTS AND TRADES, Peter Stockham (ed.). Extremely rare 1807 volume describes to youngsters the crafts and trades of the day: brickmaker, weaver, dressmaker, bookbinder, ropemaker, saddler, many more. Quaint prose, charming illustrations for each craft. 20 black-and-white line illustrations. 192pp. 4⅝ × 6. 27293-1 Pa. $4.95

VICTORIAN FASHIONS AND COSTUMES FROM HARPER'S BAZAR, 1867–1898, Stella Blum (ed.). Day costumes, evening wear, sports clothes, shoes, hats, other accessories in over 1,000 detailed engravings. 320pp. 9⅜ × 12¼. 22990-4 Pa. $13.95

GUSTAV STICKLEY, THE CRAFTSMAN, Mary Ann Smith. Superb study surveys broad scope of Stickley's achievement, especially in architecture. Design philosophy, rise and fall of the Craftsman empire, descriptions and floor plans for many Craftsman houses, more. 86 black-and-white halftones. 31 line illustrations. Introduction. 208pp. 6½ × 9¼. 27210-9 Pa. $9.95

THE LONG ISLAND RAIL ROAD IN EARLY PHOTOGRAPHS, Ron Ziel. Over 220 rare photos, informative text document origin (1844) and development of rail service on Long Island. Vintage views of early trains, locomotives, stations, passengers, crews, much more. Captions. 8⅞ × 11¾. 26301-0 Pa. $13.95

THE BOOK OF OLD SHIPS: From Egyptian Galleys to Clipper Ships, Henry B. Culver. Superb, authoritative history of sailing vessels, with 80 magnificent line illustrations. Galley, bark, caravel, longship, whaler, many more. Detailed, informative text on each vessel by noted naval historian. Introduction. 256pp. 5⅜ × 8½. 27332-6 Pa. $6.95

TEN BOOKS ON ARCHITECTURE, Vitruvius. The most important book ever written on architecture. Early Roman aesthetics, technology, classical orders, site selection, all other aspects. Morgan translation. 331pp. 5⅜ × 8½. 20645-9 Pa. $8.95

THE HUMAN FIGURE IN MOTION, Eadweard Muybridge. More than 4,500 stopped-action photos, in action series, showing undraped men, women, children jumping, lying down, throwing, sitting, wrestling, carrying, etc. 390pp. 7⅞ × 10⅝. 20204-6 Clothbd. $24.95

TREES OF THE EASTERN AND CENTRAL UNITED STATES AND CANADA, William M. Harlow. Best one-volume guide to 140 trees. Full descriptions, woodlore, range, etc. Over 600 illustrations. Handy size. 288pp. 4½ × 6⅜. 20395-6 Pa. $5.95

SONGS OF WESTERN BIRDS, Dr. Donald J. Borror. Complete song and call repertoire of 60 western species, including flycatchers, juncoes, cactus wrens, many more—includes fully illustrated booklet. Cassette and manual 99913-0 $8.95

GROWING AND USING HERBS AND SPICES, Milo Miloradovich. Versatile handbook provides all the information needed for cultivation and use of all the herbs and spices available in North America. 4 illustrations. Index. Glossary. 236pp. 5⅜ × 8½. 25058-X Pa. $5.95

BIG BOOK OF MAZES AND LABYRINTHS, Walter Shepherd. 50 mazes and labyrinths in aH—classical, solid, ripple, and more—in one great volume. Perfect inexpensive puzzler for clever youngsters. Full solutions. 112pp. 8⅛ × 11. 22951-3 Pa. $3.95

PIANO TUNING, J. Cree Fischer. Clearest, best book for beginner, amateur. Simple repairs, raising dropped notes, tuning by easy method of flattened fifths. No previous skills needed. 4 illustrations. 201pp. 5⅜ × 8½. 23267-0 Pa. $5.95

A SOURCE BOOK IN THEATRICAL HISTORY, A. M. Nagler. Contemporary observers on acting, directing, make-up, costuming, stage props, machinery, scene design, from Ancient Greece to Chekhov. 611pp. 5⅜ × 8½. 20515-0 Pa. $11.95

THE COMPLETE NONSENSE OF EDWARD LEAR, Edward Lear. All nonsense limericks, zany alphabets, Owl and Pussycat, songs, nonsense botany, etc., illustrated by Lear. Total of 320pp. 5⅜ × 8½. (USO) 20167-8 Pa. $6.95

VICTORIAN PARLOUR POETRY: An Annotated Anthology, Michael R. Turner. 117 gems by Longfellow, Tennyson, Browning, many lesser-known poets. "The Village Blacksmith," "Curfew Must Not Ring Tonight," "Only a Baby Small," dozens more, often difficult to find elsewhere. Index of poets, titles, first lines. xxiii + 325pp. 5⅜ × 8¼. 27044-0 Pa. $8.95

DUBLINERS, James Joyce. Fifteen stories offer vivid, tightly focused observations of the lives of Dublin's poorer classes. At least one, "The Dead," is considered a masterpiece. Reprinted complete and unabridged from standard edition. 160pp. 5³⁄₁₆ × 8¼. 26870-5 Pa. $1.00

THE HAUNTED MONASTERY and THE CHINESE MAZE MURDERS, Robert van Gulik. Two full novels by van Gulik, set in 7th-century China, continue adventures of Judge Dee and his companions. An evil Taoist monastery, seemingly supernatural events; overgrown topiary maze hides strange crimes. 27 illustrations. 328pp. 5⅜ × 8½. 23502-5 Pa. $7.95

THE BOOK OF THE SACRED MAGIC OF ABRAMELIN THE MAGE, translated by S. MacGregor Mathers. Medieval manuscript of ceremonial magic. Basic document in Aleister Crowley, Golden Dawn groups. 268pp. 5⅜ × 8½. 23211-5 Pa. $8.95

NEW RUSSIAN-ENGLISH AND ENGLISH-RUSSIAN DICTIONARY, M. A. O'Brien. This is a remarkably handy Russian dictionary, containing a surprising amount of information, including over 70,000 entries. 366pp. 4½ × 6⅛. 20208-9 Pa. $9.95

HISTORIC HOMES OF THE AMERICAN PRESIDENTS, Second, Revised Edition, Irvin Haas. A traveler's guide to American Presidential homes, most open to the public, depicting and describing homes occupied by every American President from George Washington to George Bush. With visiting hours, admission charges, travel routes. 175 photographs. Index. 160pp. 8¼ × 11. 26751-2 Pa. $10.95

NEW YORK IN THE FORTIES, Andreas Feininger. 162 brilliant photographs by the well-known photographer, formerly with *Life* magazine. Commuters, shoppers, Times Square at night, much else from city at its peak. Captions by John von Hartz. 181pp. 9¼ × 10¾. 23585-8 Pa. $12.95

INDIAN SIGN LANGUAGE, William Tomkins. Over 525 signs developed by Sioux and other tribes. Written instructions and diagrams. Also 290 pictographs. 111pp. 6⅛ × 9¼. 22029-X Pa. $3.50

ANATOMY: A Complete Guide for Artists, Joseph Sheppard. A master of figure drawing shows artists how to render human anatomy convincingly. Over 460 illustrations. 224pp. 8⅜ × 11¼. 27279-6 Pa. $9.95

MEDIEVAL CALLIGRAPHY: Its History and Technique, Marc Drogin. Spirited history, comprehensive instruction manual covers 13 styles (ca. 4th century thru 15th). Excellent photographs; directions for duplicating medieval techniques with modern tools. 224pp. 8⅜ × 11¼. 26142-5 Pa. $11.95

DRIED FLOWERS: How to Prepare Them, Sarah Whitlock and Martha Rankin. Complete instructions on how to use silica gel, meal and borax, perlite aggregate, sand and borax, glycerine and water to create attractive permanent flower arrangements. 12 illustrations. 32pp. 5⅜ × 8½. 21802-3 Pa. $1.00

EASY-TO-MAKE BIRD FEEDERS FOR WOODWORKERS, Scott D. Campbell. Detailed, simple-to-use guide for designing, constructing, caring for and using feeders. Text, illustrations for 12 classic and contemporary designs. 96pp. 5⅜ × 8½. 25847-5 Pa. $2.95

OLD-TIME CRAFTS AND TRADES, Peter Stockham. An 1807 book created to teach children about crafts and trades open to them as future careers. It describes in detailed, nontechnical terms 24 different occupations, among them coachmaker, gardener, hairdresser, lacemaker, shoemaker, wheelwright, copper-plate printer, milliner, trunkmaker, merchant and brewer. Finely detailed engravings illustrate each occupation. 192pp. 4⅝ × 6. 27398-9 Pa. $4.95

THE HISTORY OF UNDERCLOTHES, C. Willett Cunnington and Phyllis Cunnington. Fascinating, well-documented survey covering six centuries of English undergarments, enhanced with over 100 illustrations: 12th-century laced-up bodice, footed long drawers (1795), 19th-century bustles, 19th-century corsets for men, Victorian "bust improvers," much more. 272pp. 5⅜ × 8¼. 27124-2 Pa. $9.95

ARTS AND CRAFTS FURNITURE: The Complete Brooks Catalog of 1912, Brooks Manufacturing Co. Photos and detailed descriptions of more than 150 now very collectible furniture designs from the Arts and Crafts movement depict davenports, settees, buffets, desks, tables, chairs, bedsteads, dressers and more, all built of solid, quarter-sawed oak. Invaluable for students and enthusiasts of antiques, Americana and the decorative arts. 80pp. 6½ × 9¼. 27471-3 Pa. $7.95

HOW WE INVENTED THE AIRPLANE: An Illustrated History, Orville Wright. Fascinating firsthand account covers early experiments, construction of planes and motors, first flights, much more. Introduction and commentary by Fred C. Kelly. 76 photographs. 96pp. 8¼ × 11. 25662-6 Pa. $8.95

THE ARTS OF THE SAILOR: Knotting, Splicing and Ropework, Hervey Garrett Smith. Indispensable shipboard reference covers tools, basic knots and useful hitches; handsewing and canvas work, more. Over 100 illustrations. Delightful reading for sea lovers. 256pp. 5⅜ × 8½. 26440-8 Pa. $7.95

FRANK LLOYD WRIGHT'S FALLINGWATER: The House and Its History, Second, Revised Edition, Donald Hoffmann. A total revision—both in text and illustrations—of the standard document on Fallingwater, the boldest, most personal architectural statement of Wright's mature years, updated with valuable new material from the recently opened Frank Lloyd Wright Archives. "Fascinating"—The New York Times. 116 illustrations. 128pp. 9¼ × 10¾. 27430-6 Pa. $10.95

PHOTOGRAPHIC SKETCHBOOK OF THE CIVIL WAR, Alexander Gardner. 100 photos taken on field during the Civil War. Famous shots of Manassas, Harper's Ferry, Lincoln, Richmond, slave pens, etc. 244pp. 10⅝ × 8¼.
22731-6 Pa. $9.95

FIVE ACRES AND INDEPENDENCE, Maurice G. Kains. Great back-to-the-land classic explains basics of self-sufficient farming. The one book to get. 95 illustrations. 397pp. 5⅜ × 8½. 20974-1 Pa. $7.95

SONGS OF EASTERN BIRDS, Dr. Donald J. Borror. Songs and calls of 60 species most common to eastern U.S.: warblers, woodpeckers, flycatchers, thrushes, larks, many more in high-quality recording. Cassette and manual 99912-2 $8.95

A MODERN HERBAL, Margaret Grieve. Much the fullest, most exact, most useful compilation of herbal material. Gigantic alphabetical encyclopedia, from aconite to zedoary, gives botanical information, medical properties, folklore, economic uses, much else. Indispensable to serious reader. 161 illustrations. 888pp. 6½ × 9¼. 2-vol. set. (USO) Vol. I: 22798-7 Pa. $9.95
Vol. II: 22799-5 Pa. $9.95

HIDDEN TREASURE MAZE BOOK, Dave Phillips. Solve 34 challenging mazes accompanied by heroic tales of adventure. Evil dragons, people-eating plants, bloodthirsty giants, many more dangerous adversaries lurk at every twist and turn. 34 mazes, stories, solutions. 48pp. 8¼ × 11. 24566-7 Pa. $2.95

LETTERS OF W. A. MOZART, Wolfgang A. Mozart. Remarkable letters show bawdy wit, humor, imagination, musical insights, contemporary musical world; includes some letters from Leopold Mozart. 276pp. 5⅜ × 8½. 22859-2 Pa. $6.95

BASIC PRINCIPLES OF CLASSICAL BALLET, Agrippina Vaganova. Great Russian theoretician, teacher explains methods for teaching classical ballet. 118 illustrations. 175pp. 5⅜ × 8½. 22036-2 Pa. $4.95

THE JUMPING FROG, Mark Twain. Revenge edition. The original story of The Celebrated Jumping Frog of Calaveras County, a hapless French translation, and Twain's hilarious "retranslation" from the French. 12 illustrations. 66pp. 5⅜ × 8½. 22686-7 Pa. $3.95

BEST REMEMBERED POEMS, Martin Gardner (ed.). The 126 poems in this superb collection of 19th- and 20th-century British and American verse range from Shelley's "To a Skylark" to the impassioned "Renascence" of Edna St. Vincent Millay and to Edward Lear's whimsical "The Owl and the Pussycat." 224pp. 5⅜×8½. 27165-X Pa. $4.95

COMPLETE SONNETS, William Shakespeare. Over 150 exquisite poems deal with love, friendship, the tyranny of time, beauty's evanescence, death and other themes in language of remarkable power, precision and beauty. Glossary of archaic terms. 80pp. 5³⁄₁₆ × 8¼. 26686-9 Pa. $1.00

BODIES IN A BOOKSHOP, R. T. Campbell. Challenging mystery of blackmail and murder with ingenious plot and superbly drawn characters. In the best tradition of British suspense fiction. 192pp. 5⅜ × 8½. 24720-1 Pa. $5.95

THE WIT AND HUMOR OF OSCAR WILDE, Alvin Redman (ed.). More than 1,000 ripostes, paradoxes, wisecracks: Work is the curse of the drinking classes; I can resist everything except temptation; etc. 258pp. 5⅜ × 8½. 20602-5 Pa. $5.95

SHAKESPEARE LEXICON AND QUOTATION DICTIONARY, Alexander Schmidt. Full definitions, locations, shades of meaning in every word in plays and poems. More than 50,000 exact quotations. 1,485pp. 6½ × 9¼. 2-vol. set.
Vol. 1: 22726-X Pa. $15.95
Vol. 2: 22727-8 Pa. $15.95

SELECTED POEMS, Emily Dickinson. Over 100 best-known, best-loved poems by one of America's foremost poets, reprinted from authoritative early editions. No comparable edition at this price. Index of first lines. 64pp. 5³⁄₁₆ × 8¼.
26466-1 Pa. $1.00

CELEBRATED CASES OF JUDGE DEE (DEE GOONG AN), translated by Robert van Gulik. Authentic 18th-century Chinese detective novel; Dee and associates solve three interlocked cases. Led to van Gulik's own stories with same characters. Extensive introduction. 9 illustrations. 237pp. 5⅜ × 8½.
23337-5 Pa. $6.95

THE MALLEUS MALEFICARUM OF KRAMER AND SPRENGER, translated by Montague Summers. Full text of most important witchhunter's "bible," used by both Catholics and Protestants. 278pp. 6⅝ × 10. 22802-9 Pa. $10.95

SPANISH STORIES/CUENTOS ESPAÑOLES: A Dual-Language Book, Angel Flores (ed.). Unique format offers 13 great stories in Spanish by Cervantes, Borges, others. Faithful English translations on facing pages. 352pp. 5⅜ × 8½.
25399-6 Pa. $8.95

THE CHICAGO WORLD'S FAIR OF 1893: A Photographic Record, Stanley Appelbaum (ed.). 128 rare photos show 200 buildings, Beaux-Arts architecture, Midway, original Ferris Wheel, Edison's kinetoscope, more. Architectural emphasis; full text. 116pp. 8¼ × 11. 23990-X Pa. $9.95

OLD QUEENS, N.Y., IN EARLY PHOTOGRAPHS, Vincent F. Seyfried and William Asadorian. Over 160 rare photographs of Maspeth, Jamaica, Jackson Heights, and other areas. Vintage views of DeWitt Clinton mansion, 1939 World's Fair and more. Captions. 192pp. 8⅞ × 11. 26358-4 Pa. $12.95

CAPTURED BY THE INDIANS: 15 Firsthand Accounts, 1750–1870, Frederick Drimmer. Astounding true historical accounts of grisly torture, bloody conflicts, relentless pursuits, miraculous escapes and more, by people who lived to tell the tale. 384pp. 5⅜ × 8½. 24901-8 Pa. $8.95

THE WORLD'S GREAT SPEECHES, Lewis Copeland and Lawrence W. Lamm (eds.). Vast collection of 278 speeches of Greeks to 1970. Powerful and effective models; unique look at history. 842pp. 5⅜ × 8½. 20468-5 Pa. $13.95

THE BOOK OF THE SWORD, Sir Richard F. Burton. Great Victorian scholar/adventurer's eloquent, erudite history of the "queen of weapons"—from prehistory to early Roman Empire. Evolution and development of early swords, variations (sabre, broadsword, cutlass, scimitar, etc.), much more. 336pp. 6⅛ × 9¼. 25434-8 Pa. $8.95

AUTOBIOGRAPHY: The Story of My Experiments with Truth, Mohandas K. Gandhi. Boyhood, legal studies, purification, the growth of the Satyagraha (nonviolent protest) movement. Critical, inspiring work of the man responsible for the freedom of India. 480pp. 5⅜ × 8½. (USO) 24593-4 Pa. $7.95

CELTIC MYTHS AND LEGENDS, T. W. Rolleston. Masterful retelling of Irish and Welsh stories and tales. Cuchulain, King Arthur, Deirdre, the Grail, many more. First paperback edition. 58 full-page illustrations. 512pp. 5⅜ × 8½.
26507-2 Pa. $9.95

THE PRINCIPLES OF PSYCHOLOGY, William James. Famous long course complete, unabridged. Stream of thought, time perception, memory, experimental methods; great work decades ahead of its time. 94 figures. 1,391pp. 5⅜ × 8½. 2-vol. set.
Vol. I: 20381-6 Pa. $12.95
Vol. II: 20382-4 Pa. $12.95

THE WORLD AS WILL AND REPRESENTATION, Arthur Schopenhauer. Definitive English translation of Schopenhauer's life work, correcting more than 1,000 errors, omissions in earlier translations. Translated by E. F. J. Payne. Total of 1,269pp. 5⅜ × 8½. 2-vol. set. Vol. 1: 21761-2 Pa. $11.95
Vol. 2: 21762-0 Pa. $11.95

MAGIC AND MYSTERY IN TIBET, Madame Alexandra David-Neel. Experiences among lamas, magicians, sages, sorcerers, Bonpa wizards. A true psychic discovery. 32 illustrations. 321pp. 5⅜ × 8½. (USO) 22682-4 Pa. $8.95

THE EGYPTIAN BOOK OF THE DEAD, E. A. Wallis Budge. Complete reproduction of Ani's papyrus, finest ever found. Full hieroglyphic text, interlinear transliteration, word-for-word translation, smooth translation. 533pp. 6½ × 9¼.
21866-X Pa. $9.95

MATHEMATICS FOR THE NONMATHEMATICIAN, Morris Kline. Detailed, college-level treatment of mathematics in cultural and historical context, with numerous exercises. Recommended Reading Lists. Tables. Numerous figures. 641pp. 5⅜ × 8½. 24823-2 Pa. $11.95

THEORY OF WING SECTIONS: Including a Summary of Airfoil Data, Ira H. Abbott and A. E. von Doenhoff. Concise compilation of subsonic aerodynamic characteristics of NACA wing sections, plus description of theory. 350pp. of tables. 693pp. 5⅜ × 8½. 60586-8 Pa. $13.95

THE RIME OF THE ANCIENT MARINER, Gustave Doré, S. T. Coleridge. Doré's finest work; 34 plates capture moods, subtleties of poem. Flawless full-size reproductions printed on facing pages with authoritative text of poem. "Beautiful. Simply beautiful."—*Publisher's Weekly.* 77pp. 9¼ × 12. 22305-1 Pa. $5.95

NORTH AMERICAN INDIAN DESIGNS FOR ARTISTS AND CRAFTS-PEOPLE, Eva Wilson. Over 360 authentic copyright-free designs adapted from Navajo blankets, Hopi pottery, Sioux buffalo hides, more. Geometrics, symbolic figures, plant and animal motifs, etc. 128pp. 8⅜ × 11. (EUK) 25341-4 Pa. $7.95

SCULPTURE: Principles and Practice, Louis Slobodkin. Step-by-step approach to clay, plaster, metals, stone; classical and modern. 253 drawings, photos. 255pp. 8⅛ × 11. 22960-2 Pa. $10.95

THE INFLUENCE OF SEA POWER UPON HISTORY, 1660–1783, A. T. Mahan. Influential classic of naval history and tactics still used as text in war colleges. First paperback edition. 4 maps. 24 battle plans. 640pp. 5⅜ × 8½.

25509-3 Pa. $12.95

THE STORY OF THE TITANIC AS TOLD BY ITS SURVIVORS, Jack Winocour (ed.). What it was really like. Panic, despair, shocking inefficiency, and a little heroism. More thrilling than any fictional account. 26 illustrations. 320pp. 5⅜ × 8½.

20610-6 Pa. $7.95

FAIRY AND FOLK TALES OF THE IRISH PEASANTRY, William Butler Yeats (ed.). Treasury of 64 tales from the twilight world of Celtic myth and legend: "The Soul Cages," "The Kildare Pooka," "King O'Toole and his Goose," many more. Introduction and Notes by W. B. Yeats. 352pp. 5⅜ × 8½.

26941-8 Pa. $8.95

BUDDHIST MAHAYANA TEXTS, E. B. Cowell and Others (eds.). Superb, accurate translations of basic documents in Mahayana Buddhism, highly important in history of religions. The Buddha-karita of Asvaghosha, Larger Sukhavativyuha, more. 448pp. 5⅜ × 8½. ,

25552-2 Pa. $9.95

ONE TWO THREE . . . INFINITY: Facts and Speculations of Science, George Gamow. Great physicist's fascinating, readable overview of contemporary science: number theory, relativity, fourth dimension, entropy, genes, atomic structure, much more. 128 illustrations. Index. 352pp. 5⅜ × 8½.

25664-2 Pa. $8.95

ENGINEERING IN HISTORY, Richard Shelton Kirby, et al. Broad, nontechnical survey of history's major technological advances: birth of Greek science, industrial revolution, electricity and applied science, 20th-century automation, much more. 181 illustrations. ". . . excellent . . ."—Isis. Bibliography. vii + 530pp. 5⅜ × 8¼.

26412-2 Pa. $14.95